"This book provides a solid overview of HRM practices in the Asia-Pacific region. Importantly, it delineates HRM practices in countries that often are not the location of the majority of research done in the field of HRM. This book is a wonderful contribution towards a more global understanding of HRM, and should be on the bookshelves of scholars and practitioners who work in the area of international human resource management."

Mark E. Mendenhall, *J. Burton Frierson Chair of Excellence in Business Leadership, University of Tennessee, Chattanooga*

"This book offers an excellent overview of major HRM issues in the Asia-Pacific context. The unifying framework provides the essential theoretical framework, while the country case studies provide valuable insights about differences and similarities across countries and regions. An important resource for any comparative HRM course."

Vladimir Pucik, *Professor of International Human Resources and Strategy, International Institute for Management Development, Lausanne*

"People are the key to success in business and being able to manage human resources effectively in the most important economic growth area of the world is crucial. This is a cutting-edge contribution that provides a real understanding of the cross-national HRM differences created by the great cultural and institutional variation of Asia-Pacific. Foreign investors as well as students and researchers will find this book indispensable in finding out how to deal with the most valuable resource of any firm."

Professor Jan Selmer, *Hong Kong Baptist University*

"This book brings together some fascinating insights on the recent developments as well as the challenges of managing people in the Asia-Pacific region. In their well-thought-out analyses, the authors have succeeded in bringing out the unique features that characterize and shape HR practice in each country. The Asia-Pacific region is a vast and multi-layered context, one that poses huge challenges to researchers and students of international HRM. Budhwar and his team have risen to this challenge, and provided us with a superb piece of work."

Ken N. Kamoche, *City University of Hong Kong*

# Managing Human Resources in Asia-Pacific

Developments in Human Resource Management (HRM) in the west are now well documented. In the Asia-Pacific region HRM is still evolving, yet there remains an absence of systematic analyses that comprehensively explore the dynamics of HRM in Asia-Pacific. This book fills that gap.

*Managing Human Resources in Asia-Pacific* paints the picture of HRM in 11 Asia-Pacific countries, highlighting the challenges faced by HR professionals as well as the contextual differences, the dynamics and the growth of HR within each of these countries. Written by people living and working in the region, the countries covered are China, South Korea, Japan, Hong Kong, Taiwan, India, Thailand, Vietnam, Malaysia, Singapore and Australia. There are also chapters on the transfer of HRM to MNC affiliates in Asia and the agenda for future research and policy.

A truly groundbreaking addition to the subject area, this authoritative new text will be welcomed across the board by academics, students and practitioners in the field of HRM.

**Pawan S. Budhwar** is Reader in HRM and Organizational Behaviour at Aston Business School, UK.

## Routledge Global Human Resource Management Series

*Edited by Randall S. Schuler, Susan E. Jackson, Paul Sparrow and Michael Poole*

**Routledge Global Human Resource Management** is an important new series that examines human resources in its global context. The series is organized into three strands: Content and issues in global Human Resource Management (HRM); Specific HR functions in a global context; and comparative HRM. Authored by some of the world's leading authorities on HRM, each book in the series aims to give readers comprehensive, indepth and accessible texts that combine essential theory and best practice. Topics covered include cross-border alliances, global leadership, global legal systems, HRM in Asia, Africa and the Americas, industrial relations and global staffing.

**Managing Human Resources in Cross-Border Alliances**
*Randall S. Schuler, Susan E. Jackson and Yadong Luo*

**Managing Human Resources in Africa**
*Edited by Ken N. Kamoche, Yaw A. Debrah, Frank M. Horwitz and Gerry Nkombo Muuka*

**Globalizing Human Resource Management**
*Paul Sparrow, Chris Brewster and Hilary Harris*

**Managing Human Resources in Asia-Pacific**
*Edited by Pawan S. Budhwar*

# Managing Human Resources in Asia-Pacific

Edited by
Pawan S. Budhwar

Routledge
Taylor & Francis Group

LONDON AND NEW YORK

First published 2004
by Routledge
11 New Fetter Lane, London EC4P 4EE

Simultaneously published in the USA and Canada
by Routledge
29 West 35th Street, New York, NY 10001

*Routledge is an imprint of the Taylor & Francis Group*

Typeset in Times New Roman and Franklin Gothic
by Keystroke, Jacaranda Lodge, Wolverhampton
Printed and bound in Great Britain
by TJ International Ltd, Padstow, Cornwall

*British Library Cataloguing in Publication Data*
A catalogue record for this book is available from the British Library

*Library of Congress Cataloging in Publication Data*
Managing human resources in Asia-Pacific / edited by Pawan S. Budhwar.
    p. cm.
Includes bibliographical references and index.
1. Personnel management—Asia.  2. Personnel management—Pacific Area.
3. Human capital—Asia—Management.  4. Human capital—Pacific
Area—Management.  I. Budhwar, Pawan S.
    HF5549.2.A75M36 2004
    658.3′0095—dc22

ISBN 0–415–30005–3 (hbk)
ISBN 0–415–30006–1 (pbk)

To Laxmi and Gaurav with all my love.

To those who have interest in the management of human resources in the Asia-Pacific region.

# Contents

# Illustrations

## Figure

## Tables

# Contributors

**Johngseok Bae** is Associate Professor of Management at Korea University Business School, 5–1 Anam-Dong, Sungbuk-Gu, Seoul, 136–701, Korea.

**Clemens Bechter** is Associate Professor at the School of Management, PO Box 4, Klong Luang, Pathum Thani 12120, Thailand.

**Ingmar Björkman** is a Professor at the Swedish School of Economics and Business Administration, PO Box 479, 00101 Helsinki 10, Finland.

**Pawan S. Budhwar** is Reader in Organizational Behaviour and HRM at Aston Business School, Aston Triangle, Birmingham, B4 7ET, UK.

**Andrew Chan** is Associate Professor, Office – AC G7421 at the Department of Management, City University of Hong Kong, Tat Chee Avenue, Hong Kong.

**Fang Lee Cooke** is Lecturer in Employment Studies at the Manchester School of Management, UMIST, PO Box 88, Manchester, M60 1QD, UK.

**Yaw A. Debrah** is Reader at the School of Business and Management, Brunel University, Uxbridge, Middlesex, UB8 3PH, UK.

**Naresh Khatri** is Assistant Professor in Health Management and Informatics at the School of Medicine, 324 Clark Hall, University of Missouri, Columbia, MO 65211, USA.

**Steven Lui** is Assistant Professor, Office – AC G7423 at the Department of Management, City University of Hong Kong, Tat Chee Avenue, Hong Kong.

**Kamel Mellahi** is Lecturer in Strategic Management at Loughborough University Business School, Loughborough University, LE11 3TU, UK.

**Margaret Patrickson** is Associate Professor at the University of South Australia, The International Graduate School Of Management, City West Campus, Office – WL5-33, PO Box 2471, Adelaide, South Australia 5001, Australia.

**Truong Quang** is Associate Professor at the School of Management, Asian Institute of Technology, PO Box 4, Klong Luang, Pathum Thani 12120, Thailand.

**Chris Rowley** is Reader in Human Resource Management and Employee Relations at the Faculty of Management, Cass Business School, City University, 106 Bunhill Row, London, EC1 8TZ, UK.

**Debi S. Saini** is Professor of Human Resource Management at the Management Development Institute Gurgaon, Haryana, India.

**John Salmon** is Lecturer, HRM Section at Cardiff Business School, Colum Drive, Cardiff, CF10 3EU, UK.

**Sununta Siengthai** is Associate Professor at the School of Management, PO Box 4, Klong Luang, Pathum Thani 12120, Thailand.

**Wahyu Sutiyono** is Lecturer at the International Graduate School of Management, University of South Australia, City West Campus, North Terrace, Adelaide, SA 5006, Australia.

**Le Chien Thang** is a Lecturer at the School of Industrial Management, HCMC University of Technology, Ho Chi Minh City, Vietnam.

**Geoffrey T. Wood** is a Professor at Middlesex Business School, Middlesex University, N11 1QS, UK.

**Pei-Chuan Wu** is Assistant Professor in Management and Organization at NUS Business School, Office – FBA1 B1-03E, National University of Singapore, 1 Business Link, Singapore 117592.

# Foreword

Routledge Global Human Resource Management is a series of books edited and authored by some of the best and most well-known researchers in the field of human resource management. This series is aimed at offering students and practitioners accessible, coordinated and comprehensive books in global HRM. To be used individually or together, these books cover the main bases of comparative and international HRM. Taking an expert look at an increasingly important and complex area of global business, this is a groundbreaking new series that answers a real need for serious textbooks on global HRM.

Several books in this series, Routledge Global Human Resource Management, are devoted to human resource management policies and practices in multinational enterprises. Some books focus on specific areas of global HRM policies and practices, such as global leadership, global compensation, global staffing and global labour relations. Other books address special topics that arise in multinational enterprises such as managing HR in cross-border alliances, developing strategies and structures, and managing legal systems for multinational enterprises.

In addition to books on various HRM topics in multinational enterprises, several other books in the series adopt a comparative approach to understanding human resource management. These books on comparative human resource management describe the HRM policies and practices found at the local level in selected countries in several regions of the world. The comparative books utilize a common framework that makes it easier for the reader to systematically understand the rationale for the existence of various human resource management activities in different countries and easier to compare these activities across countries. This framework considers a range of national factors including culture, institutions, industrial sector, and dynamic changes in the environment. These books therefore help us to both understand the factors that still lead to unique HRM solutions in different countries around the world, the essential elements of localisation, but also the opportunities for transfer of best practice. This book, *Managing Human Resources in Asia-Pacific* edited by Pawan S. Budhwar, is an excellent example of one of these books on comparative human resource management. In this book the reader will find detailed descriptions of human resource management activities in eleven key countries in the Asia-Pacific. Pawan Budhwar helps surface the many complex arguments involved in the convergence-divergence debate as it applies to the Asia-Pacific region. In this task, he has brought together a series of prestigious authors of the various country chapters, who have been carefully selected for being experts in the subject area in their chosen countries and for being able to write clearly and concisely. Each chapter is complete with useful and timely references that enable the reader to delve into each country in even more detail than provided in the chapter. Overall, Pawan Budhwar has given the reader a very valuable book that provides information on the human resource management activities and experiences influencing fully half the world's population.

This Routledge series, Global Human Resource Management, is intended to serve the growing market of global scholars and professionals who are seeking a deeper and broader understanding of the role and importance of human resource management in companies as they operate throughout the world. With this in mind, all books in the series provide a thorough review of existing research and numerous examples of companies around the world. Mini-company stories and examples are found throughout the chapters. In addition, many of the books in the series includes at least one detailed case description that serves as a convenient practical illustrations of topics discussed in the book.

Because a significant number of scholars and professionals throughout the world are involved in researching and practicing the topics examined in this series of books, the authorship of the books and the experiences of companies cited in the books reflect a vast global representation. The authors in the series bring with them exceptional knowledge of the human resource management topics they address, and in many cases the authors have been the pioneers for their topics. So we feel fortunate to have the involvement of such a distinguished group of academics in this series.

The publisher and editor also have played a major role in making this series possible. Routledge has provided its global production, marketing and reputation to make this series feasible and affordable to academics and practitioners throughout the world. In addition, Routledge has provided its own highly qualified professionals to make this series a reality. In particular we want to indicate our deep appreciation for the work of our series editor, Francesca Poynter. She, and her predecessor Catriona King, have been behind the series from the very beginning and have been invaluable in providing the needed support and encouragement to us and to the many authors in the series. She, along with her staff, has helped make the process of completing this series an enjoyable one. For everything they have done, we thank them all.

Randall S. Schuler, Rutgers University
Paul Sparrow, Manchester University
Susan E. Jackson, Rutgers University
Michael Poole, Cardiff University

# Preface

Over the last decade or so, many volumes have been written regarding the management system(s) of Asia-Pacific economies. This has been mainly in response to the dramatic rise of Asia-Pacific economies after World War II, led by Japan in the 1950s, the Tiger nations in the 1960s, major ASEAN members in the 1970s, China and Vietnam in the 1980s and 1990s respectively and finally India in the 1990s. The main focus of such volumes has been to understand and explain the main driving forces contributing to the "economic miracle" of the region. The Asian economic crisis of the late 1990s raised a number of questions regarding the suitability of the management system(s) of the countries affected by the present crisis. On the other hand, rapid developments in the field of human resource management (HRM), globalization of business and the increased acceptance of HRM function as an important contributor towards the firms' performance demand the need to examine HRM systems in different cross-national contexts. At present such literature is dominated by writings on western developed nations – a region which is economically aging very rapidly. The Asia-Pacific region is now considered to be very important for the global economy and as such, both academics and practitioners are interested in finding out more about the nature of HRM system(s) and the factors affecting them in this region. This will contribute both to better theory and practice development. This book attempts to fill this gap in the literature.

Due to the context specific nature of HRM, one should expect cross-national variations between the HRM systems of Asia-Pacific nations. It is important for managers to be aware of such differences and to realize that HRM strategies vary significantly from country to country and that the strategies used to manage human resources (HRs) in one country are sometimes ineffective or irrelevant in another country. They need to develop an understanding regarding the dynamics of managing HRs in different parts of the globe. However, students are taught what are generalizable HRM concepts and practices which have a strong base in the Anglo-Saxon context. Similarly, multinational companies (MNCs) tend to adopt an ethnocentric (due to control and coordination reasons amongst others) approach towards the management of their HRs in different subsidiaries operating in the Asia-Pacific region. In the present globalized world, the applicability of such concepts and practices to different local contexts is clearly questionable.

The challenges regarding the management of HRs in the Asia-Pacific countries are complex and demanding. Academics can play a significant role in this regard by providing relevant information to policy-makers and researchers. It is also important for business students, as future business leaders, to gain an understanding of the different issues relating to HRM in the region. An attempt has been made in this book to highlight in detail how national HRM systems are unique and deeply rooted in the sociocultural and institutional context of each of the countries covered.

Thus, the objective of this book is to provide the reader with an understanding of the dynamics of HRM in eleven countries in the Asia-Pacific region: China, South Korea, Japan, Hong Kong, Taiwan, India, Thailand, Vietnam, Malaysia, Singapore and Australia. It is intended that the reader acquires not only an understanding about the HRM functions in these countries, but more awareness of the diverse and unique configurations of national factors (cultural, institutional and business environment) which dictate HRM in cross-national settings. Such awareness will enable the reader to better understand the "context-specific" nature of HRM in these countries and the need to acknowledge the strength of cross-national HRM differences.

To achieve this objective, all the contributions have been written around a set framework. It highlights the historical developments of the HRM function, the influence of core national factors (i.e. national culture, national institutions, dynamic business environment and business sector) on HRM policies and practices, key challenges facing the HRM function and the future of HRM function in the countries covered. This book consolidates in a single source the dynamics of management of human resources in the Asia-Pacific countries, i.e. questions pertaining to the "what," "why" and "how" of HRM in the region. All the chapters in this volume are original contributions to the field and were specially commissioned for the book.

It is hoped that this volume will serve as a catalyst to the development of further theoretical insights and appropriate techniques of HRM in this area. The subject area of the book is suitable for both undergraduate and postgraduate HRM and International Management courses. In addition, this book will be of interest to cross-national HRM researchers and practitioners.

Two main reasons gave rise to this book. First, the scarcity of a single volume that highlights the scenario of HRM in the Asia-Pacific context which can be used on relevant courses. Second, this is a product of long discussions with the series editors and a number of colleagues on the need for such a book.

I would like to thank all those who have in various ways helped to make this project a success, and extend my special gratitude to the series editors for giving me the opportunity to work on this project. I would also like to thank all the contributors for their enthusiasm and promptness which helped me to complete this work. My special thanks to all the reviewers for responding readily to my requests and for providing invaluable comments on the chapters. I would also particularly like to thank Catriona King (formerly with Routledge), who initially commissioned this project, Francesca Poynter and Rachel Crookes at Routledge for their help and assistance at various stages of the production of this volume.

Pawan S. Budhwar, Aston Business School, Birmingham

# 1 Introduction: HRM in the Asia-Pacific context

PAWAN S. BUDHWAR

## Introduction

Over the last couple of decades or so, a number of Asia-Pacific economies have witnessed unprecedented levels of economic growth (Japan and Korea experienced this much earlier) and the region has been a major contributor to global prosperity and stability. The economic crisis of the late 1990s suddenly halted this remarkable economic run. Importantly, it highlighted a number of characteristics of the affected economies which needed major changes so as to enable them to assimilate into the global economy (Arndt and Hall, 1999; Yip, 2000). Already a number of efforts have been made to achieve this (see Chen, 2002); however, several macro-level phenomena unique to each of the economies in the region (such as their political set-up, regulatory set-up, very high level of corruption, and family matters) are creating major hindrances in this regard (see *The Economist*, 2002; Lau, 2002; Tsui-Auch and Lee, 2003). Nevertheless, at present, the Asia-Pacific region produces more goods and services than either North America or the European Union and this trend is expected to accelerate in the years to come. Moreover, out of the twenty-five most important emerging markets, ten or more are regularly from the Asia-Pacific region (see *The Economist*, 2003). Further, they attract an enormous amount of foreign direct investment (FDI). Despite the fact that global FDI inflows declined in 2002 for the second consecutive year, FDI in Asia and the Pacific declined the least in comparison to other regions of the world, and China with a record inflow of $53 billion became the world's biggest host country (for more details see UNCTAD, 2003). It is also predicted that most new members of the newly affluent nations will come from the Asia-Pacific in the twenty-first century (see Tan, 2002). Despite all this, most of the Asia-Pacific economies (excluding Japan, Australia and to some extent Korea) have a long way to go before they can be considered on a par with their western counterparts in both economic development and management professionalism. For example, many Asia-Pacific countries have reached a stage of development where their future source of growth will not lie primarily with the inflow of FDI, but with innovation, research and development and generating their own FDI. Moreover, many of the advanced Asia-Pacific countries (for example, Singapore, Korea and Taiwan) have lost their cheap labor and property advantage to some of the emerging economies in the region (such as China, India and Thailand). A possible way forward for them is to shift their economic activities from mass production to development hubs (see Tan, 2002). Such developments have serious implications for the human resource management (HRM) function in the region, especially when human resources (HRs) are known to play a significant role in the economic development of nations (see Tayeb, 1995; Debrah *et al.*, 2000).

This book highlights the dynamics of HRM systems in eleven Asia-Pacific countries: China (short for People's Republic of China), Korea (short for South Korea), Japan, Hong Kong, Taiwan, India, Thailand, Vietnam, Malaysia, Singapore and Australia. The remainder of this chapter is structured as follows: the next section highlights the key issues reported in the literature related to the field of HRM in the region. It then discusses the framework adopted by the contributors writing their country-specific chapters for this volume. Lastly, it presents the structure of the book and introduces each of the chapters.

## Developments in Asia-Pacific HRM

The developments in the field of HRM in the west are now well documented (see for example, Legge, 1995; Poole and Warner, 1998; Schuler and Jackson, 1999; Sisson and Storey, 2000). In comparison, the field of HRM is still evolving in the Asia-Pacific region. A thorough literature search highlights the absence of a systematic analysis which can present a comprehensive picture regarding the dynamics of HRM here. Indeed, there are a number of reliable country-specific studies which have emerged with the economic development of a particular country in the region (Ang, 1997). For example, there is plenty of literature on Japanese management systems (see for example, Ouchi, 1981; Sano *et al.*, 1997) and on various aspects of management of human resources in the Australian context (see De Cieri and Kramar, 2003). The existing literature also highlights that, of late, much research has been conducted and published on issues related to HRM in other advanced countries of the region such as Singapore, Hong Kong, Taiwan and Korea (see for example, Rowley, 1998). At present, much research is being published on different aspects of management in the Chinese context (see Brown, 1996; Warner *et al.*, 2002). Research publications on other important emerging markets such as India, Malaysia, Thailand, Indonesia and the Philippines are also emerging, though at a very slow and infrequent pace. Still, the overall balance is strongly in the favour of HRM in advanced industrial societies in the western world (Lau, 2002).

The increased acceptance of the contribution of human resources towards the achievement of firms' objectives (see Schuler and Jackson, 1999) on the one hand, and the increased interest of both academics and practitioners regarding the management of human resources in different parts of the world (due to globalization) on the other, stress the need for more research and publications to provide a reliable and comprehensive picture of HRM systems relevant to different parts of the world (Brewster *et al.*, 1996; Dowling *et al.*, 1999; Dowling and Welch, 2004). This certainly applies to the Asia-Pacific region (see Ng and Warner, 1999) due to its significant contribution towards the global economy (in different ways, such as supplier of cheap resources), and its being the largest consumer market in the world, able to attract maximum FDI and host the operations of maximum foreign firms.

Of course there is broad information available regarding different aspects of HRM in the region. However, in the present context, the validity of a number of established ideal-typical management models is questionable; for example, the three pillars of the Japanese employment system (i.e. permanent jobs, seniority pay and enterprise union) and the management models of Singaporean Chinese and Korean business groups (see Rowley, 1998; Tsui-Auch and Lee, 2003). To understand such changes, there is now a need to highlight the major factors that determine HRM policies and practices in the Asia-Pacific region in the present global context. Such an evaluation will further contribute to the development of HRM theories and relevant policies and practices (Budhwar and Debrah, 2001a). An attempt has been made in this volume to highlight the key determinants of HRM in the respective countries.

Academics have responded positively to the challenges raised by the globalization of business by investigating a number of issues and problems related to HRM in the Asia-Pacific context (see El Kahal, 2001). Adopting a neo-institutional approach, Moore and Jennings (1995) examine the pattern of HRM systems in eleven Asia-Pacific Rim countries. Neo-institutional theory focuses on the way in which innovations in behavior, technology and structure become accepted and widely used (i.e. the process through which innovations become recognized, formalized and then legitimized in the society). Along with this perspective, the authors also stress the role of local culture and conditions for HRM while studying the employment relationships in the chosen countries. Pursuing a similar theme and emphasizing cultural values, Kao et al. (1999) stress the need to indigenize the management practices in Asian organizations. The authors challenge the applicability of western management and organization theories in the Asian context (something which has been tested and confirmed for many years; see for example, Kanungo and Jaeger, 1990). Continuing with the cultural perspective, Kidd et al. (2001) examine the key HR issues faced by western firms operating in the Asian context and the challenges faced by the local firms in the post-Asian economic crisis of the late 1990s. The authors assert that, due to the cultural and institutional differences, foreign firms operating in China find it hard to implement their headquarters' HRM practices in their Chinese subsidiaries. On the other hand, studies by Björkman and Lu (1999) reveal contradictory results. They show the successful implementation of global standardized HRM practices in foreign firms operating in the Chinese context. Similar results have been recently reported by Budhwar and Björkman (2003) in their study of foreign firms operating in India. Such results indicate that certain levels of standardization of HRM systems are perhaps taking place around the globe. Still, most research findings regarding the transfer of HRM practices from headquarters of multi-national corporations (MNCs) to different regional subsidiaries emphasize some sort of adjustment to the local context (see for example, Bae et al., 1998). In such conditions, it becomes important that HR managers responsible for decisions regarding HRM practices and policies in subsidiaries operating in the Asia-Pacific region be aware of the key factors which significantly influence HRM systems in the respective countries.

Rowley and associates (see Rowley and Lewis, 1996; Rowley, 1998; Rowley and Benson, 2002; Benson and Rowley, 2003; Rowley et al., forthcoming), Warner (1998, 2002) and Amante (1998) amongst others, have examined the issues of convergence–divergence in the Asia-Pacific context. Over the last few years, research evidence has helped to supplant the convergence view with the knowledge that managerial attitudes, values, behaviors, and efficacy differ across national cultures (see for example, McGaughey and De Cerie, 1999); recent investigations in the Asia-Pacific region (see for example, Warner, 2000, 2002) emphasize the notion of 'soft convergence' (partial impact) as an outcome of globalization. From the MNC's perspective, the implementation of global standardized HRM practices and policies (with local adjustments) is also an indication of soft convergence. Globalization and international trade and finance place pressures on firms to standardize practices and policies (Rowley and Benson, 2002). However, considering the sheer variations (such as population, geography, economies, economic development phase, labor markets, sociocultural, legal and political setup, and HRM systems) in the Asia-Pacific region, it will not be sensible to talk about significant or 'hard convergence' (for more details see Hofstede, 2001; Warner, 2002). Possibly, a thorough cross-national analysis of the key factors which form the basis of national HRM systems (such as national culture, institutions and dynamic business environment) and the level (both depth and acceptance) at which a given HR practice is adopted in different settings can help to examine the convergence–divergence thesis in a more meaningful manner (see Begin, 1997; Budhwar and Sparrow, 2002).

Another important issue which has attracted the attention of both academics and practitioners over the years has been the unique characteristics of different business groups (such as *chaebols* in Korea, *keiretsus* in Japan or Chinese family businesses) operating in different countries in the Asia-Pacific region which have contributed a great deal to their economic success. Details of such characteristics are provided in individual chapters of this volume (also see Floyd, 1999, for a comparison of eastern versus western management practices). These business groups have deep roots in the core institutions (such as family structure, Confucianism), and sociocultural background of their respective societies (see for example, Whitley, 1996) and accordingly have their own HRM systems (see Begin, 1997; Rowley, 1998). The economic crisis of the late 1990s and the present competitive environment have raised questions regarding the validity of such ideal-typical family business management models in the present context (see Tu et al., 2002; Tsui-Auch and Lee, 2003). Before the economic crisis, such groups, although professionalized in their management systems, retained family control and corporate rule. However, the pressure created by the economic crisis is forcing the groups to relinquish these by absorbing more professional managers at the top. A similar pattern is emerging in the Indian private business houses where top positions are being offered to the best available professionals and a more formal and rationalized approach to HRM is being adopted (see Budhwar, 2003). However, this phenomenon is still evolving across many Asia-Pacific countries and there is a scarcity of reliable literature in this regard (White, 2002). Such information is highlighted in this volume.

Similarly, globalization has affected the industrial/employment relations system of Asia-Pacific countries (see for example, Verma *et al.*, 1995); most countries of the region (like many others around the globe) have experienced a decline in union membership (see Kuruvilla *et al.*, 2002); changes in industrial relations in the Asian context are also contributing to adjustment from previously salient constraints (labor peace and industrial stability) to the new imperative of enhancing firm-level competitiveness through both numerical and functional flexibility (Kuruvilla and Erickson, 2002). A similar pattern was observed in western industrialized nations, suggesting the possibility of convergence. However, such indications are based on limited sources and need to be seriously questioned. Nevertheless, it is clear that globalization and the Asian economic crisis of the late 1990s have certainly affected the employment relations of Asia-Pacific countries in one way or the other, such as employment security (for more details see Debrah, 2002; Hadiz, 2002).

Based on the above discussion and the existing literature (which is not reviewed here as it is beyond the scope of this chapter and the volume), at least two conclusions can be drawn. First, the significant contribution of the Asia-Pacific region towards global economic development is now well acknowledged (see for example, Kim and Koo, 1997; Yip, 2000). Second, it is clearly evident that the existing HRM research in the Asia-Pacific context (probably not applicable to Australia) is both limited and not conducted in a systematic manner within a clear framework to include those countries which may enable a conclusive and comprehensive picture. As a result, it does not generally provide insight into underlying processes and contribute to theory development (see White, 2002). In the present global context, highlighting of region/country-specific phenomenon would help to generate theory for global-relevant issues. It can also contribute to validate region-specific constructs (for example, Chinese, Indian, or Korean) to study local and global issues (see Lau, 2002). A possible way forward is to conduct a systematic analysis starting from a basic level and leading to an advanced level, thereby helping to provide a comprehensive analysis and a more reliable picture of the scene. How this may be conducted is discussed in the next section.

## Framework for analyzing cross-national HRM

Before discussing the framework adopted for developing the country-specific chapters for this volume, it will be useful to highlight the complex context of the Asia-Pacific region which makes it difficult to conduct a meaningful cross-national HRM analysis. A number of scholars (see for example, Rowley, 1998; Hasegawa, 2002; Warner, 2002, among others) highlight the complex setting of the Asia-Pacific region. One of the more common mistakes committed by both academics and policy-makers is the use of terms such as "Far-East," "Asian" or "Asia-Pacific" in a very general sense (i.e. it is applied to a group of nations existing in the region). However, it is important to acknowledge that each nation within the region has an independent set of socioeconomic components differing from one another in content and arising inevitably from the interplay of social relations unique to themselves. Hence, there is a clear need to see the management phenomena as part and parcel of the distinctive political, socioeconomic, cultural and institutional systems of each country (Morishima, 1995; Rowley, 1998; Hasegawa, 2002).

Further, countries in the Asia-Pacific region are at different stages of industrialization and economic development. The region covers a range of geographical, economic and cultural spheres. Though writers (such as Leggett and Bamber, 1996; Ng and Warner, 1999; Bamber et al., 2000) divide the countries of the region into three broad categories, i.e. advanced economies (Japan, Australia and New Zealand), newly industrialized economies (such as Korea, Taiwan, Singapore and Hong Kong) and less developed countries or those which are in the earliest phase of industrialization (such as China, India, Malaysia, Thailand and the Philippines) on the basis of their economic development. However, while analyzing HRM systems here, such a categorization is unhelpful and should be avoided, as countries within these categories significantly vary on core aspects of national culture (for example, Japan and Australia), institutional framework (such as the nature of the family business groups of Korea and Singapore or Taiwan, which vary significantly; see Tu et al., 2002) and core business sectors (such as the software sector of India and the manufacturing sector of China). These are the main national factors which significantly determine national HRM systems (see Budhwar and Sparrow, 2002).

In order to develop a conceptual framework for examining HRM in a cross-national context involving both developed and developing nations (as in the case of the Asia-Pacific region), it is important to define HRM in the broadest sense. There are some reasons for this. First, the existing literature suggests that the concept of HRM is relatively new and possibly non-existent in some regions of the developing world. Second, several distinctive HR models may exist within firms in a particular country, each of which depends (along with a number of other factors, such as different institutions and national culture) on a number of distinct "internal labour markets" (Osterman, 1994; Boxall, 1995; Hendry, 1996). Within each labor market, HRM incorporates a range of subfunctions and practices which include systems for workforce governance, work organization, staffing and development and reward systems (Begin, 1992). HRM is therefore concerned with the management of all employment relationships in the firm, incorporating the management of managers as well as non-management labor.

In line with these views, different scholars in the field of HRM have put forth a number of frameworks for conducting international/cross-national HRM research (for an extensive review, see Jackson and Schuler, 1999; Budhwar and Debrah, 2001b; Budhwar and Sparrow, 2002; Schuler et al., 2002). Based on a critical analysis of the existing frameworks and extensive research in the field, Budhwar and associates (see

Budhwar and Sparrow, 1998, 2002; Budhwar and Debrah, 2001a, 2001b) have proposed a framework for examining cross-national HRM. They have identified three levels of factors and variables which are known to influence HRM policies and practices and are worth considering for cross-national examinations (for details see Budhwar and Sparrow, 2002). These are:

1 national factors (involving national culture, national institutions, business sectors and dynamic business environment);
2 contingent variables (such as age, size, nature, ownership, life-cycle stage of organization);
3 organizational strategies (such as those proposed by Miles and Snow and Porter) and policies related to primary HR functions and internal labor markets.

However, considering the infancy stage of HRM in many Asia-Pacific countries and the argument that HRM in a cross-national context may best be analyzed by examining the influence of national factors (Brewster *et al.*, 1996; Budhwar and Sparrow, 1998), it is proposed to examine the impact of the main national factors on HRM in the eleven selected Asia-Pacific countries. A similar approach was successfully adopted by Budhwar and Debrah (2001a) to examine the HRM systems in thirteen developing countries. The broad national factors such as culture and institutions form the macro environment of organizations in a national context. All the contributors of country-specific chapters for this volume have made a sincere effort to highlight the influence of the national factors (where possible) on the national HRM system in their respective countries. For a detailed explanation regarding the rationale for the selection of various factors and variables included in the framework, see Budhwar and Sparrow (2002). The core aspects of each of the four national factors are available in Table 1.1.

## Plan of the book

It is difficult to include all the countries of the Asia-Pacific region in one volume. However, by including a wide range of countries, it is hoped to present the reader with a rich flavor of the core aspects of HRM systems and the possible trends and patterns that are emerging for each country and how these are shaped by key national factors. Highlighting the scenario of HRM in the Asia-Pacific region and key issues related to it, this volume is divided into two parts. The first part deals with country-specific chapters (chapters 2–12) and the second part with issues related to transfer of HRM from MNC's headquarters to their subsidiaries in the Asia-Pacific region (chapter 13) and key HRM challenges faced by firms operating in the region (chapter 14).

Most of the contributors are either natives of the country for which they have authored the chapter or have worked and researched for long periods in the respective country. This helps to minimize the "western bias" in such projects and has enabled the authors to present a more realistic picture. Each of the country-specific chapters follows a common pattern. This has been developed keeping in mind the broad objective of the

*Table 1.1* Details of aspects of national factors determining cross-national HRM

| National culture | Institutions | Industrial sector | Dynamic business environment |
| --- | --- | --- | --- |
| Socialization process | National labor laws | Common strategies, business logic and goals | Competition |
| Common values, norms of behavior and customs | Trade unions | Regulations and standards | Business alliances |
| Influence of pressure groups | Politics | Sector-specific knowledge | Changing composition of workforce |
| Assumptions that shape managers perceptions, insights and mindset | Educational and vocational training set-up | Informal and formal bench marking | Restructuring |
| Management style | Labor market | Cross-sector cooperation | Focus on total customer satisfaction |
| Meaning of work and values | Professional bodies | Common developments in business operations | Facility of information |
| Personal dispositions, attitudes and manners | International institutions | Labor or skill requirements | Technological change |
| Approaches to cultural diversity | Industry by itself | Merger activity | Globalization of business |
| Match to the organization culture | Employers federation | Workforce mobility | |
| | Consulting organizations | Capital mobility | |
| | Placement organizations | | |
| | Trade bodies | | |
| | Government institutions | | |
| | Local authorities | | |
| | Voluntary bodies | | |

book, i.e. to highlight the dynamics of the HRM systems in the respective countries. All the authors have made a reasonable attempt to structure their country-specific contributions around the following topics:

1 historical development in HRM/IR/PM/personnel administration;
2 role and importance of, and degree of partnership in, HRM in most companies;
3 key factors determining HRM practices and policies (such as law, politics, national culture, competitive business environment, different institutions, economy, etc.), with a review of most of the HR practices, such as pay, staffing, training, etc.;
4 present changes taking place within the HR functions (over the past five years) and the factors responsible for the same;
5 key challenges facing HRM;
6 determine what is likely to happen to HR functions in the next five years;
7 details of websites and current references for the latest information and developments in HRM that will provide more information to the reader over the years.

In chapter 2, Cooke highlights the profound changes which have taken place in the Chinese traditional personnel administrative system over the last five decades or so. She discusses how the personnel function in China remained centralized until the early 1980s and how the "three systems" reforms, along with other programs (for example, "competing for the post," downsizing, restructuring, early retirements) initiated fundamental changes in the Chinese HRM policies during the mid-1990s. Cooke also illuminates our understanding about the rapidly changing dynamics of the labor-market in China and the movement away from harmonious management–labor relations to one characterized by conflicting interests, rising disputes and increasing inequality in contractual arrangements between management and labor. The rapidly changing business environment in China has contributed to the movement from state-owned enterprises to joint venture and private-owned enterprises. She succinctly highlights the main factors responsible for such changes and highlights the role of political, legal, cultural and economic factors in the development of HR functions in China.

Chapter 3 details the dynamics of HRM in South Korea. Here, Rowley and Bae use the three stages (i.e. pre-1987, 1987–1997, and post-1997) and two dimensions of rewards and evaluation and resourcing and flexibility to discuss the developments in Korean HRM. They also discuss the emergence of employee involvement and partnership in HRM at both macro (national) and micro (firm) levels. Rowley and Bae also discuss the historical and political background of Korea and highlight the foundations of Korean corporations, the "*chaebols*," and how they manage employment relations. In addition, they discuss the Asian economic crisis and the problems and strains it brought to the *chaebols*. Next, the chapter highlights the scenario regarding a number of HRM functions in Korea and the changes taking place there. Finally, the future of HRM in Korean companies is analyzed.

In chapter 4, Salmon presents the past and present scenario of HRM in Japan. He discusses the pressures forcing changes to established Japanese management models (i.e. lifetime employment, seniority-based promotion, HR development and the enterprise union). Salmon then highlights the implications of the decade-long recession on the field of HRM in Japan and discusses the employers' responses to the same. He also points out the key challenges faced by HRM functions in the present-day Japanese organizations.

Chapter 5 highlights employment relations in Hong Kong over the last thirty years. Chan and Lui have structured their discussion around three time periods – the 1970s, 1980s and 1990s (i.e. from a manufacturing base to a full service-base) – to report the developments in HRM in Hong Kong. They also discuss the de-industrialization and the re-commercialization processes and their impact on HRM in Hong Kong. Further, Chan and Lui highlight the post-1997 restructuring phase and its implications for the HRM functions. Next, they discuss the core pattern of HRM in small and medium enterprises; local Chinese family businesses; and multinational corporations. The chapter then highlights the influence of different institutions and globalization on the HRM system in Hong Kong. Finally, the authors discuss the future of HRM in Hong Kong.

In chapter 6 Wu adopts a historical perspective to present the dynamics of the HRM system in Taiwan. She asserts that Confucian work principles still dominate working relationships in Taiwan. Wu discusses the three stages of development of HRM in Taiwan (i.e. pre-mid-1960s, 1965–1985, and post-mid-1980s). Wu's chapter reveals that, in comparison to China and Korea, Taiwan seems to have a more formal and established HRM function. She also indicates the growing strategic nature of Taiwanese HRM. Further, Wu has enriched her discussion by providing the support of empirical studies and important statistics regarding the influence of environmental factors on HRM; changes in the Taiwanese HRM functions over the last five years; and key challenges facing HRM. Lastly, she discusses the scenario of the main HRM functions in selected Taiwanese firms.

Chapter 7 is concerned with HRM in India. Here, Saini and Budhwar present an overview of the socioeconomic environment of India and its impact on Indian HRM. The authors highlight the roots of HRM functions in India and how they have evolved over the last eight decades or so. The discussion then focuses on the debate regarding differences in personnel management, HRM and HR development. Using the framework introduced in this chapter, the authors highlight the influence of national culture, national institutions supporting industrial relations, legal framework, vocational educational and training setup, and other factors on Indian HRM. Later in the chapter, the discussion is focused on the possible direction for HRM in India from different perspectives (organizational, individual and national).

In chapter 8 Siengthai and Bechter present the evolution and development of HRM functions in Thailand. They contend that over the years the role of HRM has changed from a traditional payroll function to a business partner. While discussing these changes, the authors highlight the influence of key factors such as the Thai national culture and the economic environment on the Thai HRM system. This is followed by a critical analysis on HRM in Thailand before and after the economic crisis of the late 1990s. Later in the chapter, results from a number of empirical studies are presented to highlight the scenario of HRM in both Thai and multinational firms. A separate section is devoted to labor management relations in Thailand. Like most chapters, this also highlights the main challenges facing HRM functions and the possible way forward in the Thai context.

Chapter 9 provides a critical analysis of HRM systems and practices in Vietnam. Quang and Thang show how a mixture of different cultural and political institutions and the economic structure of the country impact Vietnamese HRM. The authors discuss the scenario of HRM both before and after the renovation period of 1986 (before which Vietnam followed a centrally planned economic model). Next, the current status of HRM functions in Vietnam is analyzed. A special emphasis is laid on industrial relations in the country. Finally, the chapter highlights the changing role of HRM and the key challenges before it in the new economic environment.

In chapter 10 Mellahi and Wood discuss the dynamics of HRM in Malaysia. They highlight the roles of political setup, sociocultural context and government initiatives in the development of a national HRM system. The authors discuss the significant impact of both Islamic and Chinese Malaysian work-related values on Malaysian employment policies and practices. Mellahi and Wood also highlight the scenario of industrial relations and labor markets in the Malaysian context. The chapter then discusses the national HR development strategy (Vision 2020) and the present state of HRM functions.

Chapter 11 is about HRM in Singapore. Khatri highlights the impact of economic development strategy, national administrative systems, multinationals and various cultural aspects on Singaporean HRM policies and practices. While doing so, he highlights a number of significant differences between various categories of employees (such as local versus foreign). The author highlights issues such as labor turnover, participation of both females and older employees in the workforce and management of Singaporean expatriates as the main challenges facing Singaporean HRM functions. Next, the chapter presents the current state of HRM policies and practices in both local and foreign firms operating in Singapore. Finally, the possible direction of Singaporean HRM is discussed.

Patrickson and Sutiyono detail in chapter 12 the scene of HRM in Australia. They initially present an overview of Australian HRM systems in the context of the changing economic and technological business environment. Then they highlight the main characteristics of the Australian workforce and the recent contextual changes (such as the legal) and their implications for HRM policies and practices. The changing context of Australia is also contributing to a decline in the number of unions, making HRM more formal, and with an increased emphasis on diversity management. The authors then discuss the core HRM functions and the possible changes taking place in the same. Some useful references to small enterprises (which are dominant in the Australian context) are also made in the chapter. Finally, they highlight the main challenges facing HRM in Australia in the 2000s.

Chapter 13 is devoted to discussion on the theme of transfer of HRM from MNC's headquarters to their Asia-Pacific subsidiaries. This chapter is mainly included in the volume because of the interest of many MNCs in the region. Moreover, the topics covered in this chapter form part of current debates and a clear consensus on the same is still not reached. Björkman highlights a number of conceptual and theoretical issues related to the topic. He then presents a concise review of the existing literature related to the characteristics of MNC HRM practices and determinants of HRM policies and practices in MNC affiliates. Later, in the chapter, Björkman sketches out the possible direction in the field with a special reference to the Asia-Pacific context.

In the last chapter, Debrah and Budhwar discuss the current HRM challenges in the Asia-Pacific region. It is believed that these issues will be the focus of future research and will help to further enhance our understanding of HRM in the Asia-Pacific.

## Acknowledgment

I thank Chris Rowley and Yaw Debrah for their useful comments on an earlier version of this chapter.

## References

Amante, M.S.V. (1998) "Converging and diverging trends in HRM: The Philippine 'Halo-Halo' approach," in C. Rowley (ed.) *Human resource management in the Asia Pacific region*, London: Frank Cass, pp. 111–132.

Ang, S.H. (1997) "Fourteen years of research in the Asia Pacific Journal of Management," *Asia Pacific Journal of Management* 14: 89–97.

Arndt, H.W. and Hall, H. (1999) (eds.) *Southeast Asia's economic crisis: Origins, lessons and the way out*, Singapore: Institute of Southeast Asian Studies.

Bae, J., Shyh-jer, C. and Lawler, J.J. (1998) "Variations in human resource management in Asian countries: MNC home-country and host-country effect," *International Journal of Human Resource Management* 9: 653–670.

Bamber, G., Park, F., Lee, C., Ross, P.K. and Broadbent, K. (2000) *Employment relations in the Asia-Pacific: Changing approaches*, London: Thompson Learning Press.

Begin, J.P. (1992) "Comparative HRM: A systems perspective," *International Journal of Human Resource Management* 3: 379–408.

Begin, J.P. (1997) *Dynamic human resource systems: Cross-national comparisons*, Berlin: Walter de Gruyter.

Benson, J. and Rowley, C. (2003) "Conclusion: Changes in Asian HRM: Implications for theory and practice," *Asia Pacific Business Review* 9 (4): 186–195.

Björkman, I. and Lu, Y. (1999) "The management of human resource in Chinese–Western joint ventures," *Journal of World Business* 34: 306–324.

Boxall, P.F. (1995) "Building the theory of comparative HRM," *Human Resource Management Journal* 5: 5–17.

Brewster, C., Tregaskis, O., Hegewisch, A. and Mayne, L. (1996) "Comparative research in human resource management: A review and an example," *International Journal of Human Resource Management* 7: 586–604.

Brown, R. (ed.) (1996) *Chinese business enterprise* (4 vols), London: Routledge.

Budhwar, P. (2003) "Culture and management in India," in M. Warner (ed.) *Culture and management in Asia*, London: Curzon Press, pp. 66–81.

Budhwar, P. and Björkman, I. (2003) "A corporate perspective on the management of human resources in foreign firms operating in India," 2003 International HRM Conference, 4–6 June 2003, Limerick, Ireland.

Budhwar, P. and Debrah, Y. (2001a) "Introduction: HRM in developing countries," in P. Budhwar and Y. Debrah (eds.) *HRM in developing countries*, London: Routledge, pp. 1–15.

Budhwar, P. and Debrah, Y.A. (2001b) "Rethinking comparative and cross national human resource management research," *International Journal of Human Resource Management* 12: 497–515.

Budhwar, P. and Sparrow, P. (2002) "An integrative framework for determining cross national human resource management practices," *Human Resource Management Review* 12: 377–403.

Budhwar, P. and Sparrow, P. (1998) "National factors determining Indian and British HRM practices: An empirical study," *Management International Review* 38, Special Issue 2: 105–121.

Chen, M. (1995) *Asian management systems*, London: International Thomson Business Press.

Chen, M. (2002) "Post-crisis trends in Asian management," *Asia Business & Management* 1: 39–58.

De Cieri, H. and Kramar, R. (2003) *Human resource management in Australia: Strategy, people and performance*, Sydney: McGraw Hill.

Debrah, Y.A., McGovern, I. and Budhwar, P. (2000) "Complementarity or competition: The development of human resources in a growth triangle," *International Journal of Human Resource Management* 11 (2): 314–335.

Debrah, Y.A. (2002) "Introduction: Migrant workers in Pacific Asia," *Asia Pacific Business Review* 8 (4): 1–18.

Dowling, P.J. and Welch, D.E. (2004) *International dimensions of human resource management*, 4th edition, Cincinnati: South-Western College Publishing.

Dowling, P.J., Welch. D.E. and Schuler, R.S. (1999) *International dimensions of human resource management*, 3rd edition, Cincinnati: South-Western College Publishing.

*The Economist* (2002) "Timid Tigers," 15 June: 77–78.

*The Economist* (2003) "Emerging-market indicators," 19 April: 106.

El Kahal, S. (2001) (ed.) *Business in Asia Pacific: Text and cases*, Oxford: Oxford University Press.

Floyd, D. (1999) "Eastern and Western management practices: Myth or reality?" *Management Decision* 37 (7): 628–632.

Hadiz, V.R. (2002) "Globalization, labour, and economic crisis: Insights from Southeast Asia," *Asia Business & Management* 1: 249–266.

Hasegawa, H. (2002) "Editorial," *Asia Business & Management* 1: 1–4.

Hendry, C. (1996) "Continuities in human resource processes in internationalization and domestic business management," *Journal of Management Studies* 33: 475–494.

Hofstede, G. (2001) *Culture's consequences: Comparing values, behaviours, institutions and organizations across nations*, London: Sage.

Jackson, S.E. and Schuler, R.S. (1999) "Understanding human resource management in the context of organizations and their environment," in R. Schuler and S. Jackson (eds.) *Strategic human resource management*, London: Blackwell, pp. 4–28.

Kanungo, R.N. and Jaeger, A.M. (1990) "Introduction: The need for indigenous management in developing countries," in A.M. Jaeger and R.N. Kanungo (eds.) *Management in Developing Countries*, London: Routledge, pp. 1–19.

Kao, H.S.R., Sinha, D. and Wilper, B. (1999) (eds.) *Management and cultural values: The indigenization of organizations in Asia*, New Delhi: Sage.

Kidd, J.B., Li, X. and Richter, F.-J. (2001) (eds.) *Advances in human resource management in Asia*, Basingstoke: Palgrave.

Kim, Y.-S. and Koo, H.K. (1997) "Asia-Pacific region in changing global economy," *Human Systems Management* 16 (4): 285–291.

Kuruvilla, S. and Erickson, C.L. (2002) "Change and transformation in Asian industrial relations," *Industrial Relations* 41 (2): 171–227.

Kuruvilla, S., Das, S., Kwon, H. and Kwon, S. (2002) "Trade union growth and decline in Asia," *British Journal of Industrial Relations* 40: 431–461.

Lau, C.-M. (2002) "Asian management research: Frontiers and challenges," *Asia Pacific Journal of Management* 19: 171–178.

Legge, K. (1995) *Human resource management: rhetorics and realities*, Basingstoke: Macmillan Business.

Leggett, C. and Bamber, G. (1996) "Asia-Pacific tiers of change," *Human Resource Management Journal* 6 (2): 7–19.

McGaughey, S.L. and De Cerie, H. (1999) "Reassessment of convergence and divergence dynamics: Implications for international HRM," *International Journal of Human Resource Management* 10 (2): 235–250.

Moore, L.F. and Jennings, P.D. (1995) (eds.) *Human resource management on the Pacific Rim – Institutions, practices and attitudes*, Berlin: De Gruyter.

Morishima, M. (1995) "Embedding HRM in a social context," *British Journal of Industrial Relations* 33: 617–640.

Ng, S.-H. and Warner, M. (1999) "Human resource management in Asia," in B. Morton and P. Joynt (eds.) *The global HR manager*, London: IPD.

Osterman, P. (1994) "Internal labor markets: Theory and change," in C. Kerr and P.D. Staudohar (eds.) *Markets and institutions*, Cambridge, MA, and London: Harvard University Press, pp. 303–339.

Ouchi, W. (1981) *Theory Z: How American business can meet the Japanese challenge*, Reading, MA: Addison-Wesley.

Poole, M. and Warner, M. (eds.) (1998) *The IEBM handbook of human resource management*, London: International Thomson Business Press.

Rowley, C. (1998) "Introduction: Comparison and perspectives on HRM in the Asia Pacific," in C. Rowley (ed.) *Human resource management in the Asia Pacific region*, London: Frank Cass, pp. 1–18.

Rowley, C., Benson, M. and Warner, M. (forthcoming) "Towards an Asian model of human resource management? A comparative analysis of China, Japan and South Korea," *International Journal of Human Resource Management*.

Rowley, C. and Benson, J. (2000) "Convergence and divergence in Asian human resource management," *California Management Review* 44 (2): 90–109.

Rowley, C. and Lewis, M. (1996) "Greater China at the crossroads: Convergence, culture, and competitiveness," *Asia Pacific Business Review* 2 (3): 1–22.

Sano, Y., Morishima, M. and Seike, A. (eds.) (1997) *Frontiers of Japanese human resource management practices*, Tokyo: The Japan Institute of Labour.

Schuler, R.S. and Jackson, S.E. (eds.) (1999) *Strategic human resource management*, London: Blackwell.

Schuler, R.S., Budhwar, P. and Florkowski, G.W. (2002) "International human resource management: Review and critique," *International Journal of Management Reviews* 4 (1): 41–70.

Sisson, K. and Storey, J. (2000) *The realities of human resource management*, Buckingham: Open University Press.

Tan, T.T. (2002) "Introduction to special issue of JBR on Asian business research," *Journal of Business Research* 55: 797–798.

Tayeb, M. (1995) "The Competitive advantage of nations: The role of HRM and its socio-cultural context," *International Journal of Human Resource Management* 6: 588–605.

Tsui-Auch, L.S. and Lee, Y.-J. (2003) "The state matters: Management models of Singaporean Chinese and Korean business groups," *Organization Studies* 24: 507–534.

Tu, H.S., Kim, S.Y. and Sullivan, S.E. (2002) "Global strategy lessons from Japanese and Korean business groups," *Business Horizons* (March–April): 39–46.

UNCTAD (2003) *World Investment Report 2003*, http//www.unctad.org

Verma, A., Kochan, T.A. and Lansbury, R. (eds.) (1995) *Employment relations in growing Asian economies*, London and New York: Routledge.

Warner, M. (1998) "China's HRM in transition: Towards relative convergence?" in C. Rowley (ed.) *Human resource management in the Asia Pacific region*, London: Frank Cass, pp. 19–33.

Warner, M. (2000) "Introduction: The Asia-Pacific HRM model revisited," *International Journal of Human Resource Management* 11: 171–182.

Warner, M. (2002) "Globalization, labour markets and human resources in Asia-Pacific economies: An overview," *International Journal of Human Resource Management* 13: 384–398.

Warner, M. (2003) "Introduction: Culture and management in Asia," in M. Warner (ed.) *Culture and management in Asia*, London: RoutledgeCurzon, pp. 1–23.

Warner, M., Wong, L. and Lee, G.O.M. (2002) "Editorial," *International Journal of Human Resource Management* 13: 379–383.

White, S. (2002) "Rigor and relevance in Asian Management research: Where are we and where can we go?" *Asia Pacific Journal of Management* 19: 287–352.

Whitley, R. (1996) *Business systems in East Asia: Firms, markets and societies*, London: Sage.

Yip, G.S. (2000) *The Asian advantage: Key strategies for winning in the Asia-Pacific region*, Reading, MA: Addison-Wesley.

# 2 HRM in China

FANG LEE COOKE

## Introduction

HRM in China is as new as its market economy, with its traditional personnel administrative system undergoing a period of profound change. This chapter first outlines the historical development in personnel management and the role of trade unions and the Workers' Congress in China. It then analyzes the legislative, social, cultural and business factors that shape the HRM practices in terms of recruitment, training, working-time arrangements and pay. This is followed by a discussion of the major changes in recent years in the HR functions such as recruitment and performance appraisal. The chapter then contemplates key challenges facing HRM in China, notably the thorny issue of motivation-performance-reward, skill shortage and its associated problems of recruitment, retention and training, and the absence of strategic HRM. The chapter finally explores the implications of all these for HRM functions in the near future.

Throughout the chapter, relatively heavy references are made to state-owned enterprises (SOEs) and public sector organizations, although the private sector will also be discussed as much as possible. This is because the state has been a major employer in the past and because SOEs and public sector organizations are the areas where HRM has experienced the most radical changes in recent years under the economic and social (welfare) reforms. This chapter will also use the term HRM in a broad sense, although the term "personnel management" is used to describe personnel administrative policies prior to the 1980s when radical economic reforms started, leading to the proliferation of business ownership in addition to the state sector. It must be noted here that, while the concept of HRM has grown in popularity in recent years, there is considerable divergence in the ways in which "human resource management" is interpreted and understood in China. However, the scope of this chapter does not warrant the space to debate the origin and various versions of the concept in detail, a task made more difficult due to the lack of such a debate among academics and practitioners in China, who tend to accept the concept uncritically as a progressive given.

# Historical development in personnel management in China

Personnel management in China has a 50-year history following the founding of the "New China" in 1949 under the Communist Party. For the first three decades until the end of the Cultural Revolution, the personnel management system was highly centralized by the state under the planned economy regime. Personnel management during this period exhibited two major features in terms of its governance structure and content of the personnel policy.

First, the personnel policies and practices of organizations were strictly under the control of the state through regional/local labor departments. Centralization, formalization and standardization of the personnel policies and practices were the primary tasks of the Ministry of Labor (for blue-collar workers) and the Ministry of Personnel (for white-collar and managerial staff). The state not only determined the number of people to be employed and sources of recruitment, but also unilaterally set the pay scales for different categories of workers. State intervention also extended to the structure and obligations of the personnel functions at organizational level and managers of all levels were only involved in the administrative function and policy implementation under rigid policy guidelines (Child, 1994; Cooke, 2003a).

Second, for most people, entering employment was a "once-in-a-lifetime" event with "lifelong" job security. Wages were typically low but compensated by a broad range of workplace welfare provisions, including housing, pension, health, children's schooling, transportation to and from work, employment for spouses and school-leaving children, as part of the responsibility of the "nanny" employer (Warner, 1996a; Cooke, 2000).

These characteristics were once dominant in the personnel management system of the country because, until the 1980s, the vast majority of the Chinese employing organizations were state-owned, with a minority being collectively-owned and even fewer, privately-owned (see Table 2.1).

Today, four broad types of business ownership coexist in China's economic regime with the latter three rapidly gaining larger proportions:

1　state-owned enterprises;
2　collectively-owned enterprises in cities, townships and rural areas;
3　privately-owned firms and self-employed businesses;
4　foreign businesses, Sino-foreign joint ventures, and Sino-foreign cooperative enterprises (including investment from Hong Kong, Macao and Taiwan).

The changing composition structure of business ownership since the 1980s with the shrinking share of state ownership and the rapid growth of private and foreign-related firms undoubtedly has major implications for the patterns of personnel management and industrial relations at a macro level (see discussion below). In addition, the state sector has witnessed radical changes in its personnel policy and practice in the last two decades, as part of the Economic Reforms and the Enterprise Reforms beginning in the early 1980s. One of the major changes has been the rolling back of direct state control and the

*Table 2.1* Employment statistics by ownership in urban and rural areas in China* (figures in 100,000)

| Ownership | 1978 | 1980 | 1985 | 1990 | 1995 | 1998 | 2001 |
|---|---|---|---|---|---|---|---|
| **Number of employed in urban areas** | 951.4 | 1052.5 | 1280.8 | 1661.6 | 1909.3 | 2067.8 | 2394.0 |
| State-owned units | 745.1 | 801.9 | 899.0 | 1034.6 | 1126.1 | 905.8 | 764.0 |
| Collectively-owned units | 204.8 | 242.5 | 332.4 | 354.9 | 314.7 | 196.3 | 129.1 |
| Cooperative units | — | — | — | — | — | 13.6 | 15.3 |
| Joint ownership units | — | — | 3.8 | 9.6 | 5.3 | 4.8 | 4.5 |
| Limited liability corporations | — | — | — | — | — | 48.4 | 84.1 |
| Share-holding corporations | — | — | — | — | 31.7 | 41.0 | 48.3 |
| Private enterprises | — | — | — | 5.7 | 48.5 | 97.3 | 152.7 |
| Units with funds from Hong Kong, Macao and Taiwan | — | — | — | 0.4 | 27.2 | 29.4 | 32.6 |
| Foreign funded units | — | — | 0.6 | 6.2 | 24.1 | 29.3 | 34.5 |
| Self-employed individuals | 1.5 | 8.1 | 45.0 | 61.4 | 156.0 | 225.9 | 213.1 |
| **Number of employed in rural areas** | 3063.8 | 3183.6 | 3706.5 | 4729.3 | 4885.4 | 4927.9 | 4908.5 |
| Township and village enterprises | 282.7 | 300.0 | 697.9 | 926.5 | 1286.2 | 1253.7 | 1308.6 |
| Private enterprises | — | — | — | 11.3 | 47.1 | 73.7 | 118.7 |
| Self-employed individuals | — | — | — | 149.1 | 305.4 | 385.5 | 262.9 |

Sources: figures for 1978–1998 come from *China Statistical Abstract* (2000), Beijing: China Statistics Press, p. 37; figures for 2001 come from *China Statistical Yearbook* (2002), Beijing: China Statistics Press, p. 117.

* Since 1990, data on economically active population, the total employed persons and the sub-total of employed persons in urban and rural areas have been adjusted in accordance with the data obtained from the 5th National Population Census. As a result, the sum of the data by region, by ownership or by sector is not equal to the total (original note from *China Statistical Yearbook*, 2002, p. 117).

consequent increase of autonomy and responsibility at enterprise level in major aspects of their personnel management practice. This change was accompanied by a series of state-driven personnel initiatives which sent shock waves to individual employees as well as to the country's economy as a whole.

The objective of these initiatives was to bring to an end the planned state economy characterized by "high employment rate," "high welfare," "low wage" and "low productivity" and to introduce the market economy "with Chinese characteristics" in which competition and incentive were two major ingredients. As a result, rapid and fundamental changes in the Chinese HRM policies have taken place during the 1980s and especially 1990s (Easterby-Smith *et al.*, 1995).

In particular, the "three systems" reforms have been implemented in most (state-owned) organizations since the mid-1990s. These include: fixed duration individual and collective labor contracts instead of jobs-for-life; new remuneration systems to reflect performance, post and skill levels; and new welfare schemes in which all employers and employees are required by law to make a contribution to five separate funds: pension, industrial accident, maternity, unemployment and medical insurance (Warner, 1996a, 1999). The new welfare system is intended to shift the huge welfare burden from the (state) employers towards individual employees.

Employment contracts were introduced for both managerial workers and ordinary workers to replace the old system in which managers were appointed by their superiors and workers were employed for life. The rationale of this contract system was to allow greater freedom for both organizations and individuals in entering and/or terminating their employment relationship. It also reduced the job security of individuals so that they would be more motivated to work and to update their skill. It should be pointed out here that all employers are now required by the Labor Law of China (1995) to sign an employment contract with their workers, by adapting a standardized employment contract provided by the local labor authority to each specific post. While the initial intention of introducing the employment contract in SOEs was to increase motivation by removing job security, the purpose of signing employment contracts in the private firms is primarily to protect individual workers against irresponsible employers who may try to evade their responsibilities as employers. Many of these workers come from rural areas and have little knowledge of their employment rights. According to the Labor Law (1995), the employment contract should include: length of contract, work content, health and safety protection and working conditions, remuneration, discipline, conditions for termination of contract, and liability for violating the employment contract.

In SOEs and public sector organizations, a system called "competing for the post" was also introduced in the mid-1990s in which employees would be assessed (through tests) once a year on their competence to work (Cooke, 2000, forthcoming, 2004b). Those who came last would be laid off and further training would be given to increase their competence while they were waiting for a post. This system has effectively injected an element of job insecurity which serves as an incentive for the employees to become more competitive by "up-skilling" themselves.

The State Economy Commission issued a document in 2001 (No. [2001] 230) which required SOEs to deepen the above "three systems" reforms by placing them as their top priority. The document reasserts that SOEs are required to establish a system in which managerial workers should compete for their posts with both upward and downward mobility. SOEs are also required to establish an independent employment system without interference from other bodies. Employment contracts are signed and employees need to compete for their post through competency tests. Finally, SOEs are required to establish a reward system which provides greater links between (individual) performance and reward as a motivational mechanism.

Many of the above changes in the state-owned sectors were initiated by the state and carried out at organizational level from the top down, with little involvement from trade unions and employees. These changes also took place alongside the most radical change in the SOEs in the last decade: downsizing. Started in the early 1990s as part of the program of restructuring and revitalizing the outmoded SOEs, this initiative reached its peak in the late 1990s after Premier Zhu Rongji's announcement of his SOE reform plan in 1997. This reform program included plans to make 10 million workers redundant within three years through early retirement and performance review. Laid-off workers were expected to receive re-training for re-employment, a process in which the trade union was able to play a more visible role.

## Partnership in HRM

Only one trade union – the All China Federation of Trade Unions (ACFTU) – is recognized in China, with its formal national union structure dating back to the early 1920s in support of the Communist Party revolution. The current structure of the Chinese trade union organization has not changed drastically since 1949 (Warner, 1990), although there has been an expansion of union membership as urbanization has drawn more workers into industry (Ng and Warner, 1998). Drawing their membership from all sorts of occupations and sectors including manual and non-manual workers in factories, hospitals, schools and universities, the trade unions do not have any distinctive "trade" characteristics, as they all belong to the same "father" – ACFTU. Two major pieces of legislation provide the legal framework for the role of the union: the Trade Union Law (1950), which was replaced by the recently amended Trade Union Law (2001) in response to the rapid growth of the private sector, and the Labor Law (1995).

Traditionally, SOEs in China, which employ the majority of the workforce, have been the patron of the workers' welfare, as mentioned above. In the communist system in which labor and capital are perceived to share the same interests, trade unions in the SOEs in China play only a welfare role under the leadership of the Communist Party. They carry out this function effectively by acting as a "conveyor belt" between the Communist Party and the workers (Hoffman, 1981). Although union membership level is generally high, people join trade unions by default (to be seen as supportive to the Party and to enjoy the welfare benefits) rather than by desire. In some ways, it is a form of social exclusion not to be a union member in the state sector. For example, temporary workers (many of them from rural areas) who carry out laborious and tedious work unwanted by urban workers are usually non-union members and do not share the same level of workplace benefits as permanent workers.

In theory, trade unions have been given a newly regulated monitoring role. According to the Labor Law (1995), they are to "represent and protect the legal rights and interests of workers independently and autonomously and develop their activities according to the law" and to "monitor that employing units abide by labor disciplines and regulations." In practice, this proposition rarely materialized. Past and contemporary empirical evidence hardly supports the notion of trade union autonomy in China, whether it is for trade unions in large SOEs or in private- or foreign-owned enterprises (Warner, 1995; Ng and Warner, 1998; Warner, 2001; Cooke, 2002; Ding et al., 2002). Although union organizations have a relatively strong presence in some traditional state-owned industries, such as the railway industry (Cooke, 2000), union officials in China have generally been considered unfamiliar with the western style of collective bargaining, "with their serious lack of the necessary back-up bargaining resources, skills and capacities" (Warner and Ng, 1999: 307). Moreover, trade union officials in China are often in their post not because they are the best candidates for the job, but because they have appeared to be, for various reasons, "unsuccessful" in their previous managerial posts (Cooke, 2002).

Under the new ownership forms as a result of the privatization of SOEs in the 1990s, the welfare role of the state has largely disappeared. The seemingly harmonious management–labor relationship has been replaced with one characterized by conflicting interests, rising disputes and increasing inequality in contractual arrangements between management and labor. However, the role of the trade unions, or more specifically, the union officials' perception of their duties, remains little changed. They still continue to carry out their traditional functions such as organizing social events, taking care of workers' welfare, helping management to implement operational decisions, and co-ordinating relations between management and workers (Verma and Yan, 1995).

In the private sectors, union membership levels are far lower than those in the state sector and union activities are less popular (see Ding and Warner, 1999). Many firms do not recognize trade unions, claiming that the union's (welfare) functions are still carried out by the firm despite the absence of union organization. While labor officials often confuse the role of trade unions with that of a welfare function, demand from workers to establish a trade union may be low in part because they are unfamiliar with the concept of workplace representation but more so because of their perceived ineffectiveness of such an organization (Cooke, 2002).

According to the Labor Law (1995), the formal "representative function" of the unions is supplemented by the trade union guided Workers' Congress which is a format of workers' representation in the workplace. Initially introduced in the late 1940s, the Workers' Congress has been given an enhanced role since the 1980s as a result of the marketization programs. It has the legal right to:

Deliberate such major issues as the policy of operations, annual and long-term plans and programmes, contract and leasing responsibility systems of management; it may approve or reject plans on wage reforms and bonus distribution as well as on important rules and regulations; it may decide on major issues concerning workers' conditions and welfare; it may appraise and supervise the leading administrative cadres at various levels and put forward suggestions for awards and punishments and their appointment and approval; and it democratically elects the director.

(Liu, 1989: 5–6)

Again, in reality, the role of the Workers' Congress remains less than effective (Benson and Zhu, 2000). The Workers' Congress is required by law to hold an annual meeting in which workers can raise issues of concerns. This, however, does not often happen. Even when it is held, it is mostly a symbolic gesture and an opportunity for a banquet party for everybody involved.

In short, there is no real "partnership" between management and the trade union or "employee voice" in the management–labor relations in China. However, the dominance of state influence in the state-owned sectors and the weak presence of trade unions in employment relations in China as a whole do not mean unilateral determination of HRM practices by the (state) employers.

## Key factors determining HRM practices

Like those in other countries, HRM practices in both the state and the private sectors in China are, to a greater or lesser extent, shaped by a range of political, legal, cultural and economic factors. Major labor laws include: The Labor Law (1995), the Trade Union Law (1950, 2001), and the Provisions Concerning the Administration of the Labor Market (2000), which set out China's basic philosophy for the governance of the Labor Market. In spite of the perceived ineffectiveness of the employment regulations in China (Warner, 1996b; Cooke, 2001; Cooke and Rubery, 2002), these regulations do, at least in principle, provide a legal framework under which HRM practices, such as recruitment, training, working time and pay, should be carried out.

Regulations in recruitment are often aimed at removing gender discrimination. In recent years, external labor markets have been playing an increasingly important role in the (re)distribution of the labor resource as a result of the emergence of a market economy, sectoral restructuring, the decreasing role of the state as an employer and the consequent downsizing of its workforce. Instead of being assigned to a designated employing organization by the state when they enter employment, individuals are more likely to seek their jobs in a labor market inundated with candidates. This new way of recruitment and employment has on the one hand introduced dynamics to the country's employment system, and on the other hand brought new problems and conflicts to the system in general but more specifically to women's employment.

Although women (mostly full-time workers) make up nearly 40 percent of China's total workforce, recruitment is perhaps the most difficult barrier that women face in employment because of the current downsizing of SOEs, the mass migration of rural labor and the high unemployment rate (Cooke, 2001). Traditionally, male workers are considered to be more capable than female workers with higher participation rates, stronger adaptability, better mobility and attendance records, and a longer working life. Many employers are unwilling to recruit women because they are "inferior" to men and because of the "fuss" and cost associated with women's physiological conditions (e.g. child-bearing and caring). In order to eliminate gender discrimination, the state has issued a number of laws. These include the more recent laws such as the PRC Law on Protecting Women's Rights and Interests (1992) and the Labor Law (1995). These laws assert that men and women share the same labor rights. However, discrimination in different forms widely exists, often overtly, in the recruitment process against women who are at the higher end of the labor market as well as those who are sought for their low-cost and low-skill (Cooke, 2003a). Many job advertisements (including those issued by the public sector organizations) specify gender requirements and age limits even though the posts are suitable for both men and women, while the age limit is an attempt to avoid women job seekers of child-bearing age.

In terms of working-time arrangements, the Labor Law (1995) also specifies the number of hours (no more than 44) workers should work for in a normal working week and the number of hours of overtime they should be expected to undertake (no more than 36 per month). It needs to be pointed out here that the vast majority of workers work full time in China, as part-time working is still a relatively new concept with insufficient interest from both the employers and the workers. While these working-time regulations are followed by most state sector organizations and many large private enterprises (Zhang *et al.*, 2002), they are often not adhered to by small business employers or township and village enterprises (TVEs). In general, workers in the private service sector such as retail and catering businesses work much longer hours than the norm, a situation compounded by the low level of rest days and holidays that are given to the workers. For example, Cooke's study (forthcoming) of small retail shops found that few shops gave their workers one day per week for their rest days. Instead, the majority of shops gave their workers 2 or 3 days of rest per calendar month. Most owners did not allow their workers to take their statutory holidays, such as the Chinese New Year, because they were the busiest periods for the businesses.

In terms of training, there has always been a high level of state involvement/intervention in the training policies and practices of SOEs and public sector organizations (Cooke, forthcoming, 2004b). Since the start of economic reforms in 1979, a national network of Cadre Management Training Institutes has been established providing compulsory training courses for all (potential) managers (Warner, 1992). In 1981, the State Council of China stipulated that enterprises should allocate a minimum of 1.5 percent of the total wage bill as funding for employee education and training (Lu, 1987). In 1990, The Ministry of Labor issued another statutory requirement: "The Regulations for Worker's Technical Grade Examination." The examination content includes work attitude, performance and level of skill/competence. The regulations establish a system that links training, testing, deployment and remuneration together. In 1995, the "Temporary

Regulations on Continuous Education for Professional and Technical Personnel in China" was introduced by the state. This is seen as an important policy document for the national continuous training, which marks the beginning of the formalization of continuous training for professional and technical staff. It specifies that all senior and middle-ranking professionals and technical staff should receive at least 40 hours of off-the-job training per year, and junior ranking staff no less than 32 hours. While these regulations provide a major momentum for (state-owned) workplace training, training provisions remain generally low and are unevenly distributed across different industries (see further discussion below).

Another factor that drives training provisions is the competitive business environment. For example, the increasing globalization of business in China has brought organizations to the recognition of the need to converge with international norms/practice. We have seen, in the last few years, a heat wave of applications of ISO 9000 quality series accreditation by many business organizations in China. This has led to an increase in training in some enterprises in order to fulfil the accreditation requirements. The accession to WTO likewise brought a tidal wave of training. One of the main reasons for the increase in the training provision in the last two years has been to do with the WTO-related legal framework. However, this training is far from sufficient for the Chinese organizations to deal with the surge of demand for WTO-related knowledge.

The pay system in China demonstrates a number of unique characteristics which differ from that in other societies, characteristics such as the egalitarian culture, the relatively heavy proportion of bonus in the total package of pay, and the significant role of workers in controlling the bonus. In Mao's era, the distribution principle was based on *the equality norm* which was "expected to lead to the best group harmony and stability" (Yu, 1998: 304). The espoused policy for employee motivation was based on moral teaching and the doctrine of "serve the people." During the Deng and now post-Deng period, bonus and perks have become the driving force. However, the basic wage is still based largely on the seniority-based egalitarian wage structure which does not reflect competence, and egalitarianism in the bonus distribution remains a key characteristic in order to maintain stability and harmonization.

Pay is perhaps the only aspect of HRM in China in which grass-root workers exert extensive control in its (even) distribution. It has been noted that the most noteworthy characteristic of the Chinese perspective on distributive fairness is one of egalitarianism. Chinese workers are said to be very sensitive and to have low tolerance toward income gaps between individuals or between different groups in the same company (Shirk, 1981; Easterby-Smith *et al.*, 1995). They regard this as potentially disruptive in collective social systems that put group harmony and social adhesion as the top priority (Yu, 1998; Cooke, 2002; Taylor, 2002).

A main feature of the pay system in the state sectors is the tension between the lack of employee input in establishing the formal wage set by the state, on the one hand, and their role in maintaining the low-earning differentials among themselves, on the other (Cooke, forthcoming, 2004a). While employees have little room to oppose the formal wage structure, they play a fundamental role in preserving the egalitarian and seniority culture in the distribution of bonuses and other material incentives, regardless of the relative efficiency of individuals. Attempts from the top to increase wage differentials between individuals according to performance may be mediated during implementation at the operational level.

In the private sectors, seniority and egalitarianism still remain characteristic in employees' attitude towards pay, albeit being diluted by employers' constant attempts to introduce performance-based pay and pay confidentiality, especially in joint ventures (JVs) and foreign firms. For example, Chen's Sino-American study (1995) found that Confucian values were still evident in the continued emphasis on the social hierarchy, with a higher ranking for differential rewards according to rank and seniority in the Chinese sample. While management's attempt to keep workers' bonuses confidential has been met with workforce resistance in Cooke's study (2002), resentment to widening pay differentials was felt by workers in Taylor's study (2002). However, Braun and Warner's small-scale study (2002) of multinationals in China found that the wide implementation of bonus pay systems seemed to be more accepted in Sino-western JVs. It appears that the new emphasis of Chinese employees towards an economic logic and rejection of equality-based rules is more a product of recent environmental pressure and institutional practice than any shift in underlying cultural values (Sparrow, 2000).

In short, the HRM practices are shaped, to varying degrees, by political, legal, economic and cultural factors specific to China. While there is a trend of the legal protection being extended to cover the private and informal sectors, there are also signs that the rapid growth of private businesses and joint ventures are adding forces for change in the SOEs and public sector, especially in areas such as recruitment, reward and performance management (see further discussion below).

## Present changes within the HR functions

Existing studies on HRM in China suggest that personnel practices are in transition (Warner, 1998) from a highly centralized allocation process to a more market-oriented and merit-based system. This transition has strong implications for SOEs because of previous heavy influence of the state and current pressure from market competition (Zhu and Dowling, 2002). Until quite recently, the personnel function in SOEs was confined to job allocation, personnel record filing, and the provision of welfare benefits. The primary task for personnel management was to keep the employees politically and ideologically sound (Ding and Warner, 1999). Many of the HR functions which are familiar to their western counterparts were beyond the experience of personnel staff in China. However, economic reform and decentralization of decision-making in SOEs from the state have brought considerable changes to the HR functions in the state sectors. For example, Ding and Warner's study (1999) of twenty-four SOEs and JVs in four major cities found that the role of personnel managers has changed dramatically in both the SOEs and JVs. They were involved in making decisions in a range of HRM issues such as recruitment and selection, training, promotion, dismissal, reward and discipline. However, personnel management in the JVs exhibited more of the HRM characteristics than that in the SOEs. While personnel departments in both SOEs and JVs had extensive involvement in training, the former still had less power than the latter in the determination of reward and disciplinary actions.

Similarly, Zhu and Dowling's study (2002) found that many traditional HR policies in China have changed and that there was clear evidence that a more complex and hybrid management model was emerging as a result of increasing level of marketization and enterprise autonomy (Warner, 1998). For example, over half of the enterprises surveyed in Zhu and Dowling's study (2002) had written job analyses which were used for other HR activities such as HR planning, recruitment and selection and performance management. In addition, enterprises with different types of ownership all placed an emphasis on job-specific information for selection criteria, which demonstrated positive correlation with perceived effectiveness of staffing practices. Different external sources, such as advertising and the labor market, were used for recruitment purposes and more employees were hired on contractual basis. These findings all indicate some resemblance to HR practices used in advanced economies.

Recruitment and performance appraisal are perhaps the two aspects of HRM that have affected the personnel functions the most in governmental organizations as a result of the state-driven initiatives to modernize the workforce (Cooke, 2003b). There is a renewed emphasis on examination as a recruitment assessment mechanism in an attempt to block the influx of nepotism that has been a longstanding recruitment practice in governmental organizations in the past. The recruitment procedures specified by the state in the Provisional Regulations for State Civil Servants (1993) require that the whole examination and recruitment process be made public, including the exam content, procedure and result, so that the public can monitor its fairness. This is a bid for a fair and efficient system of recruitment and promotion that is transparent and competitive. Job applicants have to go through a competitive recruitment process that is ensured by intensive entrance examinations, coupled with other selection mechanisms, such as interviews and assessment centers. The regulations further specify that civil servants are required to have a formal annual assessment which includes written exams and performance record inspection. The assessment results are graded and referred to for promotion and reward. These new procedures of recruitment and performance appraisal create a considerable amount of planning and administrative work with which the recruitment personnel may not yet be familiar.

## Key challenges facing HRM in China

HRM in China faces several challenges. First, Chinese enterprises in general do not have a systematic approach to HRM that is consistent with their enterprise business strategy. Second, despite the oversupply of labor, many employers are experiencing recruitment and retention problems. Third, there is a lack of an effective system which links long-term motivation and performance with reward. Fourth, there is a lack of coherence and continuity in enterprise training. The growth of human capital is obviously lagging behind that of enterprise profit. However, these problems are not encountered by the public and private sectors to the same degree. While some problems are generic to both sectors, others are more specific to the public or private sectors.

In terms of approaches to HRM, domestic private firms (many of which are very young) in China share a considerable level of similarities in the development of their HR functions. They source their HRs primarily from the labor markets, especially at the start-up of their businesses. They lack a comprehensive HR strategy that provides skill training and career structure. They have not developed an organizational culture to elicit their employees' commitment and loyalty. By comparison, the state-sector organizations have a more established HR system due to the fact that they have a much longer history and have been subject to much state influence. However, many elements in their HR system have become outmoded and incompatible with recent developments in the economic environment and the labor markets. The rigidity of the HR system is also a major source of disadvantage of SOEs and public sector organizations which are faced with two major problems in their HRM: how to retain and attract talent and how to motivate existing employees.

Retention of key technical staff has been a tough perennial problem encountered by many SOEs and public sector organizations in recent years. SOE workers are now much more likely to seek high wages in non-state firms (Ding *et al.*, 2001). It is believed that foreign firms and JVs have been poaching key technical personnel from SOEs. For example, an investigation by Beijing City Economy Commission of 150 large and medium-sized enterprises in Beijing on their HR composition revealed that SOEs had lost 64 percent of their university graduates since 1982 while high-tech private firms had lost 18.5 percent (Chu, 2002). It is also reported that the four major state-owned banks have lost many of their talented people to foreign banks in China in the last few years since China relaxed its policy for foreign banks to operate there (Chu, 2002). Wang and Fang (2001) found in their study of multinational companies (MNCs) in China that the vast majority of employees in these MNCs were no more than 30 years of age and over 95 percent of them possessed at least advanced diploma educational qualifications. Over 64 percent of the Chinese employees surveyed said that the most important reason for them to join MNCs was that they felt that they could utilize their talent and realize their own value. High income was the second most important reason (62.5 percent).

In the past, many SOEs and public sector organizations tried to retain their (key) staff by imposing a penalty clause in their employment contract. Those who wished to leave their employer before the prescribed number of years was fulfilled were often faced with a heavy financial penalty and their personnel file would not be released by their defiant employer. An increasingly popular method now used to retain staff is that of "negotiated wage" on an individual basis. This involves the abandoning of the conventional wage structure that does not differentiate performance in a real sense to a more tailored package for each individual worker based on his/her competence and market value. This often results in a general wage increase for the individuals concerned (Chen, 2002). It needs to be pointed out here that in recent years, there is a reverse trend of talent "returning" to the better managed SOEs which offer more attractive salaries and individualized reward packages.

There is a great scarcity of high-performing Chinese managerial and professional staff in China (Wong and Law, 1999). While foreign firms and JVs operating at the high end of the product markets are able to recruit good quality university and polytechnic graduates as technicians and skilled workers, many domestic companies are facing recruitment problems. Graduates are unwilling to go to or stay with enterprises that offer relatively low pay and have unhealthy prospects. While the increasing fluidity of the labor market may be beneficial for individuals who are in advantageous positions, organizations may find it difficult to establish a long-term employment relationship with key workers conducive to the organization's competitiveness. Keen competition for talent also tends to drive wages upward disproportionally (thus widening the wage gap and social inequality) and encourages opportunistic behaviors.

Foreign and domestic private firms also face the dilemma of whether to train up their employees for the key skills required at the risk of having them poached or to recruit from the market with attractive employment packages. Firms that provide training may have to readjust their training plan in order to reduce the cost associated with staff turnover. For example, Motorola (China) Ltd had to reduce its training period from 6–12 months to 3 months in order to stop trainee employees (who were sent to the USA for training) from abandoning the firm to stay in the United States (Editorial Team of *Development and Management of Human Resources*, 2001). Hence, firms that successfully recruit, develop and motivate their skilled employees may have significant competitive advantages (Björkman and Fan, 2002).

Another major challenge in HRM in China is the need to change the ideology of reward, distribution and performance, as discussed earlier in this chapter. Pay has not been an effective mechanism in China to reflect workers' performance or to motivate workers (Cooke, forthcoming, 2004a) and poor performance has always been a problem haunting the SOEs (Korzec, 1992; Chiu, 2002), if less so the private firms. However, Chinese workers have often been criticized by the managers of JVs, foreign and domestic private firms for a lack of motivation and pride in their work, and for showing little interest in advancing themselves. Therefore, a difficult task for HRM is to change the behavioral patterns of workers, to make them more motivated, to make them take greater ownership and responsibility for their own work and take greater pride in their organization. This will lead to a greater level of organizational congruence and ultimately productivity.

Perhaps the most severe challenge facing HRM in China at the national level is that of the skills shortage and the insufficiency of training provision, an intertwined problem that has been touched upon several times so far in this chapter. One characteristic of the training system in China is the considerable variation of training provision between different forms of enterprise ownership and in different regions (Cooke, forthcoming, 2004b). In general, foreign firms, JVs and the state sector provide more training than other forms of business, with small private and self-employed business perhaps providing the least training. Firms located in the more developed east and southeast regions of the country provide more training in general than those in the north and west. Employees in manufacturing and public sector organizations also receive more training in general than those in the private-service sectors.

At the enterprise level, training practice displays a number of problems characterized by the lack of strategic planning and the low priority of training in organizational activities. Enterprises often carry out training without any strategic planning, costing or taking into account what the training needs of the enterprises are. Employee training is often seen as part of the non-core business for companies and the training department is often used to accommodate cadres who are deemed unsuitable for the front line of production. Training departments usually operate in a reactive mode. They are there to "fulfil the task given by the higher authority." While training officers complain that senior management of the company neglect training, criticisms often leveled at the training provision are that it is irrelevant, out-of-touch, a formality to tick the training box and an opportunity for individuals to gold plate their qualifications (Xu, 2000). Borgonjon and Vanhonacker (1994) also pointed out that the Chinese SOEs were mostly concerned about technical training, and did not yet have the capability to run management training courses.

## The future of the HR functions in China

The above key challenges facing HRM in China have profound implications for the HR functions at individual, organizational and national level. At the individual level, there is an urgent need to professionalize the HR functions. Human resource management as a discipline in higher education did not make its appearance until the mid-1990s, although it has been expanding rapidly since. In 1999, there were only thirty higher educational institutions that provided undergraduate degree courses on HRM. By July 2001, there were over ninety universities that recruited HRM undergraduates (Liao and Chen, 2002). The vast majority of HR officers in enterprises have therefore never received any formal training on HRM. Many of them came from a non-personnel background. Moreover, the nature of the personnel functions is experiencing significant changes from the reactive administrative role of the planned economy era to a more proactive and strategic role of the market economy. This is accompanied by an increasing level of labor mobility, more overt labor–management disputes, more complex reward systems, and the introduction of more labor regulations. HR personnel therefore need to equip themselves with the understanding of HR theories and labor regulations and their practical implications. They also need to understand the strategic role of HRM in relation to other functions of the organization.

At the organizational level, it is likely that in the next few years, the HR function in many Chinese organizations will continue to share its administrative and welfare roles with the trade unions. While the rapid expansion of the private sector and the recent amendment of the Trade Union Law are unlikely to change the power base (or the lack of it) of the union dramatically, the HR function has yet to develop to be part of the business strategy. The majority of entrepreneurs and CEOs in China have insufficient understanding of the strategic importance of HRM to organizational competitiveness and tend to underestimate the technicality of HRM. According to Xu (2001), their ideology of employment relationship is still largely of the transactional nature. A common mindset is that: "I have the money, I employ you, therefore you should do a good job for me." Much work needs to be done to convince them of the added value of human resources and the importance of winning employees' commitment for the success of the organization.

At the industry and national level, there is a need to establish industrial and national networks to share information of HR, to coordinate the HR functions such as skill training and recruitment, and to monitor the labor market trends and the conformity of labor regulations. Equally importantly, national professional bodies for HR professionals should be set up to link HR professionals and to facilitate the sharing of "best practices" in HRM. To date, no professional HR body exists at the national level. However, there are signs that some best practice sharing is taking place beyond the workplace level, albeit often in an unorganized manner. For example, blue-chip foreign firms and JVs are considered to have a sophisticated HR system, many elements of which are western practices transferred and adapted to suit the Chinese environment. Their HR policy and practice are often hailed by the media as good models to be followed by domestic firms in China. Delegate teams are sometimes organized by local governments or firms to visit these model companies in order to disseminate good practices.

## Conclusion

This chapter has provided an overview of HRM in China, covering most aspects of HRM and its characteristics in different types of organizations such as SOEs, public sector organizations, foreign firms, JVs, TVEs and domestic private firms. It highlighted the most unique aspects of HRM practices in China. These include: gender inequality in recruitment and selection; the weak presence of trade unions and the absence of true workers' voices; the unofficial role of grass-root workers in maintaining the egalitarian distribution system; problems of skills shortage, training, recruitment and retention; and the need to professionalize the HR functions. While the current state of HRM in China is characterized by the withdrawal of state intervention at enterprise level and a trend towards greater diversity and marketization, these are taking place in parallel with the introduction of more statutory labor regulations and the radical reforms of workplace welfare and social security provisions. In short, the emerging HRM in China presents not only exciting opportunities but also severe challenges for the role of HR at all levels. Above all, HRM in China shares similar characteristics, to some extent, with that found in other economies, but at the same time displays its own strong national characteristics.

# References

Benson, J. and Zhu, Y. (2000) "A case study analysis of human resource management in China's manufacturing industry," *China Industrial Economy* 4: 62–65.

Björkman, I. and Fan, X.C. (2002) "Human resource management and the performance of Western firms in China," *International Journal of Human Resource Management* 13 (6): 853–864.

Borgonjon, J. and Vanhonacker, W. (1994) "Management training and education in the People's Republic of China," *International Journal of Human Resource Management* 5 (2): 327–356.

Braun, W. and Warner, M. (2002) "Strategic human resource management in western multinationals in China: The differentiation of practices across different ownership forms," *Personnel Review* 31 (5): 553–579.

Chen, B. (2002) "'Negotiated wage': a method to stop staff turnover in SOEs," *Development and Management of Human Resources* 4: 11–12.

Chen, C.C. (1995) "New trends in rewards allocation preferences: a Sino-US comparison," *Academy of Management Journal* 38 (2): 408–428.

Child, J. (1994) *Management in China in the age of reform*, Cambridge: Cambridge University Press.

*China Statistical Abstract* (2000) Beijing: China Statistics Press.

*China Statistical Yearbook* (2002) Beijing: China Statistics Press.

Chiu, W.C.K. (2002) "Do types of economic ownership matter in getting employees to commit? An exploratory study in the People's Republic of China," *International Journal of Human Resource Management* 13 (6): 865–882.

Chu, L.Q. (2002) "Can your enterprise retain talent after WTO?," *Development and Management of Human Resources* 5: 7–8.

Cooke, F.L. (2000) "Manpower restructuring in the state-owned railway industry of China: The role of the state in human resource strategy," *International Journal of Human Resource Management* 11 (5): 904–924.

Cooke, F.L. (2001) "Equal opportunities? The role of legislation and public policies in women's employment in China," *Journal of Women in Management Review* 16 (7): 334–348.

Cooke, F.L. (2002) "Ownership change and the reshaping of employment relations in China: A study of two manufacturing companies," *Journal of Industrial Relations* 44 (1): 19–39.

Cooke, F.L. (2003a) "Equal opportunity? Women's managerial careers in governmental organisations in China," *International Journal of Human Resource Management* 14 (2): 317–333.

Cooke, F.L. (2003b) "Seven reforms in five decades: Civil service reform and its human resource implications in China," *Journal of Asia Pacific Economy* 8 (3): 380–404.

Cooke, F.L. (forthcoming, 2004a) "Public sector pay in China: 1949–2000," *International Journal of Human Resource Management*.

Cooke, F.L. (forthcoming, 2004b) "Vocational and enterprise training in China: Policy, practice and prospect," *Journal of Asia Pacific Economy*.

Cooke, F.L. (forthcoming) "Employment relations in small commercial businesses in China," unpublished working paper.

Cooke, F.L. and Rubery J. (2002) "Minimum wage and social equality in China," project report on *Minimum wage and employment equality in developed and developing countries*, Geneva: International Labour Organization (ILO).

Ding, D., Goodall, K. and Warner, M. (2002) "The impact of economic reform on the role of trade unions in Chinese enterprises," *International Journal of Human Resource Management* 13 (3): 431–449.

Ding, D., Lan, G. and Warner, M. (2001) "A new form of Chinese human resource management? Personnel and labour-management relations in Chinese township and village enterprises: A case study approach," *Industrial Relations Journal* 32 (4): 328–343.

Ding, D. and Warner, M. (1999) "'Re-inventing' China's industrial relations at enterprise-level: An empirical field-study in four major cities," *Industrial Relations Journal* 30 (3): 243–246.

Easterby-Smith, M., Malina, D. and Lu, Y. (1995) "How culture-sensitive is HRM?," *International Journal of Human Resource Management* 6 (1): 31–59.

Editorial team of *Development and Management of Human Resources* (2001) "Report of the Second Conference of Human Resource Development and Management in China," *Development and Management of Human Resources* 4: 9–15.

Hoffman, C. (1981) "People's Republic of China," in A. Albert (ed.) *International Handbook of Industrial Relations*, Westport, CT: Greenwood Press.

Korzec, M. (1992) *Labour and the failure of reform in China*, London: Macmillan.

Liao, C.W. and Chen, W.S. (2002) "Human resource management employee training system," *Development and Management of Human Resources* 7: 22–26.

Liu, T. (1989) "Chinese workers and employees participate in democratic management of enterprises," *Chinese Trade Unions* 2: 5–10.

Lu, H.J. (ed.) (1987) *Enterprise labour management*, Beijing: China Labour Press.

Ng, S.H. and Warner, M. (1998) *China's trade unions and management*, London: Macmillan.

Shirk, S.L. (1981) "Recent Chinese labour policies and the transformation of industrial organisation in China," *China Quarterly* 88: 575–93.

Sparrow, P. (2000) "International reward management," in G. White and J. Druker (eds.) *Reward management: A critical text*, London: Routledge.

Taylor, B. (2002) "Privatisation, markets and industrial relations in China," *British Journal of Industrial Relations* 40 (2): 249–272.

Verma, A. and Yan, Z.M. (1995) "The changing face of human resource management in China: Opportunities, problems and strategies," in A. Verma, T. Kochan and R. Lansbury (eds.) *Employment relations in the growing Asian economies*, London: Routledge.

Wang, C.G. and Fang, W. (2001) "Cultural adaptation and co-operation: An important aspect that MNCs face in China," *Xinhua Wenjai* 12: 19–24.

Warner, M. (1990) "Chinese trade unions: Structure and function in a decade of economic reform, 1979–1989," *Management Studies Research Paper No. 8/90*, Cambridge University.

Warner, M. (1992) *How Chinese managers learn*, London: Macmillan.

Warner, M. (1995) *The management of human resources in Chinese enterprises*, London: Macmillan and New York: St Martins Press.

Warner, M. (1996a) "Human resources in the People's Republic of China: The 'three systems' reforms," *Human Resource Management Journal* 6 (2): 32–43.

Warner, M. (1996b) "Chinese enterprise reform, human resources and the 1994 Labour Law," *The International Journal of Human Resource Management* 7 (4): 779–796.

Warner, M. (1998) "China's HRM in transition: Towards relative convergence?," in C. Rowley (ed.) *Human resource management in the Asia Pacific region: Convergence questioned*, London: Frank Cass, pp. 19–33.

Warner, M. (1999) "Human resources and management in China's 'Hi-tech' revolution: A study of selected computer hardware, software and related firms in the PRC," *International Journal of Human Resource Management* 10 (1): 1–20.

Warner, M. (2001) "Human resource management in the People's Republic of China," in P. Budhwar and Y. Debrah (eds.) *Human resource management in developing countries*, London: Routledge, pp. 19–33.

Warner, M. and Ng, S.H. (1999) "Collective contracts in Chinese enterprises: A new brand of collective bargaining under 'market socialism'?," *British Journal of Industrial Relations* 37 (2): 295–314.

Wong, L.S. and Law, K.S. (1999) "Managing localisation in the PRC: A practical model," *Journal of World Business* 34: 26–40.

Xu, Z. (2000) "On format, style and methods of employee training," *China Smelter Education* 6: 79–80.

Xu, Y.L. (2001) "Current situation of HRM in China," *Development and Management of Human Resources* 2: 8–10.

Yu, K.C. (1998) "Chinese employees' perceptions of distributive fairness," in A.M. Francesco and B.A. Gold (eds.) *International organisational behavior*, New Jersey: Prentice Hall.

Zhang, H.Y., Ming, L.Z. and Liang, C.Y. (2002) *The development of private enterprises in China: Report no. 3*, Beijing: Social Science Documentation Publishing House.

Zhu, C. and Dowling, P. (2002) "Staffing practices in transition: Some empirical evidence from China," *International Journal of Human Resource Management* 13 (4): 569–597.

## Useful websites

Asia-Pacific Human Resources Research Association: http://www.aphr.org
ChinaHR.com Corporation: http://www.chinaHR.com
ChinaHRD.net: http://www.ChinaHRD.net
51e-training.com: http://www.51e-training.com
The Ministry of Foreign Trade and Economic
    Co-operation of P. R. China: http://www1.moftec.gov.cn/moftec

# 3 HRM in South Korea

CHRIS ROWLEY AND JOHNGSEOK BAE

## Introduction

This chapter is concerned with human resource management (HRM) in South Korea (hereafter just "Korea"), the third largest economy in Asia and the thirteenth (2002) in the world (the eleventh largest just before the 1997 Asian financial crisis). While at first sight it may be assumed to be a "typical" Asian country in terms of its HRM, the reality is less clear-cut, with many particular practices. The key characteristics in Korean HRM revolve around practices based on "seniority" and regulation versus more flexibility in labor markets; with easier job shedding, remuneration, and greater focus on performance elements. Paradoxically, some influences (such as the Asian crisis and globalization) have generated a less homogenous HRM system in Korea.

This chapter is written around the framework and analytical structure common to others in this collection and are thus detailed as follows: first, the historical development of HRM; second, partnership in HRM; third, the key factors determining HRM practices, such as politics, national culture, the economy, business environment and different institutions along with a review of HRM practices such as staffing, pay, training and unions; fourth, changes taking place within the HRM function recently and currently, and the reasons for them; fifth, some key challenges facing HRM; sixth, what is likely to happen to the HR function; and lastly, some websites and current references for the latest information and developments in HRM.

## Historical development of HRM

The "management of people" has a long and diverse history in Korea. This needs to be set within Korea's sometimes traumatic history. Here we delineate the more contemporary HRM system (see Kim and Bae, forthcoming, for earlier periods). HRM's evolution can be analyzed within a three-dimensional framework. In this there are two critical historical incidents: the great labor struggle in 1987 and the Asian financial crisis of 1997 (Bae and Rowley, 2003; Kim and Bae, forthcoming). This produces three stages: pre-1987; 1987–1997; post-1997, each with different HRM configurations. The HRM system can be conceptualized on two dimensions: (a) rewards and evaluation; (b) resourcing and flexibility. The first dimension indicates the basis of remuneration and appraisal, i.e. seniority versus ability/performance; the second represents labor market choices, i.e. internal labor markets and long-term attachment versus numerical flexibility. Simultaneously, we can also use Rousseau's (1995) threefold typology of psychological contracts: (i) "relational," with high mutual (affective) commitment, high integration and identification, continuity and stability; (ii) "transitional," with ambiguity, uncertainty, high turnover and termination and instability; (iii) "balanced," with high member commitment and integration, ongoing development, mutual support and dynamics.

The first stage, pre-1987, was a "seniority-based relational"-type HRM. "Seniorityism" was pivotal for various HRM practices such as recruitment, evaluation, training, promotion, pay and termination. In addition, firms generally had long-term attachment to employees, who were rarely laid off. However, the first critical incident, the great labor struggle, resulted in sudden wage increases, which partly reduced competitive advantage in this dimension. This led to the second stage.

The second stage was an "exploratory performance-based"-type HRM. Firms started to specify performance terms. The fulcrum of the HRM system began changing from seniority more towards performance. From the early 1990s firms started to adopt "new HRM" (*sininsa*) systems to enhance fairness, rationalization and efficiency (Bae, 1997). Many firms revamped performance evaluation systems to make them actually function. However, adjustment on the resourcing and flexibility dimension was more rarely touched.

Finally, post-1997 a "flexibility-based transitional"-type HRM developed. With the Asian crisis, large corporations launched massive restructuring efforts, for example, mergers and acquisitions, management buyouts, spin-offs, outsourcing, debt for equity swaps, downsizing and early retirement programs. Under these circumstances both public and private policies focused more on labor market flexibility. On the other hand, the performance orientation adopted from the previous stage was consolidated. Hence, a more performance-based approach was internalized by organizational members (Bae and Rowley, 2001). At first, the HRM system after the crisis was more like Rousseau's (1995) "Transitional" type. Top management and HRM professionals lost their sense of direction regarding the future of HRM. However, from the beginning of the twenty-first century, firms started to became more like Rousseau's (1995) "Balanced" type. This model of mutual investment and support has been adopted by large, progressive corporations, such as Samsung and LG. At the same time, firms began to utilize a dual strategy of "balanced" type for core employees; and "transitional" type for contingent workers (Bae and Rowley, 2003).

## Partnership in HRM

Ideas of increased employee involvement and partnership have more recently emerged at dual levels. Examples at the macro level include the neocorporatist-type Presidential

Commission on Industrial Relations Reform (1996) and the tripartite Labor–Management–Government Committees (*nosajung wiwonhoe*) on Industrial Relations (1998) (Yang and Lim, 2000). At the micro level are examples such as LG Electronics which examined practices in plants in the USA (Saturn, Motorola) and Japan. LG Group used the concept of "partnership" in its post-1998 employee relations reforms (see Park and Park, 2000). There is also a national Labor Management Council (LMC) system (Kwon and O'Donnell, 2001).

Some indicators of employment relations, such as unemployment and real wage growth, worsened after the crisis, which the Tripartite Commission was formed to resolve. This was an unusual case, given the hostile relationships among employee relations systems' actors and the government's policy direction toward a more market-based approach. Since 1998 several commissions have been initiated:

1  15 January 1998: the First Tripartite Commission with Mr. Han Kwang-ok as Chairperson held its first session
2  6 February 1998: the Tripartite Commission held the 6th session and adopted the Social Compact to overcome the crisis and agreed on ninety items, including consolidation of employment adjustment-related laws and legalization of teachers' trade unions
3  3 June 1998: the Second Tripartite Commission with Mr. Kim One-ki as Chairperson held its first session
4  24 February 1999: the Korean Confederation of Trade Unions (KCTU) withdrew from the Tripartite Commission
5  1 September 1999: the Third Tripartite Commission was launched with Mr. Kim Ho-jin as Chairperson and held its first plenary session
6  8 August 2000: the Fourth Tripartite Commission was launched with Mr. Chang Young-chul as Chairperson
7  9 August 2002: the Fifth Tripartite Commission was launched with Mr. Shin Hong as Chairperson.

Although an assessment of the commissions is difficult, it may be summarized by the shorthand label of "early effective, later malfunctioning" (Kim and Bae, forthcoming). The Social Compact was groundbreaking, the first autonomous tripartite agreement in Korean labor history. Although this helped the government to enhance its capacity for crisis management and to tackle the Crisis, the Commission did not produce any significant agreements thereafter. Therefore, while the experiments with tripartite systems were meaningful, they were not entirely successful.

There are also examples at the micro level, such as LG Electronics and Samsung SDI.[1] Both are in the electronics industry, have histories of severe labor disputes and are successful. During workplace innovations towards a high performance work organization (HPWO), these *chaebols* took quite different routes and modes. The 1997 crisis had

---

1  These are mainly from Kim and Bae (forthcoming).

pushed their management to make these workplace innovations. Both management and employees developed more cooperative and participative employee relations. Management changed from paternalistic and authoritarian styles and attitudes towards being more progressive and participative. Unions and employees were also effectively involved in the process of workplace innovation. Full cooperation of the union leadership or employee representatives helped to establish a new work production system. While unionized LG Electronics adopted a team production mode with a labor–management partnership, non-union Samsung SDI had a lean production mode emphasizing TQM, Six Sigma and other management-initiated innovations. Thus, trade union status made a difference in the process of HPWO adoption in terms of speed, method and persistence.

In the case of LG Electronics, from 1990 to 1994, labor–management cooperation remained at the affective and attitudinal level. However, at the next stage (1995 to the present), the partnership of labor and management changed towards a more structural and institutionalized level. In the high-tech electronics industry most competitors are non-union, such as Samsung Electronics in Korea; IBM, Motorola, and HP in the USA. The initial adoption process was slow in LG Electronics due to strong union resistance, whereas Samsung SDI more speedily adopted new approaches. While LG Electronics used a more bottom-up approach, with the involvement of frontline employees, Samsung SDI chose a management-centered top-down approach. However, when the HPWO is established, we expect the team production mode to be more strongly institutionalized in the unionized setting, which is more likely to prevent easy abandonment. Although LG Electronics shows very active union participation in workplace (i.e. lowest) and collective bargaining (i.e. middle) levels, it is not practiced in the strategic (i.e. highest) level, such as product development, new investment and corporate restructuring. This may be a future agenda for labor and management. Samsung SDI operates successfully an extensive system of open communications, information sharing, and non-union employee representation. Although this has cultivated well the attitudinal aspects of employee relations (i.e. labor–management cooperation), its structural and institutional aspects (i.e. employee participation through formal mechanisms), have not yet fully developed.

## HRM practices: key determinants and review

This section is divided into two main parts: first, key factors influencing HRM practices; second, a review of those HRM practices.

## Influences on HRM

Several key factors have influenced HRM. These include politics, national culture, the economy, business environment, different institutions and so on.

## *Historical and political background*

This north-east Asian country now occupies almost 100,000 km² of the southern Korean peninsula (6,000 miles from the UK). Korea's very homogeneous ethnic population rapidly urbanized and grew, more than doubling since the 1960s, from 20.2 million (1966) to 47.6 million (2002). Of these, nearly 10 million are in the capital, Seoul (more than double 1966's 3.8 million), the dominant center for political, social, business and academic interests.

Korea's nickname of "the country of the morning calm" became increasingly obsolete with massive, speedy economic development. From the 1960s Korea was rapidly transformed from a poor, rural backwater with limited natural or energy resources, domestic markets and legacy of colonial rule and war with dependence on US aid, to one of the fastest growing economies in a rapidly expanding region. Gross domestic product (GDP) real annual growth rates of 9 percent from the 1950s to the 1990s (with over 11 percent in the late 1980s) took GDP from US$1.4 billion (1953) to US$437.4 billion (1994) (Kim *et al.*, 2000). Per capita GDP grew from US$87 (1962) to US$10,543 (1996) and gross national product (GNP) from US$3 billion (1965) to US$376.9 billion (1994). From the mid-1960s to the 1990s annual manufacturing output grew at nearly 20 percent and exports over 25 percent, rising from US$320 million (1967) to US$136 billion (1997) (Kim and Rowley, 2001). Korea became a large manufacturer of a range of products from "ships to chips," in both more "traditional" (steel, shipbuilding, cars) and "newer" (electrical, electronics) sectors. Employment grew and unemployment levels declined, to just 2 percent by the mid-1990s.

How did the former "Hermit Kingdom" reach this position? The "Three Kingdoms" (39BC onwards) were united in the Shilla Dynasty (from AD668), with the Koryo Dynasty (935 to 1392) followed by the Yi Dynasty, ended by Chosun's annexation by Japan in 1910. The colonization experience, along with the forced introduction of the Japanese language, names and labor, inculcated strong nationalist sentiments, a central psychological impetus for the later economic dynamism (Kim, 1994: 95). While colonized, Koreans were restricted to lower organizational positions and excluded from managerial roles. Other Japanese influences came via infrastructure developments, industrial policy imitation, application of technology and techniques of operations management and Korean émigrés (Morden and Bowles, 1998). Some later HRM indicated these Japanese influences, including lifetime employment and seniority pay, although with some distinctions. For instance, employee loyalty was ". . . chiefly to an individual, be it the owner or chief executive" (Song, 1997: 194), with little to organizations as such, in contrast to Japanese organizational commitment. While limited to regular, particular male employees in large companies, normative practice extended this to other firms (Kim and Briscoe, 1997).

After 1945 came partition, with US military control until the South's independence government in 1948 followed by further widespread devastation with the Korean War from 1950 to 1953. The large US military presence, and continued tensions with the

North remain. Furthermore, many Koreans studied the American management system, especially as the country was the destination of most overseas students. This impacted on managerial, business and academic outlooks, perspectives and comparisons. Korea also experienced 25 years of authoritarian and military rule, which only ended in 1987. Additionally, many business executives were ex-officers, while many male employees served in the military, and had regular military training, while some companies maintained reserve army training units.

## Cultural influences

The role of national culture, including Confucianism, had and continues to have a powerful, multi-faceted and ingrained influence on Korean society in general and is embedded in HRM in particular (see Rowley and Bae, 2003). This can be seen in summary in Table 3.1.

## Economic environment

The importance of Korea's economic background, rapid development and the particular structure and organization of capital and links to the state, are all important to HRM's operating context. This developmental, state-sponsored, export-orientated and labor-intensive model of industrialization (Rowley and Bae, 1998; Rowley et al., 2002) was reinforced by exhortations and motivations (often with cultural underpinnings, as noted earlier). These included the need to escape the vicious circle of poverty, compete with Japan, repay debts and elevate Korea's image and honor.

In late 1997 the contagion of the Asian crisis hit Korea, with devastating impacts on economic performance, employment, although both quickly recovered, and HRM. This was partly because the post-crisis IMF "bailout" loan came with stipulations of labor-market changes, for instance to end lifetime employment and allow job agencies. Furthermore, the economy opened up to greater penetration from foreign direct investment (FDI), which in turn brought exposure to HRM practices to supplement the experiences of Korea's own multinational companies (MNCs) operating in other countries.

Key aspects of this economic performance and context may be seen in Tables 3.2 and 3.3. The different age and gender impacts are important to note. Basically, older and male workers remain more exposed to the vagaries and impacts of unemployment, especially in a system with only a limited safety net and culturally influenced opprobrium. Finally, despite the post-crisis economic regeneration, a worrying survey by Dong-a Ilbo (reported in The Economist, 2003) indicated recent public apprehension: 89 percent agreed that the economic situation in mid-2003 was either worse (54 percent) or at least similar (35 percent) to that in 1997.

Table 3.1 Characteristics and paradoxes of culture and management in Korea

| Cultural influences | Concepts | Meanings | Management behaviors and managerial characteristics | Paradoxes |
|---|---|---|---|---|
| | Inhwa | Harmony, solidarity | Company as family-type community | Sharp owner–manager–worker distinctions |
| | Yongo | Connections:<br>hyulyon: by blood<br>jiyon: by geography<br>hakyon: by education | Recruitment via common ties, solidity within inner circles, kinship-based relationships with owners | Bounded collectivism and exclusivism |
| Confucianism (family) | Chung | Loyalty, subordinate to superior | Paternalistic approach and taking care of employees and their families | Emphasis on hierarchical ranks, authoritarianism in leadership |
| | Un | Indebtedness to organization/ members | Respect, tolerance, patience adhered to in business | Loyalty/cooperation to individual not organization |
| | Uiri | Integrity to others in everyday life | Long-term relationships (e.g. lifetime employment) | Personal entertainment, gift giving, transaction opaqueness |
| | Gocham | Senior in service, an 'old-timer' | Seniority-based rewards and promotions | Tension between seniority and competence/ability |

*Table 3.1* (continued)

| Cultural influences | Concepts | Meanings | Management behaviors and managerial characteristics | Paradoxes |
|---|---|---|---|---|
| Japan | *Kibun* | Good mood, satisfactory state of affairs | Maintain harmony, not hurting someone's *kibun* | Performance management tensions |
| | *Sinparam* | Exulted spirits | Management and making efforts by sentiment-based motivation rather than rational understanding | Delinquency and low commitment without *sinparam* |
| | *Han* | Resentment/frustration felt over unjust or inequitable treatment | Confrontational and militant labor relations (e.g. employment adjustment tensions) | Passiveness, negativism and suppression |
| Military | *Chujin* | Propulsion, drive, get through something | Can-do spirit, strong driving force, rapid accomplishment of plans/goals | Lack of rational evaluations and omitting due processes |
| | *Palli palli* | Quickly quickly | Speed of action | Quality, reflection |
| | *Sajeonhyupui* | Informal consensus formation prior to making final decisions | Collaboration and participation of stakeholders in decision-making | Team ethos impacts, slow decisions, impediment to empowerment |

Source: Rowley and Bae (2003)

*Table 3.2* Recent trends in Korean employment patterns, growth and inflation (%)

| Year | Participation | Unemployment | GDP growth | Inflation |
|------|---------------|--------------|------------|-----------|
| 1990 | 60.0 | 2.4 | | |
| 1991 | 60.6 | 2.4 | | |
| 1992 | 60.9 | 2.5 | | |
| 1993 | 61.1 | 2.9 | | |
| 1994 | 61.7 | 2.5 | | |
| 1995 | 61.9 | 2.1 | | |
| 1996 | 62.0 | 2.0 | 6.8 | 4.9 |
| 1997 | 62.2 | 2.6 | 5.0 | 4.4 |
| 1998 | 60.7 | 7.0 | −6.7 | 7.5 |
| 1999 | 60.5 | 6.3 | 10.9 | 0.8 |
| 2000 | 60.7 | 4.1 | 9.3 | 2.3 |
| 2001 | 61.4 | 3.8 | 3.0 | 4.1 |
| 2002 | 62.0 | 3.1 | 6.0 | 2.7 |

Source: Korea National Statistical Office.

*Table 3.3* Trends in leaving by age in Korea (%)

| | Year | Age | | | | | |
|---|------|-------|-------|-------|-------|-------|-------|
| | | *15–20* | *21–24* | *25–29* | *30–39* | *40–49* | *50–60* |
| *All* | 1995 | 7.06 | 22.69 | 21.34 | 25.66 | 12.97 | 10.28 |
| | 1997 | 5.63 | 21.62 | 23.57 | 25.22 | 12.10 | 11.85 |
| | 1998 | 4.39 | 16.37 | 20.87 | 25.27 | 15.73 | 17.37 |
| *Male* | 1995 | 9.43 | 14.28 | 22.36 | 30.24 | 12.88 | 10.81 |
| | 1997 | 4.52 | 13.80 | 24.70 | 30.91 | 12.69 | 13.39 |
| | 1998 | 3.13 | 10.30 | 19.83 | 30.63 | 16.84 | 19.28 |

Source: Kwon (2003)

## *Capital – the* chaebol

These leading lights and drivers of the economy were family founded, owning and controlling large, diversified business groupings with a plethora of subsidiaries, as indicated in the label: An "octopus with many tentacles." They were held together by opaque cross-shareholdings, subsidies and loan guarantees with inter-*chaebol* distrust and rivalry. Much of the large business sector was part of a *chaebol* network and they exerted widespread influence over other firms, management practices and society. The *chaebols* were underpinned by a variety of elements (Rowley and Bae, 1998; Rowley *et al.*, 2002) and explained by a range of theories (Oh and Park, 2002). For some, the state–military links and interactions with the *chaebol* was the most important factor, producing politico-economic organizations substituting for trust, efficiency and the market. The state-owned banks (with resultant reliance for capital), promoted *chaebols* as a development strategy and intervened to maintain quiescent labor. These close connections were often damned as nepotism and "crony capitalism."

There were more than 60 *chaebols*, although a few dominated. At their zenith in the 1990s the top five (Hyundai, Daewoo, Samsung, LG, SK) accounted for almost one tenth (9 percent) of Korea's GDP, and the top 30 for almost one sixth (15 percent), taking in 819 subsidiaries and affiliates. Some became major international companies in the world economy, engaged in acquisitions and investments overseas, dominated by the USA and China. A sketch of the top *chaebols* illustrates their typical development and structure.

Samsung is the oldest *chaebol*, with roots in the Cheil Sugar Manufacturing Company (1953) and Cheil Industries (1954), although it started as a trading company in 1938. It developed from a fruit and sundry goods exporter into flour milling and confectionery. Over the postwar decades it spread to sugar refining, textiles, paper, electronics, fertilizer, retailing, life insurance, hotels, construction, electronics, heavy industry, petrochemicals, shipbuilding, aerospace, bio-engineering, and semiconductors. Sales of US$3 billion and staff of 45,000 (1980) ballooned to US$96 billion and 267,000 (1998) (Pucik and Lim, 2002). Samsung Electronics alone had 21 worldwide production bases, 53 sales operations in 46 countries, sales of US$16.6 billion and was one of the largest producers of dynamic random access memory semiconductors by the late 1990s. By 2002 Samsung still claimed global market leadership in 13 product categories, from deep-water drilling ships to microwaves, television tubes and microchips, and with a target to actually have 30 world beaters by 2005. In 2003 it still had 63 affiliates and assets of won 72,000 billion.

*Table 3.4* Size and businesses of the largest *chaebols* (trillion won)

| Name | Main business | Assets |
| --- | --- | --- |
| Samsung | Electronics, machinery and heavy industries, chemicals, construction | 72.4 |
| LG | Clothing, supermarkets and radio, television, electronics stores | 54.5 |
| SK | Refining, distributing and transporting petroleum products, production and sale of petrochemical products | 46.8 |
| Hyundai Motors | Manufacture and distribution of motor vehicles and parts | 41.3 |
| Hanjin | Construction, shipbuilding | 21.6 |
| Hyundai | Electronics, construction, finance | 11.8 |

Source: OECD in *The Economist* (2003)

*Table 3.5* Korean large business groups ('000 billion won)

| Name | Affiliate number | Debt–equity ratios (%) | Assets |
|------|------|------|------|
| Korea Electrical Power Corp | 14 | 72.1 | 90.9 |
| Samsung | 63 | 240.6 | 72.4 |
| LG | 51 | 206.8 | 54.5 |
| SK | 62 | 156.4 | 46.8 |
| Hyundai Motors | 25 | 168.0 | 41.3 |
| Korea Telecom | 9 | 101.7 | 32.6 |
| Korea Highway Corp | 4 | 100.4 | 26.4 |
| Hanjin | 21 | 294.4 | 21.6 |
| Korea Land Corp | 2 | 373.4 | 14.9 |
| Korea National Housing Corp | 2 | 185.2 | 14.5 |
| Hyundai | 12 | 977.6 | 11.8 |
| Gumho | 15 | 503.1 | 10.6 |
| Hyundai Heavy Industry | 5 | 219.4 | 10.3 |
| Hanwa | 26 | 238.3 | 9.9 |
| Korea Water Resources Corp | 2 | 27.2 | 9.5 |
| Koran Gas Corp | 2 | 256.0 | 9.1 |
| Doosan | 18 | 191.4 | 9.0 |
| Donghu | 21 | 312.1 | 6.1 |
| Hyundai Oilbank | 2 | 837.1 | 5.9 |

Source: Ward (2003b) based on OECD and Korea Fair Trade Commission

However, the Asian crisis brought out into the open some of the inherent and underlying problems and strains that were beginning to be felt in the *chaebols*, and the Korean model more generally. There followed the collapse of some *chaebols*, scandals and bankruptcy and the reconfiguration of others, including even the takeover of some by western MNCs. The more recent situation may be seen in Tables 3.4 and 3.5.

## *Labor*

The critical management of labor has occurred in a variety of contexts, including military governments. Importantly, labor played an integral role against occupation and supporting democratization. From the early twentieth century, low wages, hazardous conditions and anti-Japanese sentiments contributed to union formation (see Kwon and O'Donnell, 2001). From the 1920s unions increased, reaching 488 and 67,220 members (1928). The 1930s witnessed a decline with harsh repression and subordination to Japanese war production, and also internal organizational splits. Union numbers fell to 207 and 28,211 members (1935). The postwar radical union movement (the *Chun Pyung*) was declared illegal by the American military government trying to restrict political and industrial activities to encourage US-type "business unions." The subsequent strikes and General Strike resulted in 25 dead, 11,000 imprisoned and 25,000 dismissed. A more conservative, government-sponsored industry-based movement was decreed, signaling labor's incorporation by the state, conflict repression and an authoritarian corporatist approach. Thus, the government officially recognized the Federation of Korean Trade Unions (FKTU) and became increasingly interventionist, enacting a battery of laws regulating hours, holidays, pay and multiple and independent unions.

A diversity of approaches towards labor were also partly influenced by *chaebol* growth strategies (Kwon and O'Donnell, 2001). For instance, economic growth and focus on minimizing labor costs resulted in the expansion and concentration of workforces in large-scale industrial estates with authoritarian and militaristic controls. The pressure and nature of the labor process was indicated in the volume of workplace accidents, some 4,570 (1987) compared to smaller numbers in larger workforces (although with sectoral impacts, of course), such as 513 in the USA and 658 in the UK (Kang and Wilkinson, 2000). Labor resistance was generated, the catalyst for conflict and re-emergence of independent unions from the 1970s. Employers responded by disrupting union activities, sponsoring company unions and replacing labor-intensive processes by automating, subcontracting or moving overseas. From the late 1980s companies also softened strict supervision and work intensification emphasis by widening access to paternalistic practices and welfare schemes (ibid.). Nevertheless, trade unionization grew from 12.6 percent (1970), peaking at 18.6 percent (1989).

During the 1990s independent trade unions established their own national organization, with federations of *chaebol*-based and regional associations. An alternative national federation, the KCTU (*minjunochong*), emerged in 1995. It organized the 1996 General Strike (Bae *et al.*, 1997), enhancing its legitimacy. However, the economic whirlwind of the Asian crisis then hit. Trade union density fell back to 11.5 percent (1998).

## Review of HRM practices

Second, a review of HRM practices is presented. It is useful to compare the more traditional characteristics with newer ones, as in Table 3.6. We will then detail these categories that comprise much of HRM.

### *Employee resourcing*

Aspects of employee resourcing include recruitment, selection and contracts. The *chaebols*, traditionally seen as prestige employers, recruited graduates biannually with preference for management trainees from prestigious universities (Kim and Briscoe, 1997). There have been some moves from such resourcing systems towards on-going, atypical and insecure forms. For instance, flexibility was classified as "low" numerically

*Table 3.6* Influences on HRM in Korea: traditional and new compared

| Influences → | Traditional characteristics | HRM area | New characteristics | ← Influences |
|---|---|---|---|---|
| Culture (traditional) | • Mass recruitment of new graduates<br>• Job security (lifetime job)<br>• Generalist oriented | Employee resourcing | • Recruitment on demand<br>• Job mobility (lifetime career)<br>• Development of professional | Culture (modern) |
| America | • Seniority (age and tenure)<br>• Pay equality | Employee rewards | • Ability, performance (annual system)<br>• Merit pay | Globalization |
| Japan | • Evaluation for advancing in job/grade | | • Evaluation for pay increases | Asian crisis |
| Military | • No appraisal feedback<br>• Single-rater appraisal | | • Appraisal feedback<br>• 360° appraisal | State |
| State | • High induction<br>• Company specific<br>• Functional flexibility context | Employee development | • Overseas programs<br>• Differentiated training<br>• Numerical flexibility context | Management/capital/ investment (inward and outward) |
| Management/ capital | • Authoritarian corporatism<br>• Legal constraints<br>• Less involvement | Employee relations | • Enterprise based union and federations<br>• More freedoms<br>• Involvement of knowledge workers | Labor |
| Labor | • Less information sharing | | • Information sharing | |

in pre-crisis Korea (Bae et al., 1997). Since then flexibilities seemingly swiftly increased. The trend is indicated by a survey (of 300 firms) in 1997 and 1998 (Choi and Lee, 1998). During the first period, virtually one third (32.3 percent), adjusted employment. By the second period this coverage almost doubled (to 60.3 percent). For the first period, specific types of employment adjustment (firms made multiple responses) were: worker numbers (19.7 percent), working hours (20 percent) and functional flexibility (12.7 percent). By the second period these types of employment adjustment massively increased: worker numbers more than doubled (43.7 percent), while working hours (36.7 percent) and functional flexibility (24.3 percent), almost doubled. There was a more than doubling in both "freezing or reducing recruitment," from 15 percent to 38.7 percent, and "dismissal" from 7 percent to 17.3 percent, with rises in "early retirement" from 5.7 percent to 8 percent. Thus, numerical flexibility increased. Indeed, it was argued that even by 1999 the number of temporary, contract and part-time workers now comprised over 50 percent of the workforce (Kang and Wilkinson, 2000; Demaret, 2001). These employee resourcing areas can be seen in the growth and variety of types of non-permanent workers, as shown in Table 3.7.

Some company cases also highlight employee resourcing practices. Samsung Electronics' 60,000 employees (1997) were massively reduced by about one third to 40,000. LG Group in 1998 dismissed 14,000 (11.6 percent of its total) employees (Kim, 2000). Daewoo Motors shed 3,500 jobs, despite violent protests and strikes. Some 30,000 employees at public companies, like Korea Telecom, Korea Electric Power Company and Korea National Tourism Organization were to be dismissed, while another 30,000 (10 percent) of local public servants were dismissed by the end of 1998 (Park and Park, 2000).

However, there were some limits to such employee resourcing practices. At first, neither government nor *chaebols* seemed overly keen to use the new legislation (*The Economist*, 1999). This inertia may be seen in the following cases where adjustment was constrained. Korea Telecom moved towards increased adjustment via changes in job categories, transfers and promotions (Kwun and Cho, 2002). Rather than dismissal, a Samsung subsidiary asked both men and women to take unpaid "paternity leave," while Kia remained "proud" of its "no-lay-offs" agreement and Seoul District Court protected jobs by refusing to close Jinro (*The Economist*, 1999). One high-profile example concerned Hyundai Motors, whose initial plan to dismiss 4,830 of its 45,000 workers was diluted

*Table 3.7* Trends in employment status in Korea (%)

|  | 1995 | 1996 | 1997 | 1998 | 1999 |
|---|---|---|---|---|---|
| Regular workers | 58.1 | 56.6 | 54.1 | 53.0 | 48.3 |
| Temporary workers | 27.7 | 29.5 | 31.6 | 32.8 | 33.4 |
| Daily workers | 14.2 | 13.8 | 14.3 | 14.2 | 18.3 |

Source: Kwon (2003)

to 2,678 and then 1,538. The union went on strike in 1998, followed by illegal strikes and physical conflict until a negotiated compromise was reached. This provided for just 277 dismissals (with 167 of these from the canteen!), along with severance payment. As a result, while Hyundai's workforce fell to 35,000, this was mainly due to 7,226 voluntary retirements plus about 2,000 who will return after 18 months' unpaid leave (ibid.). Indeed, some collective dismissals, such as the 1,500 figure at Hyundai Motors, were regarded as "illegal" and "unreasonable" (Lee, 2000).

## Employee rewards

There has been increasing importance attached to performance in employee rewards practices. Some of the reasons for this were: pay system rigidity making labor almost a quasi-fixed cost; weak individual-level motivational effects; and changing environmental factors (Kim and Park, 1997). However, there is actually more variety here than is presented by an overly-stark "either–or" choice as Table 3.8. indicates:

Data from the earlier survey (Choi and Lee, 1998) indicated employee rewards flexibility almost quadrupled from 10.7 percent to 38.7 percent between 1997 and 1998. The table shows that about one third (33 percent) of firms had performance-based – (3) or (4) – systems. There seem to be common trends across sectors, although with some greater change in use of (4) in non-manufacturing *vis-à-vis* manufacturing. Slightly more variation by size of organization would be expected, given size is a powerful variable in many HRM areas. Somewhat counter-intuitively, (1) was used by slightly more "smaller" (although defined at a relatively high employment level here) firms, while more than twice the percentage (although still a small total percentage) compared to "larger" ones, used (4).

The example of annual pay, whereby salary is based on individual ability or performance, is another employee rewards practice. A survey (1999) of 4,303 business units (with over 100 employees) found 15.1 percent had already adopted annual pay; 11.2 percent were preparing for it; and 25 percent were planning to adopt it (Korea Ministry of Labor, 1999). Thus, just over one quarter (26.3 percent) of firms had either introduced it, or were preparing to. Indeed, just over half (51.3 percent) of firms were in some stage of changing pay systems. Again, there seemed to be common trends across organizational size.

Other evidence indicates employee rewards practices being used and considered. Some 13 percent (more than double 1998's 6 percent) of companies listed on the Korean Stock Exchange were giving share options; with some 18 percent (more than quadruple 1998's 4 percent) of l5,116 large companies sharing profits in January 2000, with another 23 percent planning to do so by year end (Labor Ministry survey in *The Economist*, 2000).

Again, we give company examples of employee rewards. The operation of annual rewards systems may also be seen in specific cases. Instances among the *chaebols* are shown in Table 3.9. All used forms of annual pay systems. Samsung and Hyosung adopted a "zero-sum" method, reducing salary for poorer performers while increasing

*Table 3.8* Variations in Korean pay systems by size and sector (%)

| System options | Sector | | Size (employees) | | All firms |
| --- | --- | --- | --- | --- | --- |
| | Manufacturing (N=210) | Non-manufacturing (N=68) | Less than 300 (N=144) | More than 300 (N=134) | |
| (1) Traditional seniorityism | 42.4 | 42.6 | 43.8 | 41.3 | 42.4 |
| (2) Seniority-based with performance factor* | 25.2 | 22.1 | 22.8 | 26.0 | 24.5 |
| (3) Performance-based with seniority factor | 29.0 | 29.4 | 27.8 | 30.5 | 29.1 |
| (4) Ability/performance-based | 3.4 | 5.9 | 5.6 | 2.2 | 4.0 |

* originally labelled "Ability-based system, but seniority-based operation."
Source: Park and Ahn (1999).

*Table 3.9* Comparison of annual pay systems among Korean *chaebols*

|  | *Doosan* | *Daesang* | *Hyosung* | *SK* | *Samsung* |
|---|---|---|---|---|---|
| *Adopted* | 1994 | 1995 | 1997 | 1998 | 1998 |
| Target group | Section chief and above | College graduates and above | College graduates and above | Deputy general managers and above | Section chief and above |
| Composition of annual pay | – Basic annual<br>– Performance | – Basic<br>– Ability<br>– Performance | – Seniority<br>– Job-based<br>– Ability<br>– Performance | – Individual annual<br>– Incentives | – Basic annual<br>– Performance (individual and group) |
| Base-up | No | Yes | Yes | No | Yes |
| Plus-sum | Yes | Yes | No | Yes | No |
| Cumulative | Yes | Yes | No | Yes | No |

Source: adapted from Yang (1999: 232).

pay by the same amount of reduced salary for better performers. Doosan, Daeang and SK used a "plus-sum" method, increasing salaries of good performers without reducing those of poor performers. Finally, some firms accumulated performance evaluation results.

In Samsung remuneration had been composed of base pay (based on seniority), plus extra benefits (long service, and so on) until it introduced its "New HR Policy" (1995) with its greater emphasis on performance. Now remuneration was composed of base pay (common pay, cost-of-living), plus merit pay (competence and performance used) (Pucik and Lim, 2002; Kim and Briscoe, 1997). LG Group introduced (1998) practices to determine pay based on ability and performance (Kim, 2000). LG Chemical brought in a system of performance-related pay at its Yochon plant (*The Economist*, 1999). Korea Telecom made some moves towards more flexibility and performance in rewards (Kwun and Cho, 2002). Hyundai Electronics introduced (1999) share options. Samsung Electronics used profit sharing.

The key lever in operationalizing these employee rewards practices is performance appraisal. Traditionally, it did not affect pay (or promotion). Given this new emphasis, however, Samsung's appraisal system was revamped and made more sophisticated in the search for greater objectivity and reliability. It was now composed of several elements, such as: supervisor's diary; 360-degree (supervisors, subordinates, customers, suppliers) appraisal; forced distribution; and two interviews (with the supervisor; "Day of Subordinate Development"). The "Evaluation of Capability Form" used was composed of interesting items, such as "Human Virtues," for example, "morality": willingness to sacrifice (sic) themselves to help colleagues (Kim and Briscoe, 1997).

Again, the extent of such employee rewards practices requires some consideration. Some practices are relatively limited in coverage and spread. For instance, data in Table 3.8 also indicated that seniority remained in large numbers of firms (nearly 43 percent). Indeed, some form of seniority – (1) or (2) – accounted for the pay systems of over two-thirds (67 percent) of firms. Likewise, data in Table 3.9 indicated most firms applied practices only to certain groups, such as managers or the higher educated. Some, such as Samsung, Daesang and Hyosung, used "base-up" methods, a uniform increase of basic pay regardless of performance or ability levels. Similarly, Hyundai's vaunted stock option policy covered just 7 percent of the workforce, while Samsung's profit sharing was restricted to "researchers" (*The Economist*, 2000). At LG, although employee evaluation systems were in place, in most instances compensation did not reflect evaluation results as it remained ". . . largely determined by seniority . . ." (Kim, 2000: 178).

Also, there are also many problems with trying to link employee rewards and performance via appraisals. These concern appraisals in general, when linked to rewards and in Asian contexts (see Rowley, 2003). For instance, well-known tendencies in human nature lead towards subjective aspects in appraisals. Furthermore, practitioner-type literature commonly recommends that appraisals should not be linked with remuneration. There are also concerns that appraisals cut against the "professional ethos." Finally, there are cultural biases of which to be aware. For example, Korean managers are often unwilling to give too negative an evaluation as *inhwa* emphasizes the importance of harmony among individuals who are not equal in prestige, rank and power, while supervisors are required to care for the well-being of their subordinates and negative evaluations may undermine harmonious relations (Chen, 2000). Another Korean value, *koenchanayo* ("that's good enough"), also hampers appraisals as it encourages tolerance and appreciation of people's efforts and not being excessively harsh in assessing sincere efforts (ibid.).

## Employee development

Korea's spectacular postwar economic growth, and some *chaebols*, have been influenced by a skilled and well-educated workforce with heavy investment in the development of HRs. It was argued that the success of companies, such as Pohang Iron and Steel, was due in part to its employee development and regular training (Morden and Bowles, 1998). Many espoused the Confucian emphasis on education with very strong commitment to it and also traditional respect and esteem attached to educational attainment. This is indicated by high levels of literacy, high proportion of scientists and engineers per head of population, and that 70 percent of the workforce graduated from high school (Morden and Bowles, 1998).

Employee development can be classified (Kim and Bae, forthcoming) as: new recruits and existing employees; in-house and external; language proficiency, job ability and character building; basic and advanced courses. Many *chaebols* put strong emphasis on training and have their own well-resourced and supported training centers. There is often many (3–6) months' in-house induction training with new employees staying at training centers or socialization camps. Here they are inculcated in company history, culture, business philosophy, core values and vision, to develop "all-purpose" general skills through which to enhance team spirit, "can-do" spirit, adaptability and problem-solving. They use *sahoon* (shared values explicitly articulated), a company song and a catch-phrase, to build up feelings of belonging, loyalty and commitment (Kim and Briscoe, 1997; Kim and Bae, forthcoming). These centers also provide on-going training and a variety of programs. For instance, in 1995 Samsung spent US$260 million on training, Hyundai US$195 million, Daewoo and LG US$130 million each (Chung *et al.*, 1997).

Some companies use invited foreign engineers to work with them and transfer skills, and some send their own trainees overseas (Kim and Bae, forthcoming). Managerial-level training focused more on molding managers to the company's core values and philosophy than to developing their job-related abilities and knowledge. Programs placed more emphasis on building character and developing positive attitudes than on professional competence. One popular way to improve job-related skills was job rotation and multi-skilled training, but these were not applied systematically and varied between industries (ibid.). Many large firms launched several programs to promote business–university partnerships. In addition, overseas training programs to provide opportunities have been introduced and many companies give employees with requisite qualifications or appraisal results opportunities to study at foreign universities, e.g. Samsung's "Region Expert" program sends junior employees overseas for one year to obtain language skills and cultural familiarity (ibid.).

## Employee relations

By 1998 there were 1.40 million union members (12.6 percent density) and an increasing number of strikes: 129; this rose to 1.48 million members (11.9 percent) and 198 strikes in 1999, and to 1.53 million members (12 percent) and 250 strikes by 2000 (Kim and Bae, forthcoming). Thus, unions can be highly militant. Furthermore, unions are strategically well located in ship and automobile manufacture as well as power, transportation and telecommunications. Conflicts had often been high profile, large scale and confrontational. For example, the 1992 week-long occupation of Hyundai Motors was ended by 15,000 riot police storming the factory (Kim, 2000).

From the late 1980s the institutions, framework and policies of employee relations all reconfigured under pressures from political liberalization and civilian governments, joining the ILO (1991) and OECD (1996), trade union pressure and the Asian crisis. Nevertheless, the frames of reference and perspectives for management remains strongly unitary. In contrast, this is less so for labor, with stronger pluralist, and even radical, perspectives evident. The position of the state is more ambiguous, especially given the background of the current president and some seeming shift from the initial pluralist stance towards a more unitary one. This may be seen in the following examples.

There were strikes by power plants and major car-makers in 2002, and a week-long truck-driver strike in early 2003. This latter dispute crippled Pusan, the world's third largest port, which handles 80 percent of Korea's ocean-going cargo, and risked manufacturers, such as Samsung and LG Chem, grinding to a halt by choking their supply and distribution channels (Ward, 2003a). The government made concessions to resolve this dispute; these included fuel subsidies, tax cuts and lower highway tools for trucks (ibid.). It was also seen as part of the new President Roh Moo-hyun's policy of resolving labor disputes peacefully through dialog. Similarly, the privatization of the national railway network has been cancelled, while the sale of the state-owned Chohung Bank stalled, both amid fierce union opposition (ibid.). These instances can be seen to support a more pluralist approach.

However, a more unitarist sentiment can also be detected. For instance, in 2002 there was imprisonment of unionists, refusal to recognize public sector unions and ending of the power workers strike after several weeks of public threats and intimidation and surrounding their Myong-dong Cathedral camp with riot and secret police. In 2003 there were high-profile disputes by truck-drivers and bankers and a four-day strike of railway workers was crushed by more than 1,000 arrests. Korea is still seen as repressive, flouting trade union rights and ILO Conventions 87 and 98 by restraining the rights to freedom of association, collective bargaining and strike action. Thus, in 2002 the President of the Korean Confederation of Trade Unions was imprisoned for two years for "obstructing business" by simply coordinating a general strike (ICFTU, 2003).

## Changes taking place within the HR function

Traditionally in the *chaebol* there were links between the HR department and the powerful chairman's office, which made many important HR decisions, "thus the HR function is closely tied to the highest level of the *chaebol*" (Kim and Briscoe, 1997: 299). More recently, HRM units in Korean firms have changed their roles from the traditional administrative aspects towards more strategic value-adding activities. This is summarized in Table 3.10.

The first change is in HRM organization. Traditionally, Korean firms had the perception that "anybody can assume HRM jobs," meaning that HR practitioners did not need any special competencies or qualifications. This reflects a "lowest common denominator" syndrome: a small fraction of HRM activities created the large proportion of value-added, whereas most activities added little value (Baron and Kreps, 1999). The shifts in this also occurred in several different ways. As aforementioned, the roles of HR professionals have changed and have become more strategic. To become business partners, HR managers started to align HRM configurations with business strategies and organizational goals. Some empirical evidence also confirms this (Bae and Lawler, 2000; Bae and Yu, 2003). In addition, firms also started to reorganize their HR units by differentiating them into several specialities and sections, i.e. HR planning, recruitment, HR support team, employee relations, and by adopting a separate shared service unit.

A second change in the HR function, related to the first, involves the efforts to enhance the competencies of HR professionals. Three different strategies are employed:

*Table 3.10* Change in perspectives on HRM in Korea (%)

| Employee champion or advocate | 29 | Current | 40 | Strategic partner |
|---|---|---|---|---|
| | 12 | Future | 68 | |
| Reactive change agent for management | 63 | Current | 17 | Proactive change agent |
| | 32 | Future | 57 | |
| Internal-oriented for organizational issues | 57 | Current | 17 | External-oriented for social issues |
| | 22 | Future | 48 | |
| Focused on operational issues in organization | 68 | Current | 14 | Focused on business goals and strategies |
| | 16 | Future | 75 | |
| Efficient management of human resources | 53 | Current | 23 | Internal consultants for line managers |
| | 38 | Future | 49 | |
| Seniority-based HRM | 70 | Current | 12 | Ability/performance-based HRM |
| | 2 | Future | 96 | |
| Results-oriented HRM | 51 | Current | 24 | Process-oriented HRM |
| | 26 | Future | 54 | |
| Task-centered HRM | 26 | Current | 50 | People-centered HRM |
| | 47 | Future | 38 | |
| Generalist orientation | 62 | Current | 11 | Specialist orientation |
| | 6 | Future | 84 | |
| Paternalism-based HRM | 71 | Current | 9 | Contract-based HRM |
| | 3 | Future | 91 | |
| Authoritarian approach | 70 | Current | 10 | Democratic approach |
| | 4 | Future | 91 | |

Source: Park and Yu (2001).

(a) initiating various education programs for HR managers (see Kim and Bae, forthcoming); (b) transferring to HRM units people who have various experiences in organizations, such as planning, sales and R&D; (c) recruiting HR professionals from outside who are trained in graduate-level programs or experienced in other organizations. All these strategies were unusual in the past.

Another change in the HR function is the outsourcing phenomenon (similar to that in some other countries such as the UK; see Rowley, 2003). Various HR activities have been outsourced, as shown in Table 3.11. Three areas highly prone to outsourcing are: (i) education and training; (ii) outplacement; (iii) HR information systems. Partly as a result of these trends, HR service firms have drastically increased (Rowley and Bae, 2003). These include outsourcing for general affairs and benefits, HR consulting, education and training, head-hunting, e-HRM and HR information system providers, outplacement, online recruiting, staffing service, and HRM (active server pages ASP) (see Table 3.11). The approximate gross sales for such businesses (in won in 2002) are (Kim, 2002): HR consulting (one trillion); staffing service (one and half trillion); on-line recruiting (200 billion); head-hunting (100 billion); and HRM ASP (50 billion).

*Table 3.11* HRM activities expected to be outsourced in Korea

| Rank | HRM activities for outsourcing | Feedback (%) |
| --- | --- | --- |
| 1 | Education and training | 85 |
| 2 | Outplacement | 77 |
| 3 | Building up and utilization of HR information systems | 77 |
| 4 | Job analysis | 68 |
| 5 | Employee recruitment and selection | 56 |
| 6 | Salary pay and operation | 53 |

Source: Park and Yu (2001).

Finally, the adoption of e-HRM is also an example of recent change in the HR function. By managing all employment-related data through such information systems, firms gained some benefits in terms of cost reduction and speed of operations. In particular, e-recruitment through which firms efficiently screen job candidates, is actively utilized.

## Key challenges facing HRM

There is a range of key challenges facing HRM. First, there are more macro ones stemming from the economy. These include the call for greater transparency and openness in corporate governance issues, and the continued reorganization of capital with *chaebol* restructuring, FDI and takeovers, and thus exposure to nontraditional HRM practices. HR practitioners can have a role in all of these.

There is also the challenge for HRM of an aging workforce (Bae and Rowley, 2003). For example, in 1990 the economically active population aged 15–19 was 639,000, by 2002 it was down to 352,000, while over the same period those aged 40–54 increased from 5,616,000 to 8,189,000. Of course, such trends are widespread, but the implications for Korea are stark given some of the traditional aspects of culture and society, not least its strong family basis and orientation, homogeneity and exclusiveness.

Second, there are challenges from the more micro HRM policy areas. This has several elements to it. One challenge is the so-called "war for talent," i.e. an attraction strategy to recruit top-quality talent. Many Korean corporations actively pursued recruiting and retaining such talent. For this purpose, *chaebols* such as Samsung, LG, SK, Hyundai Motors, Hanwha, Doosan and Kumho, provide a fast-track system, signing-on bonus, stock options, and so on. This was not an issue earlier during the "seniority-based relational" HRM system. Since the 1997 crisis, the mobility of people has increased within and across large corporations and venture firms. Corporations responded to labor-market changes with multiple strategies (Kim and Bae, forthcoming). Firms divided employees into different groups, each with their own approach: "attraction strategy" (i.e. dashing into the war for talent) and "retention strategy" (i.e. taking measures to keep core employees) for core employees; "replacement strategy" (i.e. dismissing under-performing employees) and "outplacement strategy" (i.e. providing information and training for job switching) for poor performers; "transactional and outsourcing strategy" (i.e. contract-based, short-term approach) towards atypical workers. All of these strategies had been unfamiliar to most Korean firms.

Managing contingent workers is also a challenge for HRM. At first, these types of workers reduced company costs. Yet, managing these people is becoming harder. There are several issues here, which include the shattering of the "psychological contract," recontracting, differentiated treatment (e.g. lower pay and benefits) and disharmony with regular workers, and complicated and multiple configurations. These "costs" have been seen in a range of countries, while additionally in Korea, some cultural aspects (see Table 3.1), i.e. the strong perception of the equality norm and a strong union movement, make management even more difficult.

Finally, performance-based systems have also generated HRM challenges. In some aspects, firms gained higher productivity and performance after adoption. However, it also produced downsides too. Commonly, people only become involved in activities that are evaluated by their organization – the "no evaluation, no act" syndrome or the dictum "what gets measured get done." Therefore, organizational citizenship behaviors, which used to be more common in Korean firms, are now more rarely observed. Another phenomenon is that people are more reluctant to cooperate with other teams or divisions. This has become even more critical since some profit-sharing programs were adopted. This is particularly problematic for electronics companies pursuing digital convergence as this requires high levels of cooperation and coordination. Finally, people have become more prone to focus on current and short-term goals, especially in R&D divisions or institutes. Researchers avert high-risk long-term projects, the critical foundation for future success. In short, the institutionalization of performance-based HRM is a half-success story, and one which may have an unhappy middle section and a calamitous ending.

## What is likely to happen to HR functions?

With regards to HR units, we expect re-engineering of HRM processes and decentralization. The shrinkage in headquarters HR practitioners, and increases in business division HRM, will be accelerated. Decentralization will be realized through the transfer of HRM-related activities to line managers. Again, some activities will be accomplished by outsourcing. However, the difficulties with the necessary control, coordination and consistency in HRM, with the importance of equity and fairness within and across businesses and people in such circumstances are clear (see Rowley, 2003).

As other functional areas (e.g. planning, marketing and MIS) have experienced, the HRM function might encounter a challenge from top management regarding the value added by the HRM unit. HR managers in many Korean firms are currently preparing for this challenge. Following Becker *et al.* (2001), many firms have recently developed HR performance indexes to link HRM activities and firm performance. HRM audit and review based on the HR scorecard approach will be more actively conducted. A focus on areas such as corporate governance, ethical business practices and top executive pay, as well as managing diversity, will further allow HR to add value.

Finally, as Korean firms continue to relocate production to other countries such as China, Southeast Asia and further afield, global HRM is gaining significance. Several issues here include the globalization–localization choice, transfer of the "best" people (e.g. both expatriates and inpatriates) and HR practices, and global integration and coordination. Some companies, such as Samsung Electronics, employ inpatriates from host countries to work at the head office. Other companies, like LG Electronics, send executive-level management to regional head offices (e.g. China) to establish and coordinate the whole of HRM in the region. The need for HRM to have a role in this area of cross-cultural management is clear. All these issues are examples of what is likely to happen in the next few years.

# References

Bae, J. (1997) "Beyond seniority-based systems: A paradigm shift in Korean HRM?" *Asia Pacific Business Review* 3 (4): 82–110.

Bae, J. and Lawler, J. (2000) "Organizational and HRM strategies in Korea: Impact on firm performance in an emerging economy," *Academy of Management Journal* 43 (3): 502–517.

Bae, J. and Rowley, C. (2001) "The impact of globalization on HRM: The case of South Korea," *Journal of World Business* 36 (4): 402–428.

Bae, J. and Rowley, C. (2003). "Changes and continuities in South Korean HRM," *Asia Pacific Business Review* 9 (4): 76–105.

Bae, J., Rowley, C., Lawler, J. and Kim, D.H. (1997) "Korean industrial relations at the crossroads: The recent labour troubles," *Asia Pacific Business Review* 3 (3): 148–160.

Bae, J. and Yu, G. (2003) "HRM configurations in Korean venture firms: Resource availability, institutional force, and strategic choice perspectives," working paper, Korea University.

Baron, J.N. and Kreps, D.M. (1999) *Strategic human resources: Frameworks for general managers*, New York: John Wiley & Sons.

Becker, B.E., Huselid, M.A. and Ulrich, D. (2001) *The HR scorecard: Linking people, strategy, and performance*, Boston, MA: Harvard Business School Press.

Chen, M. (2000) "Management in South Korea," in M. Warner (ed.) *Management in Asia Pacific*, London: Thomson, pp. 300–311.

Choi, K. and Lee, K. (1998) "Employment adjustment in Korean firms: Survey of 1998," Seoul: Korea Labor Institute.

Chung, K.H., Lee, H.C. and Jung, K.H. (1997) *Korean management: Global strategy and cultural transformation*, Berlin: de Gruyter.

Demaret, L. (2001) "Korea: Two speed recovery," *Trade Union World* 21 (1), December–January: 21–22.

*The Economist* (1999) "A survey of the Koreas," 10 June: 1–16.

*The Economist* (2000) "Business in South Korea," 1 April: 67–70.

*The Economist* (2003) "No honeymoon for Roh," 7 June: 60.

ICFTU (2003) "Trade union victory in South Korea," ICFTU Press Online, 4 March.

Kang, Y. and Wilkinson, R. (2000) "Workplace industrial relations in Korea for the 21st century," in R. Wilkinson, J. Maltby and J. Lee (eds.) *Responding to change: Some key lessons for the future of Korea*, Sheffield: University of Sheffield Management School, pp. 125–145.

Kim, K.D. (1994) "Confucianism and capitalist development in East Asia," in L. Sklair (ed.) *Capitalism and development*, London: Routledge, pp. 87–106.

Kim, Y. (2000) "Employment relations at a large South Korean firm: The LG Group," in G. Bamber, F. Park, C. Lee, P. Ross and K. Broadbent (eds.) *Employment relations in the Asia-Pacific*, London: Thomson, pp. 175–193.

Kim, Y. (2002) "Trends in HR service industry in Korea," *HR Professional* 1: 94–99 (in Korean).

Kim, D. and Bae, J. (forthcoming) *Employment relations and HRM in South Korea*, London: Ashgate.

Kim, D., and Park, S. (1997) "Changing patterns of pay systems in Japan and Korea: From seniority to performance," *International Journal of Employment Studies* 5 (2): 117–134.

Kim, J. and Rowley, C. (2001) "Managerial problems in Korea: Evidence from the nationalized industries," *International Journal of Public Sector Management* 14 (2): 129–148.

Kim, S. and Briscoe, D. (1997) "Globalization and a new human resource policy in Korea: Transformation to a performance-based HRM," *Employee Relations* 19 (4): 298–308.

Korea Ministry of Labor (1999) "A survey report on annual pay systems and gain-sharing plans," Korea Ministry of Labor (in Korean).

Kwon, S.-H. and O'Donnell, M. (2001) *The Chaebol and labour in Korea: The development of management strategy in Hyundai*, London: Routledge.

Kwun, S.K. and Cho, N. (2002) "Organizational change and inertia: Korea telecom," in C. Rowley, T.W. Sohn and J. Bae (eds.) *Managing Korean businesses: Organization, culture, human resources and change*, London: Frank Cass, pp. 111–136.

Lee, C. (2000) "Challenges facing unions in South Korea," in G. Bamber, F. Park, C. Lee, P. Ross and K. Broadbent (eds.) *Employment relations in the Asia-Pacific*, London: Thomson, pp. 145–158.

Morden, T. and Bowles, D. (1998) "Management in South Korea: A review," *Management Decision* 36 (5): 316–330.

Oh, I. and Park, H.J. (2002) "Shooting at a moving target: Four theoretical problems in exploring the dynamics of the Chaebol," in C. Rowley, T.W. Sohn and J. Bae (eds.) *Managing Korean businesses: Organization, culture, human resources and change*, London: Frank Cass, pp. 44–69.

Park, F. and Park, Y. (2000) "Changing approaches to employee relations in South Korea," in G. Bamber, F. Park, C. Lee, P. Ross and K. Broadbent (eds.) *Employment relations in the Asia-Pacific*, London: Thomson, pp. 80–100.

Park, J. and Ahn, H (1999) "The changes and future direction of Korean employment practices," Seoul: The Korea Employers' Federation (in Korean).

Park, W. and Yu, G. (2001) "Paradigm shift and changing role of HRM in Korea: Analysis of the HRM experts' opinions and its implication," *The Korean Personnel Administration Journal* 25 (1): 347–369.

Pucik, V. and Lim, J.C. (2002) "Transforming HRM in a Korean Chaebol: A case study of Samsung,"in C. Rowley, T.W. Sohn and J. Bae (eds.) *Managing Korean businesses: Organization, culture, human resources and change*, London: Cass, pp. 137–160.

Rousseau, D.M. (1995) *Psychological contracts in organizations: Understanding written and unwritten agreements*, Thousand Oaks/London/New Delhi: Sage.

Rowley, C. (ed.) (1998) *HRM in the ASIA Pacific region: Convergence questioned*, London: Frank Cass.

Rowley, C. (2001) "Going global? Globalization and the management of human resources," *Financial Times Mastering Management Online*, October, Issue 7: 1–3.

Rowley, C. (2002a) "Management in Korea: Background and traditions," *Financial Times Mastering Management Online*, December–January, Issue 9: 1–3.

Rowley, C. (2002b) "Management in Korea: Crisis, reforms and the future," *Financial Times Mastering Management Online*, March, Issue 11: 1–2.

Rowley, C. (2002c) "Management in Korea: Employment, policies and practices", *Financial Times Mastering Management Online*, May, Issue 13: 1–2.

Rowley, C. (2002d) "South Korean management in transition," in M. Warner (ed.) *Managing across cultures*, London: Thomson, pp. 178–192.

Rowley, C. (2003) *The management of people: HRM in context*, London: Spiro Press.

Rowley, C. and Bae, J. (eds.) (1998) *Korean businesses: Internal and external industrialization*, London: Frank Cass.

Rowley, C. and Bae, J. (2003) "Culture and management in South Korea," in M. Warner (ed.) *Culture and management in Asia*, London: Curzon Press, pp. 187–209.

Rowley, C. and Benson, J. (2000) (eds.) *Globalization and labour in the Asia Pacific Region*, London: Frank Cass.

Rowley, C. and Benson, J. (2002) "Convergence and divergence in Asian HRM," *California Management Review* 44 (2): 90–109.

Rowley, C. and Benson, J. (eds.) (2003) *HRM in the Asia Pacific region: Convergence revisited*, London: Frank Cass.

Rowley, C., Sohn, T.-W. and Bae, J. (eds.) (2002) *Managing Korean businesses: Organization, culture, human resources and change*, London: Frank Cass.

Song, B.-N. (1997) *The rise of the Korean economy*, Oxford: Oxford University Press.

Ward, A. (2003a) "Government deal ends South Korean truck strike," *Financial Times*, 16 May: 10.

Ward, A. (2003b) "South Korea's Chaebol," *Financial Times*, 9 July: 17.

Yang, B. (1999) "The annual pay systems in Korean firms," Proceedings of the International Conference of Korea Association of Personnel Administration on the Change of HRM Paradigm and Annual Pay, November, Seoul, pp. 207–239.

Yang, S.-H. and Lim, S. (2000) "The role of government in industrial relations in South Korea: The case of the Tripartite (labour–management–government) Committee," in R. Wilkinson, J. Maltby and J.-H. Lee (eds.) *Responses to change: Some key issues for the future of Korea*, Sheffield: Sheffield University Management School, pp. 113–123.

# Useful websites

There are a range of sources for the latest information and developments in HRM that can provide details to the reader over the years. These include the following:

| | |
|---|---|
| Korea Labor Institute: | http://www.kli.re.kr |
| Korea Chamber of Commerce and Industry: | http://www.kcci.or.kr |
| Ministry of Labor: | http://www.molab.go.kr |
| Ministry of Education and Human Resource Development: | http://www.moe.go.kr |
| Ministry of Science and Technology: | http://www.most.go.kr |
| National Statistical Office: | http://www.nsohp.nso.go.kr |
| Civil Service Commission: | http://www.csc.go.kr |
| Samsung Economic Research Institute: | http://www.seri.org |

There is also a range of journals in the area, especially:
*Asia Pacific Business Review*
*International Journal of HRM*
*Asia Pacific Journal of HRs*
*Asia Pacific Journal of Management*

# HRM in Japan

JOHN SALMON

## Introduction

Since the early 1980s there has been a growing debate regarding the importance of
human resource management (HRM). Much of this debate has provided conceptual and
analytical accounts that have sought to link the presence of HRM practices with
improved company performance (MacDuffie; 1995; Delaney and Huselid, 1996; Tyson,
1997). The conventional wisdom holds that the firm investing in HRM possesses a route
towards high performance in which improved employee effort can become a source of
sustained competitive advantage (Barney, 1991). It is through the implementation of
HRM that improved employee effort can be developed whereby improved performance
and value added contribute towards organizational specific human capital that is difficult
for competitors to emulate precisely (Becker, 1964). In its most developed form HRM
is viewed as a strategic management approach that seeks to link employee policies to
business strategies that pave the way towards enhanced organizational performance
(Legge, 1995). Although HRM is in essence a managerial approach, it is principally
through the organizational investments in training, employee recruitment and
selection, in addition to performance evaluation and career development that effective
employee commitment comes to contribute towards a high performance–employment
relationship.

Despite the considerable western interest in Japanese management, very little academic
attention has been paid to HRM in Japan. This is all the more significant given that Japan
is under considerable pressure to change important aspects of its employment practices in
order to cope with the changing business environment. Against a decade of low growth,
recession and rising unemployment, Japanese employers have been faced with an
increasing number of HR problems. On the one hand they have to devise HRM strategies
to address the effects of an ever greater social diversity amongst employees and their
values and lifestyles, alongside a concurrent employer-led diversification of the labor
market. Such changes have been urging a critical re-evaluation of the basic framework
of the established Japanese HRM management model. This chapter explores Japanese
HRM in regard to changes in company recruitment, training, lifetime employment and
labor-market diversification.

# The Japanese HRM model

Japan has long attached particular importance to the development of its human resources. Unlike other leading economies in Europe and North America, Japan's rapid rise to become the world's second largest national economy was achieved largely in spite of its absence of natural resources. The development, growth and centrality placed upon the management and organization of its indigenous human resources has been, as in the field of education for example, quite conscientiously cultivated as an important matter of both corporate and national public policy (Salmon, 1999). Since the early 1980s there has been a growing and largely Anglo-Saxon debate regarding the importance of HRM. Much of this debate has provided conceptual and analytical accounts that have sought to link the presence of HRM practices with improved company performance (Tyson, 1997; MacDuffie; 1995; Delaney and Huselid, 1996). The conventional wisdom holds that the firm that invests in HRM possesses a route towards high performance in which improved employee effort can become a source of sustained competitive advantage (Barney, 1991). It is through the implementation of HRM that employee effort can be developed so that improved performance and value added contribute towards organizational specific human capital that is difficult for competitors to emulate precisely (Becker, 1964). In its most developed form, HRM is viewed as a strategic management approach that seeks to link employee policies to business strategies that pave the way towards enhanced organizational performance (Legge, 1995). Although HRM is in essence a managerial approach, it is principally through the organizational investments in training, employee recruitment and selection, in addition to performance evaluation and career development that effective employee commitment comes to contribute towards a high performance–employment relationship. There are, however, a number of key differences between the Japanese and Anglo-Saxon approaches towards creating HRM. Whereas the Anglo-Saxon model of HRM has been seen in part as a corporate strategy to achieve a union-free organization by avoiding union recognition and collective bargaining (Godard and Delaney, 2000), in Japan HRM is a characteristic that is most developed in the large unionized firm (Koike, 1997; Sano, 1997; Sato, 1997; Selmer, 2001). Moreover, the Japanese unionized employment relationship has attached far greater emphasis upon the maintenance of long-term institutionalized political and societal sources of organizational stability both at the macro level as well as the micro level of the firm (Cole, 1973; Dore, 1973; Aoki, 1984, 1988; Salmon, 1992; Morishima, 1995; Pempel, 1998; Kato, 2000b)

Under conditions of low growth, however, and following a decade of the Heisei recession, there have been growing doubts about the continued sustainability of Japanese job security. The stability of lifetime employment and its centrality to the in-house growth of HR development and training have been central features of the Japanese employment relationship (Kawakita, 1997). Recent Japanese media coverage of restructuring and downsizing in the decade of recession suggests that employment security in Japan is in decline, the implication being that Japanese employees can no longer expect their companies to fulfil their commitment to job security as they resort to corporate restructuring.

The Japanese management model has been characterized largely by its institutional features: the presence of *nenko* comprising merit, age and seniority-based promotion *and* the lifetime employment principle in addition to the presence of the third pillar, an enterprise union. *Nenko* systems operate within the firm. Lifetime employment, though a feature of the large firm, takes the form of an implicit employer adherence not to dismiss members of the regular workforce. Enterprise unionism represents mainly the manual and non-manual regular workers within the company below that of the managerial grades. With only a minority of exceptions there is no real effort to organize the non-regular worker such as the part-time and temporary employee. The most distinctive feature of the Japanese employment relationship is that both *nenko* and lifetime employment provide the necessary conditions for the long-term development of firm-specific human capital within the firm. Core workers are carefully selected from an annual intake of young inexperienced new recruits chosen from prestige high schools and universities and who are expected continually to strive to enhance their careers within the company by improving their capabilities through extensive in-house training and company-based personal development.

Abegglen was one of the first western scholars to draw attention to the concept of lifetime employment (1958); the expansion of the lifetime employment norm is largely associated with a period of high economic growth (Cole, 1973). Its widespread societal acceptance in Japan, however, is not simply determined by the interests of employers. It owes much to the judicial rulings of the Japanese courts that placed limitations on the rights of employers to dismiss employees. An important body of case-law rulings created by the Japanese courts during the 1950s and 1960s encouraged employers to seek alternatives to employment dismissals (Sugeno 1992: 162; Hanami, 1994). During the 1970s' economic crisis, government public-policy initiatives were implemented to promote employer acceptance of employee security within the firm (Kume, 1998). Union militancy has also played its part. Some of the most violent industrial disputes in the early postwar period in Japan have been fought against rationalization and mass lay-offs (Moore, 1983). For Japanese unions, job security has long been an important consideration for the creation of a cooperative relationship with the employer while long-term employee tenure within the firm has been a necessary requirement for gaining employee recruitment and commitment for creating firm-specific HR development within the firm.

## HR development

Skill formation and internal career development among regular workers have been the central features of the Japanese model of HRM. In-house learning and the particular centrality placed upon on-the-job training (OJT) (Okazaki-Ward, 1993; Koike, 1997) are distinctive hallmarks of the Japanese management system and the cornerstone of the development of human capital (Sato, 1997; Selmer, 2001) for inexperienced high-school leavers and university graduate recruits. Careful recruitment and selection, socialization into the company culture and late promotion has provided the career span for long-term training in firm-specific skills and leadership development. OJT also helps foster worker cooperation through team working, information sharing and the Japanese preference for face-to-face communication through small group activities at workplace level (Rohlen, 1985). Change in the business environment, however, has led firms to rethink their competitive strategies and product-line portfolios. There is a greater need to diversify product lines and create new business opportunities, raising problems for company training and development.

Following recruitment and induction, new employees embark upon a specified systematic program of skill formation and learning that involves job rotation and programmed instruction under the direction of their immediate supervisors, line managers and in accordance with the strategic requirement of the personnel department. It is the personnel department budget that specifies the required hours and duration of the allotted training time for each inexperienced employee. The schedule of training leads to certified knowledge that is meticulously recorded in the career profile for each individual worker. Learning takes place by working alongside a more experienced worker within the workgroup. Initial training requires high levels of off-the-job training (Off-JT) particularly where specialist knowledge is required or a public license is needed to handle particular types of equipment. Health and safety legislation may also call for specialized formal Off-JT training and the need to have certified evidence of a particular skill and ability (arc-welding, for example, cannot be learned exclusively by OJT). The company-based career development program sets out the agreed blueprint for each individual's learning schedule (Okazaki-Ward, 1993). The training process is subject to regular appraisals and guidance from supervisors, with attempts to get a close fit between the individual learning schedule and the long-term needs of the firm. OJT is also used in the preparation of candidates in line for promotion to higher positions. New responsibilities are learned from the direct experience of working with a senior manager. Much of the OJT training in the workplace remains informal. It takes place outside the programmed training budget and emerges as part of the normal shared collective effort within the workgroup, with tacit learning development, guidance and interaction with more experienced senior members of the workgroup.

## Limits of HR development

OJT is widely used among blue-collar workers in manufacturing who are trained in performing manual job tasks that are defined by the type of job description and the nature of the plant technology. OJT is more extensive in the largest firms where multi-skilling, job rotation and problem-solving maintenance tasks are widely developed. Only a quarter of small firms utilize OJT compared to over a half of large firms. Though OJT is utilized in the training of white-collar employees, it has proved to be much less effective (Koike, 1997) White-collar workers with higher-education backgrounds have job tasks less subject to routine, involving greater discretionary judgments and requiring greater capacities to process knowledge (Sato, 1997). The relationship between job content and training is far less transparent than for blue-collar workers (Koike, 1997). One consequence has been that more generalized responsibilities have left much of their work activities relatively undisturbed during the period of high growth. Under low growth, however, and the rising seniority-based wage curve, greater attention has been placed upon the performance of the white-collar worker. The revolution in information technology and the pressure for organizational efficiency has heightened white-collar job insecurity.

## HRM and white-collar workers

The traditional Japanese approach towards the recruitment of white-collar staff places considerable value on the social and attitudinal characteristics of candidates. Selection criteria tends to seek "cooperative spirit," cultural orientation and reliance on new recruits coming from the same high schools and universities as the existing workforce. This reliance upon a closed institutional network for company recruitment has helped to sustain the corporate culture and foster company loyalty, nurturing the "company man." It has, however, led to claims of favoritism and the privilege of old-boy networks (Kameyama, 1997). Moreover, it appears ill-fitted to broaden to a more socially diverse employment relationship suited to the changes taking place in today's Japan. Moreover, the selective screening of candidates places less weight on particular capabilities of new entrants. White-collar recruitment stresses generalist abilities but gives insufficient attention to the possession of professional and specialist skills.

Faced with low growth, business strategies required new products. Over half of firms have sought to find new growth through creating new fields of business. The OJT system has been found ill-suited to adapt to new business ventures. Direct recruitment of new graduates is not feasible for new businesses where developed abilities and work experience are required, while established experienced company workers with high levels of firm-specific skills may be ill-fitted to the requirements of new business. New products increase training costs as more Off-JT is required but do little to address the employment opportunities of existing workforces. Some 70 percent of firms who have found themselves in this situation have resorted to hiring experienced mid-career workers from the external labor market. Company employees, who possess embedded knowledge of company culture, work practices and procedures, often lack specific knowledge or experience of sales and marketing or the particular skills needed for new business areas.

Firms as well as employees are increasingly seeking more specialized and professional skills and abilities that give them a stronger advantage in meeting more diversified business strategies (Kawakita, 1997). In terms of internal career development, however, low growth considerably increases the anxieties of regular workers. Ironically the lifetime employment norm, with its implicit expectation of a career in the same company, has come to pose a threat to older workers. Unlike America and Britain there are no Japanese agreements that provide rules regarding lay-off by seniority. Despite the high commitment to the training of regular workforces, the largest proportion of investment is understandably directed at younger workers. Low growth, however, reduces opportunities for young workers to find positions in big companies as regular workers. Promotion opportunities intensify inter-worker competition while the prospects of being temporary or permanently transferred or encouraged to take early retirement increase. Against a more competitive global business environment, Japanese firms are now changing their hiring practices. They are increasingly resorting to cost-cutting measures that involve expanding their pool of non-regular workers and in some cases recruiting cheaper non-regular workers to undertake regular work assignments. Fears about the increased uncertainty of lifetime employment along with the growth of non-regular, part-time, temporary and agency work are giving rise to greater fears about future employment security with a demoralizing effect on regular employees (Osawa, 2001; Sato, 2001; Weathers, 2001)

## Defending the employment norm

The fear of rising unemployment following the 1973 international oil crisis marked an important stage in the development of the Japanese approach towards HRM. The Japanese response to what was regarded as a major threat to the high-growth Japanese employment model saw a number of initiatives being undertaken to deal with the prospect of increased unemployment. The Labor Standards Law requires that a 30-day notice or payment in lieu of notice is required to dismiss an employee. Mass redundancies were met with unrest and militant union opposition during the early postwar period. In the 1950s and 1960s, the courts began to develop a body of case law that bolstered the lifetime employment norm (Sugeno, 1992). The courts accepted the principle that a dismissal could be "an abuse of the employer's right to dismiss" in which the courts would establish whether there was "just cause" (Hanami, 1994: 35). Dismissals could be declared null and void by the court unless the employer could prove that they were "objectively reasonable and socially appropriate" measures. The burden of proof is placed upon the employer rather than the employee. Such judgments set limits on the employer's capacity particularly to dismiss full-time regular workers. Employers seeking adjustments in their workforce were obliged by the courts to demonstrate how they had sought to avoid dismissals. This judicial requirement encouraged employers to develop alternative measures short of dismissal to sustain employment. Companies began reducing overtime working, curtailing the recruitment of new workers and avoiding the non-renewal of part-time and temporary worker contracts (Schregle, 1993). In some cases workers were re-trained, temporarily or permanently posted to other sections of the company or sent to subsidiaries and supplier firms. Restricting the powers of employer discretion to freely dismiss workforces led to creative ways to retain and redeploy regular employees whose employment security and long-term HR value were prized by the firm. The concern to protect employment, however, led to direct public policy initiatives that sort to avoid employer recourse to unemployment. Radical policy alternatives to redundancy were enshrined in a series of statutory initiatives introduced in the 1970s. These were intended not only to encourage the retention of the lifetime employment norm but were also designed to placate the possibility of a revival of increased trade union opposition to the potential response to large-scale redundancies (Kume, 1998; Takanashi *et al.*, 1999). A major government initiative seeking to sustain job security at the level of the firm occurred following the statutory changes in the use of unemployment insurance funds.

The Revision of the Employment Insurance Law (1974), The Special Measures for Laid-off Workers in Targeted Depressed Industries (1977), along with the creation of The Employment Stabilization Funds (1977) saw the beginning of an ambitious public policy attempt to avoid unemployment by promoting employment security and retention within the firm. Significantly these changes received the support of the main opposition political parties who were closely allied to the main trade unions. Japanese trade unions have long prioritized job security. Trade union involvement in the public policy defense of employment security led to the increased influence of organized labor in the policy-making process. Domei, the more moderate national union center with the majority of its membership among the private sector industrial unions, and eventually Sohyo, the more radical union center representing the small firms and more militant highly unionized public sector unions, came to support the new policy measures.

It was against the background of the oil shock, with the fear of rising inflation and the concern about increased job losses that public policy endeavors sought to preserve employment stability by containing rising unemployment. It is estimated that two-thirds of wages in small firms and half of large firms' wages were subsidized from unemployment insurance funds to allow employers to re-train rather than dismiss workforces (Takanashi *et al.*, 1999). The trade unions restrained the level of their annual *shunto* wage demands. The public policy goal remained the stabilization of employment during a period of recession and employment adjustment by retaining existing employees in work and through the maintenance and continued training of employees within the firm rather than resorting to the Anglo-Saxon alternative of "hire and fire" and mass lay-offs.

The specific effects of the new policy approach included the creation of employment adjustment benefits, payments for employee education and training and financial support for employee transfers to subsidiary companies, in order to sustain the welfare of employees by protecting them from unemployment. The combination of statutory measures sat alongside the body of case law in the context of the overriding concern to maintain good industrial relations in a period of severe international crisis. This enabled the creation of a pattern of employment adjustment that sought to preserve the Japanese model of long-term in-house training and thereby sustain the internalization of employee commitment through the protective development of employee careers within the firm.

## The corporate community

By the early 1980s the characteristics of Japanese HRM were firmly in place. Employee involvement, small group activities and joint participation schemes initiated in the 1960s continued to expand and flourish throughout the 1970s and 1980s. In the aftermath of the oil crisis the international business environment became more competitive. The trade union movement began to lose its militancy particularly among the large industrial unions in the internationally exposed private sector export industries. Japanese strike levels that had been among the highest in the advanced industrial economies during the 1960s fell to among the lowest after 1980. Yet while the domestic economy still operated under conditions of acute labor shortages in the second half of the 1980s, the expansion of new company recruits covered by lifetime employment status increased sharply (Chuma, 2002). The large firms continued to see the competitive development of the firm in terms of expanding the specific in-house core competencies of employees as the principal source for establishing Japanese international competitive advantage. Security of employment continued to be a key component for the employment relationship. The combination of policy intervention to sustain employment within the firm and the avoidance of a major confrontation with organized labor during the period of employment adjustment saw a more cooperative stance emerging among the private sector industrial unions.

In 1987 there was a historic unification of the formerly divided labor movement when the four major national centers created "Rengo." This led to high expectations that a unified voice of Japanese organized labor could initiate progressive improvements in the employment relationship that would benefit not just union members but the wider Japanese society. The international crisis, however, had led many of the leading Japanese companies to improve their contacts with their enterprise unions. Joint consultation and communication committees were installed at company, plant, and workplace levels with their enterprise union-elected representatives. The improved channels of communication between management and the company unions combined with union attachment to the employers' implicit responsibility to maintain job security for regular employees began to appear to moderate the company union stance towards employers. In the 1980s, the Japanese employment relationship came to be redefined in terms of "companyism" or the "corporate community" (Dore, 1973; Tabata, 1997). These new ways of theorizing the Japanese management model placed primary importance on worker attitudes, values, motivations and level of identification with their company. Such an approach posed an alternative to the prevailing orthodox view that Japanese management was a product of Japan Inc. (van Wolferen, 1989) in which the Japanese state bureaucracy and big business interests had master-minded the high growth strategy of Japanese "exceptionalism" (Johnson, 1982). "Companyism" drew the debate back to the employment relationships by highlighting worker loyalty and commitment to the firm manifested in the concept of "company man." The late 1980s became the high watermark of the Japanese model.

## The rekindling of HRM

Reforms to the *nenko* wage structure began during the 1980s. In the 1990s in the context of low growth, *nenko* innovations have tended to relocate salary determination away from the more predictable fixed annual entitlements and allowances based on seniority towards a far greater emphasis on individual ability and greater use of merit evaluations. The biannual bonus package, though formally subject to negotiation with the company trade union, has become subject to a greater level of discretionary allocation based on individual ability.

Prospects for promotion have considerably diminished in the 1990s. Slow growth reduces the increase in new management positions. Promotion opportunities diminish further by intensification of lean management organization and delay of middle management as a consequence of increased international competition. The response of the leading Japanese firms has been to reconceptualize the basis for HR development. This has involved a move away from the single channel management hierarchical structure to permit promotion according to work specialism and professional expertise. The clearest example may be seen in research and development. Under the traditional structure, promotion required leaving an established area of expertise in order to be promoted to a higher administrative post. The new trend that emerged in the mid-1990s sought to promote specialist expertise on an equivalent management wage grade enabling specialist knowledge workers to continue to develop their expertise rather than abandon it for a management promotion. A further change has been the introduction of new criteria for individual effort either to gain higher positions within a grade or by being promoted into higher grades. In some instances "ghost" promotion has taken place where long-serving employees who would have been promoted in periods of higher growth are granted promoted status. Workers are able to use their status of foreman or supervisor in the management rank but have no employees to supervise. Ghost promotion helps to satisfy the considerable importance attached to status in Japanese society. It permits workers to place their new position on their business cards, an important consideration to gain credibility in social and personal relations outside the firm. They are also able to claim the respect by being addressed within the firm by their new rank.

The movement away from the traditional seniority-based wage system has been a gradual factor in the development of the *nenko* wage. The rethinking of the Japanese approach has had to come to terms with low growth and the limitations of the famed OJT system of broad skill accumulation where radical new business strategies have developed to meet new markets. One aspect of the pressure for change has been the more pervasive utilization of management by objectives. Although the duration of job tenure for regular workers still remains high in Japan, the main change in *nenko* is the shift away from the seniority system that had produced stable annual increments related to each year of service and biannual bonuses. The new wage systems have become much more merit and performance-orientated. Income is more tied to individual performance. Pay systems stress individual ability to undertake job duties. The expanded use of *satai* assessment based on measuring achievement, job ability and attitude has become a growing feature in the Japanese workplace that can lead to unfavorable assessment and the lowering of salaries.

## Heisei recession: the lost decade

The impact of recession during the 1990s and the sharp decline of trade union membership and influence have significantly weakened the bargaining stance of Japanese industrial unions. The annual *shunto* wage round has faced much stiffer opposition from the employers. The content of current wage negotiations has seen the reduction in the traditional fixed elements in the basic wage, and the decline of the value of annual increments based on tenure. The determination of annual pay is being settled by a greater variable lump sum in the salary structure. The future direction of the Japanese employment relationship appears to be directed towards greater levels of internal expertise and professional knowledge as new criteria for advancement in the firm. The shift to reward through personal ability and away from a pattern of predictable fixed increments has had an impact on union influence. Union weakness has eroded both moral and union representation. The sharp rise in personnel issues caused by restructuring and increased employment transfers has placed considerable burdens on union officers with greater time spent in involvement in company participation meetings. Even the largest Japanese unions face severe difficulties finding rank and file members willing to put themselves forward for election to union officer posts (Kato, 2000).

Between 1950 and 1980, unemployment remained at 1 or 2 percent during most years. Throughout the 1990s it rose to a historic postwar high, reaching 5 percent in 2001. Gross domestic product (GDP) averaged only 1.6 percent in the 1990s compared to 11.1 percent in the 1960s, 5.3 percent in the 1970s and 4.5 percent in the 1980s. At current low levels, competitive survival comes into question. The response of Rengo to rising unemployment levels is to seek to establish work-sharing in an attempt to sustain the retention of employment.

## The employer offensive: diversification of the labor market

Employer response to the recession has been to set an agenda for change in the employment relationship. The "Japanese-style management for a new era" published in 1995 by the leading Employers Organization, Nikkeiren (Nikkeiren, 1995), advocated a threefold classification in the traditional employment model. Long-term employees would form the core workforce. The second tier would be made up of specialist workers hired only for their specific skills and professional abilities but for shorter periods of employment. The third group would be the flexible workforce with lower skills, little training and irregular employment contracts and would include part-time, temporary and largely female workers. Such a structure would retain the lifetime model for the core workforce but lower the employer obligation for employment retention among specialists and lesser-skilled employees, particularly during adverse business conditions. The Worker Dispatching Law in 1985 was introduced for specialized occupations. The 1999 revision substantially extended the types of occupation to come under contract to employment agencies. These marked the biggest changes in the Labor Standards Law since their enactment in 1947 and have helped to pave the way for a deregulation of the Japanese labor market. Both Nikkeiren and the statutory labor law reform reflect a fundamental rethinking about the future direction of the Japanese management model in an era of low growth. Socioeconomic changes effecting young worker attitudes combined with greater diversification of the Japanese employment relationship has seen a marked change in the HRM model.

The Japanese management model now has to determine how to maintain competitiveness in a global economy while adjusting to the conditions of low growth in what has become a mature domestic economy. Many employees are faced with employment insecurity; employers with the high cost of lifetime employment, an aging workforce, and with companies still burdened by long-term recession (Chuma, 2002). Many long-serving blue-collar and white-collar employees who have invested their livelihood in their company have limited value beyond the parameter of their firm.

## Conclusion

The debate about the importance of HRM has been tied to improved company performance (Delaney and Huselid, 1995; MacDuffie, 1995; Tyson, 1997). HRM has been seen as a route towards improved employee effort and sustained competitive advantage (Barney, 1991). Although HRM is in essence a managerial approach in Japan it is principally through the organizational investments in training, employee recruitment and selection, in addition to performance evaluation and career development, that effective employee commitment is being reconfigured to contribute towards a high performance–employment relationship

The Japanese management system is under considerable pressure to change. Much of the current diversification of employment is aimed at reducing labor costs. Many of the features that provided high growth in the past have come to be questioned in relation to economic maturity, recession and low growth. The Japanese approach towards HRM has in turn had to adapt to the changing business environment. For regular employees and particularly the white-collar baby-boomers, the prospects for promotion are diminishing. Ironically the pioneering of high-performance lean-management organization that did so much to elevate Japanese international competitiveness also brought about flat management structures that have limited the growth of career opportunities. The response of the leading Japanese firms has been to reconceptualize the basis for HR development. Although Japanese unions, employers and public policy initiatives continue to stress the retention of the long-term institutionalized commitment to employment within the firm, the emphasis now being placed upon the need for specialists and professional expertise suggests more value will be given to identifying individual ability and personal performance, and future rewards and career development will come to be more closely tied to personal evaluation as the basis for motivation.

## Acknowledgment

The author wishes to acknowledge support from the Japan Foundation.

## References

Abegglen, J. (1958) *The Japanese Factory: Aspects of its social organisation*, Glencoe, IL: The Free Press.

Aoki, M. (1988) *Information, incentives and bargaining in the Japanese economy*, New York: Cambridge University Press.

Aoki, M. (1994) "The Japanese firm as a system of attributes: a survey and research agenda," in M. Aoki and R. Dore (eds.) *The Japanese firm: Sources of competitive strength*, Oxford: Oxford University Press, pp. 1–11.

Banno, J. (1997) "The historical origins of companyism: From westernization to indigenization," in J. Banno (ed.) *The political economy of Japanese society*, vol 1, Oxford: Oxford University Press, pp. 1–13.

Barney, J. (1991) "Firm resources and sustained competitive advantage," *Journal of Management* 17: 99–120.

Becker, G.S. (1964) *Human capital*, New York: National Bureau of Economic Research.

Chuma, A.H. (2002) "Employment adjustments in Japanese firms during the current crisis," *Industrial Relations* 41 (4) (October).

Cole, R.E. (1973) *Japanese blue collar; the changing tradition*, Berkeley: University of California Press.

Delaney, J.T. and Huselid, M.A. (1996) "The impact of human resource management practices on perceptions of organisational performance," *Academy of Management Journal* 49 (4): 949–969.

Dore, R. (1973) *British factory–Japanese factory*, London: Allen and Unwin.

Endo, K. (1998) "'Japanization' of performance appraisal system: A historical comparison of the American and Japanese systems," *Social Science Japan Journal* 1 (2): 247–262.

Godard, J. and Delaney, J.T. (2000) "Reflections on the 'High performance' paradigm's implications industrial relations as a field" *Industrial and Labor Relations Review* 53 (3) (April 2000).

Hanami, T. (1994) *Managing Japanese Workers*, Tokyo: The Japan Institute of Labour.

Johnson, C. (1982) *MITI and the Japanese miracle: The growth of industrial policy, 1925–1975*, Tokyo: C. E. Tuttle.

Kameyama, K. (1997) "Human resource management in Japan: Recent trends in recruitment and hiring activities," *Labour Issues Quarterly* 37 (Autumn).

Kato, T. (2000a) "Recent transformation of participatory employment practices in Japan," *NBER Working Paper*, 7965 (October), pp. 1–79.

Kato, T. (2000b) "The end of lifetime employment in Japan?: Evidence from national surveys and field research," *Journal of Japanese and Industrial Economics* 15: 489–514.

Kawakita, T. (1997) "Corporate strategy and human resource management," in M. Sako and H. Sato (eds.) *Japanese labour and management in transition: Diversity, flexibility and participation*, London: Routledge.

Koike, K. (1995) "Learning and incentive systems in Japanese industry," in M. Aoki and R. Dore (eds.) *The Japanese firm: Sources of competitive strength*, Oxford: Oxford University Press.

Koike, K. (1997) *Human resource development*, Tokyo: The Japan Institute of Labour.

Kume, I. (1998) *Disparaged success: Labor politics in postwar Japan*, Ithica, NY: Cornell University Press.

Legge. K. (1995) *Human resource management: Rhetorics and realities*, London: Macmillan Press.

MacDuffie, J.P. (1995) "Human resource bundles and manufacturing performance: Organisation logic and flexible production systems in the world auto industry," *Industrial and Labour Relations Review* 48 (2): 197–221.

Moore, J. (1983) *Japanese workers and the struggle for power 1945–1947*, Madison, WI: University of Wisconsin Press.

Morishima, M. (1995) "Embedding HRM in a social contract," *British Journal of Industrial Relations* 33 (4) (December): 617–640.

Nikkeiren (1995) *The current labor economy in Japan*, Japan Federation of Employers' Associations.

Nitta, M. (1998) "Employment relations after the collapse of the bubble economy," in J. Banno (ed.) *The political economy of Japanese society*, vol. 2, Oxford: Oxford University Press, pp. 267–284.

Okazaki-Ward, L. (1993) "Management education and training," *Japan*, London: Graham and Trotman.

Osawa, M. (2001) "People in irregular modes of employment: Are they really not subject to discrimination?," *Social Science Japan Journal* 4 (2): 183–199.

Pempel, T.J. (1998) *Regime shift: Comparative dynamics of the Japanese political economy*, Ithica, NY: Cornell University Press.

Rohlen, T.P. (1985) "The company work group," in E.F. Vogel (ed.) *Modern Japanese organisation and decision-making*, Berkeley: University of California Press.

Salmon, J. (1992) "The impact of developments in welfare corporatism upon Japanese workplace trade unionism," *International Journal of Human Resource Management* 3 (2): 247–266.

Salmon, J. (1999) "Rethinking Japanese HRM: Researching HRM. Where are we Going?," paper presented to BUIRA conference.

Sano,Y., Morishima, M. and Seike, A. (1997) (eds.) *Frontiers of Japanese human resource practices*, Tokyo: The Japan Institute of Labor.

Sato, H. (1997) "Human resource management systems in large firms: The case of white graduate employees," in M. Sako and H. Sato (eds.) *Japanese labour and management in transition: Diversity, flexibility and participation*, London: Routledge, pp. 80–103.

Sato, H. (2001) "Atypical employment: A source of flexible work opportunities?," *Social Science Japan Journal* 4 (2): 161–181.

Schregle, J. (1993) "Dismissal protection in Japan," *International Labour Review* 132 (4).

Selmer, J. (2001) "Human resource management in Japan: Adjustment or transition?," *International Journal of Manpower* 22 (3): 235–243.

Shibata, S. (2002) "Wage and performance appraisal systems in flux: A Japan–United States comparison," *Industrial Relations* 41 (4): 629–652.

Sugeno, K. (1992) *Japanese labour law*, Tokyo: University of Tokyo Press.

Tabata, H. (1997) "Industrial relations and the union movement," in J. Banno (ed.) *The political economy of Japanese society*, vol. 1, Oxford: Oxford University Press, pp. 85–108.

Takanashi, A. (1999) *Japanese employment policies*, The Japan Institute of Labour.

Tyson. S. (1997) "Human resource strategy: A process for managing the contribution of HRM to organisational performance," *The International Journal of Human Resource Management* 8 (3): 277–290.

Van Wolferen, K. (1989) *The enigma of Japanese power*, London: Macmillan.

Weathers, C. (2001) "Changing white-collar workplaces and female temporary workers," *Social Science Japan Journal* 4 (2): 201–218.

## Useful websites

The Japan Institute of Labor:     http://www.jil.go.jp/index-e.htm
Japanese Trade Union Confederation (JTUC-Rengo):   http: //www.jtuc-rengo
Main Japanese Labor Economic Indicators:     http://.jil.go.jp/estatis/eindex.htm

# 5 HRM in Hong Kong

ANDREW CHAN AND STEVEN LUI

## Introduction

To understand the current challenges and future prospects of HRM in Hong Kong, we take a historical perspective in this chapter and review Hong Kong's wider cultural, social and economic context since the 1970s. We will recount the unfolding of HR practices as the city evolved from an entrepôt, to an enclave economy to a metropolitan business and financial center. In the latest words of officials of the Hong Kong government, the vision of Hong Kong is to reposition itself as the world's most service-oriented knowledge economy that capitalizes on its strength in value-added producer services in order to complement the growth of the Chinese economy in the future.

We agree with Budhwar and Debrah (2001) that HRM practices are largely driven by external factors – in Hong Kong the most important are economic conditions, company size and the owner's background and culture. In spite of much discussion over the aims of HRM in the academic literature, we consider for the purpose of this chapter that HRM in Hong Kong comprises a set of practices in the service of the employers to maintain employment relationships.

The preferences and shifts in company policies regarding manpower and succession planning, recruiting, training, performance and compensation management are predominantly determined by whether the owner's business is prospering, striving or merely surviving. In a free economy like Hong Kong, where 90 percent of employers are small enterprises, HR policies and practices have a direct casual relationship with business realities. It makes sense, therefore, to maintain an optimum employment relationship through versatile HR practices.

This chapter sketches a profile of the key features influencing the development of HRM in Hong Kong. In the eyes of its Hong Kong practitioners, HRM refers to management practices purposefully used to regulate employment relationships in sizable organizations, including Chinese family business conglomerates, the Hong Kong civil service, quasi-governmental organizations, and subsidiaries of foreign companies in Hong Kong. The academic distinction between personnel management and human resource management has been well debated in the literature (Armstrong and Long, 1994; Legge, 1995; Bach and Sisson, 2000; Boxall and Purcell, 2003). In the context of our characterization of HRM in Hong Kong and the theme of this volume, we take the view that the distinction is moot.

This chapter is organized into four parts. We will first trace the development of HR in Hong Kong during the last 30 years in order to make sense of what happens in workplace employment relations today. We will then account for the role of HR in different business settings. This is followed by a discussion of three selected contingent factors that impinge on some of the key developments of HR practices in the unique setting of Hong Kong. Lastly, we review the prospects and challenges facing HRM in Hong Kong today.

# The development of HRM in Hong Kong

## Manufacturing base (1970s)

Hong Kong flourished as a British colony for trading in its early days. After three decades of rapid expansion in manufacturing, Hong Kong had successfully transformed itself from an entrepôt into a low-cost manufacturing center by the 1970s, exporting mainly garments, textiles, electronic products, and toys to the rest of the world (Chiu et al., 1997; HKTDC, 1998). This transformation was buttressed by the closure of China to the outside world after the communist takeover and the large labor pool thus made available to Hong Kong by the influx of legal and illegal immigrants from China (Cheung et al., 2000). The 1960s and 1970s were the heyday of Hong Kong's industrialization, with high growth rates of both industrial exports and income. In 1971, the manufacturing sector generated 28.2 percent of the GDP and employed 47.0 percent of economically active persons (Chiu et al., 1997).

The majority of manufacturing companies were labor intensive. These companies tended to be small, export-oriented, and engaged in cost-based competition (Enright et al., 1999). Government statistics show that in 1978, 78 percent of the manufacturing firms in Hong Kong employed fewer than 20 workers, and only 4 percent had more than 100 employees (HKDTC, 1998).[1] In an early study of labor relations in Hong Kong, England (1989) reported that the working conditions in these small factories were generally bad with cramped space, unsafe practices and long working hours. Their businesses depended mainly on subcontracted orders and required highly flexible employment practices that could adjust to fluctuation in the orders. Most workers were therefore employed as semiskilled or unskilled labor on a temporary basis, and were provided with little training and few welfare benefits. Although the employment

---

1  In the Year 2002, out of about 320,000 registered companies in Hong Kong, 87.8 percent hired less than 10 members of staff; 1.1 percent hired 50–99 employees, and only 254 companies (0.08 percent) had 500 or more staff members.

conditions were better in larger firms, the labor relationship was still maintained by personal paternalism rather than formal employment contract (England, 1989: 70–73).

Human resource management in this period was largely administration oriented, perceived as less strategic, and so personnel management would be a more fitting characterization. Recruiting labor was not a problem, as there was a plentiful supply from the refugee pool and the postwar baby boom in Hong Kong (Chen, 2000). Low-level recruiting was often carried out informally through word of mouth or personal relationships. On the other hand, managerial positions in large companies and senior ranks in the civil service were often filled by expatriates coming to work in Hong Kong.

> At more senior levels, civil servants enjoy indirect compensation which is not normally given to civil servants in other countries. This indirect compensation (or "fringe benefits") is largely the result of Hong Kong's colonial legacy. Benefits are paid to all expatriates in the British colonial service. These include the provision of housing and the payment of a tenancy allowance. Air passages for leave (and on resignation) are paid to expatriate civil servants and their families on the directorate scale. In addition, education allowances and passages are paid for the civil servants' children who are educated overseas.
>
> (Scott, 1984: 23)

Motivation and compensation of semi- and unskilled labor were not a problem. Workplace training was often minimal, as worker mobility was high, and employers were hesitant to provide training for workers in a free labor market with high worker mobility (Ng and Ip, 1999). The work environment deterred workers from organizing themselves for collective bargaining. Instead, trade unions in Hong Kong in their early days were extensions of China's internal political strife (England, 1989). Civil disturbances in 1967 led to the enactment of the Employment Ordinance in 1968. This ordinance later became the foundation of other labor legislation in Hong Kong (Ng and Wright, 2002).

## Early service-base (1980s)

During the 1980s, the growth of manufacturing in Hong Kong slowed as small-scale manufacturing companies faced protectionism from advanced economies and a shortage of affordable land and factory space within the city. To maintain their cost advantage, these companies started relocating their labor-intensive production facilities to China where land and labor were abundant. Their logistics and support functions, however, they kept in Hong Kong. Thus a small company of a dozen employees in Hong Kong might comfortably oversee the running of a factory with several production lines and hundreds of workers in China (HKTDC, 1998). At the same time, Hong Kong gradually built itself up as a trade support center. It became a hub for traders and businessmen looking for financial services such as seed money from merchant banks and help from investment banks with initial public offerings when they wanted to become publicly listed. Taking advantage of China's open-door policy, many companies engaged in re-export activities to and from China in the early 1980s, and Hong Kong regained its role as a very active entrepôt.

The Sino-British Joint Declaration, which detailed the reversion of sovereignty over Hong Kong to China 13 years later, was signed in 1984. Ever since then, Hong Kong's social, economic, and cultural integration with China has gathered momentum. This created uncertainty among the population, and led to high emigration, creating a brain drain of managerial and professional labor to countries like Canada, New Zealand, and Singapore, especially in the ten years between 1984 and 1994. This resulted in a widespread surge in real wages, and increased costs in the service sector from 1986 onward (Chen, 2000).

The completely different development in the service and the manufacturing sectors posed two HR issues. First, as manufacturing companies managed their operations between Hong Kong and its hinterland in South China, they needed a specific set of HR practices to optimize employment relationships, having to deal fairly in the midst of intricate issues of workplace diversity, pay differentials, and differences in legal systems between the two places. Second, the thriving service sector demanded more skilled human resources than the residual labor-intensive manufacturing sector, and this created a scarcity in the labor market. A falling birth rate in Hong Kong, emigration among the middle class and tightened border controls on illegal entrants from China added to the problem (Chiu and Levin, 1993; Chen, 2000).

The Hong Kong government at that time used various measures to address the critical issue of labor scarcity. These included the setting up of a quasi-governmental body, the Vocational Training Council, in 1982. The council was responsible for identifying manpower and training needs and providing training in industrial, technical, and management skills to the Hong Kong workforce. This was followed by the expansion of tertiary education opportunities for secondary school graduates, with a target of placing 18 per cent of the eligible age group in degree or subdegree programs. The government also launched successive labor importation schemes throughout the early 1990s for the purpose of addressing labor shortages in specific industries (Ng and Wright, 2000).

At the company level, more effective channels of recruiting were explored. Newspaper advertisement was the most often used recruitment method. Interestingly, Chinese newspapers were generally used for lower-level employment, while local English newspapers were used for senior-level employment. This segregation has continued into the 2000s. Employment agencies became more popular, and executive search firms came to be used for top-level vacancies, at least by larger companies, which also started to invest more in training and development in order to retain employees and to reduce turnover. Relatively more structured succession planning and promotion from entry-level positions became slightly better accepted among private enterprises.

Kirkbride and Tang (1989) have provided a general review of HR practices in Hong Kong based on a survey of 361 companies conducted in 1988. They concluded that HR policies in Hong Kong were not very sophisticated when compared with those in other developed countries. In-house training focused narrowly on technical and vocational ability, and management development was seldom provided. Although formal appraisal systems were common, they were often accompanied by employee collusion and inadequate appraisal training. In terms of time spent on HR issues, respondents in that survey reported spending most of their time in recruitment, followed by employee relations, manpower planning, pay administration, training, and appraisal. The importance of recruitment again reflected the scarcity of labor in society at the time.

## Full service-base (1990s)

The 1990s saw Hong Kong successfully positioning itself as an international commercial, business, and financial center. The deindustrialization of Hong Kong was followed by a recommercialization process that had been taking place continually in the financial, banking, and business subsectors throughout this decade. According to government economists, Hong Kong drew more than 80 percent of its GDP from commercial and service-oriented activities, one of the highest percentages in the world (Ng and Ip, 1999). On the other hand, manufacturing shrank below 10 percent of GDP (Chen, 2000). Enright *et al.* (1999) have argued that Hong Kong focused on developing value-adding producer services that supported the production of goods and services by others, as opposed to consumption services. As producer services were subject to increasing returns to scale and attracted further services to cluster together, it became logical for more multinational corporations (MNCs) to choose Hong Kong as their regional headquarters. During the 1990s, more than 2,000 MNCs had regional offices or headquarters in Hong Kong, including over 200 Fortune 500 companies.

Another feature of Hong Kong's service sector was its external orientation, as a service hub to China and Asia. The repercussions of the 4 June 1989 crackdown on student demonstrators in Beijing haunted HR managers well into the 1990s in the run-up to the reversion to China of sovereignty over Hong Kong. During this period, there was still considerable labor shortage in many sectors, intensified by the brain drain of professionals and other workers. It was at this time that companies of all sizes began to provide more internal training and more promotion opportunities.

On a macro level, the government set up the Employee Retraining Board in 1992 to deal with the mismatch of skills between industrial workers and service jobs. As the business situation became more complex, with globalization, rapid environmental changes, and increased competition, a closer partnership between HR and firm strategy became more accepted, and this paved the way for HR managers to play a more strategic role within their organizations.

In 1995, the government established the Equal Opportunities Commission with the aim of protecting individuals against prejudice that might arise from their age, sex, gender, religion, family status, or physical and mental handicaps. Antidiscrimination regulations were subsequently passed regulating recruitment (such as newspaper job advertisements). This has kept Hong Kong's labor regulations in line with international norms in terms of workplace and employment standards.

HR practices have become more sophisticated to satisfy the needs of a service economy. For instance, Ng (1997) noted that increased training and internal promotion were being provided to junior staff. Snape *et al.* (1998) found the use of performance appraisal was more widespread in Hong Kong than in Britain, but that the process tended to be more directive and less participative in Hong Kong. McCormick (2001) rightly pointed out a need to use more term-based appraisals to suit the local collectivist and group culture.

However, a survey of over 1,000 medium and large companies showed that only 33 percent employed full-time HRM personnel in 1991. Of these, 3.9 percent were appointed at a strategic job level (HKVTC, 1992). Two subsequent large-scale surveys in 1995 (see Tang *et al.*, 1995) and 1998 (Cheung, 1998) conducted by the Hong Kong Institute of HRM depicted the limited influence of HR in Hong Kong companies on strategic issues such as manpower planning, changes in work organization, and new technology introduction. These two surveys showed that while HR was becoming more important, it still played a limited role in a strategic sense. This perception has now changed, as we shall see.

## Post-1997 restructuring phase

In 1997, Hong Kong reintegrated with China as a Special Administrative Region, maintaining its own laws and institutions. The Asian financial crisis of 1997 struck a huge blow to Hong Kong's externally-oriented service-based economy. The post-crisis environment in Asia was one of rapid globalization. Traditional interfirm relations were reshuffled, and the industrial environment became highly competitive (Kidd *et al.*, 2001). Other complex issues like returning emigrants, labor importation schemes, unemployment, a depressed property market, and the outbreak of SARS aggravated the problems of post-1997 Hong Kong. The unemployment rate remained around 8 percent between May 2002 and June 2003. HR faced tremendous challenges in this phase.

Companies in Hong Kong painfully adjusted to this new business environment with revised HR measures (Fosh *et al.*, 1999; Cheung *et al.*, 2000). They became more cautious in recruitment and moved towards performance-based compensation. Companies also needed to tackle new HR issues such as downsizing and employee retrenchment. Kamoche (forthcoming) examined the hotel industry in Hong Kong after the 1997 Asian financial crisis and identified the simultaneous need for more structure and flexibility in HR practices. He further cast doubt on Hong Kong organizations' ability to meet this need. Chu and Siu (2001) reported how some small companies in Hong Kong faced the crisis by first cutting staff development funds and wages, using lay-offs only as the last resort. On the other hand, industrial conflicts in large companies were notable.

For instance, the pilot pay dispute at Cathay Pacific Airlines in 1999 and the labor disputes, pay cuts, and redundancies at Pacific Century CyberWorks Ltd. in 2002.

Another major development was the introduction of the Mandatory Provident Fund (MPF) in 2000. Under this scheme, both employers and employees were required to contribute to the employees' retirement benefits. It was a belated government response to the call for basic provision of employee benefits for the general labor force. Similar schemes had been set up much earlier in other Asian countries such as Malaysia in 1951 and Singapore in 1955, but the MPF in Hong Kong has retained features of high risk and a privatized nature (Ng and Wright, 2002). However, its introduction amidst an economic downturn drew criticism that it represented an extra burden in the cost of running a business.

While we have portrayed this slightly gloomy picture of the nagging issues faced by HR managers in the field, another representative sample of the HR community, however, perceived things slightly differently. A survey conducted by the Hong Kong Institute of HRM among their member companies in 2001 showed that HR practices were often deployed with a strategic purpose (Cheung, 2001). More companies were found to have adopted strategic HRM than traditional HRM. Training was often provided to employees to address changes in products, new technology, and organizational reengineering. Results-oriented performance appraisal with targets to meet was more widely used with all levels of staff. There was also more outsourcing of HR functions, particularly in training, development, and recruitment. The survey amply reflected the vibrant environment and the challenges to HRM.

## The role of HRM in different business settings

Next we will examine the changes in the HRM function and the unique sets of issues HRM has faced in different business settings in Hong Kong over those four phases. We characterize these changes through looking at a spectrum of relative degrees of HRM partnership that underpinned HR policies and practices — from strategic partnership or one end to pragmatic administration at the other. This relative continuum of HR involvement in the business strategy is attributable to the size and the ownership of the firms (Chiu and Levin, 1993; Shaw *et al.*, 1993). We outline the contours of HRM partnership found in three types of firms in Hong Kong: small and medium enterprises, large family businesses, and multinational corporations.

## Small and medium enterprises

As in other Asian economies, a dual labor market exists in Hong Kong (Ng and Wright, 2002), and it is made up of a primary and a secondary sector. The large private firms, the civil service and the quangos constitute the primary sector, while the small and medium enterprises (SMEs) constitute the secondary sector. SMEs make up the majority of businesses in Hong Kong. In 2000, SMEs in the manufacturing sector (fewer than 100 persons) constituted 98.6 percent of all manufacturing establishments and took up 62.7 percent of total manufacturing employment. Similarly, SMEs in the service sector (fewer than 50 persons) constituted 98.3 percent of all service establishments and accounted for 61.3 percent of total service employment (Hong Kong Information Service Department, 2002).

Compared with the primary sector, HR practices in the secondary sector are *ad hoc*, much less structured, and less formalized (Ng and Wright, 2002). Because of their small size, these firms subscribe to a lean regimen in their personnel and administration that often results in only the sheer essentials of what may be called the core HR functions. Based on the research findings on SMEs in Hong Kong (Saha, 1987; Kirkbride and Tang, 1989; Cheung, 2001), most SMEs provide limited on-the-job training for their employees, as these employees can move around easily in Hong Kong's free labor market. To retain employees, firms generally resort to a high pay strategy. This decision partly leads to a high cost structure in these firms, and it greatly reduces their competitiveness in times of economic adversity.

To summarize, the role of HR in SMEs is minimal. HR is mainly non-strategic, administration focused, and has low influence on a firm's operations, as far as small companies in Hong Kong are concerned.

## Local Chinese family businesses

Local Chinese family businesses employ a significant number of employees. Their early success was usually built on businesses in textiles, garment manufacturing, and trading. Some of these family businesses have grown alongside the Hong Kong economy to expand into new markets. Their key decision-makers and management have reached the third generation succeeding their founders at the turn of the last century. A few of these firms are much larger than SMEs, and their HR policies are more comprehensive and formalized. However, their HR policies are different from those promulgated by the strategic partnership model. Redding (1993: 155) and Westwood and Chan (1992) have suggested that the Chinese heads and their businesses encapsulate the ethnocentric values of Confucian paternalism, patriarchy, and personalism. These are manifested in three key relationships: power connected to ownership, a distinct style of benevolently autocratic leadership, and personalistic as opposed to neutral relations. Their management style is paternalistic, with centralized decision-making, emphasizing harmony and compliance (Westwood and Chan, 1992), seniority, loyalty, mutual obligation, and informal networking at the workplace (Redding and Wong, 1986; Shaw *et al.*, 1993; Snape *et al.*, 1998). By no means deprecating, this Chinese management style propagates unique employment relationships marked by a delicate blend and balance between a western outlook and traditional Chinese values. For instance, these firms may recruit from a variety of sources, but selection is pragmatically based on personal recommendation. They may establish clear job descriptions and levels of reporting, but remuneration would reflect seniority and degree of loyalty rather than performance. Usually, these firms can enjoy a strong internal labor market with entry to the organizations at low levels, and the frequency and scale of training and development being more *ad hoc*.

These HR features or employment relationships engender a clear sense of goals among employees, who could expect that their hard work, dedication, and loyalty are repaid, and many practitioners believe that such work values have contributed to the early success of these Chinese family firms. However, the HRM functions are still found to be separated from the decision and power core of the businesses and from other business operations in the company, performing an administrative rather than a strategic role. This may pose problems as these companies expand overseas and face increasing market uncertainty. The strategic role of HRM becomes more significant in multinational corporations than in Chinese family business conglomerates and SMEs.

## Multinational corporations

Over 3,000 overseas companies had regional headquarters or offices in Hong Kong in 2002 (Hong Kong Census and Statistics Department, 2002). The majority of them came from the USA, Japan, and the UK, with China coming up the list recently. Their major lines of business were in the wholesale and retail trades, and in business services. Their reputations and high profile gave MNCs a prominent presence in Hong Kong.

Among other needs in managing HR, MNCs need to deal with expatriation, repatriation, adjustment, and adaptation of home-based practices to blend with local norms and host-nation laws and regulations. As MNCs are relatively more experienced in managing international HR, the role of their HRM function is more strategically oriented compared with the other types of Hong Kong companies that we have discussed. Most often cited in literature are the former's well-developed management training programs and their structured performance-based reward systems (Dowling *et al.*, 1999).

Research has consistently pointed to the differences in HRM between foreign firms and local firms operating in Hong Kong. For instance, Shaw *et al.* (1993) found that British and American firms were more likely than local firms to use formal performance appraisal and more technical methods of job evaluation. Ng and Chiu (1997) found that British and American firms were more likely to adopt women-friendly HR practices. Ngo *et al.* (1998) extended the comparison to Japanese firms and found that they were more likely to adopt seniority-based compensation than local Hong Kong firms, but had no differences in the provision of training and development, or in retention-oriented compensation. Fields *et al.* (2000) found that foreign firms tended to spend more effort in securing and retaining managers. Contrary to the above, McGraw (2001), however, found relatively minor differences in HR practices between local and foreign firms, and supported a global convergence of HR practices.

# Contingent factors shaping HRM

At the beginning of this chapter, we have referred to Budhwar and Debrah (2001) who suggest a way forward to research international HRM. There, the factors that affect HRM practices in any country or culture are categorized into national factors, organizational strategies and policies, and other contingent variables. As we trace the historical development of HRM in Hong Kong, three such contingent variables stand out to be influential in shaping the present state of HRM practices in the workplace: the legal and institutional factors, the China factor, and globalization.

## Legal and institutional factors

The free market principles underlying the economy, coupled with the weak bargaining power of the labor unions and Chinese paternalism engendered what Ng and Wright (2002) called an "institutional permissiveness" in the workplace. Institutional permissiveness refers to loose and informal regulating institutions in the labor market, which help to maintain harmonious industrial relations. This is reflected in the weakness or lack of legal regulations. The Hong Kong government regulates the labor market and employment mainly through the Employment Ordinance of Hong Kong. Intervention has been minimal, apart from setting up initiatives for long-term manpower development. Neither does the government favor laws mandating trade unionism, nor a minimum wage for labor.

According to government statistics, there were 601 trade unions at the end of 2001. Of these, only 93 had declared a membership of over 1,000. The role of trade unions in Hong Kong has remained weak. Snape and Chan (1999) offer three reasons for this: the small size of establishments in manufacturing and private sector services, cultural resistance of workers towards joining unions and openly challenging their employers, and employers' hostility towards unions.

Surveys show that the role of unions in private sector pay negotiations has been limited (Tang *et al.*, 1995; Cheung, 1998, 2001). Instead of work-related issues, unions engage mostly in activities outside the workplace, such as organizing recreational and social activities, and providing educational and health services to members. In the absence of strong trade unions, collective bargaining has been weak, leading to the low level of strikes and industrial conflict in Hong Kong (England, 1989).

However, collective bargaining has become more common after the Asian financial crisis. Several high-profile strikes were reported in large private companies, such as the cases of Cathay Pacific and PCCW Ltd. mentioned earlier. Ng (1997) suggests that this may signal a change in the way conflict is handled between firms and their employees, as a more western-style adversarial approach is adopted.

The consequence of institutional permissiveness for HR managers is that they can adopt a set of highly versatile and flexible HR practices based on individual employment contracts (Cheung *et al.*, 2000; Ng and Wright, 2002). Firms can adjust their compensation based on individual performance and prevailing market conditions. In this way, firms have high leverage in their HR policies, especially in SMEs. Conversely, individuals can negotiate their wages and salaries according to their individual bargaining power.

## The China factor

The economic and political development of Hong Kong is closely linked to China. This factor impacts HR development through the labor supply and business opportunities for businesses of all types. Two waves of immigration from China provided the needed labor in Hong Kong at crucial moments (Chen, 2000). The first wave of immigrants came to Hong Kong in the early 1950s, when the Communist Party came to power. The huge influx of refugees brought capital and entrepreneurial skill. This generation of immigrants formed the source of labor throughout Hong Kong's industrialization in the following decade. The second wave of immigration during the 1970s, consisting of illegal immigrants, provided a large pool of cheap labor to Hong Kong at its time of rapid industrialization.

The China factor has also been influential in attracting MNCs to Hong Kong. In order to tap into the huge China market for their products, MNCs have often opted to set up their headquarters in Hong Kong to test the water. These MNCs brought with them new HR skills and procedures. Local companies benefit from their presence through imitating these HR practices. Indeed, some researchers suggest that MNCs may have been the "major impetus towards increasing personnel sophistication" in earlier days (Kirkbride and Tang, 1989: 46).

## Globalization

The effect of globalization on Hong Kong may be much stronger than elsewhere because of Hong Kong's externally oriented and open economy. To increase its legitimacy as a global business partner, Hong Kong has adopted international industrial regulations and set up human rights watchdogs such as the Equal Opportunities Commission. This commission has adopted a mainly non-coercive approach, focusing on conciliation and public education rather than invoking its statutory power to issue enforcement notices against non-compliance (Ng and Wright, 2002).

Globalization opens Hong Kong to external market forces, and its influence in directing HR development in Hong Kong was particularly crucial in the 1970s and 1990s. In the 1970s, Hong Kong's manufacturing firms moved their operations first into Southern China and then to Southeast Asia. At that time, this development solved the labor scarcity problem. With hindsight, we suggest that this might have slowed down the development of HRM in Hong Kong, especially in training and development. In the 1990s, facing a fast changing global market, firms had to be adaptive, fast to change, and efficient. Globalization resulted in China becoming the global production site, supporting Hong Kong's service role. In our view, China's entry to World Trade Organization in 2001 has clearly provided an impetus for any firm to use more developed HR practices, and will accelerate their need for high-quality employees in the years to come.

# The future prospects of HRM in Hong Kong

## Bleak future or a silver lining?

The last part presents a point-counterpoint about the future of Hong Kong and implications for the future of HRM. Let us first sketch aspects of what may make up the bleak outlook and dire situation, before we counterpoise this with a contrary thesis.

In many people's eyes, Hong Kong's lackluster economy over the five years 1999–2003 has exhibited its worst performance in many decades. The poor economic environment and the brief disruption of the outbreak of SARS in 2003 have been coupled with salary cuts, redundancies, lay-offs, early retirement schemes, downsizing, and corporate restructuring in large firms and small enterprises. Insolvencies have become more common. In the HR field, practitioners have been busy looking at ways to rationalize manpower, minimize expense, and freeze hiring in order to sustain a low-cost operating environment. Like the business sectors, the civil service has also been affected by this trend. With a forecast budget deficit between 2003 and 2007, the Hong Kong government has frozen all civil services hiring except policemen beginning from 2003, slashed salaries across the board by 1.5 percent in 2002, and proposed a further pay-cut of 3 percent each year in 2004 and 2005. The government's target is to reduce the staff establishment from 180,000 in 2000/01 to c. 160,000 by 2006/7, through, among other things, natural attrition and early retirement schemes.

Hong Kong's biggest private sector employer, the telephone company Pacific Century CyberWorks Ltd., uses incentive schemes to lure employees to depart and set up their own businesses to bid for project-based assignments and subcontracting work farmed out by their former employer. Many HR practitioners are dealing with downsizing programs, budget and salary cuts, and early retirement schemes. They are fine-tuning appraisal and performance management, and putting very few resources into training and development – but there are exceptions.

Some employers hire aggressively. For example, in the business and financial sectors, insurance, transport and logistics, information systems, and property development. The qualifications and quality of people hired in these fields are on the rise. For these employers and their HR managers, the situation in the next five years will be different. Broadly speaking, medium and long-term HR planning should be aware of the declining birth rate (60,000 births in 1994 as against 80,000 in 1986) and a graying population. (Those aged 65 or above were 200,000 and 480,000 respectively in 1984 and 1994, and projected to be 700,000 in 2004.) Macro-measures like labor re-training, continuing education, importation of skilled labor, experts and professionals and the luring of investment emigrants are in full swing or being vigorously studied.

## The metropolis thesis

In both the press and the academic literature, analyses have pointed to the dire conditions facing Hong Kong's economy. The future of the city seems bleak, and recovery is not yet in sight. Some economists, however (e.g. Enright *et al.* 1997; Enright *et al.*, 1999) emphasize the contrarian view that Hong Kong is in transition to a truly metropolitan service economy. As this gradually materializes, the HR scenario in Hong Kong companies will present new sets of challenges.

While Hong Kong retains the distinctive "one country, two systems" for 50 years until 2047, it will continue to offer to businesses incentives like a low tax base, a liberal environment for movement of capital, and freedom of exchange of information. As in other metropolitan economies, high value-added activities will continue to replace low value-added activities. The physical production stages of manufacturing will play a less prominent role in Hong Kong's GDP (5.8 percent of GDP in 2000). Proponents of this metropolis scenario argue that Hong Kong's strength is that it has established itself as a regional center and one of the most service-oriented economies in the world, with producer services that support Hong Kong's offshore production operations.

If we look at some relevant figures, they tell us that in 2003, Hong Kong's services sector accounted for 86 percent of Hong Kong's GDP.[2] This is similar to the percentage of GDP occupied by the service sector in the New York metropolitan area in 1994 (Enright *et al.*, 1999). The metropolis thesis compares Hong Kong and Greater London, whereby as a city Hong Kong's 1997 GDP of US$170.1 billion exceeded that of Greater London. Hong Kong is backed up by the vast Pearl River Delta hinterland consisting of city economies that were formerly rustic townships. Three of these representative cities have now turned into closely collaborative cities that have a combined GDP greater than that of Shanghai. Seen from the perspectives of regional economics and competitive advantage, Hong Kong is unlike Singapore in that the latter does not have a "friendly" hinterland to absorb the benevolent centrifugal windfalls from its economic activities. Dodwell (2001: 254) invites us to ponder the following scenario:

> If opportunities are appropriately exploited and managed, future scenarios of the shared region (Hong Kong and the Pearl River Delta hinterland) are exciting in the extreme. As more Hong Kong residents settle in the delta townships – commuting daily to work as

2  Percentages of services in GDP in 2003 are: 72 percent in USA, 67 percent in the UK, 62 percent in Japan, 65 percent in Singapore, 50 percent in Shanghai, 45 percent in Shenzhen, 35 percent in the People's Republic of China.

would a commuter from Connecticut or New Jersey into New York – and as these commuters mingle with an increasing well-off middle-class local workforce, there is the prospect of attractive PRD communities emerging. . . . Managed well, the region can become one of the most prosperous in the world, as the PRC progressively liberalizes in the decades ahead. Many metropolitan regions worldwide fail to capture cooperative strategies . . . this cooperation will take time and careful democracy, but it is essential if the region is to emerge as one of the world's leading metropolitan economies, and as Asia's "world city."

These profiles give out important signals to HR practitioners and their senior policy-makers and strategists. Even though the "threat" of deindustrialization of Hong Kong has materialized, groups of economists close to the government (e.g. Enright *et al.*, 1997, 1999) argue that "opportunities" always exist for Hong Kong if it suitably concentrates on value-adding producer services and related activities. Similar changes have been experienced in cities like New York and Tokyo. The outward relocation of manufacturing activities does not represent a "decline" of this sector as far as Hong Kong capitalists are concerned. In the 2003 policy address, Mr C.H. Tung, Chief Executive of Hong Kong, has sanctioned the idea that the city's preferred role would be the management and coordination center for Southern China.

As a metropolitan business center that provides value-added services, Hong Kong-based service providers and the offices of multinationals should be geared up to reap the first-mover advantage. Opportunities to compete for the provision of financial, business, and professional services in China are highly likely. Markets there tend to be fragmented by China's restrictions on foreign firms. As the regulatory environment changes and service sectors open up further under China's WTO accession, Hong Kong firms and their HR functions are advised to concentrate on performing even higher value services in attracting, hiring, and keeping the workforce in the fields of banking, finance, accounting, consulting, and other kindred activities.

## A knowledge workforce for a knowledge economy

Given the importance of knowledge-intensive and highest value-added activities in businesses, HR priorities should be prepared to place even more resources on supporting these activities. Helping the business sectors meet their needs, university education should focus on training personnel for logistics management, process engineering, information systems, finance and management. We suggest to HR practitioners that the skills that will be in greatest demand are those involved in managing organizations, coordinating across borders, generating and processing information, and communicating with international partners. For Hong Kong firms and their HR managers, the strategic focus will be on identifying long-term HR needs. If they are to compete in the knowledge and information economy, they had better become highly efficient in information processing: they must begin by knowing what staff they need, with what skills, how they can find and re-train them as needed, and how they can motivate them to work more effectively and raise their awareness of lifelong skills for future roles. In-house career counseling and advice about training needs and opportunities will be very much needed.

Unlike metropolitan destinations such as New York, Tokyo, and London, where property and other costs fall gradually from the city center out to the furthest suburbs, Hong Kong is situated on the coastline of the Pearl River Delta with its boundary drawn against the mainland where costs remain relatively low. In our view, the past and future of Hong Kong HRM policies and practices are predominantly subject to external contingent factors (e.g. economic conditions and business sentiment). From colony to special administrative region, from window to China to metropolitan driver for its hinterland cities, Hong Kong's macro-environment mandates that it strengthen its role as a business and financial nerve-center and as a hub for services producers. In that regard, the rhetoric has shifted from "colony" to "territory" to "tiger" to "city" to "metropolis."

At a practical level and of more immediate concern to HR managers, HRM sourcing is advised to look more carefully at the wide pool of talents, experts, and professionals resident in South China, Taiwan, and among ethnic Chinese and other overseas nationals familiar with China. This skilled workforce is what Hong Kong seriously lacks now. Of prime importance in the 2003 policy address of the chief executive was the need to make it attractive for mainland Chinese specialists and skilled workers and experts to come with their families to work in Hong Kong. This emphasizes establishing even closer ties and integration with the Pearl River Delta hinterland. The metropolis thesis clearly requires a repositioning of HR-related policies for many companies. This will become clear on the eve of the sixth anniversary of the handover in June 2003, when the Closer Economic Partnership Agreement (CEPA) is announced. This will allow for zero tariffs on exports coming from Hong Kong entering mainland China. Service firms in Hong Kong, for example, in the fields of legal services, accountancy, banking, advertising, transport and logistics, and management consultancy, will enjoy the benefits of "no trade barriers" and hence be able to set up their businesses. With these impending openings in late 2003, HRM's future in Hong Kong has acquired a new definition with a new set of implications.

A glimpse of these important changes can also be seen in the new immigration policy proposed by the Hong Kong government in February 2003. Whether Hong Kong will attract and retain the required manpower, whether it is an attractive place for mobile professionals, remains to be seen. The rationale behind this policy asserts that skilled and professional people will make up the most critical portion of Hong Kong's knowledge workforce. Immigrants are welcome because, in the long term, a continually renewing and thriving population is needed to overcome problems as a result of the low birth rate and the graying of Hong Kong citizens. Incentives to lure "investment immigrants," whether they are ethnic Chinese or not, are now openly offered under the new immigration policy. The time will come for HR managers in Hong Kong to revisit expatriation and kindred international HRM issues, once hot topics in the 1980s. This time their internal customers may well be local Hong Kong Chinese moving across the border to work in the mainland, as well as indigenous Chinese coming to work in Hong Kong from all parts of China and the rest of the world.

# References

Armstrong, M. and Long, P. (1994) *The reality of strategic HRM*, London: IPM.

Bach, S. and Sisson, K. (2000) *Personnel management: A comprehensive guide to theory and practice*, 3rd edition, Oxford: Blackwell.

Boxall, P. and Purcell, J. (2003) *Strategy and human resource management*, London: Palgrave.

Budhwar, P.S. and Debrah, Y.A. (eds.) (2001) *Human resource management in developing countries*, London: Routledge.

Chen, E.K.Y. (2000) "The economic setting," in D.G. Lethbridge and S.H. Ng (eds.) *The business environment in Hong Kong*, Hong Kong: Oxford University Press, pp. 3–46.

Cheung, G., Ho, E.Y.Y., Ng, S.K. and Poon, C.Y.W. (2000) "Business restructuring in Hong Kong," in D.G. Lethbridge and S.H. Ng (eds.) *The business environment in Hong Kong*, Hong Kong: Oxford University Press, pp. 154–184.

Cheung, S. (1998) *Human resource management practices in Hong Kong survey report 1998*, Hong Kong: Hong Kong Institute of Human Resource Management.

Cheung, S. (2001) *2001 human resource management strategies and practices in Hong Kong*, Hong Kong: Hong Kong Institute of Human Resource Management.

Chiu, S.W.K., Ho, K.C. and Lui, T.L. (1997) *City states in the global economy: Industrial restructuring in Hong Kong and Singapore*, Oxford: Westview Press.

Chiu, S. and Levin, D.A. (1993) "From a labour-surplus to a labour-scarce economy: Challenges to human resource management in Hong Kong," *International Journal of Human Resource Management* 4 (1): 159–189.

Chu, P. and Siu, W.S. (2001) "Coping with the Asian economic crisis: The rightsizing strategies of small- and medium-sized enterprises," *International Journal of Human Resource Management* 12 (5): 845–858.

Dodwell, D. (2001) "Hong Kong and the Pearl River Delta: The makings of an Asian world city," in J. Weiss (ed.) *Tigers' roar: Asia's recovery and its impact*, New York: M.E. Sharpe, pp. 250–255.

England, J. (1989) *Industrial relations and law in Hong Kong*, 2nd edition, Hong Kong: Oxford University Press.

Enright, M., Scott, E. and Dodwell, D. (1997) *The Hong Kong advantage*, Hong Kong: Oxford University Press.

Enright, M., Scott, E. and Leung, E. (1999) *Hong Kong's competitiveness beyond the Asian crisis*, Hong Kong: HKTDC Research Department.

Fields, D., Chan, A. and Akhtar, S. (2000) "Organizational context and human resource management strategy: A structural equation analysis of Hong Kong firms," *International Journal of Human Resource Management* 11 (2): 264–277.

Fosh, P., Chan, A.W., Chow, W.W.S., Snape, E. and Westwood, R. (1999) *Hong Kong management and labour: Change and continuity*, London: Routledge.

Hong Kong Census and Statistics Department (2002) *Report on 2002 annual survey of regional offices representing overseas companies in Hong Kong*, Hong Kong: Census and Statistics Department.

Hong Kong Information Service Department (2002) *Hong Kong: The facts*, Hong Kong: HKISD.

Hong Kong Trade Development Council (1998) *Hong Kong's manufacturing industries: Current status and future prospects*, Hong Kong: HKTDC Research Department.

Hong Kong Vocational Training Council (1992) *1991 survey report on manpower and training needs of human resources management personnel*, Hong Kong: Vocational Training Council.

Kamoche, K. (forthcoming) "Riding the typhoon: The HR response to the economic crisis in Hong Kong," *International Journal of Human Resource Management*.

Kidd, J., Li, X. and Richter, F. (2001) "Affirmation of the central role of human resource management in Asia," in J.B. Kidd, X. Li and F.J. Richter (eds.) *Advances in human resources management in Asia*, New York: Palgrave, pp. 1–24.

Kirkbride, P. and Tang, S.F.K. (1989) "Personnel management in Hong Kong," *Asia Pacific Human Resource Management* 27 (2): 43–57.

Legge, K. (1995) *Human resource management: Rhetorics and realities*, Basingstoke: Macmillan.

McCormick, I. (2001) "Performance appraisals in Asia," *HR Focus* 4: 20–21.

McGraw, P. (2001) "Human resource management in Hong Kong: Convergence or divergence," in S. Gray, S. McGaughey and W. Purcell (eds.) *Asia Pacific issues in international business*, Cheltenham: Edward Elgar, pp. 235–252.

Ng, C.W. and Chiu, W. (1997) "Women-friendly HRM good for QWL? The case of Hong Kong based companies," *International Journal of Human Resource Management* 8 (5): 644–659.

Ng, S.H. (1997) "Reversion to China: Implications for labour in Hong Kong," *International Journal of Human Resource Management* 8 (5): 660–676.

Ng, S.H. and Ip, O. (1999) "Manpower," in L.C.H. Chow and Y.K. Fan (eds.) *The other Hong Kong report 1998*, Hong Kong: Chinese University of Hong Kong Press.

Ng, S.H. and Wright, R. (2002) "Hong Kong," in M. Zanko (ed.) *Handbook of human resource management policies and practices in Asia-Pacific economies*, Cheltenham: Edward Elgar, pp. 167–259.

Ngo, H.Y., Turban, S., Lau, C.M. and Lui, S. (1998) "Human resource practices and firm performance of multinational corporations: Influences of country origin," *International Journal of Human Resource Management* 9 (4): 632–652.

Redding, G. (1993) *The spirit of Chinese capitalism*, Berlin: de Gruyter.

Redding, G. and Wong, G.Y.Y. (1986) "The psychology of Chinese organizational behaviour," in M.H. Bond (ed.) *The psychology of the Chinese people*, Hong Kong: Oxford University Press.

Saha, S.K. (1987) "Human resource management practices in Hong Kong," *Hong Kong Journal of Business Management* 5: 51–68.

Scott, I. (1984) "A profile of the civil service," in I. Scott and J.P. Burns (eds.) *The Hong Kong civil service: Personnel policies and practices*, Hong Kong: Oxford University Press, pp. 17–35.

Shaw, J.B., Tang, F.Y.T., Fisher, C.D. and Kirkbride, P.S. (1993) "Organizational and environmental factors related to HRM practices in Hong Kong: A cross cultural expanded replication," *International Journal of Human Resource Management* 4 (4): 785–815.

Snape, E. and Chan, A. (1999) "Hong Kong trade unions: In search of a role," in P. Fosh, A.W. Chan, W.W.S. Chow, E. Snape and R. Westwood (eds.) *Hong Kong management and labour: Change and continuity*, London: Routledge, pp. 255–270.

Snape, E., Thompson, S., Yan, F.K.C. and Redman, T. (1998) "Performance appraisal and culture: Practice and attitudes in Hong Kong and Great Britain," *International Journal of Human Resource Management* 9 (5): 841–861.

Tang, S., Lai, E. and Kirkbride, P.S. (1995) *Human resource management practices in Hong Kong: survey report 1995*, Hong Kong: Hong Kong Institute of Human Resource Management.

Welch, D. and Schuler, R. (1999) *International human resource management*, Cincinatti, OH: South-Western.

Westwood, R. and Chan, A. (1992) "Headship and leadership," in R. Westwood (ed.) *Organizational behaviour: Southeast Asian perspectives*, Hong Kong: Longman, pp. 118–143.

## Useful websites (as of July 2003)

### Government departments

| | |
|---|---|
| Hong Kong Government: | http://www.gov.hk |
| Labour Department: | http://www.info.gov.hk/labour |
| Government Information Services Department: | http://www.info.gov.hk/isd/index.htm |
| Hong Kong Trade Development Council: | http://www.tdc.org.hk |
| Employees Retraining Board: | http://www.erb.org |
| Vocational Training Council: | http://www.vtc.edu.hk |

### Non-government organizations

| | |
|---|---|
| Hong Kong Management Association: | http://www.hkma.org.hk |
| Hong Kong Institute of Human Resources: | http://www.hkihrm.org |
| China Staff: | http://www.asialaw.com |

# 6 HRM in Taiwan

PEI-CHUAN WU

## Historical background

Taiwan is the largest island in the arc of mountainous islands in the western Pacific off the eastern coast of Asia, situated between Japan and the Philippines. Shaped like a sweet potato, the island of Taiwan is separated from mainland China by approximately 130 km at its closest point and is about 36,006 km$^2$ in size.

Until the seventeenth century, Taiwan was largely isolated from mainland China and the rest of the world. It was the Dutch and Spanish who first arrived and set about colonizing parts of the island. In 1662, Cheng Cheng-Kung defeated the Dutch and then ruled the island for 22 years until his family surrendered to the Ching Dynasty in 1683. Under the Ching administration, Taiwan was viewed as a gateway to the seven south-eastern provinces in China and a key trading base (*The Republic of China Yearbook*, 2002).

In 1885, Taiwan was made the twenty-second province of China. However, as a result of the 1895 Treaty of Shimonoseki, it was ceded to Japan and was not returned to Chinese sovereignty until the Japanese surrendered at the end of World War II. The Japanese regime transformed Taiwan into a relatively modern society with a better economic infrastructure. However, the social cost was high as the Taiwanese were treated as second-class citizens and the island's economic development only benefited the ruling power.

## Economic development

As a small island with only one-third of its land area usable, Taiwan has always relied heavily on its human resources. The island's population grew from 6 million in 1945 to 22 million by 2002, making it one of the most densely populated areas in the world today. In 2000, 8.62 percent of the population was over 65, which is close to the world average. As the population growth rate has decreased since the 1980s and life expectancy has increased, standing at 75 in 2001, it is expected that Taiwan will become an aging society in the near future.

*Table 6.1* Selected key economic and labor market indicators in Taiwan

| Variables | 1965 | 1970 | 1975 | 1980 | 1985 | 1990 | 1995 | 2000 | 2001 | 2002 |
|---|---|---|---|---|---|---|---|---|---|---|
| GNP per capita (US$) | 217 | 389 | 964 | 2,344 | 3,297 | 8,111 | 12,653 | 14,188 | 12,876 | 12,900 |
| Economic growth rate (%) | 11.0 | 11.3 | 4.4 | 7.1 | 5.6 | 5.5 | 5.9 | 5.9 | −2.2 | 3.5 |
| Unemployment rate | 3.3 | 1.7 | 2.4 | 1.2 | 2.9 | 1.7 | 1.8 | 3.0 | 4.6 | 5.2 |
| Total labor force (1,000s) | 3,891 | 4,654 | 5,656 | 6,629 | 7,651 | 8,423 | 9,210 | 9,783 | 9,830 | 9,965 |
| Labor force participation rate (LFPR) | 58.2 | 57.4 | 58.2 | 58.3 | 59.5 | 59.2 | 58.7 | 57.7 | 57.2 | 57.3 |
| LFPR: male | – | – | – | 77.1 | 75.5 | 74.0 | 72.0 | 69.4 | 68.5 | 68.2 |
| LFPR: female | – | – | – | 39.3 | 43.5 | 44.50 | 45.3 | 46.0 | 46.1 | 46.6 |

Source: Council for Economic Planning and Development, Executive Yuen. Directorate General of Budget, Accounting and Statistics.

Over the past 50 years, Taiwan has enjoyed the most rapid period of economic growth in its history (see Table 6.1 for macro-economic and labor statistics), its GDP increasing from US$1.7 billion in 1952 to US$309.4 billion by 2000.

Under the Japanese regime and in the early days of the Kuomintang (KMT) administration, agriculture was the major industry, hiring 56.7 percent of the labor force in 1951. The manufacturing industry became increasingly important in the following decades, reaching a peak in 1987 when it employed 42.8 percent of the labor force. Since then, the figure has gradually decreased, standing at 35.2 percent in 2002. On the other hand, the percentage of workers employed by the service industries has grown sharply, from 27.0 percent in 1951 to 57.3 percent in 2002. The agriculture industry now employs only 7.5 percent of the labor force.

Average monthly working hours decreased from 204 in 1985 to 181 in 2001. On the other hand, average monthly earnings in manufacturing increased from NT$4,044 in 1976 to NT$38,277 in 2001. The relatively high postwar economic growth rate led to acceleration in labor costs and an increased tendency for people to take lower-skilled work. This resulted in a labor shortage problem in the mid-1980s that forced many manufacturing companies to transfer their operating plants to countries with lower labor costs, such as China. In 1990, the government approved the employment of foreign workers from Southeast Asia to ease Taiwan's problems. The unemployment rate, consistently low from 1965 to 2000, currently stands at 5.2 percent, the highest in Taiwan's history.

In 1997, Taiwan managed to resist the effects of the Asian financial crisis by diversifying into the high-tech industry. However, in the past decade, China has become the main destination of Taiwanese investment. It is expected that not only will traditional manufacturing companies continue to move their operations to China, but so will companies in the high-tech and service industries.

## The government

The strength of Taiwan's economy in recent years has been due partly to government policy. After the Japanese occupation, Taiwan was ruled by the KMT regime for 50 years. During this period, Taiwan's success was driven by sound government policy as well as a stable external environment. From 1950 to 1965, two policies were critical to the island's economy: aid from the USA and land redistribution.

Between 1965 and 1987, Taiwan experienced rapid growth via an export promotion policy. In 1987, the government lifted the state of martial law and opened up non-government civilian contact between Taiwan and China. During the same period, Taiwan gradually shifted its focus to high-tech and chemical-intensive industries. By 2000, China had become Taiwan's second largest trading partner after the USA.

In 1988, President Lee Teng-Hui came to power and began to implement a series of widespread reforms. In 1996, Lee was re-elected in Taiwan's first-ever presidential election. Four years later, President Chen Shui-Bien (a member of the Democratic Progressive Party) won the second direct presidential election, ending 50 years of KMT rule. Under Chen's administration, investment in China is discouraged and official talks between Taiwan and China remain stagnant. However, the government has recently adopted a more open China policy and limited transportation links have been allowed between two small islands and the mainland.

Another major event affecting Taiwan's economy was its entry into the World Trade Organization (WTO) in 2002. While this promises to give the nation a more significant say in the world economy, in the short term, the domestic market may suffer.

## The culture

When Taiwanese characteristics are judged from the perspectives of the two previously well-documented frameworks, the whole picture of Taiwanese value orientation appears unclear and inconsistent. Hofstede's (1980) study showed a large power distance and a low level of individualism. The survey conducted by Chinese Culture Connection (1987) revealed a medium level of human-heartedness and moral discipline, a low level of integration and a high level of Confucian dynamism. As these studies were all carried out more than 20 or 30 years ago, there is a need today to explore the stability and change in value orientations in Taiwan after a relatively long period of industrialization and after significant social changes.

Empirical studies indicate that Taiwanese students' motivational patterns have changed over the last few decades (separate studies were conducted in 1963, 1975 and 1987) as they now show more tendencies towards exhibition, autonomy and change, and less towards deference, order, dominance, endurance and aggression (Hwang, 1989). A similar trend has been detected among Taiwanese people in general in that their need for individual-oriented achievement motivation is higher now than that for social-oriented achievement motivation (Yu, 1990). Hsu's (1987) study of work goals showed that Taiwanese managers are more self-centered compared to Singaporean managers. They tend to place more importance on organizational rewards than the job content and relationships, and pay little attention to job significance. Yang (1986) concluded that Taiwanese society is gradually transforming into one that emphasizes individual needs more (e.g. autonomy, exhibition, heterosexuality, etc.) and collective needs less (e.g. order, abasement, nurture, endurance and social approval). Individual needs or characteristics are now possibly more in tune with the so-called "modern" values of Taiwanese society, while collateral needs or values are more similar to the stereotypes of "traditional" Chinese values.

Yang's (1992) findings further suggest that some indigenous collectivistic values still survive in modern society; they can coexist and will not necessarily disappear despite the rise of individualism. Furthermore, certain traditional values should not be viewed as a stumbling block to modernization or social development (Yau, 1988). Rather, some values, such as familism, which is embedded in traditional Chinese values, are reinforced and sustained across generations in Chinese societies (Yang, 1986). Indeed, the values of harmony and familism will help companies to implement techniques such as total quality management, face-to-face communication and feedback, and a cooperative learning climate.

It is therefore more important for researchers and practitioners to explore the human resources management (HRM) model in the context discussed above. First of all, with the above discussion in mind, it is expected that the hardship and familism stressed by Confucianism will dominate top management's values, which may influence the design of HRM systems. Second, the Taiwanese value of harmony will have positive associations with participatory programs such as quality circles, goal-setting, feedback, participation in decision-making, and so on. Harmonious attitudes will lead to a more cooperative relationship between management and labor. The greater the level of harmonious industrial relations, the greater the effectiveness of implementing HRM policies in organizations. Finally, with the changing values of Taiwanese society, especially among the younger generation, organizations with an open and commitment-based HRM system will earn more support from their employees. Indeed, under the new government rules, the new democratic system and the new phase of economic development on the island, a looser and more democratic atmosphere is expected to arise, both in the workplace and in non-work domains. Strategic HRM policies on the island have been implemented over the past decade to address these needs. We will now continue our discussion of HRM systems in Taiwan.

## Pre-2000 HRM practices

The development of HRM systems in Taiwan can be divided into three different stages (Yao, 1999). The first stage, occurring well before the mid-1960s, coincided with the country's focus on the agriculture industry. At that time, companies were more concerned with the traditional and administrative roles of HRM. The major role of the HRM function is book-keeping, especially in the conventional areas of compensation, attendance and leave records, health records, recruitment and evaluation. Negandhi's (1973) findings reflected HRM themes in Taiwan in this particular stage in that he concluded that the HRM systems used by local Taiwanese companies were less developed than those of US and Japanese subsidiaries. At that time, local Taiwanese companies were adopting fairly simple and loose HRM practices. For example, no manpower policies were documented, there was no independent personnel department, there were no clear criteria for promotion opportunity, seniority was more important than performance in promotion, monetary rewards were emphasized, and so on. Companies would not spend a large amount of money on training and development unless it was absolutely necessary. The role of HRM at this stage was insignificant.

The second stage was the learning period (1965–1985). During this time, many multinational companies, mainly from the USA and Japan, set up subsidiaries in Taiwan.

It was also at this time that Taiwan sought to become labor-intensive by focusing on the manufacturing industry. Indeed, the island's fastest economic growth rate occurred during this period. Yeh's (1991) field study conducted in 1984–1985 found that local companies had learned quickly from their Japanese and US counterparts, and had then adapted accordingly. For example, local Taiwanese companies were similar to the American subsidiaries in terms of two recruiting criteria of new hires (technical education and general education). They were similar to the Japanese subsidiaries in their preferences of hiring new graduates, obtaining referrals from current employees, using technical competence and seniority in promotion, adopting quality circles and emphasizing group activities. However, Taiwanese firms occupied the middle position in many other HRM practices, such as bonus payment, job autonomy, lay-off policies and the emphasis on training. The HRM system in Taiwan during this period was seen to be more established and to display a hybrid style.

Stage three encompassed the years following the mid-1980s. When the field of HRM introduced the idea that business strategy was important to the HRM system in the USA, organizations in Taiwan started to bring HRM issues into the boardroom. It was also during this period that Taiwan's industry became more service-oriented and more focused on IT, with many IT firms, such as Acer and Mitac, being set up. The functions of HRM were viewed as more significant. Some companies changed the personnel department into the HRM department, some set up an independent HRM department and some installed a vice president as the head of HRM. Wu (1990) examined the role of HR managers in the top 500 manufacturing firms in Taiwan. Her study found that 88 percent of the firms had a formal personnel department and 80 percent of the heads of the HRM function bore the title "manager" or lower. The average size of the personnel department was small, with 47 percent employing fewer than six staff. The strategic role of HRM was not clear and the contribution of the HRM function to firm performance was considered fairly low compared to other functional areas. More recently, Huang (2001) found that 44 percent of companies in Taiwan have HRM practices linked closely to a firm's strategic function. The role of HRM in many companies, therefore, gradually transformed from an administrative one into a strategic one, and there was a shift from a reactive to a proactive approach in planning HRM activities to meet changing business needs. The HRM function at this stage was not yet at the strategic level, but it was moving towards a more strategic role. Meanwhile, two professional HRM associations were established, namely the Chinese Human Resource Management Association and the Human Resource Development Association of ROC. These associations help to organize public seminars and workshops in HRM-related areas.

Clearly, HRM in Taiwan had developed smoothly – from insignificance to hybridity – well before it incorporated the strategic role of the HR function. In the past 15 years, HRM in Taiwan has undergone many changes, especially in its role as a strategic partner and in its capability of being transformed. In the following section, we will discuss major findings in the field of HRM in Taiwan that have implications for the future.

# HRM practices in the twenty-first century

In 2002, I conducted a questionnaire survey of strategic HRM issues in leading companies in Taiwan. A directory of Taiwan's leading companies published by the local *CommonWealth* magazine was used for sampling. Companies with less than 40 full-time employees were excluded. In total, the sample was made up of 553 firms from the manufacturing industry and 553 firms from the service industry. The contact for the study was the HR manager in each firm. I mailed each HR manager a cover letter and a questionnaire measuring strategic HRM activities. From the 1,106 companies, 198 questionnaires were returned. Missing data reduced the final dataset to 190, representing a reasonable response rate of 17 percent. Among the 190 firms in the sample, 152 were Taiwanese-owned, 18 were western-owned and joint ventures, and 20 were Japanese subsidiaries and joint ventures. The sample represented 128 (67 percent) manufacturing firms. The questionnaire measured four important issues of HRM: environmental factors influencing HRM decisions, changes in the HRM function during the past five years, current HRM practices and key challenges of HR functions in the next five years. We shall discuss these issues in the following section.

# Environmental factors and HRM

The survey asked the HR managers to rank the environmental factors according to the extent to which they influenced their companies' HRM practices. Based on a six-point scale ranging from extremely unimportant to extremely important, Table 6.2 shows the results across the three groups.

The Taiwanese-owned companies considered the business environment, business strategy and top management's values as most important when formulating HRM policies. They paid least attention to employees' points of view, the labor representative committee and unions, and the political situation. For the western-owned companies, the top four factors were top management's values, laws and regulations, business strategy and the business environment. The least significant factors were cultural values, the labor representative committee and unions, and the political situation. The Japanese-owned companies ranked the business environment as the most significant factor, followed by the economic situation, and then laws and regulations. They paid least attention to cultural values, employees' viewpoints, the labor representative committee and unions, and the political situation.

Although the three groups had different priorities, it was clear that the business environment and business strategy were important for them all when it came to forming HRM policies. Thus, the linkage between business strategy and HRM is important in Taiwan, and is contingent upon there being a dynamic business environment. Another similarity was the minor perceived influence of the political situation and unions, and the labor representative committee. Although there is a tension in the relations between China and Taiwan, any political instability is diluted by the close business relationship

*Table 6.2* Ranking of factors that influence HRM practices in foreign subsidiaries/joint ventures and local firms in Taiwan

| HRM practices | Taiwanese-owned firms Mean (1) N = 152 (Ranking) | Western-owned firms Mean (2) N = 18 (Ranking) | Japanese-owned firms Mean (3) N = 20 (Ranking) | F-value (Sig) | Tukey's B |
|---|---|---|---|---|---|
| Laws and regulations | 5.02 (4) | 5.39 (2) | 5.20 (3) | 1.33 (0.27) | |
| Political situation | 3.86 (10) | 2.89 (10) | 4.05 (10) | 6.30 (0.002) | 2–1, 2–3 |
| Societal/cultural values | 4.12 (8) | 3.94 (8) | 4.20 (8) | 0.44 (0.64) | |
| Economic situation | 4.99 (5) | 5.17 (4) | 5.30 (2) | 1.33 (0.27) | |
| Business environment | 5.13 (1) | 5.33 (3) | 5.35 (1) | 1.30 (0.28) | |
| Organizational culture | 4.74 (6) | 5.06 (5) | 4.90 (5) | 1.36 (0.26) | |
| Union/labor representative committee | 3.56 (11) | 3.89 (9) | 4.10 (9) | 2.23 (0.11) | |
| Company's business strategy | 5.07 (2) | 5.33 (3) | 4.95 (4) | 1.14 (0.32) | |
| Top management's values and objectives | 5.05 (3) | 5.44 (1) | 4.65 (6) | 4.48 (0.01) | 2–3 |
| Competitors' HRM policies | 4.39 (7) | 4.56 (7) | 4.30 (7) | 0.37 (0.69) | |
| Employees' viewpoints | 4.08 (9) | 4.83 (6) | 4.20 (8) | 4.05 (0.02) | 2–1, 2–3 |

between the two sides. The role of unions and the labor representative committee is also not influential when firms set up HRM policies, partly because firms in Taiwan usually stress the importance of harmony. Many firms simply do not have unions, or employees do not proactively join unions. In the current study, the union concentration rate was 32 percent. This figure is in line with the estimated unionization of 30 percent in Taiwan reported by previous studies (Warner, 2000). Most Taiwanese companies have an informal labor representative committee to deal with benefit-related issues.

Finally, the major difference across the three groups was in their willingness to listen to their employees' viewpoints. Not surprisingly, the western-owned firms were more open to their employees than were the Taiwanese-owned and Japanese-owned firms. Employee participation opportunities in regard to HRM-related issues are still limited in Asian companies. The embedded culture of high power distance could be one of the major contributors to this.

## Changes in the HRM function

In the current study (see Table 6.3 for details), 43 percent of the participating firms had an independent personnel department (20 percent) or an independent HR department (23 percent). The remainder had an HR unit/department under administration or management. The average size of the personnel/HR function was 7.5 and about half of them (53 percent) hired less than four personnel staff. About 32 percent of the heads of HR functions bore the title "senior manager" or higher, and the majority of them (75 percent) reported directly to the company's managing director, vice president or president. The average size of the HR department found in this study is similar to that of previous studies (Wu, 1990). However, there was a higher tendency for the HR manager to be engaged in business planning.

The major change was in regard to the HRM function itself. As can be seen from Table 6.3, 28 HR managers described a transition from the traditional personnel function to a more strategic HR role. They argued that the role of the HR function became more important by being integrated with strategy formulation and implementation processes. This was in line with their direct link to senior managerial levels. Companies are aware of the significance of human capital and their contribution to organizational performance. By incorporating HR functions into business planning and strategy formulation and implementation, firms can gain an overview of their HR strengths and weaknesses, and make necessary changes. The changes in HR functions in terms of being a strategic partner and sharpening HR staff professionalism are in line with the transitional strategic HRM patterns after 1985 in Taiwan.

The second major change was in regard to the HRM policies in all important areas, including recruitment, retention, compensation, appraisals, training and development, e-HRM, and international HRM. The factors leading to the restructuring of HRM policies were the new organizational forms developing in the region and the shortage of

*Table 6.3* Changes in the HRM function over the past five years

| Major changes | Frequency | Ranking |
|---|---|---|
| Changes in the HRM function | 32 | 1 |
| HR outsourcing | 1 | |
| Changes from personnel function to strategic HRM function | 28 | |
| The size and role of HR reduced because of economic downturn | 1 | |
| The size and role of HR increased because of new structure | 2 | |
| | | |
| Changes in company structure | 25 | 3 |
| Ownership | 3 | |
| Leadership – from family members to managers | 1 | |
| Company size | 1 | |
| Organizational structure – delayering, lay-offs, re-engineering (lay-offs and restructuring; HR focusing more on lay-off policy than recruiting) | 20 | |
| | | |
| HRM policies | 26 | 2 |
| High sales growth rate in certain functional units – different manpower demands across functional units | 1 | |
| Recruitment – lay-offs | 6 | |
| Attracting and retaining workers | 1 | |
| Training and development | 15 | |
| Career management | 1 | |
| New performance appraisal – equity | 1 | |
| Moving from membership to performance-based | 1 | |
| Benefit programs – health insurance and labor insurance | 1 | |
| E-HRM | 1 | |
| International HRM | 1 | |
| | | |
| Psychological contract | 6 | 4 |
| Movement towards a commitment-based HRM system | 1 | |
| Increasing employees' level of satisfaction | 1 | |
| Equal opportunity against sexual discrimination | 1 | |
| Promoting loyalty and commitment | 3 | |

multiskilled labor. In 1993, Lin (1997) conducted a mail survey of large companies in Taiwan and found that recruitment and selection, training and development, and HR planning were the current and future focuses of HR functions at that time. Labor shortages of both skilled and unskilled workers are the major reasons for the focus on recruitment and training. As mentioned earlier, the government introduced foreign workers in 1990 to lessen the problem.

The current survey reveals certain shifts of focus in the same areas of training and development, and recruitment. For example, in the areas of training and development, the key changes were to upgrade employees' competencies and to develop more multiskilled workers. Thus, how to train the workers to have cross-functional skills was important. Another important issue was recruitment. The focus of recruitment in the past five years has shifted from how to attract people to how to lay off employees. The lay-off policy has become significant because many Taiwanese companies have not had experience laying off employees during the past 20 or 30 years. However, due to the economic downturn in the region and the business opportunities in China, firms with negative profits have been experiencing difficulty keeping all employees. The issue of how to reduce high labor costs by cutting the workforce and using foreign workers has been at the center of the debate.

The third major change was in regard to organizational forms. This includes changes in organizational structure, delayering, lay-offs, mergers and acquisitions, and leadership. The majority of the companies had successfully transformed into flatter organizations during the past five years through organizational restructuring. The average number of organizational levels in the companies assessed in the present study was eight, compared with ten to twenty layers in the past. These new organizational forms allow better communication, are less hierarchical and give frontline employees more power.

Finally, changes in the workplace involve issues of how to restore employees' psychological contract. Five managers pointed out the importance of increasing employees' levels of loyalty, satisfaction and commitment. The level of commitment had been low due to the new lay-off policy used by the companies. Furthermore, the old membership system had been replaced with a performance-based system in some companies, which would certainly affect employees' belief in the firms.

## Selected HRM practices

Regarding HRM practices, 41 items (on a six-point scale ranging from very inaccurate to very accurate) were used to measure seven HRM areas, namely selection, career management, training, performance appraisals, empowerment, incentive pay and benefits. Table 6.4 gives a comparison of selected HRM practices (only significant levels <0.01 are be shown) between foreign subsidiaries and joint ventures, and local Taiwanese companies. The findings are discussed below.

In line with the results of a previous study by Hsu and Leat (2000), this study did not find significant differences in most staffing-related areas across Taiwanese-owned, Japanese-owned and western-owned firms. Their study demonstrated that Taiwanese-owned firms adopted selection techniques as rigorous as did their counterparts. The most significant difference between the three types of firms was the amount of money they spent on selecting the right employees (p = 0.09). The Taiwanese-owned firms appeared to spend the least money on this area. Apart from this minor difference, the findings in regard to

*Table 6.4* HRM practices of significantly different items between foreign subsidiaries/joint ventures and local firms in Taiwan

| HRM practices | Taiwanese-owned firms Mean (1) N = 152 | Western-owned firms Mean (2) N = 18 | Japanese-owned firms Mean (3) N = 20 | F-value (Sig) | Tukey's B |
|---|---|---|---|---|---|
| Large amount of money spent on staffing | 3.40 | 3.80 | 3.92 | 2.42 (0.09) | |
| Training needs analysis | 4.14 | 4.72 | 4.02 | 2.74 (0.06) | 2–3 |
| Appraisals based on quantifiable results | 4.47 | 4.89 | 4.12 | 2.42 (0.09) | 2–3 |
| Performance feedback | 3.71 | 4.94 | 3.93 | 7.65 (0.001) | 2–1, 2–3 |
| Formal appraisals | 4.39 | 5.19 | 4.48 | 3.16 (0.04) | 2–1, 2–3 |
| Goal-setting | 4.33 | 4.92 | 4.20 | 2.50 (0.08) | |
| Employees' views of HRM policies | 4.12 | 4.77 | 4.13 | 2.47 (0.08) | |
| Open communication | 4.53 | 5.02 | 4.67 | 2.36 (0.09) | |
| Stock ownership plans | 3.90 | 2.80 | 2.45 | 7.30 (0.001) | 1–2, 1–3 |
| Pay based on external equity | 3.58 | 2.63 | 3.60 | 5.23 (0.006) | 2–1, 2–3 |
| Performance-related pay | 4.21 | 5.15 | 4.42 | 4.71 (0.01) | 2–1, 2–3 |
| Large pay dispenser | 4.03 | 4.85 | 4.27 | 3.34 (0.38) | |
| Flexible benefits | 2.92 | 2.48 | 2.25 | 2.42 (0.09) | |

selection were similar. The three groups of firms did not show any statistically significant differences in selectivity, including selection techniques, validation of selection tools, selection processes and selection criteria. In addition, all firms guaranteed employment and job security.

A series of policies regarding career management was measured. This included an internal promotion policy, performance-based promotion, career counseling, career opportunities and career information offered by the firms. Although the western-owned firms practiced career policies more extensively than did the other two groups, there were no significant differences found across the three groups in all sub-areas of career management.

In the areas of training and development, only one minor difference was identified across the three groups. With regard to the degree to which training needs were conducted systematically, the Japanese-owned firms (mean = 4.02) ranked lowest, followed by the Taiwanese-owned firms (mean = 4.15) and then the western-owned firms (mean = 4.72). Other areas in training and development, such as the extensiveness and effectiveness of the training programs, the training volume received by employees, and initial training for new hires, revealed similar levels of utilization.

Performance appraisals were probably one of the most heterogeneous areas in this survey. Of the five policies relating to appraisals, three appeared to show significant differences across the three groups. The western-owned firms focused more on objective, quantifiable results than did their Taiwanese-owned and Japanese-owned counterparts. They also provided face-to-face appraisal interviews and feedback to their employees more extensively than did the other two groups. The findings indicated that Taiwanese-owned firms were the most reluctant to offer feedback to their employees. The two Asian groups were far behind their western-owned counterparts in this sensitive area. The problems of "protecting face" and "establishing a good relationship with employees" might explain why this practice was not carried out. In addition, formal and systematic appraisals were practiced more extensively in the western-owned firms (mean = 5.19) than in the other two groups. Not surprisingly, the Taiwanese-owned firms were bottom in this area. Another interesting related finding concerned the use of the 360-degree performance appraisal system. All three groups appeared to show a fairly low adoption of this practice (western-owned firms, mean = 2.90; Taiwanese-owned firms, mean = 2.89; Japanese-owned firms, mean = 2.62). Traditional downward appraisals were more popular.

With respect to areas of empowerment, three out of nine practices revealed significant differences across the three groups. The western-owned firms put more emphasis on goal-setting and open communication. In addition, they seemed more likely to take employees' points of view into consideration when formulating their HRM policies. In other areas of empowerment, the results were rather similar for the three groups. The responding companies were happy to provide a series of communication channels through which their employees could exchange opinions, and they would allow their employees to make their own decisions to a certain extent. However, they appeared to be more reluctant to delegate power to their employees by allowing them to participate in HRM-related decision-making processes.

In the area of incentive pay, no clear patterns were found. Stock ownership plans were used more widely by the Taiwanese-owned firms (mean = 3.90). The other two groups showed a fairly low tendency to adopt this practice (western-owned firms, mean = 2.79; Japanese-owned firms, mean = 2.45). On the other hand, the western-owned firms were more into performance-related pay than were the Taiwanese-owned and the Japanese-owned firms. Individual and group performance was more important in the western-owned firms than seniority or membership. They also had a larger salary increment for top performers to ensure the equity principle. However, the western-owned firms were more into internal equity than external equity. They often had a sound and rigorous job evaluation process to ensure internal equity, whereas the Taiwanese-owned firms were more likely to adopt an external policy. The latter group would simply make comparisons with their competitors in the industry rather than go through the whole cycle of job analysis and job evaluation.

Finally, in the area of benefits, flexible benefit programs were hardly practiced at all by any of the three groups. In most companies, the idea of allowing employees to choose what benefits they prefer is still relatively new compared to other HRM practices. The responding companies normally used a standardized benefit plan for all employees. Other forms of flexibility offered by firms such as career break schemes, flexible working hours and family-friendly programs were also not widely practiced by the participating companies.

The above findings demonstrate the development of strategic HRM in Taiwan. The data indicated that Taiwanese-owned firms adopted the same HRM techniques as their Japanese-owned and western-owned counterparts to a certain extent in most HRM areas. No significant differences were found in most aspects of the hard, quantifiable HRM practices between Taiwanese-owned and foreign-owned firms, such as selection, and training and development. On the other hand, some significant differences were detected in certain soft areas of HRM practices, such as communication, feedback, performance-related pay and performance appraisals. In line with previous research carried out in Taiwan (Farh, 1995; Chen, 1997), a trend towards convergence of HRM practices was evidenced in "hard" rather than "soft" areas of HRM.

As HRM has moved from traditional control-based systems to commitment-based systems, the stress now is on individual contributions rather than group contributions in terms of job design, performance measurement, rewards and development. There is a focus on mutuality by using face-to-face communication and by encouraging individual employees to be involved in the goal-setting and decision-making processes. This model of HRM is, in fact, a reflection of the USA's own cultural values which are highly individualistic and emphasize "doing" and "mastery." In contrast, the HRM practices used by Japanese organizations are deeply embedded in their collectivistic cultural roots, such as teamwork, quality circles and lifetime employment. This culture-HRM linkage forces us to consider seriously the innate nature of HRM and the appropriateness of

American HRM models. This implication, or explication, of the congruence between culture and HRM has triggered a growing concern about the transferability and success of specific HRM techniques from one country to another. Child (1981) argues that despite organizations in different countries becoming more similar, as measured by surface characteristics and specific structures and technologies, the behavior of people within those organizations maintains its cultural sensitivity. Thus, the impact of national cultures on HRM policies and practices is expected to be more significant in regard to soft, behavioral-based techniques rather than hard, quantifiable techniques, and this is what we observed for our Taiwanese-owned samples.

Indeed, empirical research has found that the "hard" or more easily quantifiable technologies (such as planning, staffing and training) have met with more effectiveness in the transfer or convergence process than have the "soft," behavioral and relationship-based technologies, such as career development, performance management, work design, and pay and reward systems (Yeh, 1991; Vance et al., 1992; Shaw et al., 1993; Yuen and Kee, 1993; Brewster and Hegewisch, 1994; Easterby-Smith et al., 1995). This has raised important considerations for organizations adopting or borrowing new techniques, especially from abroad.

While the above arguments suggest a culturally sensitive approach to HRM systems, they do not rule out the possibility of implementing strategic HRM systems in Taiwan. The key issue here is still the local culture. Previous work by Bae and Lawler (2000) in Korea point to a similar situation. They found that Korean culture was undergoing change, and as a result, the Koreans were more willing to accept the strategic HRM concept. They argue that "cultural changes seem to be occurring in Korea that make workers and employers more open to high-involvement work systems" (Bae and Lawler, 2000: 504). Similarly, the Chinese cultural values in Taiwan have shown some inevitable changes due to the rapid modernization process occurring in this part of the world. As a result, companies are more aware of American or western-style HRM and are adapting to it, especially to the "hard" areas of HRM.

As well as adapting to American or western-style HRM, companies in Taiwan have also paid attention to the link between business strategy and HRM. Hsu and Leat's (2000) findings indicated that HR managers would like to be involved in board meetings in developing corporate strategy. They also felt that HR policy should have a tight fit with business strategy to obtain competitive advantage. According to Huang (1998), 44 percent of companies in Taiwan have a close linkage between strategy and HRM; for example, such firms would consider HR factors when formulating business strategies. Huang's findings further demonstrate that US-owned firms attach more importance to strategic HRM than do local and Japanese-owned firms.

## The challenges

About eight years ago, Farh (1995) argued that the role of the HRM function in Taiwan would be more significant in the future, and the convergence of HRM policies towards

*Table 6.5* Challenges to the HRM function

| Major challenges | Current challenges frequency (ranking) | Future challenges frequency (ranking) |
|---|---|---|
| The HRM function | 27 (3) | 14 (4) |
| HR outsourcing | | 2 |
| Labor shortage of HR specialists | 4 | 1 |
| HR specialists' ability to deal with the new strategic HRM function | 6 | 1 |
| The link between business strategy and HRM | 14 | 10 |
| Poor company performance – insignificant HRM function | 1 | |
| Changes from personnel function to strategic HRM function | 2 | |
| | | |
| Challenges of environmental factors | 32 (2) | 36 (2) |
| Labor laws (minimum wage and equal opportunity) | 3 | 1 |
| Competitor's policy | 4 | |
| The rise of China | 3 | 8 |
| Globalization | 1 | 7 |
| Flatter organizational structure | 9 | |
| Top management's attitudes towards HR and people | 3 | 10 |
| Aging and labor cost control | 5 | 5 |
| High salary, low firm performance and high labor cost | 4 | 4 |
| Technology – automation | | 1 |
| | | |
| Challenges of HRM policies | 108 (1) | 99 (1) |
| HR planning | 6 | 2 |
| Difficulties in recruiting senior managers and professionals | 10 | 8 |
| Attracting and retaining talented, good performers | 14 | 5 |
| Freezing labor or lay-offs | 7 | 4 |
| Human resource information system | 2 | |
| Training, developing and preparing human resources | 35 | 35 |
| Succession planning | 7 | 7 |
| E-HRM | 10 | 8 |
| International HRM | 2 | 10 |
| Pay structure and incentive programs | 8 | 8 |
| Benefit programs – flexible working hours, social activities and pensions | 1 | 3 |
| Performance appraisals | 4 | 7 |
| Career management | 2 | 2 |
| | | |
| Employees and the psychological contract | 15 (4) | 21 (3) |
| Changes in work attitudes and values | | 3 |
| High employee turnover rate | 5 | 6 |
| Motivating employees to increase employee productivity | 3 | 3 |
| Developing a team work spirit and job sharing | 2 | |
| Workers are unaware of the competitive environment | 2 | |
| Forming a new corporate culture | 2 | |
| How to communicate with employees within the new system | 1 | 9 |

those of the West might need to be sensitive to a country's social, economic and political conditions. He highlighted four important future challenges for Taiwan, namely labor shortage, industry transition, changing work values and the changing role of the government. Changes in HRM functions, organizational forms, key environmental factors and the psychological contract, discussed above, were the major changes perceived by the HR managers. The current and future challenges faced by the firms in Taiwan were similar, but they had different priorities (see Table 6.5 for details).

These challenges include:

1  HRM policies. HRM policies represented the most important set of challenges for the firms. This is not surprising as so many changes have taken place in terms of external and internal factors that have triggered the reform of HRM policies. The most challenging HRM area was training and development, which includes sharpening employees' skills and knowledge, knowledge management, developing a multiskilled workforce, promoting English ability, promoting e-learning and establishing a learning environment. Recruitment was the second most challenging area, and includes attracting and retaining talented employees, and implementing lay-off policies. The shortage of labor, especially for professional and senior managerial staff, was recognized as serious since Taiwan is transforming into an IT hub. Other important challenges identified were the utilization of e-HRM, performance-based pay and appraisals, and succession planning. International HRM has been seen in terms of its important future rather than its current challenges. As more Taiwanese firms move their subsidiaries to Southeast Asia, China, the USA or Europe, the issue of international coordination and expatriation will become more relevant.

2  Environmental factors. The major current challenge was the changing organizational form. However, three important factors might hinder the development of HRM systems in Taiwan. At the top of the list would be the top management's support and attitudes towards HRM and staff. Whether the top management sees HRM as an important function and whether they see human resources as significant assets will be the key issues in the coming years. The rise of China and globalization are also important factors. As mentioned above, many Taiwanese firms moved their factories to China during the past 10 years. The close business relationship would only be strengthened by integration and coordination between headquarters and subsidiaries. Recruiting expatriates to manage the Chinese facility and to deal with local Chinese employees would be challenging. The danger of losing talented employees to business activities in China is another issue. Finally, as Taiwan has now joined the WTO, attention has to be paid to international treaties.

3  The HRM function. The HRM function was viewed as the third most important current challenge, but as the least important one for the future. The linkage between business strategy and the HRM function is still a central theme. While changes have been made to transform the personnel function into the strategic HRM function in many firms in Taiwan, the key challenges in the coming years will be the formulation and implementation of strategic HRM policies.

4 Employees and the psychological contract. This was viewed as the third most important future issue. As so many changes will need to be made when implementing a series of HRM policies, companies will need to consider the cost of the psychological contract. Since the written contract has shifted gradually to a performance-based one with no guarantee of lifelong employment, companies will need to sell and communicate the new HRM systems to their employees. As can be seen from the results, the need to talk to employees was at the top of the firms' list, followed by the high turnover rate.

The HRM function shall continue to earn more attention in firms in Taiwan in the future. We have observed changes in the HRM function itself over the past five years. The HRM policies in regard to staffing, and training and development have gradually adopted the western HRM style by using more extensive and rigorous techniques. The HRM policies in regard to pay and appraisals have moved halfway towards convergence. The Taiwan companies were aware of the performance-based pay and appraisal systems. The difficulty in implementing them would be bound to local Chinese culture in terms of providing feedback and constructive communication. In the area of participative management, many forms have been adopted in the past, such as suggestion schemes, quality circles, profit sharing, stock ownership and labor-management committees (Huang, 1997). Allowing employees to participate in many HRM-related areas is another future challenge. Whether or not companies in Taiwan will allow employees to have a significant say in HRM issues may depend on the sensitivity of the issue itself and the high power distance relationship in the country. However, as the next generation joins the job market bringing in new work values, and as the new government introduces more open and democratic policies, democracy in the workplace may change accordingly.

# References

Bae, J. and Lawler, J.J. (2000) "Organizational and HRM strategies in Korea: Impact on firm performance in an emerging economy," *Academy of Management Journal* 43: 502–517.

Brewster, C. and Hegewisch, A. (1994) *Policy and practice in European human resource management: The Price Waterhouse Cranfield Survey*, London: Routledge.

Chen, S.J. (1997) "The development of HRM practices in Taiwan," *Asia Pacific Business Review* 3 (4): 152–169.

Child, J. (1981) "Culture, contingency and capitalism in the cross-national study of organisations," in B.M. Staw and L.L. Cummings (eds.) *Research in organisational behaviour*, Greenwich, CT: JAI Press.

Chinese Culture Connection (1987) "Chinese values and the search for culture-free dimensions of culture," *Journal of Cross-Cultural Psychology* 18: 143–164.

Council for Economic Planning and Development (2000) *Taiwan statistical data book*, Taiwan Executive Yuan.

Directorate-General of Budget, Accounting and Statistics (DGBAS) (2002) *Monthly bulletin of manpower statistics, Taiwan area, Republic of China*, Taiwan: Executive Yuan.

Easterby-Smith, M., Malina, D. and Yuan, L. (1995) "How culture-sensitive is HRM? A comparative analysis of practice in Chinese and UK companies," *International Journal of Human Resource Management* 6 (1): 31–59.

*The Economist* (1998) "Taiwan and the Asian crisis," 24 January: 66–67.

Farh, J.L. (1995) "Human resource management in Taiwan, Republic of China," in L.F. Moore and P.D. Jennings (eds.) *Human resource management on the Pacific rim: Institutions, practices and attitudes*, Berlin: de Gruyter, pp. 265–294.

Hofstede, G. (1980) *Culture's consequences: International differences in work-related values*, Beverly Hills, CA: Sage.

Hsu, P.S.C. (1987) "Patterns of work goals importance: A comparison of Singapore and Taiwanese managers," *Asia Pacific Journal of Management* 4 (3): 152–166.

Hsu, Y.R. and Leat, M. (2000) "A study of HRM and recruitment and selection policies and practices in Taiwan," *The International Journal of Human Resource Management* 11 (2): 413–435.

Huang, T.C. (1997) "The effect of participative management on organizational performance: The case of Taiwan," *The International Journal of Human Resource Management* 8 (5): 677–689.

Huang, T.C. (1998) "The strategic level of human resource management and organizational performance: An empirical investigation," *Asia Pacific Journal of Human Resource Management* 36 (2): 59–72.

Huang, T.C. (2001) "Human resource management in Taiwan," in P.S. Budhwar and Y.A. Debrah (eds.) *Human resource management in developing countries*, London and New York: Routledge.

Hwang, C.H. (1989) "A follow-up study on the psychological needs of Chinese university students" (in Chinese), *Bulletin of Educational Psychology* (National Taiwan Normal University) 22: 1–21.

Lin, C.Y.Y. (1997) "Human resource management in Taiwan: A future perspective," *International Journal of Human Resource Management* 8 (1): 29–43.

Negandhi, A.R. (1973) *Management and economic development: The case of Taiwan*, The Hague: Martinus Nijhoff.

Shaw, J.B., Tang, S.F., Fisher, C.D. and Kirkbride, P.S. (1993) "Organisational and environmental factors related to HRM practices in Hong Kong: A cross-cultural expanded replication," *International Journal of Human Resource Management* 4 (4): 785–815.

Vance, C.M., McClaine, S.R., Boje, D.M. and Stage, H.D. (1992) "An examination of the transferability of traditional performance appraisal principles across cultural boundaries," *Management International Review* 32 (4): 313–326.

Warner, M. (2000) "Introduction: The Asian-Pacific HRM model revisited," *International Journal of Human Resource Management* 11 (2): 171–182.

Wu, S.H. (1990) "Human resource management and organizational effectiveness: An analysis of large manufacturing firms in Taiwan," *Proceedings of the Conference on Human Resource Utilization and Labor Productivity*, Taipei: Council of Labor Affairs, Executive Yuan (in Chinese), pp. 235–264.

Yang, K.S. (1986) "Chinese personality and its change," in M.H. Bond (ed.) *The psychology of the Chinese people*, Hong Kong: Oxford University Press, pp. 106–170.

Yang, K.S. (1992) "Do traditional and modern values coexist in a modern Chinese society?" in *Proceedings of the Conference on Chinese Perspectives on Values*, Taipei: Center for Sinological Studies (in Chinese), pp. 117–158.

Yao, D. (1999) "Human resource management challenges in Chinese Taipei," in *Human resource management symposium on SMEs Proceedings*, vol. II, 30–31, October, Kaoshung: National Sun Yat-sen University.

Yau, O.H.M. (1988) "Chinese cultural values: Their dimensions and marketing implications," *European Journal of Marketing* 22 (5): 44–57.

Yeh, R.S. (1991) "Management practices of Taiwanese firms: As compared to those of American and Japanese subsidiaries in Taiwan," *Asia Pacific Journal of Management* 8 (1): 1–14.

Yu, A.B. (1990) "The construct validity of social-oriented and individual-oriented achievement motivation" (in Chinese), unpublished doctoral dissertation, Department of Psychology, National Taiwan University.

Yuen, C. and Kee, H. T. (1993), 'Headquarters, host-culture and organisational influences on HRM policies and practices', *Management International Review* 33: 361–383.

## Useful websites

| | |
|---|---|
| China Productivity Center: | http://edu.cpc.org.tw/ |
| Chinese Human Resource Management Association: | http://www.chrma.org.tw/ |
| *CommonWealth* Magazine: | http://www.cw.com.tw/ |
| Council of Labor Affairs: | http://www.cla.gov.tw/ |
| Council of Personnel Affairs: | http://www.cpa.gov.tw/ |
| Human Resource Management Development: | http://www.hrmd.com.tw/ |
| *The Republic of China Yearbook* – Taiwan 2002. (2002) Published on the Internet, government information office, Taiwan. Online. | |
| Available HTTP: | http://www.gio.gov.tw/ |
| Taiwan Statistical Data: | http://www.dgbas.gov.tw |

# 7 HRM in India

## DEBI S. SAINI AND PAWAN S. BUDHWAR

## Introduction

This chapter presents a broad overview of the scenario of human resource management (HRM) in India. It is structured along the framework discussed in chapter 1 of this volume. To provide the required context, this section presents some relevant demographic details of the Indian economy and society. India is a republic in South Asia. It has the second highest population in the world after China, which reached the 1 billion mark in June 2000. As per the latest census of 2001, the total population of the country is 1,027 million, which includes 531.28 million males and 495.73 million females. India's share of the world population is 16.7 percent. The literacy rate among the population for seven years and above for the country stands at 65.38 percent. The corresponding figures for males and females are 75.85 and 54.16 percent respectively. The density of population (per km$^2$) is 324 and the male=female ratio is 1000:933.

Being the largest democracy in the world, India is governed by a constitution that came into force on 26 January 1950. It attained independence from the British on 15 August 1947. The country comprises of 29 states and 6 union territories. There are six main religious groups: Hindus (83.2 percent), Muslims (11 percent), Sikhs (2 percent), Christians (2 percent), Jains and Buddhists (less than 1 percent). There are over three thousand castes. India has 179 languages and 544 dialects. The constitution recognizes sixteen languages, "Hindi" and English being the two official languages. India has one of the largest English-speaking populations in the Asia-Pacific region (Budhwar, 2003).

As per the latest round of National Sample Survey (NSS) of Employment and Unemployment, the total workforce in the country is 397 million. Out of this, nearly 92 percent or more are engaged in the activities of the unorganized sector (including the so-called informal sector) while about 8 percent of the workforce is employed in the organized sector. Of the total employment, 60 percent of the workforce is engaged in agriculture. Of the 40 percent in the non-agriculture sector, the unorganized workforce is 82 percent and the remaining 18 percent or so belongs to the organized segment. Only about 12 to 15 percent of the total workforce in the country is estimated to fall in the category of wage/salary employment. Such employees constitute 6 percent of the workforce in the rural areas and about 40 percent of the workforce in the urban

(Economic Survey, Government of India 2002–2003). The second National Commission on Labour (NCL) has estimated that only 5 percent of the workforce in the age group 20–24 has acquired some kind of a formal vocational training (Government of India, 2002). This is a far lower percentage than those of developed countries, which range between 60 to 80 percent.

India is rich in both natural and human resources, even as it faces tremendous challenges in its efforts to enhance economic growth and development. It is estimated that around 200 million people in the country comprise the middle class, which is becoming larger with the liberalization of the Indian economy. This class is also viewed by the developed countries as an important market for exporting their goods from a long-term point of view. The country has multiplied its foreign direct investment (FDI) several times since adopting the New Economic Policy (NEP) in July 1991, but is still far behind its neighbor China and countries in Southeast Asia in this regard. There are now over 15,000 multinational firms operating in India and this number is increasing rapidly (for details, see Budhwar, 2001).

As global firms seek success in their Indian operations, and as Indian firms reach a higher degree of professionalism in the global context, they have to make critical decisions related to people management as strategic choices. This will necessitate an appreciation of the factors which influence HRM policies and practices in the Indian context. These factors, among others, include availability of requisite skills and competencies, required mindsets, desired values and customs, facilitative legal framework and institutions, and conducive cultural environment. They are the products of a country's socioeconomic and political realities (see Budhwar and Sparrow, 1998; Hofstede, 1993). A comprehensive understanding of such realities and insights helps a fuller comprehension of the HRM model of a country (Budhwar and Sparrow, 2002a). The contemporary HRM scenario of a country should be understood in the context of its general economic and business environment as it evolves over the years.

## The Indian economy and business environment

After independence, India put primacy on adopting self-reliance in its economic development policies and thus preferred an import-substitution model of development for 45 years or so. It set up the Planning Commission in 1950 to formulate national plans. Since then, a "mixed economy" approach (emphasizing both private and public enterprise) has been adopted until quite recently. This had the effect of reducing the incidence of entrepreneurship as well as global competitiveness – both necessary for national growth. Economic planning is carried out mainly through the five-year plans and industrial policies. Presently, the tenth five-year plan (2002–2007) and the industrial policy of 1991 are in progress.

Despite the formalities of planning, the Indian economy was perhaps in its worst state in 1991. It witnessed a double-digit rate of inflation, decelerated industrial production, fiscal indiscipline, a very high ratio of borrowing to the GNP (both internal and external) and a dismally low level of foreign exchange reserves. Those had gone down so low that they were barely sufficient to meet the bill for three weeks' imports. The World Bank and the IMF agreed to bail out India on the condition that it changed from a regulated regime to a "free market economy." To meet the challenges, the government announced a series of economic policies, beginning with the devaluation of the rupee, followed by a new industrial policy and fiscal and trade policies. A number of reforms guided by the liberalization philosophy were made in the public sector, trade and exchange policy, the banking sector and the foreign investment policy (for details, see Budhwar, 2003).

The economy has responded positively to these reforms and India is now considered as one of the largest emerging nations, having bypassed the Asian economic crisis. The World Bank forecasts that, by 2020, India could become the world's fourth largest economy. In the last few years state control and ownership in the economy have been reduced. Bold steps have been taken to correct the fiscal imbalance, to bring about structural adjustments and to attract foreign direct investment. Foreign operators can now acquire immovable property in India, employ foreign nationals in their operations in India and buy and sell shares in Indian companies. Substantial reforms have been made in the telecommunications, financial and shipping sectors, as well as in direct tax structure and industrial policy. Significant reforms have already been initiated in the insurance sector by the present government. However, India still has a long way to go before it can compete fully with some of the more economically advanced Asian nations.

Liberalization of the Indian economy has resulted in sudden and increased levels of competition for Indian firms from international firms. At the same time it has also created opportunities for resource mobilization from new sources. HRM issues have now become more important with the firms' adoption of strategies of expansion, diversification, turnaround and internationalization. These developments have direct implications for HRM in India and the Indian HR function is under severe pressure to bring about large-scale structural changes in order to cope with the challenges brought about by economic liberalization. It has to develop a domestic workforce capable of taking on the challenges thrown up by the new economic environment. In such conditions the performance of the HR function has become more important than ever (for details, see Budhwar and Sparrow, 1997).

Despite many initiatives in response to the demands of the globalization process, India is comparatively slow in implementing the reforms process. AT Kearney's, a management consultancy firm, developed a 2003 globalization index for various countries (*Times of India*, 2003: 11). It was found that the low pace of integration with the global economy together with the decline in portfolio capital investment caused India to slip to fifty-sixth rank from forty-ninth in the year 2002. Several factors have contributed to Indian business remaining much below world class. These include: lack of aspiration to be world class, lack of vision, lack of professionalism, lack of process sensitivity, lack of cost consciousness, little respect for time, and lack of a professional system of skill development, among others (Prahlad, 1998; Rao, 1999; Saini, 2000). Most enlightened employers are aware of these limitations. They also realize a greater need to tackle the problem of outdated technology, excessive workforce, inadequacy of skills, and lack of concern for customer satisfaction, and unsatisfactory levels of productivity.

Tackling these problems necessitated reorienting management systems and processes, and undertaking programs of attitudinal change. These included mixed bags of harder measures as well as attempts towards greater professionalism for HR empowerment. Vigorous downsizing of the excessive workforce became the order of the day both within the public and the private sectors. Several organizations devised voluntary retirement schemes (VRS) to facilitate the reform process. The NEP (announced in 1991), among others, envisaged the establishment of a National Renewal Fund (NRF). It was aimed to promote upgradation of skills of those affected by downsizing, finance VRS in the public sector enterprises, and support programs of skill enhancement in general. Ironically, almost no effective program of skill upgradation has been initiated so far; almost all spendings from the NRF has been confined to financing the VRS (Mishra, 2001). Even after more than a decade of liberalization policies a "skill development fund" has not been set up to facilitate a professionally managed macro program of human resource development (HRD). The aim of such a program would have been to develop appropriate skills and competencies as per social and economic demands, including changing the mindsets of the workforce so as to be in consonance with the needs of the business realities. If started, it will necessitate necessary HRD programs at the macro level and adoption of HRM strategies at the micro level.

## Evolution of human resource management

The personnel function in India originated in the 1920s with the concern for labor welfare in factories. The Trade Union Act of 1926 gave formal recognition to workers' unions. The Royal Commission of Labor, 1931, recommended the appointment of labor welfare officers and the Factories Act of 1948 laid down the duties and qualifications of labor welfare officers. Further, the Indian judiciary played an important role in expounding the correct scope of the protection envisaged to the working class by the legislation that was enacted in several spheres of industrial relations (IR) as per the spirit of the constitution. Consequent to the passage of a number of labor and industrial relations laws, personnel managers began performing IR as a very significant role; one that formed such an important part of their work that they came to be known as children of the Industrial Disputes Act 1947 (IDA). All these developments formed the foundation of the personnel function in India (Balasubramanian, 1994, 1995) and paralleled the initial developments of the British personnel function. For example, provisions similar to those provided by Cadbury in Britain were provided by the Tata group in India in the early 1920s (see Budhwar and Khatri, 2001).

After Independence, in the 1950s, two professional bodies emerged: the Indian Institute of Personnel Management (IIPM), a counterpart of the Institute of Personnel Management in the UK, was formed at Calcutta and the National Institute of Labor

Management (NILM) at Bombay. In the 1960s, the personnel function began to expand beyond the welfare aspect with three areas, labor welfare, industrial relations and personnel administration, developing as the constituent roles for the emerging profession (Venkata Ratnam and Srivastava, 1991). In the 1970s, the thrust of personnel function shifted towards greater organizational "efficiency," and by the 1980s it began to use and focus on terms and issues such as HRM and HRD. The two professional bodies, i.e. IIPM and NILM, merged in 1980 to form the National Institute of Personnel Management (NIPM) in Bombay. Thus, the status of the personnel function in India has changed over the years (Amba-Rao, 1994; Budhwar and Sparrow, 1997).

In recent years, HRD has been seen as the main tool for improving business performance. Business survival has become an important aspect of HRD efforts. The vigorous efforts by academics (such as T.V. Rao, Udai Pareek and Ishwar Dayal, among others) helped to popularize the concept of HRD among both academics and practitioners. Programs of HRD and organizational development (OD) at the individual enterprise level in public as well as private sectors are being adopted. The formation of "The HRD Network," which today has a large membership of academics and HRM and other managers, symbolizes the need to debate HR interventions and sharpen abilities of HR professionals. This network has aroused tremendous sensitivity of the need for HRD in particular and for HRM in general. Greater focus has been put on developing HRD systems to produce synergy and employee contentment. During this period, the HR profession developed by leaps and bounds in both positive and negative senses. Several organizations resorted to indiscriminate appointment of HRD managers. This period also saw an elevation in the status of personnel managers to the board level; though only in professionally managed organizations. There was also a massive upsurge in re-labelling the title of personnel manager to HRD manager and personnel department to HRD department. Interestingly, however, some employers also perceived disillusionment with their decision as they felt that the investment in HRD did not deliver any tangible results. Thus they started downsizing or even abolishing their HRD departments. Efforts are also made to outsource HR activities. This gave rise to the need for the measurement of HR performance. Thus the concept of "HR audit" came into practice. Progressive employers like Aditya Vikram Birla asked all their companies to have their HR systems audited by consultants (Rao, 1999). The concept of the HRD scorecard is being used as a device to measure effectiveness of people-development activities.

As is well known, the HRM philosophy developed in the western countries during the 1980s and the 1990s both in its hard (instrumentalist) and soft (empowerment) dimensions (Legge, 1995). Empowerment was viewed as "the elixir of the 1990s." Finally, HRM now seems to have found wide application in both western organizations and MNCs. Ironically, no such debate on HRM as a philosophy in the Indian context existed, despite the immense contribution of various trainer-academics towards the implementation of the HRD philosophy (Saini, 2000). At the organizational level, the word HRM is rarely being used; it is substituted by HRD. However, MNCs operating in India do not confine their interventions to HRD and have undertaken wider programs and strategies of HRM (see Budhwar and Björkman, 2003). Some of the leading Indian organizations have also taken the initiative in this regard and have brought out newer issues in the strategic management of their human resources. Still, one fails to understand why Indian firms continue to use different terminology to denote their HR departments or the possible logic behind this.

## Personnel management, HRD or HRM: some reflections in the Indian context

If one examines HRM books or courses taught in management schools in India, by and large it appears to be a case of old wine in new bottles; for the term "personnel management" has been replaced by HRD without much debate. Only recently some glimpses of reforms are visible in this regard. However, they are far from adequate. The writings of key scholars in the field such as Udai Pareek and T.V. Rao of the Indian Institute of Management (IIM) Ahmedabad, have helped in popularizing the term HRD in India (see for example, Pareek and Rao, 1981; Rao, 1999). But almost no attempt has been made to critically expound the term HRM as it has come to be understood in the advanced world. Pareek and Rao provide a very wide definition of the term HRD and view it as a philosophy by itself. They do not attempt to knit it into the HRM concept nor give any reasons as to why they have ignored the term HRM despite the long debate on it in the West. Almost nowhere do they differentiate between HRD and HRM. And it is certain that there is no Indianness in their explanation of the term HRD. They use the contribution of Nadler (1970) as a model in their formulations, and continue to preach his philosophy in the different versions of their text (i.e. the latest 1992 edition of Pareek and Rao, 1981; Rao, 1999). Today, Nadler's ideas have merged into the HRM philosophy. HRD is largely viewed as a developmental intervention in HRM. Almost the entire HRM community in the West has viewed it so, with very few exceptions (see, for example, Walton, 1999). Indian academics have remained silent on the fate of HRM for long, knowingly or unknowingly, which has led to an uncritical popularization of the term HRD.

As a result, when scholars look for material on the HRM discourse in India, they receive only confusing signals, especially if they wish to put HRM thinking and practice in the context of global developments. For some strange reason, even most books in the HRM area bear HRD labels or linkages (Saini and Khan, 2000). This situation is partly attributable to the dominance of training and development and the psychologist–academics in the contemporary thinking on HRD/HRM in the country. It may partly be attributable to the renaming of the central government Ministry of Education as the Ministry of HRD in the early 1980s. Looking towards the courses in HRM offered at most business schools in India, they are not sufficiently equipped to face the challenges of this emerging subject, especially its strategic connotation. We have yet to witness most business schools and university departments devising innovative courses in this area, knowledge of which is necessary for realizing the goal of professional excellence in people management; in reality the basic HRM course for general MBA students is still personnel management. Courses in strategic HRM are hardly taught even as HR managers of most professionally managed organizations in the country are using the most modern methods and interventions of HRM (see Budhwar and Sparrow, 1997; Varkky *et al.*, 2001).

Budhwar (1998) empirically investigated in 137 Indian firms the preference for the usage of specific terms to denote HR departments in the Indian context, the nature of personnel function and the differences between personnel management (PM), HRD and HRM. His results show that the majority of Indian managers see the recently changed economic environment as the most significant factor responsible for major changes in the nature of their personnel/HR function. The liberalization of the Indian economy has created a pressure on the Indian HRM function to become more creative and innovative. The HRM profession promises to commit itself to improve the efficiency and commitment of its human resources, obtain better results and improve industrial relations. This highlights, among others, the role of training and development and team or group-HRM activities. Due to such changes, the use of HRD-related terms is becoming popular and that of personnel management-related ones is going out-of-fashion. Interestingly, in MNCs operating in India, HRM is the preferred term to denote both HR departments and managers (see Budhwar and Björkman, 2003).

Indian managers define HRM as a holistic concept, which is more focused and proactive than PM; it integrates and incorporates both PM and HRD, and deals with satisfying and developing employees. HRD implies a long-term perspective for developing the potential and capabilities of HR for future organizational needs. Personnel is seen as more of a policing type of department as it is now a secondary function, also called transactional HRM. This aspect of HRM is concerned with the day-to-day activities of control, attendance, compliance with legislation, discipline aspects and IR. The majority of Indian managers believe that the future of the HRM function is good and its status is improving. Some managers, however, feel that the existing legislation can be obstructive in this regard. Perhaps they rightly lament the functioning of the 'EXIT' policy (a policy for voluntary retirement) as problematic due to the rigidities created by the IR laws (for details, see Budhwar, 2000).

## Factors influencing HRM and related challenges

## National culture

The prevailing beliefs, values, traditions and behavior patterns among Indians form part of the national culture and can be attributed to several factors. Prominent among these are social customs and practices and the perpetration by the British of elitist values during their rule over India for more than a century. Perhaps the Britishers' biggest influence in this regard was through the promotion of feudalism. Their land cultivation system involved appointing feudal lords who exacerbated the values of hierarchy and subjugation. Also, their focus was on the supremacy of bureaucracy through the institution of an administrative service called the Indian Civil Service (ICS). The working of these institutions has made a lasting impact on the psyche of common people. They have strengthened hierarchy and power distance between the rulers and the ruled. The civil servants and the feudal lords constituted elite classes in society, whose position in the social hierarchy was strengthened by the policies of the British Indian government.

After Independence, the ICS was replaced by the Indian Administrative Service (IAS) with the projected intention of humanizing it and bringing it closer to people's aspirations. However, it inherited and sustained the culture of the ICS and the state system suffered from all the vices which are attributed to bureaucracy (see Saini, 1999b). It has resulted in a two-tier system of the elite and the general public. While the law is enforced in a particular way for the former, the same law works to the detriment of the latter. Such a culture of elitism is known to have pervaded most types of organization. Such biases have been reflected even in the people management policies in general.

Feudalism created by the British promoted inequality and hierarchy amongst the urban as well as non-urban population. The caste system in India has also played a contributory role in this regard. The family-owned business houses have made full use of the inculcation of these values in society in practicing a kind of neofeudalism in industry. This is reflected in the organizational structures and social relations which reflect hierarchy, status consciousness, power distance and low individualism. These values have helped to strengthen hierarchical superior–subordinate relationships which act as a kind of mechanism of social control on the managed. Studies have shown that Indian managers attribute high priority to the importance of cultural assumptions which guide their employees' perceptions and organizational thinking. It is also revealed that the common Indian values, norms of behavior and customs exercise considerable influence on their HRM policies and practices (Budhwar, 2001).

The Indian social and cultural environment puts primacy on strong family ties that dilute individualism, resulting in greater dependence on others. This highlights the importance of interpersonal relations in people management in India, more than the importance given to it in other societies. The core bases of the management system in social and family relationships may then be attributed to various factors, including a strong caste system, an agrarian-based society, a high incidence of illiteracy, poverty and an indifference of the state system to the needs of the individual (Budhwar, 1999).

Kanungo and Mendonca (1994) have shown significant cultural differences between India and western countries on the basis of Hofstede's (1991) four initial dimensions of power distance, uncertainty avoidance, individualism and masculinity. India stands relatively high on uncertainty avoidance and power distance and relatively low on individualism and masculinity dimensions. Relatively high uncertainty avoidance implies an unwillingness to take risks and to accept organizational change. The relative low individualism implies that family and group attainments take precedence over work outcomes (Sharma, 1984). The relative high power distance implies that managers and subordinates accept their relative positions in the organizational hierarchy and operate from these fixed positions. Obedience is facilitated by the supposedly superior authority of the position holder and not by any rational basis. This is simplyis simply by virtue of the authority inherent in that status. The relative low masculinity implies that employees' orientation is towards personalized relationships rather than towards performance (Kanungo and Mendonca, 1994: 450). On the fifth dimension of long-term versus short-term orientation, traditionally, India is known as a long-term oriented nation (see Tripathi, 1990). However, results of a recent research (see Budhwar and Sparrow, 2002b) suggest that, due to the severe pressure created by the recent liberalization of economic policies and the presence of foreign operators in Indian organizations, the question of immediate survival has become more important. This explains a recent shift of emphasis towards short-termism. However, one should be cautious in generalizing any such analysis.

Nevertheless, on the same lines as the above analysis, other researchers (see, for example, Sharma, 1984; Tayeb, 1987; Sinha and Kanungo, 1997) report that, on average, Indians resist change, hesitate to delegate or even accept authority, are fearful of taking an independent decision, are possessive towards their inferiors and frequently surrender to their superiors. A possible explanation for such behavior can be traced to the long imperialist history of India. Similarly, the traditional hierarchical social structure of India has always emphasized respect for superiors, who can be elders, teachers or superiors at work, i.e. the nature of Hinduism evidenced by the caste and social system (Sahay and Walsham, 1997; Budhwar *et al.*, 2000).

From the above discussion, it may be deduced that the Indian societal culture has made a lasting impact on most management functions such as staffing, communication, leadership, motivation and control. Staffing for top managerial positions among Indian organizations (especially in the private sector) is generally restricted by familial, communal and political considerations. Authority in Indian organizations is likely to remain one-sided, with subordinates leaning heavily on their superiors for advice and directions. Motivational tools in the Indian organizations are more likely to be social, interpersonal and even spiritual (see Sparrow and Budhwar, 1997).

## National institutions supporting industrial relations

The hallmark of the Indian IR law is massive state presence through the Industrial Disputes Act 1947 (IDA). This Act empowers the "appropriate government," in its discretion, to refer an industrial dispute for adjudication either on failure of conciliation or even without any resort to conciliation. Apart from the IDA, two other laws form part of the IR law in the country: the Trade Unions Act 1926 (TUA) and the Industrial Employment (Standing Orders) Act 1946 (IESOA). While the former confers on workers and unions freedom of association and immunity against civil and criminal liability for taking industrial action, the latter seeks to ensure standardization of the terms of employment and their certification by a government officer, who is obliged to satisfy himself that they are just and fair. These sets of laws were intended to facilitate the realization of individual and collective rights of workers.

Promoting industrial peace with social justice has projectedly guided the IR policy of the government. Towards this end, apart from the legal framework, the central government has effectively used an institution called consultative tripartite conference – otherwise known as the Indian Labor Conference – consisting of representatives of employers, labor and government, whose meetings have been held annually since 1940. One of the most notable non-legislative initiatives in IR came from the government in 1958 as a result of the deliberations at this forum in the form of the Code of Discipline and the Joint Management Councils. These instruments were to be used as a formal basis for recognition of unions and collective bargaining. However, the impact of these bodies was merely transitory (Johri, 1998: 49). Legal means and interventions continued to dominate the IR policy in the country.

By conferring the working-class rights and individual labor rights, these laws, along with others, created working-class consciousness in the country. They led to a situation of clash between workers' aspirations and employers' willingness to grant benefits. Being a labor-surplus economy, the country's labor market realities helped the employers to obtain cheap labor and violate minimum labor employment standards by colluding with the labor bureaucracy. But the IDA model – which could not be replaced or even diluted despite a 55-year debate on its fate – substantially diluted collective labor rights by ensuring massive state presence in IR to control labor power. It resulted in juridification of IR (Saini, 1997, 1999b). Its influence has been so strong that arbitration as a method of industrial disputes resolution is almost dead. Employers manage IR, among others, by diluting the efficacy of labor laws through consultation as well as adoption of extra-legal means. Variegated unfair labor practices (ULPs) are committed by them in the process. Over the years the pressure of unions, opposition parties and other pressure groups, and union federations have succeeded in influencing the state agencies to enact a large number of labor laws. One finds the situation paradoxical and perplexing. On paper, even industries which have become sick beyond hope are required to comply with these laws, including payment of minimum wages and minimum bonuses. In reality the system works such that employers have learnt to get away with these legal requirements. However, MNCs and other conscientious employers want an IR framework with simpler laws that do not require them to indulge in maneuverings and shenanigans. The IR law framework in larger organizations adversely affects the cause of forging workplace cooperation so as to meet the challenges of HRM in responding to the changed needs of industry in the era of globalization.

## Unions

Being a democracy, India has at least aleast a seemingly union-friendly legal framework of IR. Despite that, unionization rate has rarely exceeded 10 percent of the total working population in all sectors. Today this rate is believed to have slipped to around 7 percent. The compulsory adjudication system of the IDA has kept the unions weak (Saini, 1995, 1999b). The first two decades after the independence witnessed rapid unionization of the organized sector in the country (both private and public). But unionization in India started declining after the famous Bombay Textile Strike which lasted more than a year and has not been officially withdrawn until today (Venkata Ratnam, 2001). This has brought a sea change in the concept of collective bargaining, which is less and less on industry basis and more on unit basis (*Business India*, 1998).

Membership of unions that are submitting returns is still low; as per the latest estimates it is barely 2 percent of the total workforce. Over 47,000 unions have a membership of 6,329,000. As per the latest available statistics, the number of members covered by collective agreements in the country is barely 1 percent of the total workforce (Mishra, 2001: 20). This is in spite of the fact that in the 1970s and 1980s the judiciary delivered several judgments in the area of industrial relations and labor laws which reflected its attitude of extreme sympathy with the working people, less to the basic principles of industrial organization.

However, in the present economic environment the existing legal framework is required to change its strong pro-labor stance. Early indications are positive in this regard. Lately, some of the recent labor judgments reflect the belief that the judiciary is more sympathetic to the employers and realizes their susceptibilities in the new environment. As noted above, the incidence of unionism is also declining. The number of strikes resorted to is much less than the lockouts (*Business India*, 1998; Mishra, 2001). This has also reduced workers' resistance to change to the new initiatives of HRM, despite patches of working-class success in resisting the individualization of IR through HRM (Ramaswamy, 2000: 219). Interestingly, in contrast to national firms, the impact of unions on the HRM policies and practices of MNCs operating in India is negligible (see Budhwar and Björkman, 2003). On the other hand, unions still significantly influence HRM policies and practices in Indian organizations. However, their stance is slowly changing and becoming more cooperative towards their employers.

The liberalization of the Indian economy has then put tremendous pressure both on the employees and employers. As a nation, India is lagging far behind in productivity standards and production of quality goods. These realities have begun influencing the mindsets of unions and union leaders who now seem to be meekly giving in to the legitimacy of the globalization agenda, as they are aware of these burning problems. Employees both in public as well as private sectors suffer from attitudinal indifference towards professionalism in work. Overall, one notices a lack of vision of being world class in India; this is largely true of government agencies as well as employers (Prahlad, 1998; Ghoshal *et al.*, 2001). In such circumstances, the possible consequence of the adoption of appropriate HRM policies will be salutary. They will lead to minimum wastage of human and financial resources at the micro level. Their adoption will also give due importance to "innovation, bench-marking, and organizing business and professional activities as per market exigencies" (Saini, 1999b: 166). But, values of "association," "industrial justice," "workers' dignity" will face crisis; "minimum standards of employment" are also becoming clouded due to the unofficial support of the state to cost-cutting preferences of employers that is hidden in the globalization agenda. But being a democracy the country cannot openly adopt policies that disapprove of these IR values.

Diluting "workplace pluralism" as a value by superimposing HRM on it may work successfully if we have a significant chunk of workforce as gold-collared. The merger of the HRM and IR agenda many possibly work effectively in such a situation. If that happens, one may also forecast greater possibility of the use of HRM as a broad model of workplace justice. Some of the best examples in this regard are the software companies in the country, which have used HRM as a model of workplace justice, which automatically keeps the law and adversarialism away. The viability of the use of soft HRM as the principal philosophy in managing human resources increases in the case of such companies which employ knowledge workers. However, without question this will be too much to ask of national firms which do not have knowledge workers. Nevertheless, to a great extent this is successfully practiced in MNCs operating in India, irrespective of having knowledge or non-knowledge-based employees (see Budhwar and Björkman, 2003). It needs a macro level of overhauling of the Indian HRM system, which seems to have been initiated due to the pressure created by new economic environment on local firms (Ghoshal *et al.*, 2001). Still, India has a long way to go in this direction.

Judging by the way the Indian government has reacted to the situation, the continuance of its sympathy to the cause of social justice in the organized sector appears only remote. This is despite the fact that there has been no labor law reform at all in the post-liberalization era. This may appear surprising to the champions of globalization. But principally, governments' unwillingness to effect labor reforms in the past decade or so is largely explained by their fragility at the central level; they have not shown the courage to antagonize the trade unions openly by undertaking these reforms. Interesting, as it may appear, most employers have been able to manage the show despite the archaic laws. However, there is always a limit to everything, including the regulatory laws for workplace functioning.

At the executive level, state governments' attitudes are changing. Many of them have announced far-reaching changes in their labor policies, which henceforth appear to be helpful and in favor of the workers. Now they tacitly support hire and fire policies, forbidding *bandhs* (stoppages), as happened in the case of Kerala, and easing of requirements for labor inspection, for example, in Rajasthan. West Bengal government (which is headed by a Marxist party) has cancelled registration of hundreds of unions for non-submission of returns to the Registrar of Trade Unions, which is contrary to its earlier position. The incidence of granting permission for closure and retrenchment (as required under the IDA) in Tamil Nadu has gone up (Venkata Ratnam, 2001).

## Workers' participation in management

Another important area of contention in IR is workers' participation in management. Today we have virtually no meaningful participation structures through law, except the works committees under the IDA, which are not fully functional (Saini, 1997). However, the Workers Participation in Management Bill 1990 is pending before the *Rajya Sabha* (upper house of Parliament). The bill is still under consideration of the Parliamentary Select Committee on Labour and Welfare (Government of India, 2002: 22). This bill seeks to give substantial voice to employees in management, but it is unlikely that, given the changed priorities of the state, it will finally be enacted, despite the fact that the bill has recently been approved by the Cabinet Committee of the Government of India; and the present Labor Minister has shown his commitment to the cause of ensuring employee participation in industry through law. A debate on the bill is current among the social partners. Analysts, however, opine that this is a mere election gimmick as parliamentary elections are due in early 2004. One problem with granting such rights at this phase of economic development is that these efforts will exacerbate building of participation rights on the edifice of adversarial values, which in any case are at a low ebb almost everywhere. Despite such fleeting glimpses of state-sponsored attempts to help rejuvenate working-class rights, one may observe an ambience of well-recognized concerns for improving efficiency and productivity through HRM. The social goals of "association," "social justice" and "participation" are likely to remain subjugated, for they are not in tune with employers' needs for flexibility and autonomy. Workers involvement as an HRM strategy, however, is at a much higher level in foreign firms operating in India (see Budhwar and Björkman, 2003). However, employee involvement interventions are not built on adversarial foundations or any legal sanctions. Rather, they are viewed as part of an organization's voluntary efforts towards promoting commitment and performance culture, and also its unitarist goals. Such unitarism is inherent in HRM philosophy. The rationale of the "involvement" interventions is rooted in Japanization, which is increasingly becoming attractive for western organizations and for those who want to follow western HRM practices in other locales.

## Urgency of IR reforms

The above developments in Indian IR augur fairly well for developing HRM; for it is difficult to sustain it in situations of zero-sum IR; this is especially important when India's HR systems and processes have to be conducive to facilitating efficiency and productivity, and eventually the export-promotion model of development. But the government's support may be said to be forthcoming indirectly, i.e. by remaining oblivious to the legal intent. The question is whether this is enough for the country's needs to attract higher levels of FDI. MNCs and other professional establishments need more tangible ways of state support, including having the changed legal framework itself. Intriguingly, it should be appreciated that one way of tackling the problem of flexibility at the micro level is the effective adoption of HRM. It has been used even alongside unions in many organizations including Reliance and Tata Steel (see Ghoshal *et al.*, 2001). This latter has nearly 50,000 workers and has downsized by some 20,000 in the past few years. But most other organizations are unable to follow this. The need for reforms in IR law for it to be facilitative to the globalization policies then remains paramount.

## The labor law framework

India has a widespread network of labor laws which are believed to be too rigid. Due to this, wages do not necessarily respond to unemployment and productivity. Globalization warrants that areas are identified that require attention for infusing greater flexibility in the formal labor market; labor law is one such area. A large percentage of Indian managers (61.5 percent) have been found to believe that Indian national labor laws influence their HRM practices the most, for their actions and prerogatives are constricted by these laws (Budhwar, 2001: 82).

Today there are over 60 major central labor laws and about 150 state labor laws in India. All these laws may be grouped into five major categories: laws relating to working conditions; laws relating to wages and monetary benefits; laws relating to industrial relations; laws relating to social security; and miscellaneous labor laws. Some of the major central labor laws are as follows:

- Apprentices Act 1961
- Beedi and Cigar Workers (Conditions of Employment) Act 1966
- Bonded Labor System (Abolition) Act 1976
- Building and Other Construction Workers (Regulation of Employment Service) Act 1996
- Child Labor (Prohibition and Regulation) Act 1986
- Cine-Workers and Cinema Theatre Workers (Regulation of Employment) Act 1981
- Contract Labor (Regulation and Abolition) Act 1970
- Dangerous Machines (Regulation) Act 1983
- Dock Workers (Regulation of Employment) Act 1948
- Dock Workers (Safety, Health and Welfare) Act 1986
- Emigration Act 1983
- Employees' Provident Fund and Miscellaneous Provisions Act 1952
- Employees' State Insurance Act 1948
- Employers' Liability Act 1938
- Employment Exchanges (Compulsory Notification of Vacancies) Act 1959
- Equal Remuneration Act 1976
- Factories Act 1948
- Industrial Disputes Act 1947
- Industrial Employment (Standing Orders) Act 1946
- Inter-State Migrant Workmen (Regulation of Employment and Conditions of Service) Act 1979
- Labor Laws (Exemption from Furnishing Returns and Maintaining Registers by Certain Establishments) Act 1988
- Maternity Benefit Act 1961
- Mines Act 1952
- Minimum Wages Act 1948
- Motor Transport Workers Act 1961
- National Commission for Safai Karamcharis Act 1993

- Payment of Bonus Act 1965
- Payment of Gratuity Act 1972
- Payment of Wages Act 1936
- Plantations Labor Act 1951
- Public Liability Insurance Act 1991
- Sales Promotion Employees (Conditions of Service) Act 1976
- Trade Union Act 1926
- Weekly Holidays Act 1948
- Workmen's Compensation Act 1923

While labor laws are a necessary area of the focus of public policy in any enlightened society, they have to change with time. Some of the major points about the structure and working of Indian labor laws are discussed below.

1  The most problematic part in this regard is that some aspects of IR law are quite anti-thetical to the needs of globalization. Among others, the Industrial Disputes Act 1947 (IDA) has become the biggest epitome of rigidity in IR in the country. Chapter V-B of this Act requires all employers employing 100 or more workers in factories, mines and plantations to seek permission from the government in matters of lay-off, retrenchment and closure. The chapter gives bureaucratic discretion, which has often been exercised not at all or on extraneous factors. There have been cases of perennially sick establishments which have not been allowed to close or retrench excess labor force on extraneous considerations. The present government has proclaimed its commitment to increase the limit of 100 workers to 1,000 for the purpose of this chapter (V-B), but had to retreat twice under the pressure of its trade union wing, i.e. the Bhartiya Mazdoor Sangh (BMS), which today is the largest trade union federation in the country. Likewise, there are problems with section 9-A of the IDA, which requires that a notice of 21 days should be given by the employer for effecting change in any service conditions of workers. This section has also resulted in workers' resistance to the flexibility needs of the employers in this regard. The IDA also gives tremendous powers to the state to intervene in labor–management relations which produces their "juridification" (Saini, 1999b) and consequently adversarialism, thus diluting the goals of HRM (Saini, 2000).

2  The Industrial Employment (Standing Orders) Act 1946 (IESOA), an important IR law, is proving to be problematic. Among others, it provides for uniformity in service conditions of all workers who are similarly placed. This is not quite in consonance with the current needs of industry where employers want to implement performance management principles and introduce new measures which discriminate between employees as per their competencies and/or performance.

3  The Contract Labor (Regulation and Abolition) Act 1970 (CLA) is another law whose structural features are being debated in academic and management circles. This law makes it very difficult to employ contract labor in permanent operations as it provides for abolition of contract labor in certain areas of employment specified by the central government. To the extent that this Act provides for regulating the service conditions of contract workers to make them reasonable, it is a welcome piece of legislation. It is

well known that contract labor is highly exploited by contractors who do not observe minimum labor standards in their employment. Often, they are even denied minimum wages, appointment letters, identity cards, etc. (Shrouti and Nandkumar, 1994: 22). They work longer hours, are virtually denied provision of any social security benefit like protection under Employees' State Insurance (ESI) and provident fund (PF) laws. The recommendations of the second NCL (2002) will be disappointing to employers in this regard; for it has recommended continuance of provisions related to prohibition of contract labor in core activities. The commission has further recommended that if contract labor has to be temporarily employed in core activities, it must be remunerated at the rate of a regular worker engaged in the same organization doing work of a similar nature. This move is being vehemently resisted by the employers.

4  The existing labor laws have different applicability in terms of industries and employees covered. Also, different sets of administrative mechanisms and dispute-resolving quasi-judicial bodies have been envisaged under various acts. For example, the definition of a worker is different under the IDA and the Factories Act. The term "wages" has been differently defined under different acts. Some laws cover employees receiving monthly wages as low as rupees 1,600 per month (e.g. the Payment of Wages Act, 1936); others cover even clerical and administrative employees (e.g. the Employees' State Insurance Act 1948; the Provident Fund Act, 1952; the Gratuity Act 1972); for some there is no wage limit for coverage (e.g. highly paid pilots are workmen under the IDA). A plethora of case law has been delivered by the judiciary to clarify these complexities in variegated situations. This has made the grasping of labor laws a very complex affair (for a detailed discussion, see Debroy, 1996). In fact, labor law complexity has converted union leaders into full time pleaders, who have set up labor law practice as a vocation (Saini, 1995a).

5  Keeping in mind the ambiguities involved, harmonization and unification of labor laws is an important area of reform. However, almost no serious efforts are being made to tackle this precarious situation. The National Labor Law Association (NLLA, 1994) came out with a proposal to enact a National Labor Code 1994 (draft), which should be a laudable effort so far as its unification agenda is concerned. But if one looks at its contents it has tried to take labor relations back to the welfare state era, which was not acceptable to the government as well as the employers. Hence, this proposed code stands shelved.

These are some of the critical issues in labor law reform which have to be addressed by the state as well as other stakeholders to facilitate shifting of labor–management relations assumptions from confrontational to cooperative mode.

## Vocational education and training

Vocational education and training in India are divided into two subsystems. At the central (federal) level, while the vocational education is under the control of the Ministry of HRD, vocational training is basically regulated by the Ministry of Labor. Partly, the former ministry also exercises some control even in matters of training. Further, some 35 ministries of the central government are involved in providing and supporting some kind of training in their respective areas of operations (Saini, 2003). Vocational education is provided at the senior secondary stage in schools. This is over and above engineering, management and other technical education that takes place under the overall supervision of the University Grants Commission (UGC) and the All India Council of Technical Education (AICTE), both of which are central statutory bodies. State governments also exercise control in matters of accreditation of education at the engineering diploma level. Among the specialized vocational training institutions, more than 4,000 industrial training institutes (ITIs) are being run today; of these, 1,654 are run by government and 2,620 are run privately. Altogether, they have a training capacity of 750,000 students (Saini, 2003). Apart from these, the Apprentices Act 1961 has been applied to some notified industries. The Act obliges the employers covered under the Act to engage apprentices in certain predetermined trades as well as those holding degrees and diplomas as per specified ratio. This scheme, however, is working much below the projected capacity, for want of proper enforcement. Various government ministries and NGOs are running vocational training schemes for the informal sector. Apart from these, companies in public and private sectors are also involved in providing skills training and their upgradation. In the "Best 25 Employers in India" survey of 2002 conducted by Hewitt Associates, the average annual training hours in these organizations range from 24 to 120 (these hours are 24 in Indian Oil Corporation, a public sector organization, 47 in Infosys Technologies, 60 in Reddy's Laboratories, 64 in Smithkline Beecham, 86 in Tata Steel, 95 in Reliance, 71 in Tata Engineering, and 120 in LG Electronics).

After the initiation of economic reforms, the issue of skill upgradation and development has assumed critical significance in enabling the Indian economy to enhance its competitive strength. The export promotion model puts a much higher level of primacy on these issues than did the model of import substitution adopted earlier. Productivity, exports and economic growth depend on the quality of technical education and training imparted apart from programs of promoting attitudinal change and process sensitivity among employees. The performance of the existing system of state-regulated vocational training in the country is far from satisfactory (Adams and Krishnan, 2003). India has lost a valuable opportunity of occupation-based knowledge and skills in a more systematic manner at a very crucial stage of its economic development; interestingly, countries such as Singapore have been far more successful in developing competitive performance through enforcing comprehensive needs-driven schemes of skill development (Debrah *et al.*, 2000).

It should be understood that for a country of India's size and economic profile it is utopian to expect miraculous poverty-alleviation results merely through the promotion of organized industrial development. The complexity of the problem requires concerted efforts for ensuring a more meaningful vocational training system for the unorganized (including the informal) sector which employs 92 percent or more of the Indian workforce. Of course, even industry is far from happy about the availability of requisite skills for the organized sector, and a better skill development system is needed for the organized sector as well.

It is noticeable that private training-provider institutions have been able to grow with a good degree of effectiveness and have some remarkable success stories (Adams and Krishnan, 2003). The government-run ITIs, on the other hand, are functioning under several constraints and this should be kept in mind while planning for effective training strategies. A recent workshop on problems of delivering effective training in the country identified the following factors as critical, most of which were found wanting in the present training implementation framework: autonomy (operational, financial), quality of skills delivery, dedication of staff, holistic approach, focus on specific target groups and skills, freedom of admission and staff policy, effective management, adequate fees, employability of skills, marketability of products, capacity building of providers, networking, needs assessment, local resource base, and scientific support in training and technology design. It emphasized focus on soft skills apart from technical and job skills. From the self-employment perspective, aspects such as latest technology, bookkeeping, and market practices were identified as focus areas (Adams and Krishnan, 2003).

As discussed above, the original idea of the setting up of the National Renewal Fund (NRF) in July 1991 NEP was an important step in providing a social safety net to labor affected by the globalization policies. The fund was to be utilized, among other things, for imparting training as a key plank for facilitating the reforms process. But in its actual working, its focus remained confined to funding the Voluntary Retirement Scheme (VRS) as a means of retrenching public sector employee's, consequent to the downsizing program of the government (Mishra, 2001). There is then a need to develop a skill-agenda at the macro level that involves professionally organized programs, duly funded by suitable agencies. The second NCL (Government of India, 2002) has emphasized the need for a modular approach in designing and imparting vocational training so that the individual aspirants receive inter-related multiple skills eventually to contribute to enterprise flexibility. This will help keep pace with the fast-changing technologies based on computerization and the IT revolution. The commission also emphasized a competency-based training system to provide avenues for competence assessment and certification at all levels of learning. This approach underscores developing specified competencies rather than the length of training time.

To operationalize these ideas, the commission has recommended the setting up of an independent regulatory authority. This body is intended to set standards of competence to be achieved at different levels of each trade. The government is collaborating with GTZ (an agency of the German government) to design a suitable law that will facilitate training as per the peculiar social and economic needs in the country. A law is soon expected to be introduced in Parliament to this effect under the name of the All India Authority of Vocational Training Act (AIAVT). This legislation is being designed to overcome various existing arrangements. If enacted, it will help reorient the existing ITI system to changing technological requirements. It is also expected to be an experience in professional excellence in the governance structure of the vocational training system in the country (for salient features of this proposed law, see Saini, 2003). However, it has been rightly emphasized that these efforts can be successful if they are well-knit and dovetailed in an appropriate "macroeconomic policy to maintain adequate aggregate demand and pace of economic growth, specifically in the non-agricultural sector" (Mathur, 2002: 17). This is one of the main challenges for HRD at the macro level that the country faces today. It remains to be seen whether the government is able to deviate from the past and show the requisite political sagacity in developing a workable skill-development agenda to facilitate the globalization process as well as poverty alleviation. The need of the hour is the government's commitment to a demand-driven, flexible and need-based training program guided by a professional rather than rule-based approach.

## Shifting agenda in the twenty-first century: possible directions for HRM in India

In the present competitive business environment the Indian HR function faces a large number of challenges as already discussed. To survive and flourish in the new dispensation, drastic changes are required at the national, organizational and individual levels. Some of these seem to be taking place, though possibly not with the required rigor and not quite in the right direction. One serious problem while making such judgments and analyses is the availability of reliable empirical research evidence.

## The national level

The previous section highlighted some of the main national factors which significantly influence HRM in India (see also Budhwar and Sparrow, 1998, 2002a). Early indications suggest that the nature and accordingly the impact of most of the national factors (especially different institutions such as trade unions, legal framework, different pressure groups and the dynamic business environment) on Indian HRM is going to change. The legislations have to be amended so as to suit the present economic environment and help both workers and employers in the "real" sense. The stance of the unions is expected to become more cooperative. The dynamic business environment is further going to dictate the nature and type of HRM systems suitable for the country. With the rapid developments in the software and IT-enabled services (ITeS) sector and an increased emphasis on business process outsourcing (BPO), one may expect the emergence of sector-specific HRM patterns. For example, this will be the case for knowledge-based industries such as software and contact centers (see Budhwar and Singh, 2003).

# The organizational level

At the organizational level the following is expected.

## *A strategic approach to HRM*

Research evidence (see Budhwar and Sparrow, 1997, 2002b; Budhwar and Khatri, 2001) regarding the strategic nature of HRM in Indian national firms suggests that there is a low representation of the personnel function at board level, and few organizations have devised formal corporate strategies. Of these, a handful seem to consult the personnel function at the outset (this compares to a norm of around 50 percent in European organizations), many involve personnel in early consultation while developing corporate strategy and many also involve personnel during the implementation of that strategy. It seems that the status of the personnel function in India has improved over a short span of 10 years or so. The number of personnel specialists moving to the position of CEO has increased over the last few years, such that one out of every six CEOs of the top fifty Indian companies has been reported as a personnel specialist (Venkata Ratnam, 1996). On the other hand, it seems that Indian firms are witnessing a significant devolvement of responsibility of HRM to line managers. This is noticeable in the areas of pay determination, recruitment, training, industrial relations, health and safety and expansion/reduction decisions. Moreover, Indian firms have been showing an increased emphasis on training and development of HR (see Budhwar and Sparrow, 2002b). However, if a strategy of devolvement is not associated with a closer integration of HRM into the business planning processes, it may create a situation of chaos in organizations as they attempt to cope with HRM implications of liberalization. Hence, the way forward is the adoption of a more strategic approach to HRM. Perhaps this agenda is already on the move and is being put into practice (see Agarwala, 2003; Singh, 2003). Certainly, this is the case with the MNCs operating in the country (see Budhwar and Björkman, 2003).

## *Structured and rationalized internal labor markets (ILMs)*

The existing literature suggests the existence of unique ILMs in Indian organizations, based on social relations, political affiliations, political contacts, caste, religion and economic power (see Budhwar and Khatri, 2001). However, considering the present dynamic business environment, Indian organizations need to pursue more rationalized HRM practices and build strong ILMs (which should solely emphasize performance and be less influenced by the aforementioned social, economic, religious and political factors). There are some indications regarding such developments (in the form of increased emphasis on training and development, preference for talent in the recruitment and performance-based compensation), however, these tend to be more in the MNCs or the private sector. Globalization dynamics require that there is a need to speed up merit- and performance-based decision-making in all sectors.

## *Open to change, sharing and learning*

In the present competitive business environment, radical changes are taking place and it is difficult to keep track of many such changes. The new economic environment, although presenting a number of threats to local firms, also offers many opportunities to learn, collaborate and adapt to the new context. To make the best use of existing conditions, Indian firms need to be flexible and demonstrate readiness to change. Regular interaction with competitors and relevant stakeholders is becoming a necessity in the modern networked organizations. In this regard, much may be learnt from HR managers working in MNCs operating in India who are very open and flexible in their approach to managing human resources. For example, a recent research investigation with sixty-five top HR managers in as many foreign firms operating in India (see Budhwar and Björkman, 2003) reported that local firms are more rigid to change, less transparent in their operations, provide less learning opportunities and operate on traditional ILMs. However, the HR managers also perceived that the scenario is rapidly changing and such a gap between the working of MNCs and local firms is going to decrease in future. This should be one of the main agenda for Indian firms. The liberalization of economic policies, globalization realities and the operating practices of foreign firms will all put pressure on Indian firms for a more professional performance. The increasing number of Indian students graduating from the developed countries and going back to India will also contribute a great deal towards resorting to a greater degree of professionalism by visionary Indian firms.

## *Crossvergence of HRM*

With the arrival of a very large number of MNCs to India one may expect an active mixing-up of different management systems (such as the Japanese or American way of doing things). In such conditions, there will be a greater possibility of standardization of managerial roles across different firms. This is an outcome of the globalization exigencies (see Debrah and Smith, 2002) or some kind of *crossvergence*, i.e. blending of work cultures (due to the active interface of diverse groups), that is taking place in India (see Ralston *et al.*, 1993; Gopalan and Stahl, 1998). Hence, one may expect cultural convergence and overlap among different types of firms operating in the country. Already, Japanese and many American firms operating in India are able to adopt their respective HR practices in their operations with minor modifications (see Budhwar and Björkman, 2003).

## The individual level

Many Indian educational institutions (such as the Indian Institute of Management and Indian Institute of Technology) are known to be producing world-class graduates. Considering the rapidly changing business environment and the emergence of a large number of MNCs in the country, a paradigm shift in the mindsets of individuals is evident. For example, tendencies for a strong preference to work in a reputed public sector organization, lifelong employment, making available only limited jobs for females, and so on, are all changing fast. The Indian worker has either preferred for a secured employment in the sluggish public sector or has been hostile to the exploitative practices of the family-run private enterprises. The HRM policies of the foreign companies have exercised considerable power in influencing this scenario. For example, the professional customer handling by the Citibank has been positively influencing the public sector banks in the country that now have to operate in a competitive environment. The Indian managers view these practices as benchmarks. Further, most foreign firms and an ever-larger number of local firms emphasize the need to attract talent. They are increasingly adopting formal, structured and rational approaches to attract, acquire and retain talent. This has significantly influenced the behavior both at the individual and organizational levels. The opportunities provided by the new sectors such as software, contact centers and ITeS on the one hand and the MNCs on the other have encouraged females to come and join the mainstream workforce. Such developments are expected to continue and will eventually help transform the adoption of HRM practices in the country.

## Conclusion

This chapter highlighted the state of people-management policies and practices in India and their roots in the country's historical background, environmental framework, institutions, contexts and styles. The analysis shows that there is remarkable progress in the professionalization of HRM in the organized sector; this is happening despite the tendency towards a shrinking percentage of the organized sector employment in the country. Attempts towards greater professionalism may be attributed partly to the progressive policies brought about and pursued by the MNCs and the professionally managed Indian organizations, including some of the public sector enterprises (see, for example, Prasad, 1996; Uppal and Singh, 2001). The attitude towards business practice in general is changing, and people are realizing how far they need to change so as to cope. Among others, the key problems that have adversely influenced the management of HR in India include lack of a vision for skill and competency development, the rigidity caused by the labor law framework, the hierarchy-driven mindsets of employers, the government's indecisiveness in matters of privatization and dis-investment, and fragility of political coalitions that adversely affect the need to take bold decisions.

Another important factor affecting the HRM policies is the deceleration in the employment growth in the organized sector and the massive underemployment in a labor surplus economy. This increases the power of employers, and enables them to shape their HR strategies towards cost reduction. Thus a greater reliance may be placed on employment of peripheral than core employees. With the weakening of the employee power, the HRM practices *vis-à-vis* this section of employees are bound to reflect hard devices including the resort to lower minimum standards of employment and commission of unfair labor practices (ULPs).

It is noticeable that the role of HRM managers is transforming from being the child of the Industrial Disputes Act to being responsible for culture building, communication, change management, performance management and measuring effectiveness of HR systems and interventions. Within the organized sector, however, the HRM practices are quite varied depending upon a diverse factors. The majority of management schools, however, have not yet responded to the challenges of the new environment in terms of evolving appropriate courses, even as the professionals have responded well to the challenges by using the most modern interventions. A shift is noticeable in the attitude of the government, from dispensing social justice to ensuring the success of the export-promotion model of development. Interestingly, this has been possible to quite an extent despite the rigid labor law framework, for it is the governmental power which activates that framework. A rapidly growing industry of HR professionals has emerged, which is increasingly becoming sensitive to the needs of aligning HRM with business needs and strategies. Apart from the strategic performance of the traditional HR functions, new transformational themes are being identified (Saini, 2000; Varkky *et al.*, 2001). These, among others, include concepts like "People Capability Maturity Model," work–life balance, diversity management, six sigma and strategic leadership.

Some of the key challenges before the Indian state include the success of the second generation economic reforms which involve changing the legal framework, including streamlining the working of the unorganized sector and providing a workable model of competency and skill development at the national level. It will be interesting to see how the new government, after the forthcoming 2004 elections, responds to the demands of this task, which has been on the reform agenda for more than a decade. Once the reforms in this sector take place, the matured HR professionals industry in the country is growing fast enough to respond to the emergent organizational justice issues, especially in professionally managed organizations. With the passage of time the number of such organizations is bound to increase. An era of people management issues being guided by appropriately carved-out HRM policies and practices is foreseeable, and the hitherto adversarial model of employee justice dispensation promoted by the present legal framework is likely to become weakened over time.

As noted earlier, Hofstede (1991) has attributed moderate uncertainty avoidance and power distance to Indian business configurations. This tends to defy initiative and thus proves counter to creativity. If HRM function grows fast it can help alter these cultural realities as well. Many MNCs are practicing progressisive HRM practices in their Indian locales, which will help foster transparency and creativity to be benchmarked by progressive Indian organizations. For example, delayering has taken place in Indian organizations such as ICICI. In many Indian organizations bosses are being addressed by first name. Undoubtedly, however, internalizing soft HR as a way of organizational life is a complex task and one must refrain from indulging in platitudinous exhortations in this regard. Creating world-class competitors is an uphill task. It necessitates building "transaction governance capacity" (TCG) and requires that the economy upgrades itself (Prahlad, 1998). MNCs have multiple options and the country needs tremendous investment in capacity-building to attract them. They will also contribute towards a faster dawn of the era of soft HRM as a way of organizational life that will help expedite the realization of the goals of efficiency, productivity, trickle-down effect and economic prosperity.

# References

Adams, S. and Krishnan, P. (2003) "Documentation of the consultative workshop on the project SCEC" under the program: Restructuring and Strengthening the National Vocational Training System (NVTS). Proceeding of a two-day workshop organized by GTZ (Germany) and DGET, Ministry of Labour, Government of India, India International Centre, New Delhi, 16–17 January 2003.

Agarwala, T. (2003) "Innovative human resource practices and organizational commitment: An empirical investigation," *International Journal of Human Resource Management* 14: 175–198.

Amba-Rao. S. (1994) "US HRM principles: Cross-country comparisons and two case applications in India," *International Journal of Human Resource Management* 5 (3): 755–778.

Balasubramanian, A.G. (1994) "Evolution of personnel function in India – A re-examination, Part 1," *Management and Labour Studies* 19 (4): 196–210.

Balasubramanian, A.G. (1995) "Evolution of personnel function in India – A re-examination, Part II," *Management and Labour Studies* 20 (1): 5–14.

Budhwar, P. (1998) "Comparative human resource management: A cross-national study of India and Britain," Ph.D. Dissertation, Manchester Business School, Manchester.

Budhwar, P. (1999) "Indian management style and HRM" in M. Tayaeb (ed.) *International business text*, London: Pitman, pp. 534–540.

Budhwar, P. (2000) "Factors influencing HRM policies and practices in India: An empirical study," *Global Business Review* 1 (2): 229–247.

Budhwar, P. (2001) "Human resource management in India" in P.S. Budhwar and Y.A. Debrah (eds.) *Human resource management in developing countries*, London: Routledge, pp. 75–90.

Budhwar, P. (2003) "Culture and management in India," in M. Warner (ed.) *Culture and management in Asia*, London: RoutledgeCurzon, pp. 66–81.

Budhwar, P. and Björkman, I. (2003) "A corporate perspective on the management of human resources in foreign firms operating in India," *2003 International HRM Conference*, 4–6 June 2003, Limerick, Ireland.

Budhwar, P. and Khatri, N. (2001) "Comparative human resource management in Britain and India: An empirical study," *International Journal of Human Resource Management* 13 (5): 800–826.

Budhwar, P. and Singh, V. (2003) "HRM in call centres in India: An exploratory study," *2003 International HRM Conference*, 4–6 June 2003, Limerick, Ireland.

Budhwar, P. and Sparrow, P. (1997), "Evaluating levels of strategic integration and development of human resource management in India," *International Journal of Human Resource Management* 8: 476–494.

Budhwar, P. and Sparrow, P. (1998) "National factors determining Indian and British HRM practices: An empirical study," *Management International Review* 38 (special issue 2): 105–121.

Budhwar, P. and Sparrow, P. (2002a) "An integrative framework for determining cross-national human resource management practices," *Human Resource Management Review* 12 (3): 377–403.

Budhwar, P. and Sparrow, P. (2002b) "Strategic HRM through the cultural looking glass: Mapping cognitions of British and Indian HRM managers," *Organization Studies* 23 (4): 599–638.

Budhwar, L., Reeves, D. and Farrell, P. (2000) "Life goals as a function of social class and child rearing practices: A study of India," *International Journal of Inter-cultural Relations* 24: 227–245.

*Business India* (1998) "Clutching at Straws," *Business India*, March 9–22.

Datt, R. and Sundharam, K.P.M. (1999) *Indian economy*, New Delhi: S. Chand & Company Ltd.

Debrah, Y. and Smith, I. (2002) "Globalization, employment and the workplace: Diverse impacts?" in Y. Debrah and I. Smith (eds.) *Globalization, employment and the workplace*, London: Routledge, 1–23.

Debrah, Y., McGovern, I. and Budhwar, P. (2000) "Complementarity or competition: The development of human resources in a growth triangle," *International Journal of Human Resource Management* 11 (2): 314–335.

Debroy, B. (1996) "The agenda for labour market reform in India," paper presented at the International Conference on Law and Economics, Project LARGE (A project of the UNDP and National Labour Law School for the Ministry of Finance, Government of India), New Delhi, 11–13 January 1996.

Ghoshal, S., Piramal, G. and Budhiraja, S. (2001) *World class in India*, New Delhi: Penguin Books.

Gopalan, S. and Stahl, A. (1998) "Application of American management theories and practices to the Indian business environment: Understanding the impact of national culture," *American Business Review* 16 (2): 30–41.

Government of India (1931) *Report of the Royal Commission on Labour*, New Delhi: Government of India.

Government of India (1969) *Report of the National Commission on Labour* (first), New Delhi: Ministry of Labour.

Government of India (2002) *Report of the National Commission on Labour* (second), New Delhi: Ministry of Labour.

Government of India (2002) *Annual report 2001–02*, New Delhi: Ministry of Labour.

Hofstede, G. (1991) *Cultures' consequences: Software of the mind*, London: McGraw-Hill.

Hofstede, G. (1993) "Cultural constraints in management theories," *Academy of Management Executive* 7 (1): 81–93.

Johri, C.K. (1998) "INDIA" in *International encyclopedia of laws: Labour law and industrial relations* (general editor: R. Blanpain), Deventer, the Netherlands: Kluwer Law International.

Kanungo, R.N. and Mendonca, M. (1994) "Culture and performance improvement," *Productivity* 35 (3): 447–453.

Legge, K. (1995) *Human resource management: Rhetorics and realities*, London: Macmillan Press.

Mathur, A. (2002) Background paper on "Skill acquisition and the Indian labour force" presented at the consultative Workshop on Employment and Labour market Reforms in India, organized by Institute of Human Development, New Delhi, 12–13 December.

Mishra, L. (2001) *Economy and labour*, New Delhi: Manak Publications Pvt. Ltd.

Nadler, L. (1970) *Developing human resources*, Reading, MA: Addison-Wesley.

Pareek, U. and Rao, T.V. (1981) *Designing and managing human resource systems*, New Delhi: Oxford and IBH.

Prahlad, C.K. (1998) "Globalization: pitfall, pain and potential" in B. Debroy (ed.) *Challenges of Globalization*, New Delhi: Rajiv Gandhi Institute for Contemporary Studies and Konark Publishers Pvt. Ltd.

Prahlad, C.K. (1999) "The Power of imagination: India's legacy and the path to the future," *Business Today*, 22 February: 115–119.

Prasad, K. (1996) *Organizational development for organizational excellence*, New Delhi: Macmillan.

Ralston, D.A., Gustafson, D.J., Cheung, F.M. and Terpstra, R.H. (1993) "Differences in managerial values: A study of United States', Hong Kong, and PRC Managers," *Journal of International Business Studies* 24 (2): 249–275.

Ramaswamy, E.A. (1994) *The rayon spinners: The strategic management of industrial relations*, New Delhi: Oxford University Press.

Ramaswamy, E.A. (2000) *Managing human resources*, New Delhi: Oxford University Press.

Rao, T.V. (1990) *HRD missionary*, New Delhi: Oxford and IBH.

Rao, T.V. (1999) *HRD audit: Evaluating the human resource function for business improvement*, New Delhi: Response Books (a division of Sage Publications).

Sahay, S. and Walsham, G. (1997) "Social structure and managerial agency in India," *Organisation Studies* 18: 415–444.

Saini, D.S. (1995) "Compulsory adjudication syndrome in India: Some implications for workplace relations" in D.S. Saini (ed.) *Labour law, work and development: Essays in honour of P.G. Krishnan*, New Delhi: Westville.

Saini, D.S. (1995a) "Leaders or pleaders: The dynamics of brief-case trade unionism under the existing legal framework", *Journal of the Indian Law Institute* 37 (1): 73–91.

Saini, D.S. (1997) "Labour court administration in India," in ILO (ed.), *Labour adjudication in India*, New Delhi: International Labour Organization – South Asian Advisory Team.

Saini, D.S. (1999a) "Human resource management strategy and workplace pluralism," *Management and Change* 3 (1): 151–168.

Saini, D.S. (1999b) "Labour legislation and social justice," *Economic and Political Weekly* (special issue on review of Labour), xxxiv (39): L-32 to L-40, 25 September.

Saini, D.S. (2000) "Introduction" in D.S. Saini and S.A. Khan (eds.) *Human resource management: Perspectives for the new era*, New Delhi: Response Books (a division of Sage Publications).

Saini, D.S. (2003) "Alleviating poverty through skills development: Lessons for law-making in developing countries," paper presented at workshop on law and poverty V, organized by CROP programme of the International Social Science Council and the Social Science Academy of Nigeria at Abuja (Nigeria) 24–26 November 2003.

Saini, D.S. and Khan, S.A. (eds.) (2000) *Human resource management: Perspectives for the new era*, New Delhi: Response Books (a division of Sage Publications).

Sharma, I.J. (1984) "The culture context of Indian managers," *Management and Labour Studies* 9 (2): 72–80.

Shrouti, A. and N. Kumar (1994) *New economic policy, changing management strategies – impact on workers and trade unions*, New Delhi: Friedrich Ebert Stiftung.

Singh, S. (2003) "Strategic orientation and firm performance in India", *The International Journal of Human Resource Management* 14: 530–543.

Sinha, J.B.P. and Kanungo, R. (1997) "Context sensitivity and balancing in Indian organization behavior," *International Journal of Psychology* 32: 93–105.

Tayeb, M. (1987) "Contingency theory and culture: a study of matched English and the Indian manufacturing firms," *Organisation Studies* 8: 241–261.

*Times of India* (2003) "Executive digest section," *Times of India*, 10 January: 17.

Tripathi, R.C. (1990) "Interplay of values in the functioning of Indian organizations," *International Journal of Psychology* 25: 715–734.

Uppal, B. and Singh, U. (2001) "Dealing with corporate uncertainties: Mergers, acquisitions and others – SAIL, a case study," in B. Varkky *et al.* (2001). *Human resource management: Changing roles, changing goals*, New Delhi: Excel Books.

Varkky, B., Parashar, P. and Brahma, G. (2001) *Human resource management: Changing roles, changing goals*, New Delhi: Excel Books.

Venkata Ratnam, C.S. (1996) *Industrial relations in Indian states*, New Delhi: Global Business Press.

Venkat Ratnam, C.S. (2001) *Globalization and labour–management relations: Dynamics of change*, New Delhi: Response (a division of Sage Publications).

Venkata Ratnam, C.S. and Srivastava, B.K. (1991) *Personnel management and human resources*, New Delhi: Tata–McGraw-Hill Publishing Company.

Walton, J. (1999) *Strategic human resource development*, London: Financial Times–Prentice Hall.

## Useful websites

| | |
|---|---|
| National Human Resource Development Network: | http://www.hrdnetworkdelhi.com |
| Academy of Human Resource Development: | http://www.academyofhrd.org |
| Monthly Magazine on Human Resource Management (India): | http://www.humancapitalonline.com |
| All India Management Association: | http://www.aima-ind.org |
| Indian portal on Human Resource Development: | http://www.humanlinks.com |
| Human Internet: | http://www.humanresources.about.com |
| HR World: | http://www.hrworld.com |
| Executive Search Engine/Career's Search: | http://www.edgeindia.com |
| Recruitment Platform for IT Professionals: | http://www.jobcurry.com |

## 8 HRM in Thailand

SUNUNTA SIENGTHAI AND CLEMENS BECHTER

## Introduction

This chapter provides an account of the historical development of HRM, industrial relations, and personnel management in Thailand. It discusses the changes in the role and the significance of HRM from a traditional payroll function to a business partner in the business operations of a country which is still struggling to achieve a sustainable economic development. Following this, it analyzes the key factors influencing the HRM practices in Thailand. To trace the current development of HRM practices, the authors have discussed the impacts of HRM policies and practices in some sample organizations based on a questionnaire survey undertaken after the financial crisis. Then, they offer their observations of the challenges to be faced by HRM, and conclude.

## Historical development in HRM/IR/PM/personnel administration

The HRM function of firms in developing countries such as Thailand has experienced a rather slow growth and development. Until recently, most companies still had a so-called "traditional" personnel management (PM) which is only a systematic approach and basically perceived as the payroll function. In this section, the development of personnel or HRM in Thailand is described.

Studies related to personnel management issues in Thailand have not received much attention except in the area of industrial relations (IR) where government policy formulation is involved and mainly commissioned by international organizations such as the International Labor Organization (ILO). The government has not intervened at the micro level of business firms' management. Only in the case of the labor movement and labor–management conflict in deadlock does the government enter the scenario. Thai labor law somehow has not been enforced effectively in all business enterprises and thus was used more as a guideline for compliance of firms through their personnel management.

The influences of military-dominated regimes in Thailand have led to a unique pattern of HRM and development practice for more than 50 years. The use of cheap, mostly uneducated labor was a key element of comparative advantage, particularly for internal investors, and a necessity for the promotion and maintenance of an unorganized workforce, weak trade unions and dominant employer authority. This has led to hierarchy between employer and employees in the organization as observed in the public organization administration. In addition, this was also a reflection of the fact that the economy was then based substantially on the labor-intensive manufacturing activities where unskilled and semi-skilled workers were the main workforce. The adequacy of "class consciousness" among workers, bringing about reliance on rural labor, and the centrality of Buddhism to the Thai culture, the practices of "middle-path," that is, no advocation for extremity, has contributed to the unique HRM and industrial relations framework of Thailand (Siengthai, 1993).

## Public administration and public enterprise management in Thailand

The first few five-year national economic plans, which started in 1961, saw substantial government investment initiatives in developing the basic infrastructure for the country. These have become large public enterprises which generate many employment opportunities for the population. They have also become something of an outlet for the capable high government ranking officials or politicians from the dominant parties as administrators and members of the board of advisors. Most of the public enterprises have played a role as the engine of economic growth in the early years of economic development of Thailand. Although the number of public enterprises has been reduced mainly through government privatization policies, the notion of public management as opposed to traditional public administration has not been realized. However, together with the regionalization and globalization movement, organizational change and development has become the main focus of these public enterprises, especially after the financial crisis which forced the Thai government to effectively implement the privatization program in spite of the strong resistance from these state-owned enterprise labor unions. Not until foreign direct investment started to flow into the country did modern management become the more common practice. This of course was in line with the fact that many people were educated in foreign countries, particularly in the home countries of the multinational companies or joint ventures. In addition, business schools were established in the country to offer training for certificates and degrees. Thus, a supply of management-educated workforce to the demand in the business sector was sufficiently effective. Hence, even within the HRM areas, more well-trained professionals have been available in the last two decades.

## The labor movement in Thailand

On reflection, the threat by the unions has been significant since 1973 when Thailand changed its political system from militarily dominant to democratic; since then, no more *coup d'états* have happened. During 1973–1975, there were many workers' strikes; unionization was their strategy to demand change in their terms and conditions of employment. Under the military government (1958–1973), the number of strikes and workers involved started to increase, especially during the second National Economic Development Plan (1969–1974). The number of strikes substantially increased in the following five-year plan, both in terms of workers involved and man-days lost. At the time, the country was started out on labor-intensive manufacturing activities, such as textiles. Understandably, the terms and conditions of employment as well as the physical work environment were not very good. Most of the business enterprises were mainly family businesses. Employers were likely to be of Chinese origin where the management style was rather autocratic. Workers were paid minimum wages, which were barely sufficient to take care of the whole family. Thus, this led to the formation of unions to demand for changes in the employment contract. The impact of the unions using industrial weapons such as strikes led to the necessity for a firm to have a formal personnel manager as well as personnel department within the organization. As the statistics suggest, the effectiveness of the union as an organization and the importance of the issues being bargained can be implied from the number of workers involved in the strikes and man-days lost each year. The fact that many union members could participate in the strikes and for a long time, reflected the unions' strengths and the financial resources they had been able to obtain. Some of the unions also had linkages with the international union organizations, making them more effective in terms of bargaining power. During the second stage of economic development in Thailand, where export-oriented policy was implemented, and at a time when Thailand experienced an economic boom (1987–1996) recorded by the Board of Investment (BOI), the number of strikes reduced initially and then increased again in 1992. It should also be noted that from 1986 onwards, employers started to use industrial weapons such as lockout to initiate productivity bargaining with the company unions, employees' associations or unions. This was due to the fierce competition from the emerging economies, leading to more demanding work schedules and changes in work organization to increase productivity. In addition to this, many industries, such as the electronics industry, had already introduced the just-in-time production system and hence the necessity to maintain good labor–management relations. Thus, if we look at the HRM practices in different sectors of the economy, we may also find different levels of effectiveness of such practices. It is further observed that after the financial crisis, the number of strikes was reduced. However, the number of workers as well as man-days lost was still substantial.

## Government policies and HRM/IR development in Thailand

The labor movement in Thailand was very strong in the public enterprise sector. Many public enterprise unions have been very well established under the Public Enterprise Labor Relations Act. However, in 1990, this act was demolished. Hence, all the public enterprise unions became regulated under the general Labor Relations Act 1975, just like any other labor unions in the private sector. In 1990, the Social Security Act was passed.

However, coverage has still not included unemployment insurance; only sickness, accidents out of the workplace, being handicapped due to accidents in the workplace, old age (retirement) insurance and maternity leave. The influence of the government in HRM and IR practices has been significant in its legal initiatives. After the financial crisis, many public enterprises come under the privatization scheme which required organizational restructuring, and so the unions' role in the organizations has become somewhat weak.

Thus, when the enterprise has to close down or lay off some employees, the company union could probably no longer operate and maintain its entity. At the higher level of labor organizations, the number of labor federations and labor union councils are found to be rather stable with some minor changes. Trade union organization progressed much further in the public enterprise sector than in the private sector proper. About two-thirds of union members work for public enterprises, with a union density rate of around 60 percent. However, with the government policy to deregulate and privatize by 2006, agreed in the ASEAN forum, the union has become low profile and inactive in some cases. On the other hand, the HRM divisions of these organizations have become more active as a partner to change.

## Management development and the HRM/IR interface

With the establishment of industrial estates to promote foreign investment, the transfer of management knowledge among member firms within certain industrial estates became more effective, as did the possibilities of effective union avoidance strategies. Needless to say, personnel management function played a significant role in reducing the interruption in the manufacturing process of firms in question. Personnel managers, particularly those with many years of work experience, were sought after. In terms of supply, many public universities had started to offer personnel administration or management as a field of study from the early stage of national economic development.[1]

With the weak industrial relations system in the country and the very fast changes from autocratic political system to democratic system through protest and civilian revolt in 1973, it is understandable that there was urgent need for specialists who could handle the workers' issues. In addition, as workers were somehow given a sense of democracy without any training on how to conduct such participation, they felt their industrial weapon was best voiced by large numbers of workers going on strike. Thus, the professionals in workers' management must then understand the political element of the issues. This may explain why personnel administration or management in Thailand seems

---

1 Remarkably, one of the very first programs was launched by the Faculty of Political Science of Chulalongkorn University. This is only to observe that the traditional personnel administration in fact derived its strong tradition from this field of study while the approach may be totally different from that of business administration.

to have its tradition from the political science approach. When the private sector grew larger, the field of management studies was offered first in the school of business or faculty of commerce and accountancy in the public universities and later in the private universities both at the undergraduate and graduate levels.

Many companies already had professionals practicing HRM by the time the Labor Relations Act was proclaimed in 1975.[2] The role of these professionals and hence the personnel department was highlighted with their contribution in reducing work stoppages in the workplace and to make sure that the companies complied with labor law. In addition to this responsibility, the personnel department was also to keep track of the payroll. Since the Fifth National Economic and Social Development Plan (1982–1986) and the Sixth Development Plan (1987–1991) when the HR development was emphasized, HRM gained a more significant role in business operations.

## The role, importance and degree of partnership in HRM

In this section, we will discuss the changes in the role and functions of HRM and then present the findings from a questionnaire survey of the degree of partnership of the HRM department.

Recent theoretical work in business strategy has given a boost to the prominence of HR in generating sustained competitive advantage. According to the resource-based view of the firm, firms can develop sustained competitive advantage only by creating value in a way that is rare and difficult for competitors to imitate. Although traditional sources of competitive advantage such as natural resources, technology, economies of scale, and so forth, create value, the resource-based argument is that these sources are increasingly easy to imitate, especially in comparison to a complex social structure such as an employment system.

In the past decades, Thailand has witnessed significant changes in her economic and social development processes. The three main sectors of the economy, namely, the public sector proper, the public enterprises, and the private sector have undergone changes over the years, under successive governments. The political developments in the country have certainly led to many critical factors that have stimulated private sector growth; not only internal factors that contribute to change but also external factors such as globalization, requirements from the international agencies, i.e. the World Bank, the ILO, and other United Nations agencies, and so on. The most significant influence of the decade was the recent financial crisis that took hold of Thailand's economic development. Many mergers and acquisitions as well as the need to downsize to increase company competitiveness have led to the significant change in the role and impact of HRM practices in Thailand.

---

2  The Labor Relations Act 1975, provides a concrete structure for the labor unions development. The act guarantees freedom of association, collective bargaining, lays down procedures for settlement of labor disputes and prohibits unfair labor practices.

## Globalization and the changing roles of HRM

The ways in which enterprises are managed to achieve organizational goals and HRM and IR initiatives in this regard, are affected by the globalization process which brings many rapid changes in the competitive environment, particularly that represented by the advancement in the new information and communications environment (ICTs). Changes in IR practices (rather than in institutions and systems) such as increased collective bargaining at the enterprise level, flexibility in relation to forms of employment as well as in relation to working time and job functions have occurred as a result of such factors as heightened competition, rapid changes in products and processes and the increasing importance of skills, quality and productivity (Silva, 2002). These factors have also had an impact on HRM policies and practices. In managing change, the key elements include employee involvement in effecting change, greater customer orientation, and ensuring that the skills of employees are appropriate to the production of goods and the provision of services acceptable to the global market. As such, managing people in a way so as to motivate them to be productive is one important objective of HRM.

The increasingly significant role of HRM in achieving management objectives is reflected in the transformation of the personnel management function (Silva, 2002). Over the last two decades, this function was often marginalized in terms of its importance in management activities and hierarchy. It has evolved from a concentration on employee welfare to one of managing people for the best possible productivity of the employee. The former role has been emphasized in the Buddhist context as it seems to be embedded in the family values and some Buddhist values for management such as compassion, kindness and some others.[3] The changing management approach can be through methods that provide employees with both intrinsic and extrinsic rewards. Therefore, today, far from being marginalized, the HRM function becomes recognized as a central business concern; its performance and delivery are integrated into line management; the aims shift from merely securing compliance to the more ambitious one of winning commitment. Therefore, HR investment has become one of the main business strategies of firms in creating their competitive advantage. These initiatives are associated with, and maybe are even predicated upon, a tendency to shift from a collective orientation to the workforce management to an individualistic one. Accordingly, management looks for "flexibility" and seeks to reward differential performance in a differential way. Communication of managerial objectives and aspirations takes on a whole new importance.

---

3 There is one principle of management taught in Buddhism called "Brahmvihaara 4." This principle says that those who are the leaders of others either in the household or in the workplace should practice the following: *Met-taa* (compassion), *Garunaa* (kindness), *Mudhitaa* (sharing the joy of success of others); and *Ubekkhaa* (let go and accept that it is up to the other's karma, when one cannot be of any further help to others even when one has already tried very hard to be so).

# HRM as a business partner

To investigate whether HRM function is regarded as a business partner in the firm operation, an exploratory and empirical study was undertaken (Siengthai and Bechter, 2001). The survey was conducted in Thailand during 1999–2000 with a sampling of firms of 200-plus employees. It was found that the majority of firms, i.e. 63.4 percent consist of 200 to 999 employees; large-sized firms by Thai industry and labor standards. Most of these firms have been established for over 10 years and operate in the manufacturing industry. The majority's sales revenues in 1999 were from 100 to 4,999 million bath. More than half of these sample firms are local Thai firms and the rest are joint ventures, with Japan-related firms dominant and some wholly foreign multinational corporations.

From the regression analysis, it was found that many HRM practices were significantly and positively related to the level of innovation in the industry (Siengthai and Bechter, 2001: 48). The same database is used to investigate the business partnership that the HRM may have within the firms. The Cronbach's Alpha Reliability Test Results of the variable (top management support variable – MGT) is 0.8620. With the scale 1–5 for each statement related to the perception of top management of the role of HRM within their firm, we found that in general, the respondents, who are mostly HR directors, other functional managers and some managing directors, agree (4.05) that the top management in their organization think that the HR strategy is an important component of an innovation strategy (Mgt3, see Table 8.1). Most of the respondents are not sure but tend to agree (3.66) that their top management values HR more than other resources (e.g. financial, Mgt4). They also are not sure but tend to agree (3.96) that their top management believes that HR policies are a source of competitive advantage (Mgt5). Finally, most of them are not sure but tend to agree (3.49) that their top management

*Table 8.1* Top management's perception of the HRM function in Thailand

| Aspect | N | Mean | S.D. |
|---|---|---|---|
| Top management: | | | |
| • believes that human resource (HR) strategy is an important component of an innovation strategy (Mgt3) | 166 | 4.05 | 0.8110 |
| • values human resources more than other resources (Mgt4) | 166 | 3.66 | 0.9881 |
| • believes that human resource policies are a source of competitive advantage (Mgt5) | 166 | 3.96 | 0.8661 |
| • considers the HR manager a strategic partner in formulating and implementing business strategy (Mgt7) | 166 | 3.49 | 0.8220 |

considers the HR manager to be a strategic partner in formulating and implementing business strategy (Mgt7).

Thus, it can be concluded that most of the HR function in these sample firms is still not regarded as being a significant partner in business strategies and implementation changes.

## Key factors influencing HRM practices in Thailand

In this section, an analytical framework can be developed for further investigation on the development of HRM in Thailand. Some further discussion is made for some of the main variables (see Figure 8.1).

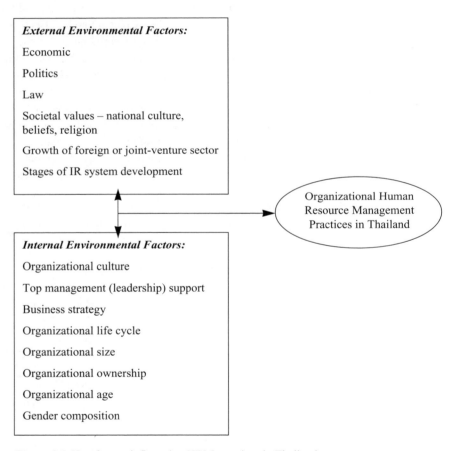

*Figure 8.1* Key factors influencing HRM practices in Thailand

# Thai cultural influences on HRM practices

Some of the Thai cultural norms that are now well recognized among expatriates include the following: *kreng jai* (Siengthai and Vadhanasindhu, 1991); *bunkhun* (reciprocity of goodness; exchange of favors); *jai yen yen* (take-it-easy); *mai pen rai* (never mind); *sanuk* (fun) and *nam-jai* (being thoughtful, generous, and kind combined). Certainly, these norms are social values emphasizing harmonious social relations and consideration for others (Kamoche, 2000: 455). They tend to reinforce the hierarchical structure (patron–client system) in the society as well as in the workplace. It therefore can be expected that in the small to medium-sized family enterprises which are still run by the first generation of founders, the HRM practices tend to be reactive rather than proactive or systematic when compared to the more developed and large-sized family enterprises where professional staffs are more prevalent.

The influences of these values are now being challenged as workers are more educated and more skilled. This is suggested by a study done by Kamoche (2000) who examined the HR challenges associated with the industrial expansion during the period of transition from the boom era to the subsequent economic downturn that saw the collapse of the economy in 1997. Based on in-depth interviews with managers across eleven major industrial sectors, his observations of office and factory practice analyze the difficulties firms face in acquiring, developing, and retaining a competent workforce. His findings suggest the following: first, there is a need for managers to re-examine their attitudes towards subordinates, especially with regard to their assumptions about low creativity/ innovativeness. Loss of valuable expertise has in the past taken place when employees quit in search of "more challenging jobs," a common explanation for labor turnover. Although the need for job security has now seemingly resolved the rampant job-hopping for the time being, it is important to institute more effective retention mechanisms in anticipation of an economic recovery. Such mechanisms should be complemented by genuine efforts to raise competence levels including allowing more scope for innovation. More specific HR initiatives include a more realistic commitment to training and career development, providing meaningful feedback on a timely basis, formalizing practices that currently rely too heavily on subjective criteria and balancing the need to "control" with the need to "develop," especially for firms operating under the traditional model.

# Economic and social development in Thailand from 1960 to 2002

The economic and social development in Thailand became the formal mission of each government since 1961 when the first National Economic Development Plan was formulated. However, the HRs or social development concern did not come into consideration until the Third Plan (1973–1978) when the notion was incorporated into the national planning and was recognized as the National Economic and Social Development Plan.

After about two decades of the planned economic development, Thailand made a sharp turn in its economic development process in 1987 (Siengthai, 1996). Between 1988 and 1990, it exhibited three consecutive years of double-digit growth and kept the growth rate over 6 percent annually up until 1997. Manufacturing emerged as a leading sector contributing to this economic growth both in terms of value added and export earnings. This is a totally different direction when compared to the period between 1977 and 1987. The source of growth then stemmed mainly from domestic demand and the engine of growth was primarily from import substitution.

The explanation for the main determinant of Thailand's accelerated growth in the past decade was the 1985 appreciation in the value of the yen, which made Japanese production more costly. The Japanese companies were then forced to look for new lower-cost production locations. In 1987, Japanese investment approved by Thailand's Board of Investment (BOI) exceeded the cumulative Japanese investments for the preceding 20 years. Thailand had in fact become the largest recipient of Japanese FDI in ASEAN. Needless to say, the influence of so-called "Japanese management practices" was observed after a certain turbulent time in industrial conflicts at the beginning of their first wave of investment in Thailand. In the late 1980s, other newly industrialized economies (NIEs) also relocated their production bases to Thailand.

The export of Thai manufactures was based on "low wage" labor and abundant natural resources. Until 1980, Thailand was considered a relatively land-abundant country. The closing of land frontiers, towards the end of the 1970s, has encouraged labor migration to urban areas, primarily to Bangkok. The first group of laborers released from the agricultural sector were the female workers who had provided a large pool of trainable and inexpensive labor. This, in fact, became the main factor contributing to Thailand's comparative advantage in the 1980s. Currently, shifting of production bases is taking place as a result of the trade preferential treatment of the major export markets such as the USA.

Domestically, the shift of Thailand's production and export structure in the last decade towards more dependence on industry (manufacturing) and services also changed the country's comparative advantage *vis-à-vis* other countries over the course of development. Although Thailand may still have an advantage in its agricultural sector, which is very large, i.e. over 60 percent, its semi-skilled labor-intensive manufactured exports have been declining rapidly. This is due to the fact that there are more newcomers in the labor-intensive industries in the world market, such as those countries in East and South Asia.

During the economic boom period, a tight labor-market situation was experienced, particularly in construction and agriculture. Substantial foreign labor was imported into the casual labor market (Siengthai, 1994). The same situation applies to skilled labor. There are industry-specific shortages of workers with secondary and vocational education. These are typically in areas where large-scale and formally organized enterprises are located. At the professional level, the shortage of university-trained labor with scientific or technological background is well documented. This reveals the mismatch in demand and supply both in terms of quantity and quality. Excess demand in this market had been partially met by imported engineers and technicians from Taiwan, the Philippines and South Asian countries. Thus, during this period, HRM strategy has had to deal with an international and diverse workforce. In addition, much job-hopping and personnel poaching has been evidenced, particularly a substantial intersectoral mobility from the public to the private sector, especially academicians teaching certain subjects and who are needed by private sector firms. The earnings gap between the private and the public sectors has widened. The push of economic growth came significantly from foreign direct investment (FDI) as the government set up the Board of Investment to promote investment and to create employment for its working population.

The Thai economy has grown rapidly and has become increasingly internationalized. During the Sixth Plan period, Thai economic growth has skyrocketed with gross domestic product (GDP) expanding at an average of 10.5 percent per year, twice the Plan target, representing the highest average growth rate of the past twenty-five years. Furthermore, the economic structure has become more outward-oriented and internationalized, as indicated by the increase in the proportion of international trade to GDP from 60 percent in 1986 to 80 percent by 1991 (NESDB, The Seventh Economic and Social Development Plan, 1992–1996).

Thailand, however, enjoyed rapid economic growth for only about a decade until mid-1997 when the financial crisis took place. The financial crisis was attributed to two main causes: lack of transparency and accountability (Campbell, 2000; Erickson and Kuruvilla, 2000; Lee, 2002). The report made by the World Bank suggested that such failings in Thailand's public and private sectors was a major cause for the nation's political, economic, and social crises, arguing that a system based on the principles of good governance and greater social responsibility would have averted the crisis, and succeeded in creating more sustainable and equitable development (Lee, 2002: 281). Thus far, the economic recovery has not been fully realized. In addition, many restructuring programs are still on-going in various traditional sectors in the economy. These major changes in organizational restructuring together with the advent of new information and communications technologies (ICTs) have led to changes in the role of HRM in most leading firms as well as the recognition of its impact on the organizational effectiveness.

In sum, key factors which have brought about the high growth rates before the financial crisis in mid-1997 include growth of the export sector, investment and tourism, all of which had grown considerably faster than the projected rates.

## Current economic conditions in Thailand

As can be seen from Table 8.2, the country is evidently recovering from the financial crisis. Private consumption is increasing gradually, which will induce more investment for production and services. In general, GDP is increasing at a positive rate. The external debt of the country is reducing. Trade balance is positive. The population grows steadily at about 1 percent per annum. The same applied to labor force growth. Unemployment is reducing. Wage levels are reflected in the minimum wages in each region of Thailand which are also rising (Table 8.3). This shows the higher purchasing level and ability to pay on the part of the employer. In addition, inflation has jumped from 1.7 to 5.7 in 2002. Thus, it is rather startling and calls for attention on the part of the government. However, it is likely that with the government's reinforcement on corporate good governance and self-sufficienct economic development policies, Thailand is likely to be able to achieve a sustainable economic development growth in the next decade.

## Organizational structure

There have been changes in the structure of many organizations in the recent past. Many large organizations have restructured and implemented the business process re-engineering to cope with the fierce competition which comes with the ICTs. These changes have been implemented to improve the efficiency and reduce costs of operation. Organizations have attempted to become flatter, hence the notion of empowerment and broadbanding in compensation management noted in many cases. The changes in organizational structure also lead to the need for multi-skilled employees, so avoiding workforce redundancy. Large organizations in the service sectors, such as banks and particularly some small and medium-sized banks, have developed their HR systems in a similar way to the government bureaucratic system (Lawler and Siengthai, 1997).

In the case of Thailand, public enterprises and foreign multinational enterprises (MNEs) initially played the leading role in promoting the country's development. However, indigenous firms, many of which are MNEs in their own right, have been dominant in the economy (Lawler et al., 1997).

Within the set of foreign MNEs, the relevant distinction is between the policies pursued by Japanese subsidiaries and those pursued by subsidiaries of western MNEs. In many ways, these systems are consistent with stereotypical notions of western and Japanese styles of HRM, although there are modifications necessitated by the Thai environment. In addition, efforts by western and Japanese MNEs to impose HRM systems in an ethnocentric fashion in their Thai operations have, on occasion, generated significant cultural clashes in the workplace.

Indigenous Thai firms fall into at least two categories with respect to HRM policies. Most private sector firms began as family-owned enterprises closely tied to the Sino-Thai community (Lawler et al., 1997). There are a number of large firms that continue to be managed in this manner, and the employment and personnel practices that these companies pursue are typically quite distinct from those companies with a broad base of investors, especially publicly traded firms (Thai corporations). A third category within the set of indigenous firms consists of numerous state-owned enterprises.

Table 8.2 Thailand's economy at a glance[a]

| | 1999 | 2000 | 2001 | 2002 | 2003 (Q1) |
|---|---|---|---|---|---|
| Population (millions, average) | 61.80 | 61.88 | 62.31 | 62.96 | 63.21 |
| Labor force (mil.)[b][1] | 32.72 | 33.22 | 33.92 | 34.25 | 34.37 |
| Unemployed[2] | 0.49 | 283.7 | | | |
| GDP at 1988 Price | 2,872.0 | 3,005.4 | 3,063.7 | 3,224.6 | n.a. |
| (%) | 4.4 | 4.6 | 1.9 | 5.3 | n.a. |
| GDP at current price (baht, billions) | 4,637.1 | 4,916.5 | 5,123.4 | 5,433.3 | n.a. |
| (%) | 0.2 | 6.0 | 4.2 | 6.0 | n.a. |
| Growth of GDP[c] | 4.4 | 4.6 | 1.8 | 0.7 | n.a. |
| GNP per capita (baht) | 72,981.0 | 77,551.0 | 80,083.0 | 84,246.0 | n.a. |
| Trade balance (US$, billions) | 9.3 | 5.5 | 2.5 | 3.4 | 1.9 |
| Current account balance (US$, billions) | 12.5 | 9.3 | 6.2 | 7.6 | 3.0 |
| Balance of payment (US$, billions) | 4.6 | –1.6 | 1.3 | 4.2 | –2.0 |
| Private consumption[c] | 2,591,129.0 | 2,751,901.0 | 2,903,664.0 | n.a. | n.a. |
| Total external debt (US$, millions) | n.a. | 79,715.0 | 67,511.0 | 59,456.0 | n.a. |
| Balance of payment on current account (% in GDP) | 10.1 | 7.7 | 5.4 | 3.8 | n.a. |
| Inflation | 0.3 | 1.6 | 1.7 | 5.7 | n.a. |

Sources: Department of Local Administration and National Statistical Office

1 Population for 2002 was recorded on 25 April 2003. And figure in parentheses represents percentage changes from the same period of the previous year.
2 Since 1996, the concept of "Labor Force" was revised to cover persons with the age of 15 years and over, as opposed to the original concept of 13 years and over.

a   All figures from BOT unless indicated otherwise.
    http://www.bot.or.th/bothomepage/databank/EconData/Thai_Key/Thai_Key.xls
b   http://www.nso.go.th/eng/stat/lfs/lfstab8.htm
c   http://www.adb.org/Documents/Books/Key_Indicators/2000/tha.pdf

*Table 8.3* Minimum wage of some selected provinces in Thailand (baht per day)

|  | 1999 | 2000 | 2001 | 2002 |
|---|---|---|---|---|
| Bangkok, Samutprakarn, Nonthaburi and Pahumthani | 162 | 162 | 165 | 165 |
| Phuket and Nakorn Pathom | 162 | 162 | 162 | 165 |
| Chonburi | 140 | 140 | 143 | 146 |
| Chiangmai, Phang Nga and Ranong | 140 | 140 | 143 | 143 |
| Rayong | 130 | 130 | 130 | 133 |

Thus, the difference of ownership of firms may well have a significant impact on the HRM policies and practices in Thailand. Another empirical study undertaken by Kongchan (2001) in the past five years found that among the 215 sample companies, HRM in the majority of Thai companies was found at divisional level both in the manufacturing and service sectors. The main responsibilities were to take care of basic functions of HRM: recruitment and selection, training and development, and so on. He found that there was no difference between manufacturing and service sector in recruitment and selection. Selection process mostly involved both HR managers and line managers. The most popular recruitment sources were walk-in applicants, followed by employee referral and newspaper advertisements. Interview was most frequently used as a selection device. With respect to training and development, there was some difference between that in the industrial and service sectors. In the industrial sector, the majority of them had definite plans for training programs, both long term and short term, while in the service sector, the majority of the companies had only short-term plans.

## Development of the IR system

Prior to 1975, workers associations had already been established. However, trade unions had been legalized since 1975, and strikes legal since 1981. The trade union movement has been weak, both in coverage and in workplace industrial relations. Most unions are recognized at the enterprise level. Union membership has not been growing extensively and rapidly, in fact, it has been declining recently; only a few industrial unions are in operation. For the past two decades, Thai unions have been encountering various obstacles both in terms of employers' recognition and their own operations. More than 90 percent of unions are currently in financial difficulties, with inter-union rivalry, lack of training for union members, non-cooperation from members, union leaders' conflicts, intervention of union activities. Lack of financial resources, in particular, means that unions are reliant on either larger unions, federations, councils or outside organizations for assistance (Siengthai, 1999).

Currently, in the Thai context, collective bargaining is not effectively resorted to as an ideal process of decision-making between employer and employees. Most conflicts are resolved only when employees resort to the power structure, which acts as a third party to intervene and thus make their demands to the employers materialize. Based on the principle of collective bargaining, employer and employees should attempt to negotiate between themselves. Both parties should respect the mutual rights and duties of each other, act with sincerity and in good faith, realize the factual situation, and make every effort to resolve the problems by means of negotiation in lieu of other means which may create conflict between both parties.

Here again, the concept of patron–client is apparent. Most of the workers' organizations have to demonstrate or publicize conflict in order to gain support from the public and put pressure on employers to concede to their demands. For most non-union member employees, when they are not satisfied with their jobs or are unfairly treated, often they choose to quit rather than to bargain with their employers. This is more evident when the Thai economy is experiencing an economic boom.

As far as the target of joint consultation and collective bargaining with conciliation-based harmony between management and employees and company stability are concerned, the difference in roles between consultation and collective bargaining will be insignificant. What the management should be aware of is the potential abuse of such management prerogatives. From a study undertaken (Siengthai, 1999), it was found that the management in many enterprises has delegated more rights and authority in decision-making to their subordinates. For example, trade union participation in recruitment, orientation, disciplinary procedures, working conditions, labor relations improvement, and so on.

Thailand has not yet reached a the good industrial relations system because of the lack of conflict resolution mechanisms that can provide satisfaction to both employers and employees (Siengthai, 1999). Many conflicts at the enterprise level have involved many people and caused unnecessary industrial productivity loss. In addition, the employees' organizations (unions) themselves still have a number of problems to be solved.

## HRM in Thailand before and after the financial crisis

This section discusses the HRM practices in the state enterprises, Thai local firms and those of the multinational corporations operating in Thailand. The data are based on the interviews and survey undertaken with some state enterprises,[4] in-depth interviews with a sample of firms as well as from the surveys and case studies conducted in various industrial sectors in the Thai economy previously.

4 This forms part of the results of the previous studies undertaken by this author and some by others on the State Railways Authority of Thailand, Petroleum Authority of Thailand, Electricity Generating Authority of Thailand (EGAT), Krungthai Bank, Telephone Authority of Thailand (TAT).

# HRM in the public enterprises

Many of the public enterprises have been very well established. Most of them seem to adopt the personnel administration policies and practices from the "proper" public sector. The compensation and training programs are more intensive than the public sector. The government has privatized more than 40 public enterprises and reduced the number of SOEs from more than 100 to 59 (Indhapanya, 2001). However, SOE reform has not been undertaken as part of a concerted, board economic reform effort.

In terms of compensation, many top-performer public enterprises[5] have brought in the concept of a "balanced scorecard" (Kaplan and Norton, 1996) which emphasizes the balance of various management functions in the organization by retaining financial measurement as a critical summary of managerial and business performance. This concept highlights a more general and integrated set of measurements that link current customer, internal process, employee, and system performance to long-term financial success. The government's privatization scheme has led to the critical role of HRM. This is largely due to the fact that all of the Thai public enterprises are unionized. Thus, the implementation of the privatization has been handled with high sensitivity to the workers' needs as represented by their unions. The positive-sum approach reflected in more intensive HR development activities to provide re-training for those who experience obsolescence in skills has been observed. In some cases, the early retirement or the mutual separation program has been offered to employees based on individual performance appraisal.

# HRM in Thai local firms

It may be said that virtually all the private Thai firms began as family-owned and controlled enterprises (Lawler and Siengthai, 1997). To date, some of the Thai larger corporations are still managed by the wealthy families. Historically, most of the Thai firms were also established by Chinese immigrants. Hence, it is not surprising to find that the ideology of the "Chinese management system" is one of social control. These organizations tend to be hierarchical and autocratic, but formal systems of control such as standard operating procedures and well-defined organizational structures are generally absent (Lawler and Siengthai, 1997: 75). The control mechanism reflects the status differences in Thai society rather than any intentionally imposed system. Thus, even though Thailand is a Buddhist society, the entrepreneurial Chinese families have introduced some degree of Confucian ideology into the workplace. These practices for Chinese family-owned enterprises are, however, complemented by traditional Thai cultural practices in the workplace (Siengthai and Vadhanasindhu, 1991).

---

5  The Ministry of Finance of Thailand has set up some key performance indicators for public enterprises where some of the top performers will release more autonomy in terms of financial management.

However, in the past decade, the economic boom before the financial crisis had led to the development and growth of the private sector of the economy as evidenced by local firms becoming public companies and listed in the Securities Exchange of Thailand (SET). The rapid growth of the economy was also brought about by foreign direct investment in the form of multinational enterprises and joint ventures.

An empirical study undertaken by Kongchan (2001) found that among the 215 sample companies, HRM in the majority of Thai companies was found at divisional level both in industrial and service sectors. The main responsibilities were to take care of basic functions such as recruitment and selection, training and development, and so on.

## Recruitment and staffing

Kongchan (2001) found that there was no difference between manufacturing and service sector in recruitment and selection. Selection processes mostly involved both HR managers and line managers. The most popular recruitment sources were walk-in applicants, followed by employee referral and newspaper advertisements. Interview was the most frequently used selection device. However, as it was found earlier in another study, if the organization is highly visible in the economy, such as a bank, there will be little difficulty in attracting well-educated and well-trained applicants (Lawler and Siengthai, 1997). Particularly since the financial crisis, the labor market is a buyers' market. Thus, it is not surprising that many organizations may now resort to reactive recruiting strategies, unlike earlier, when most large business organizations had to implement proactive recruiting strategies such as campus recruiting. Yet, with the availability of the new ICT environments, many firms have started e-recruiting by posting their job vacancies on a website as well.

With respect to staffing, the process in family enterprise organizations is simplified by its reliance on familial relationships. Thus, virtually all higher level positions in an organization are occupied by family members (Lawler et al., 1997). While family members generally fill almost all of the upper-tier positions in these organizations, middle and even lower-tier positions are typically filled by those who have connections with family members. Unless these organizations are rapidly expanding, recruiting is generally not a major problem, as turnover tends to be slight. When it is necessary to hire from outside the family, these firms rely almost exclusively on referrals from trusted individuals (family members, close family friends, influential business or government officials, or current employees). Indeed, lower-tier workers are often recruited from the relatives of current workers or domestic servants. This process of using personal or family connections to locate a job is referred to in Thai as *mee sen* (literally "to have strings").

## *Training and development*

With respect to training and development, in an earlier study of the banking industry which concentrated on local banks, it was found that most in the sample provide orientation programs for their new employees (Lawler and Siengthai, 1997). Later on, these employees are expected to be acculturated into the bank's system through on-the-job training. Banks generally provide formal training programs for employees at the supervisory level and up (Siengthai, 1989). From the surveys as well as casual observations, large organizations generally have their own training centers and provide formal training programs. Whereas for the executive development, these large organizations also provide formal training programs as well as sending their executives abroad for short-term training programs. It is interesting to observe in the banking industry that there are variations in sophistication of training across major banks. For small and medium-sized banks, they have organized continuing training programs for their middle-level managers from all branches. These are usually called "Mini-MBA" and are about 300 hours of intensive training (Lawler and Siengthai, 1997). They are usually run jointly with the schools of business of some particular universities. In smaller-sized banks that are not included in our interview survey, where the personnel department does not have its own training facilities, employees at the supervisory level are usually sent to the training programs offered by the universities. In general, bank employees who want to pursue their graduate studies may do so but very few receive financial support from the banks. All banks now prefer to hire their employees with bachelor's degrees.

It is interesting to observe the changes in the workforce composition before and after the financial crisis. Before the financial crisis in mid-1997, with the competition from non-bank institutions in the labor market for the same pool of skilled workforce, many banks in Thailand had lowered their employee qualifications requirement to a vocational college diploma in the business administration area. This certainly necessitated more focus on HR development activities to maintain the bank's competitiveness. In the previous two decades (before the crisis), there had been job-hopping, particularly at entry level and some at middle-level management, where employees left to join non-bank institutions which provided better offers. To ensure that they will recuperate from their investment in training their personnel, some banks have requested that their employees sign a contract that requires them to pay back in terms of time or cash if they quit the organization after receiving training. However, after the financial crisis, it was observed that many local banks received more applicants with higher degrees, such as MBA degrees or even those graduated from abroad.[6] Needless to say, all banks enjoy an abundant pool of professional applicants nowadays. But ironically, they need to handle at the same time the so-called "redundant" workforce.

---

6 From the field interviews recently undertaken.

In a recent survey undertaken by Kongchan (2001), it was found that with respect to training and development, there was some difference between the manufacturing and service sectors. In the manufacturing sector, the majority had definite plans for training programs both short term and long term, while in the service sector, the majority of companies had only short-term plans.

## Performance appraisal

For performance appraisal, the majority of both manufacturing and service sectors had performance appraisal once a year (Kongchan, 2001). Some of them had performance appraisal twice a year. The main objective of the appraisal was as a basis in pay-rise decision-making, followed by performance improvement. The persons responsible for appraisal in most companies were immediate supervisors. Both qualitative and quantitative criteria were used in performance appraisal.

In a study of HRM in the banking industry before the financial crisis, it was found that most banks in the sample had an annual performance appraisal, some, twice a year. For some banks this is for the HR development purposes. Most banks use their performance appraisals for administrative purposes, such as for pay-rise and promotion considerations. Large banks generally have very elaborate systems of performance appraisal, such as self-evaluation versus supervisor evaluation. However, this is not very common. Large banks, whose systems are very well-designed, provide feedback to their employees after they have been evaluated. If the subordinates do not agree on any points, they can appeal to their supervisor and to the upper management. All banks have a formal system of employee performance appraisal in that they have forms designed to measure or appraise employees for particular qualities or competencies. Some may emphasize teamwork, creativity, business code of ethics, and so on, other than interpersonal skills, managerial skills or technical skills.

## Career planning

In terms of career planning, it was found that there were no career planning programs in most industrial companies. In service companies, the majority of them had career-planning programs but they were not systematic.

## Compensation

In the study by Lawler and Siengthai (1997) on the Thai banking industry, compensation in the sample banks varied. Most banks followed the market rate in each market segment. For example, the Thai local banks have their own market rates which are different from those of foreign banks. Thus, in order to be able to attract the job applicants, most banks will follow the market rates and will vary their fringe benefits to make their offers more attractive than their counterparts in the banking industry. The issue of external equity of pay seems to be an important one at the entry level. However, once employees of a bank, they will also be compensated for their special skills, such as computer programming, accounting, or such. In general, for the Thai local banks, promotion from within has created a large internal labor market. In contrast, the internal labor market is not so structured in the foreign banks. All banks provide bonuses to their employees but generally no other financial gains. They do not have profit-sharing plans. Some incentive plans may be observed in that most banks now consider their branches as their sales points and have these operate as profit centers. Thus, those which perform well will receive a larger percentage to be allocated to their own subordinate in the branch at the time of performance appraisal. So it may be said that limited gain sharing is practiced.

Kongchan (2001) found in his survey that most companies both in manufacturing and service sectors offer incentives on an individual basis. The criteria used for evaluation are productivity. The incentive and reward are perceived as equitable to other companies. In term of preparation for globalization, most of the manufacturing companies have implemented some changes in the work system and processes while service companies have focused on HR development. Many manufacturing companies use quality circles (QC).

## Labor–management relations

In the study by Lawler and Siengthai (1997), it was found that most banks in the sample have unions; only some local banks such as the Bangkok Bank of Commerce and the Thai Danu Bank do not.[7] In all foreign banks in the sample, there are unions. However, unions are usually organized at the bank tellers and non-supervisory level. According to the Labor Relations Act 1975, employees at the supervisory level cannot become union members. It may be said that unions in the banking industry are generally weak and their collective bargaining with the employers mainly involve wages and fringe benefits. The unions are not very militant. The formation of bank unions is usually through a bank employees' "network." In many banks in the sample, unions have been long established. It may be said that their relationship with the management has been collaborative (Lawler and Siengthai, 1997). In one case (Bank of Asia), a union was newly formed after the

---

7  In the study (1997), the HR managers or assistant managers of the following banks were interviewed: Thai local banks – Bangkok Bank of Commerce, Bank of Asia, Krungthai Bank, Siam Commercial Bank, Thai Danu Bank, and Thai Farmers Bank; for foreign banks – Bank of America, Chase Manhattan Bank, Citibank, N.A. and Sakura Bank, Ltd. The interview was actually carried out in 1994. After the financial crisis, some of the local banks have been acquired and merged with foreign banks, i.e. Thai Danu Bank is now DSB Thai Danu after the merger with DBS (Singapore), while Bangkok Bank of Commerce was transformed into Thailand Assets Management Co. under the government policy directives.

bank entered the Security Exchange of Thailand and the bank's shareholder structure was changed. The owner withdrew from the management activities and promoted a professional manager to the top executive position (managing director). Furthermore, the bank started to recover after a long period of profit loss. It was because of this, together with the structural change of the bank, that the HRM indicated that the union had then become militant. However, some cultural elements seem to facilitate their relationship with the management. For example, the union representatives addressed the manager by their seniority in age and work experience in their interaction with the management. Thus, a certain level of consideration was given to the management side. This makes the management feel they can negotiate and work out an agreement which would satisfy the needs of both sides. The impact of deregulation policy to increase competition in the labor market has also made many banks more responsive to their employees' needs so that they can maintain their workforce. Some banks have also brought unions into their participative system of management (Lawler and Siengthai, 1997).

## HRM in the multinational enterprises

There are many MNCs and joint ventures in Thailand, but the major investor MNCs are those from Japan and the USA. In the earlier days of foreign investment in Thailand, most investments were in the form of foreign direct investment whereas nowadays a substantial proportion of investment is also in the form of equity. The US firms were among the first group of investors who came to Thailand and in fact had established a special treaty with the country to have 100 percent ownership.

It was found that in terms of recruitment, the western firms prefer to buy skills from outside to fill in the existing openings (Lawler et al., 1997). Foreign firms, on average, tend to favor those with US degrees. However, there has been more practice of promoting from within and filling in the vacancies by the employment agencies' search. This means that there is an opening bid for the positions available, as opposed to internal promotion in the Japanese joint-venture firms. Furthermore, Japanese management tends to invest heavily in on-the-job training for their employees at all levels, while in the American firms, there tends to be more training and development at mainly managerial and professional levels. Some multinational firms in Thailand, such as those in the construction industry, will recruit new employees through apprentice programs offered to students who have performed satisfactorily during their training period, meeting the requirements and demands of the company. In addition, they have their own training centers. Technicians and experts from parent companies come to train engineers, foremen, and supervisors as the demand for certain new skills or knowledge arises. Companies also send their employees abroad for technical and marketing training, normally to Asian countries such as Singapore, Philippines, Malaysia, and India. However, after the financial crisis, the companies have had to cut the budget for this purpose. Staff in head office are permanent but those who work only for short-term projects are laid off after completion if new projects are not in the offing, although normally, they are transferred to new projects where possible. The companies have a flexible policy towards the transfer of contracted employees from one project to another as well as from one place to another. Therefore, this finding implies that, while there is a broad career path for the employees in Japanese firms, there is a narrower career path in American firms. For example, a worker in the Japanese firm can be trained on the job and eventually reach supervisory level; in rare cases, particularly in the early days, can that employee with the most outstanding supervisory skills climb up to a lower level managerial position. This, however, was in the days when Japanese joint-venture companies were not so much favored by Thai workers. On average, this is seldom the case in American firms, because they tend to prefer specialization more than the general skills preferred by Japanese firms. This ties into the fact that in Japanese firms, compensation is linked to seniority or length-of-service with the company, simply because on-the-job training means the company has invested in the individual a broad range of skills to tap into later during length of service to the company. It is also a means to maintain these employees with the company. On the contrary, seniority or length-of-service within firms does not play a great role in the US joint ventures in Thailand. Here firms do not generally invest much in training at the lower levels; more so for the higher level employees. This has created a dual structure of wages or pay in the American firms, obviously determined by a different policy on training or investment in human capital, but also explained by it being usually harder to find the right experiences in the labor market, compared to the lower level skills and experiences where the number is more plentiful. In terms of evaluation or appraisal, there is a different approach. In the US-based firms, there is a tendency to have performance evaluation aimed at short-term results while in the Japan-based firms, the evaluation is more long-term. So, even though there is periodic evaluation, it is intended as a feedback mechanism for individuals to improve their performance rather than used as a determinant of continuation of contract.

For the US-based or western firms, wages or compensation are usually higher than the market wage rates. Therefore, these western firms generally do not experience difficulty in acquiring the best skills available in the market. This is different from the Japanese firms which are about the same size as Thai local firms, but as job security is preferred, they also attract the workforce. Over time, there have been improvements in the management practices of the Japan-based firms in Thailand.

Clegg and Gray (2002) investigate the Australian expatriate management issues in Thailand. They examine the role of HR policies in ensuring that the right people are chosen to represent MNCs in overseas locations as in the provision of pertinent support policies, such as preparation for overseas assignments and cross-cultural training. Their sample is composed of Australian expatriates in Thailand. The questionnaire survey was conducted by members of the Australian–Thai Business Council in Thailand in 1999. The findings provide some insights for expatriate management policy, including the notable conclusions that the market for expatriates is changing and becoming more demanding and that the imperatives of the emerging global market for human capital require a much more structured approach to expatriate management development. For the selection process, attention was paid to cultural aspects of the work environment. Not enough attention, however, was paid to the team dynamics based on the selected team members (Clegg and Gray, 2002: 612). In their survey, the results reveal that a third of respondents had their spouses involved in the selection process. In terms of performance appraisal processes, most of the respondents judged that their technical skills and maturity to cope with a foreign posting were key factors in gaining them the position they currently held. For a significant majority of respondents (i.e. 65 percent), a host-country manager was involved in the appraisal process. In regard to the added stresses of the foreign environment in the performance appraisal process, many respondents noted that the compensation covered this facet of the expatriate experience while an appraisal was purely on financial results, i.e. the "bottom line." The appraisal looks at the achievement of objectives within this context.

With respect to compensation, there are a variety of different approaches regarding expatriates. Factors influencing the differentials between the expatriates and those working at the headquarter office include personal and upheaval, cultural incongruities that must be managed and often political risks faced. These result in the structure of a package being considerably different than for an equivalent role in Australia. The issues include currency denomination, provision of housing and additional perquisites to compensate for the change in lifestyle.

Kongchan (2001) found in his comparative study of HRM between local Thai firms and the multinational corporations (MNCs) as follows. The units which are responsible for HRM in Thai and multinational companies are mostly found at divisional level, with the divisional manager as the one who is responsible for the main functions. In particular, HR division in American companies more than other companies is involved in strategic planning, followed by European companies, and Thai companies. HR division in Japanese companies is involved in strategic planning less than others. In terms of HRM planning, no difference is found between Thai and multinational companies. Most of the HR executives are involved in strategic planning at high level and most of the companies consider HR as a very important factor in strategic planning. In terms of HR planning, no difference is found either. Generally, the process starts with the unit that needs more staff submitting its request to the HR department. However, manpower decisions are mostly made by high-level executives or committee. The higher participation in manpower planning in terms of having representatives from all divisions concerned with such decision-making processes is, however, higher in the American companies. In terms of the recruitment and selection process, American-related companies are found to delegate more of the selection decisions to line managers. With respect to recruitment of executives, most companies utilize both internal and external sources. For external recruitment, American and European companies use recruiting firms in higher percentage than Thai companies, who prefer personal referral to other approaches. At operational level, Thai, Japanese, and European companies mostly perform their own recruitment, while American companies conduct their own recruitment as well as using outside services. For Thai companies, walk-in applications are most popular, followed by internal search. For Japanese companies, the following approaches are used: walk-in applications, newspaper advertisements, and campus recruitment. In American companies, walk-in is the most popular approach but internal searches are also used. American companies are found to use training and development for long-term planning more than other firms. With respect to performance appraisal, there is no difference between Thai and multinational companies. Most of them have appraisal once a year with a major objective being payrise, followed by performance improvement. Both qualitative and quantitative criteria are used in performance appraisal. Most of the companies reported that they informed their employees of objectives and criteria. In addition, they also have training for appraisers (Kongchan, 2001). American companies provided involvement of employees in the appraisal process in higher percentage as compared to other companies and clearly had more career planning programs than others. Most of the Japanese companies did not have career planning programs. This could have been due to the fact that most of them are basically manufacturing units and operational bases much larger than the professional level employees. Thai and European companies have reported having career planning programs but not formalized ones. In terms of reward systems, there was no difference between Thai and multinational companies (Kongchan, 2001). Productivity or performance was mainly used as a basis for rewarding. In terms of preparation for globalization, changes in work process or system were mostly used by Thai and Japanese companies. Americans emphasized on HR development while European companies focused on IT and communication improvement more than other approaches.

## Current development of HRM in Thailand

Since the Asian financial crisis in 1997, the HRM issues have been given more importance than ever. In the public sector, the Ministry of Education is being developed under the Reform Program. There is a plan by the current government to merge the Ministry of Education with the Ministry of University Affairs so that the overall planning and implementation of educational programs can be fully integrated and allow more efficient and effective use of the national resources. It is hoped that the system of education will be more adaptable to the needs of the labor market and changes in technology. It is hoped that the new system will be able to produce the basic skills and enhance the potential workforce to be able to adapt to the needs of the society and economy.

In mid-1997, when Thailand was severely hit by the financial crisis, many companies had to restructure and downsize. Cases of lay-offs were experienced by many of them who had been playing in the international markets either through exporting their products, investing overseas, or even making loans from international sources through the BIBF office. In addition, most of these firms were well-established firms that were now in their maturity and the market was saturated. Thus, they suddenly found themselves faced with the necessity to go through these rapid changes in the environment. Together with the international agreement on trade, all this has led to the more active and significant role of HRM within firms. Moreover, the professionalism of HR managers has also been enhanced substantially.

A study of one large conglomeration in Thailand[8] suggested that the redefined business strategy of dividing the firm into two main business activities, namely, full-cycle agriculture and technology-related business, has led to more investment in human resources as part of the company's policies (Chawewatanasskul, 1998).

Studies on business firms' HRM strategies and practices have revealed that, for those that do have business strategies, they adjusted their HR strategies and practices to cope with the economic crisis (Laohathanakul, 1999; Vorapongse, 2001). For example, with respect to recruitment, most organizations had settled retrenchment, turnaround strategies by recruiting only certain necessary positions and the selection process had become very rigorous. They became more strict in the probationary evaluation of the new employees. In the real estate sector (Vorapongse, 2001), for example, most firms have recruited more employees mainly from the external labor market to support the expansion of the company. This is on the basis of specific qualifications, knowledge, competence, and experience. In terms of remuneration, most companies have suspended or reduced monthly payments, bonuses, annual salary increases, overtime, strict overtime payments, reductions in work hours/days, payment for time not worked, sub-contraction, or/and reduction in welfare or activities. Vorapongse (2001) found that in the real estate sector, most companies set the compensation level according to the standard of living. Bonuses are paid depending on the profits made. With respect to welfare and fringe benefits, most organizations provide welfare and fringe benefits, some of which are required by law and some not. Performance appraisal is based on the profits made by the company and performance achieved by the individual employees (Vorapongse, 2001). Laohathanakul (1999) found that these companies have turned to in-house training and on-the-job training as a result of the recession. These HR development policies have also been evidenced by the public enterprises under the privatization scheme, such as the Telephone Organization of Thailand (TOT), The Communications Authority of Thailand (CAT), the Electricity Generating Authority of Thailand (EGAT), and so on. (Bothidaht, 2001; Kongsanchai, 2001; Chirarattananon et al., 2002). They have also attempted a workforce redeployment and/or job rotation. However, lay-off is used as the last resort for most firms.

Many organizations, both private and public enterprises, have currently made use of the new ICTs to enhance the efficiency and effectiveness of their HRM practices. Many have started to have the so-called "e-HR." Others are following suit but with the attempt to first restructure their organization. It may be said that, for most large-sized firms, the following HRM strategies have been proposed:

1 early retirement program;
2 redeployment program;
3 more effective performance management;
4 core competencies appraisal program.

---

8 This is the Charoen Pokaphand Group which is one of the largest corporations in Thailand.

Perhaps, one good thing for firms faced with financial crisis is that the phenomenon of job-hopping is not a problem any more. Certainly, with some scarce skills, job mobility is still high. Most firms are now trying to maintain the core workforce and outsourcing of some activities is more common. In fact, casual observation suggests that many large corporations have started to divest some units into another legal entity. This results in both downsizing and increased efficiency of operation due to a higher level of autonomy of decision-making and speed of market services. The divestiture is, in a sense, more of the network organizations' creation. As in the beginning, most of the projects or bidding will be granted to the divested unit. Later on, when this is better organized both in terms of services and human resources, more variety of services are then available to the market in general. This means that the HRM function also has to be separated from the parent organization. It may or may not follow that of the parent organization as the nature of the business may not be the same; this also explains why the split would be an advantage in terms of HRM.

Some business organizations have now changed the title of "human resource department" to that of "resourcing department." This seems to suggest that the traditional concept of personnel management and even that of just HRM take on a broader perspective. This is in line with the view which advocates that an organization will gain its competitive advantage through development and sustainability of its renewable and inimitable resources like HR.

However, as has been observed, in the business operations, the HRM function of firms in Thailand has experienced a rather slow growth and development. Until recently, most companies still had a traditional personnel management which was only the systematic approach and basically perceived as the pay-roll function. On the part of the private sector, business companies are now incorporating HR issues into their strategy formulation more than they used to. This is partly due to the following (Siengthai, 2002: 34):

1 The market scenario changes rapidly. Firms are unavoidably faced with rapid changes in the external environment. Many which are now engaged in the export markets will have to be more strategic in their perspective as they will need to cope with some external shocks.
2 In addition, with the availability of information technology and telecommunications infrastructure known as new information and communication technologies (ICTs), firms can now be more responsive to their customers through these technologies which enhance better communication between producers of goods and services and their customers.
3 As the country is moving towards the higher technology production level and more quality service industries, human resource management is becoming a more critical success factor of such a development path.
4 With the advent of new technologies, firms are also finding themselves incapable of taking the opportunities because their existing workforce have not been trained or upgraded in term of skills to cope with technology. The changes brought about in the

new economy, therefore, present a challenge for them to bring human resource management into their focus.

5 Innovation and productivity improvement will be the important issues for firms to enhance their comparative advantage in the global market.

6 Another aspect which Thailand has yet to achieve is a good industrial relations system. Currently, there is still a lack of conflict resolution mechanisms which provide satisfaction to both employers and employees.

7 Last but not least, Thailand has always experienced a high rate of female labor force participation. In the last decade, women managers also have increased in number in various sectors, particularly those in the service industries. It is, therefore, another agenda for the human resource managers to pay attention to the issue of workforce diversity so that an organization will be able to utilize its human resources effectively for organizational performance.

## The challenges faced by the HRM function

Many challenges are brought about by the globalization process to the HRM function. At the regional level, industrialization and globalization has been expected to bring about the convergence of HRM/IR systems (Lee, 2002: 278). It may be summed up as the management of change for the organization. The HRM function must be more proactive and take initiatives in this new role as a business partner. Among these changes are the deregulation policy or privatization scheme by the government as the external environmental changes, the restructuring or downsizing policies of firms, the advantage of the new ICTs and firm policies to exploit it, the shift from low-wage to high-wage and high-skilled labor as well as the need for management development to cope with these changes, the workforce diversity which comes with the globalization process and the regionalization process allowing free flow of products, capital and labor; and at the micro level of firm operation, the need to link between the HRM and the financial performance of the companies, organizational innovation and productivity improvement, the empowerment of employees, project-based contracts, the management of workforce redundancy, the bipartite labor–management relations, and so on.

There is a need for Thailand to move away from the notion of low wages as a source of competitiveness and begin to invest more in the development of a skilled workforce, calling for far-reaching reforms in the educational system (Kamoche, 2000). Such efforts are likely to be hindered by existing cultural norms. For example, the hierarchical *nakrian–ajarn* (student–teacher) relationship turns the student into a passive recipient of knowledge and probably creates a culture of dependence in which the student (or in this case employee) is taught that it is impolite to question the *ajarn* (or employer). If the HR is to make a significant contribution to economic recovery and industrial development, it will be important to institute change that creates more inquisitiveness and a willingness to challenge conventional wisdom in education, and more scope for management and employees to engage in constructive dialog as to how best to tackle their difficulties. This will entail reviewing the sustainability of existing patterns in organizational paternalism.

However, with the government policy to deregulate and privatize by 2006, which has been agreed in the ASEAN forum, the union has become low profile and to some extent inactive. On the other hand, the HRM divisions of these organizations have become more active as partners in that change process.

As observed in recent years, the impact of the financial crisis is still prevalent. The government as well as the private sector organizations are still working on the recovery of the economy. Together with the fierce competitive environment, it is foreseen that organizations will unavoidably keep on shedding the redundant workforce that has resulted from bringing in more labor-saving technology such as IT and the automation of certain services functions in the organization. Even though the introduction of such technology will create the need for some certain skilled labor, the workforce needed would not be equivalent to the earlier period of economic development. The other implications of this is the increase in overhead costs as the higher skilled employees will also imply higher wages and salaries, hence, the need for organizational restructuring to become flatter and for large corporations to continue to enhance customer responsiveness.

The dual economy in Thailand will become more evident as there will be a digital divide between organizations which now take advantage of the new ICTs and those which are still run by the traditional management approach and are basically small-scale family business enterprises where there is no formal HRM system. For those which are now moving into more high-tech-led operations, the new competitive landscape will necessitate that they resort to more of the individualized terms and conditions of employment for higher skilled and scarce employees.

A discernible trend in management is observed to be towards a greater individualization of the employer–employee relationship (Silva, 2002). It implies less emphasis on collective and more emphasis on individual relations. This is reflected, for instance, in monetary and non-monetary reward systems. In IR, the central monetary reward is wages and salaries, one of its central themes (effected by collective bargaining) being internal equity and distributive justice and, often, standardization across industry. HRM increasingly places emphasis on monetary rewards linked to performance and skills through the development of performance and skills-based pay systems, some of which seek to individualize monetary rewards (individual bonuses, stock options, and so on). HRM strategies to secure individual commitment through communication, consultation, and participatory schemes underline the individualization thrust, or at least effect, of HRM strategies. On the other hand, it is also legitimate to argue that HRM does not focus exclusively on the individual and, as such, does not promote only individual employment relations (Silva, 2002). Though much of HRM is directed at the individual, at the same time there is a parallel emphasis on teamwork, whether in the form of quality circles or functional flexibility, and above all, on the individual's commitment to the organization, represented not just as the sum of the individuals in it, but rather as an organic entity with an interest in survival. The potential conflict between emphasizing the importance of the individual on the one hand, and the desirability of cooperative teamwork and employee commitment to the organization, on the other, is glossed over through the general assumption of unitarist values (Silva, 2002).

The concept of the HR system as a strategic asset has implications for both the characteristics and the effects of such a system. Strategic assets are " the set of difficult to trade and imitate, scarce, appropriable, and specialized resources and capabilities that bestow the firm's competitive advantage" (Amit and Shoemaker, 1993: 36). Becker *et al.* (2001: 3–4) assert that the development of HRM practices can be represented as the following evolutionary processes: (i) the personnel perspective; (ii) the compensation perspective; (iii) the alignment perspective; (iv) the high-performance perspective. According to them, "the personnel perspective" refers to practices by firms which hire and pay people but do not focus on hiring the very best or developing exceptional employees. "The compensation perspective" refers to firms that use bonuses, incentive pay, and meaningful distinctions in pay to reward high and low performers. "The alignment perspective" is represented by senior managers who see employees as strategic assets, but they do not invest in overhauling HR's capabilities. Therefore, the HR system cannot leverage management's perspective. Finally, there is "the high-performance perspective" where HR and other executives view HR as a system embedded within the larger system of the firm's strategy implementation. The firm manages and measures the relationship between these two systems and firm performance.

On reflection, in the case of Thailand, we may be able to say that the development of the HRM function and the perception of the other departments in the majority of firms are more likely to have developed to the second stage or that of compensation perspective. However, the globalization process has brought about changes in its role and its image is now being perceived more as a business partner in large organizations.

## Conclusion

This chapter has provided the historical development of HRM, IR, and personnel management in Thailand. It discusses the changes in the role and the significance of HRM from a payroll function to a business partner in the business operations in the country which is still struggling to achieve a sustainable economic development. The empirical evidence suggests that currently, although the role of HRM practices has become more highlighted as contributing to achieve competitive advantage of the firms, the top management perception of this function as a business partner is still not very positive as most of the survey respondents suggest. Following this, the key factors influencing the HRM practices in Thailand are identified. The authors then offer their observations of the challenges ahead to be faced by HRM and also provide the readers with some websites (see p. 172) where information on HRM practices and development in Thailand may be accessed for future reference.

In sum, most of the HR functions in these sample firms are still not regarded as a significant in their business strategies and change implementation. Thus, it is suggested that the HR managers should try to enhance their professional competencies. They should have the understanding of the overall business and communicate more often and effectively with the chief executive officer (CEO) and other executives of the company by being more proactive in their HRM.

## Acknowledgments

The authors would like to express their thanks and appreciation to many executives and managers who have contributed through provision of time and insights in various in-depth interviews conducted over the years. Their thanks are also extended in particular to John J. Lawler and John D. Kasarda as well as many others with whom they have had research project collaboration in the past. The authors appreciate Decha Dechawatanapaisal, Siliphone Sisavath, and Sittichai Noibua for their library research assistance and some fieldwork. Part of this study has been funded by the Asian Institute of Technology as an initiation research grant to which they owe their gratitude and appreciation. Finally, they thank the anonymous referees for their comments and suggestions.

## References

Amit, R. and Shoemaker, P. (1993) "Strategic assets and organisational text," *Strategic Management Journal* 4 (1): 33–46.
Appold, S.J., Siengthai, S. and Kasarda, J.D. (1994) "The effect of culture and staffing patterns on firm performance: An investigation of MNEs in Thailand," research paper supported through grants from the Carnegie-Bosch Institute at Carnegie Mellon University, Citibank, N.A. and the Kenan Institute of Private Enterprise at the University of North Carolina at Chapel Hill.
Becker, B., Huselid, M.A. and Ulrich, D. (2001) *HR scorecard: Linking people, strategy and performance*, Boston, MA: Harvard Business School Press.
Beer, M. (1997) "The transformation of the human resource function: Resolving the tension between a traditional administrative and a new strategic role," *Human Resource Management* 36 (1): 49–56.
Bothidaht, P. (2001) *Preparing for organization change: A case study of TOT*, a research study in partial fulfillment for the degree of Master of Business Administration (Executive MBA Program), Asian Institute of Technology, Pathumthani, Thailand.
Burke, W.W. and Church, A.H. (1992) "Managing change, leadership style, and intolerance to ambiguity: A survey of organization development practitioners," *Human Resource Management* 31 (4): 301–318 (Winter).
Cameron, K.S. (1994) "Strategies for successful organizational downsizing," *Human Resource Management* 33 (2): 189–212 (Summer).
Campbell, D. (2000) "Recovery from the crisis: The prospects for social dialogue in East Asia," in *Proceedings of the 12th IIRA World Congress*, vol. 5, Tokyo.
Chawewatanasskul, N. (1998) *Human resource development in the 21st century of C.P.*, Master's Degree of Public Administration, Chulalongkorn University.
Chiararattananon, S. *et al.* (2002) "Electricity supply industry (ESI) structure and corporatization: A case study of Electricity Generating Authority of Thailand (EGAT)," a commissioned report submitted to EGAT by AIT.
Clegg, B. and Sidney, J.G. (2002) "Australian expatriates in Thailand: Some insights for expatriate management policies," *International Journal of Human Resource Management* 13 (4): 508–623 (June).

Devanna, M.A. and Tichy, N. (1990) "Creating the competitive organization of the 21st century: The boundary less corporation," *Human Resource Management* 29 (4): 455–472 (Winter).

Duangjai, I. (2000) "Human resource management during the economic boom and the economic downturn period: A case study of the Viriyah Insurance Co. Ltd," Master's Degree thesis, Chulalongkorn University.

Ehrlich, C.J. (1997) "Human resource management: A changing script for a changing world," *Human Resource Management* 36 (1): 85–90 (Spring).

Erickson, C.L. and Kuruvilla, S. (2000) "Industrial relations and the Asian economic crisis: An analysis of the short term impacts and long term implications for industrial relations systems," in the *Proceedings of the 12th IIRA World Congress*, vol. 5 Tokyo.

Indhapanya, B. (2001) "The roles of service marketing and human resources development for the new market rules in the next decade of the provincial electricity authority," a research study submitted in partial fulfillment of the requirements for the degree of Master of Business Administration (executive MBA Program), Asian Institute of Technology, Pathumthani, Thailand.

Jatupornruangrit, S. (2001) "Human resources management by information technology system: Case study of PTT Co. Ltd," Master's Degree thesis, Chulalongkorn University.

Kamoche, K. (2000) "From boom to bust: The challenges of managing people in Thailand," *International of Human Resource Management* 11 (2): 452–468 (April).

Kaplan, R.S. and Norton, D.P. (1996) *Translating strategy into action: Balanced scorecard*, Boston, MA: Harvard Business School Press.

Kongchan, A. (2001) "Human resource management in Thai firms and multinational corporations in Thailand," a research report, Chulalongkorn University.

Kongsanchai, T. (2001) "Creating competencies for strategic TOT services," a research study in partial fulfillment of the requirements for the degree of Master of Business Administration (executive MBA Program), Asian Institute of Technology, Pathumthani, Thailand.

Laohathanakul, Voraratana (1999) "Human resource management during the economic crisis," Master's Degree of Public Administration, Chulalongkorn University.

Lawler, J.J. and Siengthai, S. (1997) "Human resource management strategy in Thailand: A case study of the banking industry," *Research and Practice in Human Resource Management* 5 (1): 73–88.

Lawler, J.J., Siengthai, S. and Atmiyananda, V. (1997) "Human resource management in Thailand: Eroding traditions," in C. Rowley (ed.) *Human Resource Management in the Asia Pacific region*, London: Frank Cass.

Lee, J.S. (2002) "Asia in the 21st century: Challenges and opportunities in work and labour," in T. Hanami (ed.) *Universal wisdom through globalization: Selected papers from 12th IIRA World Congress*, Tokyo, May 2000.

Park, Y.B. and Siengthai, S. (2000) *Financial crisis, labour market flexibility and social safety net in Korea and Thailand*, proceedings of the 12th International Industrial Relations Association (IIRA) Congress in Tokyo, Japan, May 2000.

Poapongsakorn, N. *et al.* (1996) "The impact of new production technology on employment in Thailand: A case study of the textile industry," a report prepared by the Thailand Development Research Institute for the Ministry of Labour Protection and Social Welfare, September (text in Thai).

Siengthai, S. (1988) "Changes in wages and income level in Thailand in the last two decades," a report prepared for the National Wages and Incomes Committee, the National Advisory Council for Manpower Development, June 1988 (text in Thai).

Siengthai, S. (1989) "Human resource development: A strategic factor in the manufacturing and services industries in ASEAN," monograph prepared under the ASEAN Affairs Program, ASEAN Economic Research Unit, Institute of Southeast Asian Studies, Singapore.

Siengthai, S. (1993) *Tripartism and industrialization of Thailand*, a research paper prepared for the ILO, December (2nd revision in May 1994).

Siengthai, S. (1996) "The impact of globalization on human resource management practices: A case study of textile industry," a paper prepared for the International Industrial Relations Association 3rd Asian Regional Congress, 30 September–4 October, 1996, Taipei, Taiwan.

Siengthai, S. (1999) *Industrial relations and recession in Thailand*, a research report prepared for the ILO, BKK.

Siengthai, S. (2000) "Localization of MNCs management in Thailand," published in the Report of the Asian Club Foundation Round Table Discussion, 27–28 January 2000, Tokyo, Japan.

Siengthai, S. (2002) "HRM agenda in Thailand" *The Analyst* (published in New Delhi, April–May) 1 (2): 32–34.

Siengthai, S. and Bechter, C. (2001) "Strategic human resource management and firm innovation," *Research and Practice in Human Resource Management* 9 (1): 35–57.

Siengthai, S. and Leelakulthanit, O. (1993) "Women in management in Thailand: A participation for national prosperity," *International Studies of Management and Organization* 23 (4): 87–102.

Siengthai, S. and Vadhanasindhu, P. (1991) "Management in the Buddhist society," in J. Putti (ed.) *Management: Asian context*, McGraw-Hill.

Silva, S. R. (2002) "Human resource management, industrial relations and achieving management objectives," paper prepared for East Asia Multidisciplinary Advisory Team, ILO, Bangkok.

Smitthikrai, C. (1998) "Recruitment and human resource management of firms in Thailand: The comparison between organizations with effective and non-effective performance," research report, Department of Psychology, Faculty of Humanities, Chiangmai University.

Srisopachit, P. (1999) "International strategy, human resource practices, and competitive advantage: A case study of the electronics industry in Thailand," unpublished dissertation submitted in partial fulfillment of the requirements for the Degree of Doctor of Business Administration, the Joint Doctoral Program in Business Administration, Faculty of Commerce and Accountancy, Chulalongkorn University.

Ulrich, D., Brockbank, W., Yeung, A.K. and Lake, D.G. (1995) "Human resource competencies: An empirical assessment," *Human Resource Management* 34 (4): 473–496 (Winter).

Vorapongse, V. (2001) "Human resource management in economic recovery. A case study of real estates business," unpublished Master's Degree thesis, Chulalongkorn University.

Wolfe, R.A. (1995) "Human resource management innovations: determinants of their adoption and implementation," *Human Resource Managemen* 34 (2): 313–328 (Summer).

# Useful websites

In recent years, the boom of IT has also enhanced the ability of the HRM association and other organizations that are involved in the manpower planning, HR development and professional development activities to share and offer their knowledge, information and services to the public at large. The following websites in Thailand are currently active:

| | |
|---|---|
| Personnel Management Association of Thailand (PMAT): | http://www.pmat.or.th |
| Thailand Management Association of Thailand (TMA): | http://www.tma.or.th |
| Ministry of Labour Protection and Social Welfare: | http://www.mol.or.th |
| Bank of Thailand (BOT): | http://www.bot.or.th |
| National Statistical Office of Thailand (NSO): | http://www.nso.or.th |
| Federation of Thai Industries (FDI): | http://www.fdi.or.th |

# 9 HRM in Vietnam

TRUONG QUANG AND LE CHIEN THANG

## Introduction – the quest for competitiveness

After many years of protracted wars and postwar readjustment and orientation, Vietnam started to rebuild its institutions in the early 1990s. There are many reasons for this late but critical undertaking. The quests for sustainable development and integration into the world mainstream both require a well-functioning governance apparatus with people working in all sectors and at all levels. Human resource management (HRM) particularly is recognized as one of the most important factors contributing to the country's overall competitiveness and long-standing socioeconomic achievement.

In this respect, an attempt to link competitiveness with management competence could be meaningful (Quang, 2001). For instance, the World Economic Forum (WE) published a survey of world competitiveness in 2001. Table 9.1 shows that Vietnam was ranked sixtieth, down from fifty-second in the previous year, which is quite in keeping with its rankings in human development (HD) and the human development index (HDI), despite a better score in the education index (IG). As suggested, for example, by continuing loss of competitive advantage to Thailand (*The Nation*, 25 June 2001), Vietnamese companies will have to take immediate and concrete measures focusing on human assets to improve their inferior positions in the international markets.

Building and managing human resources (HRs) strategically have been the center of concern for many organizations in the world in the face of increasing global competition and in the relentless search for sustainable sources of competitive advantage. Likewise, the criticality of human assets to business success has been stressed in recent years by government authorities and managers in Vietnam. This new trend has surely been driven by the initial achievement of the renovation policy (*doi moi*), which came into effect in early 1987 and aimed at transforming the country from a rigid centrally planned system into a more flexible market-oriented economy. The structural reforms necessitated by this campaign have revealed several impediments, including the deficiencies in the existing system of personnel or HRM that have been blamed for slowing down the pace of the country's development and integration process. Nevertheless, so far, little seems to be have been done about understanding the way in which HRs are managed (Kamoche, 2001), and whether or not there exists an linkage between HRM and organizational effectiveness.

*Table 9.1* Vietnam's competitiveness and human development indices

| Country | Competitiveness ranking (CR)* | Human development ranking** | Human development index (HDI)** | Education index (EI)** |
|---|---|---|---|---|
| Finland | 1 | 10 | 0.930 | 0.99 |
| USA | 2 | 6 | 0.939 | 0.98 |
| Norway | 6 | 1 | 0.942 | 0.98 |
| UK | 12 | 13 | 0.928 | 0.99 |
| Belgium | 19 | 4 | 0.939 | 0.99 |
| France | 20 | 12 | 0.928 | 0.97 |
| Japan | 21 | 9 | 0.933 | 0.93 |
| China | 39 | 96 | 0.726 | 0.80 |
| Taiwan | 7 | – | non-UN | non-UN |
| Hong Kong | 13 | 23 | 0.888 | 0.83 |
| Korea | 23 | 27 | 0.882 | 0.95 |
| Singapore | 4 | 25 | 0.885 | 0.87 |
| Malaysia | 30 | 59 | 0.782 | 0.80 |
| Thailand | 33 | 70 | 0.762 | 0.84 |
| Philippines | 48 | 77 | 0.754 | 0.91 |
| Vietnam | 60 | 109 | 0.688 | 0.84 |
| Indonesia | 64 | 110 | 0.684 | 0.79 |
| Cambodia | – | 130 | 0.543 | 0.66 |
| Laos | – | 143 | 0.485 | 0.52 |
| Myanmar | – | 127 | 0.552 | 0.75 |

(* = in 2001, N= 75; ** = in 2002, N = 174)

Sources: IMD, 2001; UN Human Development Index, UNDP Human Development Report, 2002
Note: The UNDP uses the Human Development Index (HDI) to measure the quality of life of nation, as a more meaningful way to complement the comparison based on GDP/head. A nation HDI is composed of life expectancy, adult literacy and GDP per capita. The HDI of Vietnam was 0.539 (1995), 0.644 (1997), 0.671 (2000), 0.682 (2001), and 0.688 (2002) respectively out of 174 countries.

The shortage of knowledge and practice of HRM has been well manifested in the slow development of restructuring reforms of government apparatus and state-owned enterprises (SOEs), especially the equitization process (the Vietnamese version of partial privatization) and the mediocre performance of the majority of organizations in Vietnam, public and private alike. It is also reflected in the magnitude of problems that foreign investors have had to confront in Vietnam with regard to human issues in management as a result of the mismatch between expectation and reality.

A study of the characteristics of Vietnamese sociopolitical and economic structure and the development of the country's economy in transition might help to shed light on the critical issue of HRM.

## Cultural and political structure

In relative terms, China, Japan, Korea, and Vietnam are considered part of the same cultural region, influenced by a common Confucian heritage (Hung *et al.*, 1999). These cultures tend to be more collectivist and hierarchical than western cultures (Hofstede, 1997). In addition, authors studying Vietnamese cultural values show a judgmental consensus that the Vietnamese culture is typified as high power distance (acceptance of authority), high collectivism (value group membership), moderated uncertainty avoidance (value security), and high context (Swierczek, 1994). As suggested by Hofstede (1998), for countries once under Chinese rule, Vietnamese culture is reflected in large power distance but medium to weak uncertainty avoidance.

Recent studies suggest that contemporary Vietnamese culture is experiencing a subtle change from its traditional culture as a result of socioeconomic development in the last few decades. Ralston *et al.* (1999), in a comparative study of the managerial values of Vietnamese managers with those of Chinese and US managers, found that the Vietnamese were higher on collectivism than the other groups but a recent moving toward a market-oriented economy from an historical communistic economy and Confucian cultural philosophy has resulted in a mixed set of values that incorporates both old and new, and which may be characterized as a paradoxical composite embracing both Collectivism and Individualism (Ralston *et al.*, 1999: 670). Other authors reckoned similarly that despite the influence of socialist ideology, Vietnamese employees in the postwar period tend to veer towards individualism in that they have no common goals nor shared objectives and emphasize individual achievement (Quang, 1998; Tuan and Napier, 2000).

The discrepancy in cultures between regions and the shared heritage of long periods of colonialization (under the Chinese and the French) and internal conflicts have left their mark on all types of organizations in terms of leadership and management styles, and managerial practices. A blend of such "good" behaviors and practices as "the noble man," "hierarchy," "mandarin career," "respect for seniority," and "middle of the way" (Chinese); "divide and rule," "elite system," and "individualism" (French); "grassroots democracy" and "delegation" (American); and "egalitarianism" and "collective decision and responsibility" (socialism) may still be seen ubiquitously in all organizations throughout the country.

The cultural tradition and the sociopolitical environment as described above are reflected in several aspects of the organization/employee relationship such as adherence to rules, common values and norms, less individual-oriented pay, and harmony (Zhu, 2002), which will be discussed in more detail later.

Politically, Vietnam is still basically a one-party system with the Communist Party of Vietnam (CPV) in absolute control since 1954 in the north and since 1975 in the whole country. The CPV is itself positioned at the top with its politburo and permanent secretariat. The CPV Central Committee is the all-important decision-making body, under which all local committees constituted by party members are located. Both the politburo and secretariat, together with the Central Committee, control and guide the National Parliament (Legislature), the Cabinet (Executive) and other satellite organizations such as the Fatherland Front, the Trade Union, the Youth/Women/Farmers Associations, and more. This parallel structure goes all the way down to village level, where the executive people's committees and people's council, all closely linked to the Party's local committees, are established. Elections, which occasionally take place, are all to be understood within such a political structure. The CPV Congress, which is held once every five years, decides on the course of strategic orientation, to the national political programs, to foreign policies to be carried out by all organizations and individuals in the society.

The political system in Vietnam is based on consensus and collective decision-making (*tap trung dan chu* or democracy centralism), which are the principal tenets of socialism. The dominance of the CPV and the rule of the socialist principles still have strong influences on all activities of Vietnamese society and business with regard to structure, culture, and HRM.

## Socioeconomic structure

Vietnam is certainly not a poor country in terms of human resources. It has a large population of *c.* 80 million (in 2000), a 94 percent literacy rate, and a dynamic and relatively well-educated workforce. The total labor force is *c.* 38.2 million, more than half of them under 25 years of age. The gender distribution is 50.6 percent female and 49.4 percent male (International Data Base, 2002).

The young and imbalanced population structure in favor of females has shaped the composition and conditions of the Vietnamese workforce, which is characterized by high unemployment pressure, significant women gender expectations, labor flexibility and mobility.

As shown in Table 9.1, Vietnam's human resource development index (HRDI) is comparatively high and continues to improve over the years as the leverage of the continuing reform process. As a matter of fact, due to the HDI achievement status, Vietnam is no longer considered an "underdeveloped country" by UNCTAD in 2003, despite a still modest GDP *per capita* of US$420, which is still far below the required level of US$1,035 (Vietnam News Agency, 16 May 2003). This leads to a mismatch between supply and demand in the labor market. One of the clearest examples of this paradox is that, while a large proportion of the manufacturing industry makes extensive utilization of cheap and unskilled labor, many essential sectors of the economy have been left untapped due to a serious lack of skilled labor.

To be sure, Vietnam has achieved significant economic improvement in recent years, which is widely attributed to the success of its *doi moi* policy. The on-going economic renovation campaign has profoundly changed the country's business landscape, first by freeing the state from direct involvement at the enterprise level with management of the economy and then by giving enterprises greater autonomy to cope with the move towards a market economy. The major drives are to streamline the state-owned enterprises, unleash local private sector potential and attract foreign investment. The economy has responded favorably to the new treatments. The GDP grew slightly at 3.6 percent in 1997, immediately after the introduction of the new policy, and continued to accelerate at a rate of between nearly 5 and 6 percent in the next four years before it soared to a level of 8 percent between 1992 and 1994. Noticeably, the economy experienced the most dynamic period when the GDP growth rate almost reached the 10 percent mark in 1995 and 1996. Unfortunately, the well-publicized Asian crisis in 1997 put a brake on this improvement and brought down the GDP growth rate to 8.2 percent, then to 4.8 percent in 1999. The economy showed signs of gradual recovery when the GDP growth rate jumped to 6.8 percent in 2000 and re-emerged with a firm increase of 6.8 and 7 percent in the ensuing years (*Vietnam Economic Times*, 2003).

The long period of constant growth and the comparatively stable political conditions have been the two most important factors in attracting a growing number of foreign investors and engaging the private sector in the country's development process in the last decade.

Nevertheless, in spite of significant achievements due to the *doi moi* policy, most of the Vietnamese economy still rests largely on agriculture and industry. The service sector has begun to gain ground only in the last decade, especially in hospitality and foreign trade sectors. The irrational distribution of human resources is reflected in the official plan as demonstrated in Table 9.2, given the growth in the service sector.

*Table 9.2* Sectoral composition and distribution of labor in Vietnam

|  | 2001 | 2005 (plan) |
|---|---|---|
| *% Share of GDP* | | |
| Agriculture | 23.3 | 20.0 |
| Industry | 37.8 | 38–39 |
| Services | 39.0 | 40–41 |
| | | |
| *% Labor utilization* | | |
| Agriculture | 60.5 | 57–58 |
| Industry | 14.4 | 20–21 |
| Services | 25.1 | 20–23 |

Source: CIEM, 2002; GSO, 2002; MOLISA, 2002; TBKTSG, 16 January 2003.

In terms of ownership, the current Vietnamese economic structure represents three main sectors: state-owned, domestic private (non-state), and foreign invested. Organizations in each sector differ substantially in ways of people management, as has the impact of HRM effectiveness on organization performance. On the other hand, since state-owned enterprises (SOEs) are still considered the backbone of the country's economy, HRM practices in Vietnam bear many characteristics of this sector up until now.

In 1999, the state-owned sector contributed the highest to GDP (49 percent), followed by the private sector (41 percent), and foreign-invested sector (10 percent). In order of importance, the three sectors provided 9, 90 and 1 percent of total employment respectively, of which the non-state sector (the household and farm sector) still occupies a large part (Table 9.3).

*Table 9.3* GDP and employment by type of ownership in Vietnam, 1999

| % of GDP | GDP by ownership | | Employment by ownership | |
|---|---|---|---|---|
| | Share in 1999 | Growth '96–'99 | Share in 1999 | Growth '96–'99 |
| Total GDP | 100.0 | 7.0 | 100.0 | 3.4 |
| Public (state and collective) | 49.4 | 6.9 | 9.0 | 1.5 |
| Non-state (total) | 40.5 | 5.1 | 90.4 | 3.4 |
| Household and farms | 33.2 | 4.9 | 89.0 | 3.3 |
| Private companies | 7.3 | 9.7 | 1.4 | 12.1 |
| Foreign-invested | 10.2 | 18.1 | 0.6 | 38.5 |

Source: NCSSH, 2001: 33–34.

From the above figures, the state-owned sector generates roughly 5.5 percent to GDP per 1 percent of the total workforce employed on average, while this number is 5.1 percent for private companies and 17 percent for foreign-invested companies. By and large, these figures suggest a better level of productivity in the foreign-invested sector as a result of the high degree of HR utilization as compared to other sectors. In the absence of available figures for subsequent years, it is difficult to make a projection on the productivity improvement of each sector. However, despite its small size and start-up position, the growing number of private enterprises in current years demonstrates a surge in the output/workforce ratio of this sector.

## Management system before the renovation period

Prior to 1986, Vietnam followed a centrally planned economy, in which the Central State Planning Committee determined resource allocation in the whole country. Accordingly, performance targets were distributed to the production units following a rigid bureaucratic and hierarchical management system. Managers in the state enterprises (no private business was allowed) strictly complied with orders coming down from the center, having very little room to exercise their own leadership and management competencies (Quang and Vuong, 2002). SOEs did not necessarily acquire labor with the adequate set of skills and were invariably overstaffed because labor administration arranged employees for individual firms (Doanh and Tran, 1998). It is understandable, therefore, that enterprises did not have much latitude to motivate or discipline their "own" employees/workers since the latter were not directly recruited and managed by them. The enterprise's function of personnel management only focused on basic activities such as distribution of wages, provision of welfare and routine promotion of workers and cadres (*can bo cong nhan vien*) from lower ranks to higher ranks according to centrally set regulations. In the absence of a contractual employment basis, the reward system had only an indirect relationship to enterprise and individual labor effort (Zhu, 2002). Under these circumstances, HRM in modern terms was neither known nor practiced.

The key features of such management systems in the pre-*doi moi* period are evident in Table 9.4.

Until the reunification of the country in 1975, HRM western-style was practically non-existent in all types of organization in Vietnam in terms of concept and practice. In fact, under the centrally planned system, in which private ownership was not permitted, there existed no such distinction between the public and private sectors since the state was the

*Table 9.4* Characteristics of the management system before the renovation period in Vietnam

| Items | Characteristics |
| --- | --- |
| Planning term | Short range (1–2 years) |
| Control devices | Punching clocks; frequent observations |
| | Quantity control |
| | Some quality control (minor) |
| Authority definition | Unclear |
| Degree of decentralization/delegation | Low |
| Leadership style | Paternalistic; autocratic |
| Trust and confidence in subordinates | Medium; "men of the system" |
| Personnel policy | Not stated; not transparent and regulated |
| Communication pattern | Top-down |
| Training programs | Mostly on-the-job training; often not effective and relevant to jobs |
| Motivation | Monetary and psychological |
| Employee morale | Not always high |
| Absenteeism | Low |
| Productivity | Low |

Source: Quang and Vuong (2002).

sole owner of all means of production and employer of all enterprises. All employees or workers were operating according to a unified set of disciplines and were rewarded the same country-wide. Even after having undergone several phases of the "enterprise re-structuring" which started almost simultaneously with the renovation campaign, many organizations and enterprises have still been struggling to do away with the "bad" practices of "full employment" (*bien che*), "subsidy" (*bao cap*), "collective responsibility" (*trach nhiem tap the*) and the like in order to opt for a more effective system of management.

The heritage of a rigid system has gradually given way to more relevant concepts and practices in management, as the Vietnamese economy has been moving closer to a market-oriented economy, albeit with "socialist principles" as described in the next section.

## HRM in transition

As the country has aimed at ambitious targets for development (e.g. to become an "industrialized" country in 2020) and integration (e.g. to become an official member of WTO in 2005), the current development pattern shows many deficiencies to be overcome. The fact is that Vietnam is not short of labor in general, but of skilled personnel, capable of handling work required in developed industries (Quang, 1997). This requires a shift in basic thinking and practices of HRM in a system that had been deep-rooted in a "collective ownership" system for many decades. A review of the HRM evolution throughout the phases of the country's transition into a market-oriented economy will help clarify this change.

## 1975–1990: a "command" personnel administration

Although the overall campaign to renovate the country's economy had already started in early 1987, the real impact was only experienced at the beginning of the 1990s. Under the "command' system, management of HRs was also centralized. Each enterprise had a personnel department (often called "organization department," *Phong To chuc*) which concerned itself more with political and social issues than functional activities. Its main tasks were to keep employee records and to deal with promotion, salary, and benefits at all levels, including the management of the enterprise. The working principles of this system were centralization, secrecy, relationships, and experience (not professionalism). Ideally, the head of the department was a compromise figure for all parties involved, including the party cell, the enterprise management, and the peripheral organizations, such as trade union chapter and other representative associations.

To ensure organization stability, the system guaranteed lifetime employment for all, which provided job security for the employees, but made it inflexible for managers in staffing decisions. Key positions in the enterprises were filled up by discharged revolutionaries and returning graduates from the Soviet Union or Eastern Europe, more on political merit than professional qualifications. As it was based on the "promotion from within" principle, little attention was paid to external sources of recruitment and selection. Word-of-mouth, connections and employee's referral were the most practiced methods. Job advertisement in the media was not available since advertising was not possible until the market concept was adopted. Family history profile and contribution record to the revolution was carefully scrutinized in the selection process and retained in the long-term memories of the heads of department for future promotion and appointment. The pay system was centrally fixed and standardized for all levels to ensure egalitarism. Pay and merit increase were not based on performance, but on seniority, responsibility, and personal judgment. Merit increase was seen as a "distribution of favor" from both the giver and the receiver. No formal appraisal session was planned or held on a regular basis. Training only took place in on-the-job forms, and personal development and career planning were neglected, with the exception of approved potential high-ranking persons. Employee relations were grounded in the socialist basic principle of "collective ownership," which was extensively exhorted to nurture a sense of responsibility and commitment of the workers to their organization.

As it was generally agreed, this mechanistic and egalitarian approach in managing people did not stimulate personal creativity, productivity, and devotion to the common causes of the organization. The poor performance and low level of employee satisfaction in the state-owned sector, with more than a half of SOEs being loss makers or marginally profitable (World Bank *et al.*, 2000: 30), was in part attributed to the failure of this system. The urgent need to turn SOEs into more effective and efficient enterprises to support the country's transitional move have paved the way for the second, but more promising, stage of HRM in Vietnam.

## 1990–the present: learning and building a HRM system

Facing a near-bankrupt economy, the government of Vietnam (GVN) initiated a set of radical reforms to overhaul the whole economy in late 1986. The private companies were recognized for the first time as an integrated part of a "multi-sector" economy in parallel to an overall restructuring of the existing SOEs. In 1988, the government took a step further to welcome foreign investment in an effort to achieve not only quantitative, but also qualitative growth. In the last decade, there have been some positive movements toward improving the organizational effectiveness and human resources development which are described below:

● The number of SOEs has been reduced from 12,000 in 1990 to about 5,300 in 1999. Many of them were consolidated, merged or equitized (a Vietnamese version of partial privatization) for better performance or dissolved due to ineffectiveness (World Bank *et al.*, 2000). As a condition for their existence, the remaining SOEs were urged by the government or tried themselves to work more effectively by adopting modern managerial techniques and improving their competitiveness.

- Only a few years after the promulgation of the Enterprise Law (*Luat Duanh nghiep*), which allows private enterprises to operate on a "level playing field" along with other sectors of the economy, the number of newly registered private companies has risen to 75,000, providing jobs to 2 million people by the end of 2003. More interestingly, the private sector has surpassed the privileged public sector in contributing about 40 percent of the country total GDP as compared with 38 percent by the SOEs (Nyugen, 2003).
- The continuing efforts of the GVN to make Vietnam an attractive destination for foreign investors have resulted, during a period of ten years (1990–2000), in 2,501 projects with a total capital of US\$ 36 billion from more than 700 companies and multinational corporations from 60 countries all over the world (*World Investment Report*, 2001). In 2000, FDIs contributed 12.7 percent to the country's GDP and provided 350,000 jobs nation-wide (*Vietnam 2001 Economic Report*, 2003). The influx of foreign investment has brought modern technologies and managerial expertise into the country, providing "role models" for other sectors in terms of management effectiveness.

Although the enterprises in the three sectors share the same concern about improving performance, there are substantial gaps in the levels of practicing HRM due to difference in the business objectives, historical background and operating conditions of each enterprise.

## Role and status of personnel management and/or HRM

Certainly, the advent of a large number of foreign companies into the Vietnamese market within only a short period of time has effactually changed the business landscape of this country, especially in the perception and the practice of effective management. Western managers and Vietnamese counterparts often show a sharp discrepancy in their philosophy and the way they manage the human resources stock in their companies.

As noted by a researcher, Vietnamese companies are guided by the harmony of long-term relationship and mutual responsibility. In this setup, the employer is expected to take care of employees who show their full commitment and loyalty to the employer (Kamoche, 2001). A direct result of this distinction is that, while foreign-invested companies are striving to bring western practices into organizations, SOEs (in many cases a business partner of joint-ventures) usually do not emphasize formalizing the best HR practices but instead put the company's "social obligations" above the "economic needs" as traditionally required in the "corporate family" concept. Failing to appreciate the need for compromise between these two distinct cultures and business practices might lead to internal conflict and waste of resources. In case one side attempts to impose "best practice" on the other and is blamed by its business partner of being "ethnocentric," it could even be a reason for breaking up the business venture (Quang, 1998b).

The difference in the levels of HRM practices in the three sectors are as follows:

1  In the state-owned sector: Despite its dominant position in the economy and all the privileges enjoyed from the government, the management effectiveness of the majority of SOEs is far from at desired levels. There has been little improvement to the current HRM system due to management incompetence and high resistance to change.
2  In the private sector: Many of the SMEs are initiated and run by young, dynamic, and flexible entrepreneurs. They are willing to work better, eager to learn, but often lack managerial and strategic experience, especially in the area of HRM, to consolidate their business development after the start-up phase. Due to lack of capital, they also overlook the benefits and necessity of training and development.
3  In the foreign-invested sector: Joint-ventures and 100 percent-owned foreign companies stand out for the most advanced HRM practices. With the exception of a few cases, in which the joint venture suffers from internal conflict with its local partner, a fully-fledged HRM department is set up and professional HRM activities are carried out following international standards (mostly from the headquarters).

## Current HRM practices in Vietnam

Modernization of HRM has just recently started to gain momentum in Vietnam. In fact, in tandem with the marketing concept, HRM has been included in the MBA teaching curriculum as a core subject, first introduced in 1993 by foreign-aided programs such as the Swiss-AIT Management Development Program (SAV, financed by the Swiss government) and the Centre Franco Vietnamien de Formation à la Gestion (CFVG, financed by the French government) (Quang, 1997: 276). These programs, followed by several other government-to-government and institution-to-institution programs, offer regular and short training courses that facilitate the development of key skills of future managers based on market economy principles and modern managerial techniques. The influx of foreign investment into the country has added another dimension to the Vietnamese business environment by introducing western-style HRM principles and practices in their daily operations. The discrepancy in HRM practices between sectors may be seen in the ways the enterprises acquire, utilize, develop, and maintain their human resources.

## Recruitment and selection (R & S)

In a society where mutual trust is the norm, as in Vietnam, the use of personal contacts and referrals should be preferred because existing employees would only recommend those whom they know well, or else they would put their reputation at risk. Along with economic development, modern methods have been adopted to optimize the process effectiveness. Many companies resort to a wide range of recruitment options to improve their competitive advantage: meeting with students, participating in the university annual career days and "employment markets," offering internship opportunities, posting job openings directly at colleges, using recruitment agencies' facilities, and placing advertisements in the media (*Saigon Times Weekly*, 2002a, 2002b; *Saigon Times*, 2002). Recruitment centers, which involve an "unknown" third party, invite skepticism in the eyes of HRM managers and are not used very often, although they might provide a large number of applicants, for example, for labor-intensive works.

Prior to 2002, foreign companies were required by Article 132 of the Labor Code to recruit local workers only through a registered employment agency. In practice, many firms recruited employees directly and then formalized it later with the agency. To tackle this loophole, the revised Labor Code allows foreign-invested enterprise to recruit Vietnamese employees either directly or through a third-party agency on the condition that it must notify the local Labor Management Office of all new hires (*Vietnam Economic Times*, 2002; *Vietnam News*, 2002). Along with the economic change, the labor market has shown a significant shift toward more open views, especially among the youth, on greater, more flexible and prevalent opportunities than just stability, as before (An, 2002).

As selection criteria, companies usually look for academic records, long-term commitment, and discipline. To be more specific, discipline is understood as the deference to authority, dependability, and punctuality. Long-term commitment is highly valued because weathering a long wartime period has imprinted in Vietnamese the need to establish a trusting relationship (Kamoche, 2001). Experience is widely said to be the key to selection decision. However, this is not always a reliable factor as many companies have found only later that the newly recruited "experienced" people did not work well (*Saigon Times*, 2002). To avoid such a blunder, corporate employers in Ho Chi Minh City prefer to recruit fresh graduates from colleges and provide intensive and practical training as a substitute for experience requirement. Beside qualifications-related criteria, kinship and nepotism may come actively into play when decisions are made in local companies. In private companies, place of birth may be favorably considered by recruiting executives, because it provides a psychological attachment and a sense of solidarity.

An interview is the only formal selection method used in most enterprises. Under the public pressure to make it more transparent and equal, efforts to further formalize selection procedures include complex entrance examinations and a lengthy introduction/training period, especially in government agencies and state-owned enterprises. SMEs often start up with core personnel drawn from close friends or family members of the company founders without going through any formal selection steps, but often confront serious employment problems in the growth phase. On a better footing, well-established companies like P&G, Unilever, British Tobacco Co., Johnson & Johnson, etc. frequently launch aggressive campaigns to recruit young graduates at college campuses, use appropriate tests and interviews to screen applicants and set up their own assessment centers to select potential managers for their HR needs. The MNCs are in particular motivated to "localize" their operations by recruiting local nationals in order to reduce excessive overheads caused by high expatriate content and to convey a "good citizen" image to government officials (Quelch and Dinh-Tan, 1998).

Generally speaking, staffing activities in Vietnamese enterprises are not as effective as in foreign-invested companies (*Vietnam Economic Times*, 2001). Since SOEs still enjoy several kinds of subsidy and protection from the government, many of them employ an excessive number of workers and become victims of their own "full employment" commitment. This is aggravated by a high ratio of senior workers who have not yet reached the mandatory retirement age but cannot be re-trained for the new job requirements (*Vietnam Economic News*, 8 June 1999). Under the pressure of the current restructuring campaign, it is likely that those SOEs with overstaffing problems will give recruitment and selection a high priority in their agenda.

The effectiveness gap in staffing is further apparent in the management appointment process between sectors. While HRM managers in the private and foreign-invested sectors are given full authority in management staffing, high-level appointments in the state-owned enterprises are still handled according to government-prescribed procedures (Tan Duc, 2001). Accordingly, the prime minister appoints both the members of the board of management and the CEO, while the "owner" minister holds the decision on the positions of director and deputy directors of state-owned corporations and enterprises. More often than not, the CEO has limited authority in the matter of management staffing. She or he can appoint a head of department only after a consensus is reached with the party cell secretary and other concerned people who together form the locus of power in the enterprise. A direct consequence of this is internal conflict, sectarian views, and authority crisis, which might prevent the enterprise leadership from mobilizing human resources effectively in achieving the common goals.

## Training and development (T & D)

Until recently, cheap labor used to be claimed by the GVN as one of the main sources of the country's competitive advantage to lure foreign investment. This perception has been adjusted toward the real needs of the market, since the critical question of labor productivity was virtually left out of consideration.

In fact, there is a serious shortage of skilled labor in Vietnam to support the drive toward better performance of enterprises and the country development process. According to a report by the HCMC Department of Labor, War Invalids, and Social Affairs (MOLISA), only about one third of the enterprises in operation are satisfied with the qualifications of their new recruits (*Saigon Times Weekly*, 2002c). Criticism aims at training institutes and universities for being unable to meet the real market demand for technical and managerial skills (Kamoche, 2001). Another report by the Ministry of Sciences, Technology, and Environment in 2000 put the blame on the incompetence of the current system: large in number but weak in quality, a team of "old guards" (60 percent of university graduates are over 45, and the average age of professors and associate professors is 57, while there is no team of young and capable experts to replace them), concentrated in urban areas (80 percent in HCMC and Hanoi), with outdated facilities and equipment (far inferior than in most enterprises), and disconnected from the industrial and business community (MOSTE, 2000). In many business entry projects, foreign companies felt that shortage when they figured out that local managers and workers needed training before they were capable of meeting performance standards. Their response was, therefore, focused on extensive pre-job training activities (Schultz et al., 2000).

While the academic community in the country strongly supports the use of training as an effective measure to improve firm performance (Dinh, 1997) and the key to the survival and success of SMEs (Ho, 1999), the business community differs in their viewpoints about training. Managers at foreign-invested companies tend to see training as a motivational tool and as an investment that has a strong chance of being recouped (*Saigon Times*, 2002). On the contrary, SOEs view training as an expense and hence tend to keep the budget allocated for it as small as possible; they also fear that well-trained employees would leave the company for better paid jobs in foreign-invested companies (Quang and Dung, 1998). To be fair, the companies have no laws on which to rely in case employees whom they have trained decide to quit before the expiration date of their contract (Hai Ly, 2001).

Training objectives are perceived distinctively by sectors. A recent survey undertaken by the National University of Economics in Hanoi in 2001 to evaluate the quality of employees in state-owned and foreign-invested companies has shown that, while the former are usually concerned with diplomas, the latter are more concerned with the workplace results (*Vietnam Economic Times*, 2001).

In general, training has been widely used by companies in Vietnam; however, they differed in the use of training options. A survey done by Webster and Tausig (1999) found that 93 percent of the surveyed SMEs provided in-house training for freshmen and off-the-job training was also used. Most SMEs rely only on informal training due to budget constraints (Tran and Le, 1999). More varied training types, such as sending people to seminars, workshops, conferences, or on intensive short courses are offered in larger companies. In a survey of 162 SOEs located in HCMC and neighboring provinces, 32 percent of the respondents expressed the opinion that training and development are considered a means to provide employees with some kind of compensation, especially when such training (often under the form of a study tour) is conducted abroad (Quang and Dung, 1998). In foreign-invested companies, sending people abroad for training and applying more advanced and standardized techniques in training, e.g. orientation, job rotation, simulation and so on are widely applied, where headquarters HRM practices have been brought in with the venture.

There are several factors that may hinder the effectiveness of training efforts, but cannot be easily explained. For example, since the Vietnamese generally value education and show a strong willingness to learn, it should be easy to convert training outcomes into operating performance. In reality, after having acquired the new knowledge and skills, they often show resistance to apply them or to take risks for fear of failure (Kamoche,

2001). In any case, the benefits of training are well known by all enterprises across sectors. A recent empirical study in Hanoi revealed a positive association between training coverage and perceptual performance in 200 surveyed SMEs (Pham, 2001). Another study conducted in Ho Chi Minh City also demonstrated that in those industries such as plastics, where competition is especially high, private firms used to take collective initiative to identify their training needs and adopt proper methods to upgrade the skills of their managers and workers as a means of enhancing their competitiveness. More prosaically, the study revealed that many of the needed skills for top, middle and line managers are HRM-related (Swierczek and Lan Anh, 2000). Similar development is equally apparent in a state organization, which realized the strategic role of HRM and built a management development program for its future managers on that premium (McDaniel *et al.*, 1999).

It is also worth noting that local companies beyond the state sector have started to build their competitive edge by investing in human resources. A survey of thirty newly "equitized" companies pointed to significant improvements in employee's managerial skills and productivity as a direct result of their investment in training (*Vietnam Economic News*, 26 April 1999).

## Performance appraisal (PA)

Performance appraisal is pivotal in HRM as it provides the necessary yardstick for company management to form decisions on motivating, developing, and retaining HRs. It is certainly no less important for Vietnamese companies in search of better quality products and optimal productivity.

In this respect, different PA systems are used in local and foreign companies. SOEs are well known for their tradition of egalitarianism, where the PA system is based on central guidelines called Emulation Standards (*tieu chuan thi dua*). While this system shows its attractiveness in its simplicity, public awareness, and ease-of-use, it does little to motivate employees as it provides only a little cash and honor certificates as rewards for excellent performance. In addition, performance assessment in SOEs depends very much on the agreeableness of the subordinate–manager relationship (Kamoche, 2001); such subjectivity is apparently aimed at maintaining harmony in the organization rather than stimulating internal competition for progress. More often, peer evaluation is used to rate employee performance so as to determine the level of bonuses the latter should receive at year-end. The intention of this system is to create peer pressure which would encourage cooperative efforts among colleague workers, but it can hardly be realized in reality as peer evaluation does poorly in separating between high and low performers. There are two explanations to this phenomenon: (a) the Vietnamese culture values face-saving, which makes people reluctant to rate others unfavorably in front of others as it should be, and (b) everybody considers bonus as a chance to increase her/his income.

It is, therefore, understandable that, although many SOEs have claimed to have appraisal systems, the existing systems are the target of frequent complaints. The problems most frequently mentioned by 47 respondents in the survey of 162 SOEs mentioned above include prejudice, favoritism, insufficient knowledge of employee performance, ignored outcomes, time consuming, deteriorating relationships among workers (Quang and Dung, 1998: 98–99).

On the other hand, most private companies tend to evaluate their employee performance on both formal and informal criteria (Vo and Dinh, 1997). Also, feedback can be provided by an appraiser, but in an informal manner. The Vietnamese were said to prefer direct feedback, so long as it is confidential (Kamoche, 2001). As in foreign-invested companies, the outcomes of the job performance evaluation is taken into consideration for compensation, training, career development, and promotion, particularly where assigned targets have been consistently achieved.

## Compensation and welfare

As the general living standard in Vietnam is still low, remuneration policy can be an effective tool for companies to motivate their employees. Although there might be different applications between industries and regions, the levels of wages in all SOEs depended primarily on the educational qualifications and the length of service of the employee, rather than on his/her performance. Enterprises in the public sector have thus little discretion in designing an effective reward package to motivate their employees and reinforce desired behaviors.

In the 1990s, the *doi moi* reform brought substantial change into the system by allowing SOEs for the first time to determine the pay level according to their ability to pay (Zhu and Fahey, 1999). As a general practice, the employee now receives a pay package including a basic wage, which actually constitutes of only a small portion of a person's total income, the larger part coming from benefits and bonuses. The basic salary of an employee is formed by a combination of position, seniority, and the minimum wage regulated by the MOLISA. Merit pay is scheduled at relatively fixed periods of service of the person in the company. The other part depends on the individual and the company performance in the given year. In effect, the change brought about by *doi moi* has widened the pay differential between the lowest and the highest earner in SOEs from 3.5 times in the early 1980s to 13 times in the late 1990s.

But as mentioned above, the minimum wage bore little resemblance to reality as the emphasis was instead put on other parts of the employee's income. Interestingly enough, many SOEs were found to have paid substantially higher than the JV's required minimum wage of US$35 (Kamoche, 2001). This is understood as a necessary reaction of SOEs to halt the "brain drain" brought about by endless searches for qualified personnel by foreign companies. As a solution to this "job-hopping and poaching" phenomenon (Kamoche, 2001) and to consolidate employee "loyalty," it is suggested that the current compensation policies should be totally changed to enable SOES to attract and retain local talent, and hire foreign experts, especially in the fields of audit and consulting services (CIEM, 22 January 2003). On the other hand, compensation equality can be an issue in JVs where expats are usually brought in to perform certain tasks in the beginning phase of the venture. For example, local experts in fifteen surveyed JVs complained that they only received a fourth or a fifth of their foreign colleagues' salaries for the same work (Lai and Nguyen, 2000).

In 2002, different minimum wages were set for enterprises in the main three sectors. For SOEs, it was set between VND 210,000 (US$14) and VND 525,000 (US$37.50) with a basic top wage of VND 630,000 (US$42) a month if the year-on-year revenue growth of the enterprise was more than 5 percent. As a part of the government's wage reform project aiming at optimizing labor productivity, the GVN has recently announced that from 2003 onwards, enterprises in all sectors will be given full freedom to set their own wage levels (*Vietnam Investment Review*, 2002). As a guideline for the public sector, in the MOLISA's Directive No. 12 in January 2003, the GVN readjusted the minimum wage from VND 210,000 to VND 290,000 (Hong Khanh, 2003a) and up to VND 300,000 per month in 2005, acknowledging that the old level only covered 75 percent of the worker's "basic need." This is far too low compared to the non-state sector, where an accountant is paid monthly VND 3–4 million, an IT expert in a foreign oil exploration company about VND 7 million net, or an engineer in a soft drinks factory more than VND 10 million (Dang, 2002). The subsequent Directive 14 issued by MOLISA in June 2003 further complicates the issue of leveling wages between sectors. Accordingly, the monthly minimum wages are now fixed at VND 626,000 (US$40) for those foreign companies located in Hanoi and Ho Chi Minh City; VND 556,000 in other urban areas like Hai Phong, Bien Hoa, and Vung Tau; and VND 487,000 in other places (Hong Khanh, 2003b).

In any case, the situation in the private sector is believed to be more rational in using basic wage rates and bonus to compensate for employee efforts (Hoang, 1995). While several kinds of bonuses are provided in the form of cash in the majority of enterprises, others also use non-monetary measures to boost employee's motivation. For example, Vietnam Yellow Pages does not offer its employees a higher salary than other SOEs and foreign-invested companies, but it guarantees to treat all new recruits equally and empower them properly to fulfill their tasks (Tan Duc, 2003).

As the competition for better qualified personnel has reached a higher level, enterprises in both state and non-state sectors are trying to include other benefits in addition to their compensation offering. As in foreign-invested companies, many firms are offering a *Tet* (Vietnamese New Year) bonus equivalent of at least one month's salary for all employees who have been working with the firm for more than one year; plus additional benefits such as social security insurance, health insurance, transportation, and meal allowances. Altogether, the benefits and all the "social equality contribution" items can amount to as much as 20–30 percent of salary rates (Gross and Lepage, 2002). There is also a growing tendency among local companies to link pay to individual performance and engage the employee's long-term commitment to the companies by stock options and partnership in ownership.

Another positive outcome derived from the ongoing reform in employment relations is changing the welfare system into a social insurance system (Norlund, 1993). According to Decision No. 12/CP, issued on the January 26 1995, firms have to contribute social insurance for their workers, comprising 20 percent of total wages, of which the firm contributes 15 percent and the individual employee 5 percent. In addition, health insurance makes up 3 percent of total wages and firms are to cover the full contribution. It is reported that the majority of SOEs, as well as a large number of foreign and domestic private enterprises are complying with the government regulations and setting up insurance funds for their employees (Zhu, 2002: 119, 126).

## Industrial relations (IR)

In Vietnam, trade unions are a ubiquitous feature of organization (Kamoche, 2001), which is grounded in the socialist concept of "collective ownership." Under such a system, the trade union chapter in the firm is supposed to work together with the management, other representatives of the "people's organizations" (e.g. youth and women's associations) and the leadership of the Communist Party cell for the mutual benefits of the workers, the business, and the society. Accordingly, labor issues are governed by the Labor Code of 1994 which provides for collective bargaining, the right to strike, protection of worker's rights, and the procedure for dispute resolution (Kamoche, 2001: 643). However, the advent of foreign investments in the last decade has made the employer–employee relationship more of a trade-off exercise than a permanent agony. A survey into the current IR situation in foreign-owned companies in Vietnam reckoned that, with the exception of one US company, all the firms have a union chapter. The union density is also high, by any standards, ranging between 70 and 100 percent. Many of these firms have mutually reached a collective agreement (Zhu, 2002: 129, 130).

Obviously, a smooth and cooperative labor relationship benefits both the business and the government as it lays the ground for stability needed for further economic development. Nevertheless, labor conflicts as a result of cross-cultural difference, business intention and management styles, and so on are not rare, especially in the JVs (Quang, 1998). According to the General Confederation of Trade Unions of Vietnam, since January 1995, there were in total 422 strikes in the whole country, of which 64 took place in SOEs (15.2 percent of total), 229 in foreign-invested companies (54.3 percent), and 129 in other non-state enterprises (30.5 percent) (Tan Duc, 9 January 2003). Interestingly enough, the same source noted that, although the demands raised in the strikes could be justified, they all were "spontaneous" reactions of the workers and "not organized and led by the labor unions" according to the prescribed labor regulations and procedures. Most of the reported strikes were concerned with unsatisfactory levels of salaries, bonuses or overtime pay and abuses of workers' dignity. The most frequent were concentrated in the period prior to and after the *Tet* holidays and mainly in HCMC and the neighboring provinces such as Binh Duong and Dong Nai in the southern part of Vietnam. In particular, the strikes hit most in those invested companies from Taiwan and South

Korea, very well-known for subcontracting businesses using cheap labor such as footwear, garments, and food processing (Tan Duc, 9 January 2003: 17). In any case, as long as the GVN still insists on treating the trade union movement as an integral part of the employment relationship, the collectivist, harmony-seeking, and union-supportive culture may pose a challenge to JVs (Kamoche, 2001), which are required to allow a trade union chapter in the enterprise's premises.

## HRM in the new conditions

As the country is gaining momentum in economic development, Vietnamese companies and public have increasingly emphasized the role and importance of HRM in general and HR managers in particular. Indeed, the recent changes brought about by the "enterprise re-structuring" and FDIs have made profound impacts on HRM and HRD (Zhu, 2002) in all organizations of the country. This can vary from one organization to another, depending on their type of ownership.

To underline this point, a small cross-sector survey (N=30) was undertaken recently by these authors with the members of the Club of HRM Practitioners in Ho Chi Minh City to probe the relationship between the organization's corporate culture and the HRM effectiveness, based on three elements: awareness, practice, and strategic recognition of HRM. The preliminary result is shown in Table 9.5. Ostensibly, the level of HRM practice status, which is generally low in the public sector but higher in the private sector, largely depends on how much the enterprise recognizes the role of HRM, puts it in full practice and reflects it in the corporate long-term strategy.

*Table 9.5* HRM status across sectors in Vietnam (N=30)

| Sector | Awareness | Practice | Strategy |
| --- | --- | --- | --- |
| Government agencies | Low | Low | Low |
| State-owned companies | Low–Medium | Low | Low |
| Private-owned companies | Medium | Low | Low |
| Joint ventures | High | Medium–High | Medium–High |
| 100% foreign-owned companies | High | High | High |

The criteria for gauging the HRM current status are based on three levels:

1 Awareness:  – understanding the strategic role of HRM;
             – there is a physical HRM department/function.
2 Practice:    – the HRM handle all or part of the HRM activities;
             – the level of professionalism in organization (staff, process, procedure, etc.).

3  Strategy:   – the head of HRD department sits on management board;
            – HRM strategy is integrated in the company's strategy;
            – HRM department plays an important role in development and
              implementation of the company's strategy;
            – the company's strategy is focused on HR development.

## The role of the HRM manager

Regarding the awareness of the role of the HR manager, another survey of local
companies, undertaken in 2002, explained the complexity of the issue. Usually, local
companies did not have a HR manager position, but a combined function called
administration and personnel manager (*Truong phong Hanh chanh va Nhan su*).
In practice, personnel managers focus only on administrative, even secretarial, works
concerning personnel administration, but rarely are involved in key decisions concerning
HM matters, such as HR planning, recruitment and selection of new personnel,
compensation policy, and training and development. They also lack the essential
knowledge and skills on HRM to perform the professional tasks well. Due to the secret
nature of the perceived work, coordination or communication with other departments is
almost non-existent. More often than not, the company's director handles the personnel
matters himself, hence limiting the head of the personnel department to merely
formalizing the decisions made by the director (Chien, 2002; Tan Duc, 2002). On the
whole, the majority of these respondents, representing 208 cross-sector enterprises,
showed a better development trend in recognizing the role of the HRM Department in
Ho Chi Minh City, where the country's business is most concentrated and more
advanced than in other parts of the country (Table 9.6).

*Table 9.6* Awareness vs. actual HRM activities in Vietnamese companies (N=208,
HCMC)

| Activities | Importance ranking * | Current status** |
|---|---|---|
| HR planning | 10 | 9 |
| Develop and implement compensation plan | 9 | 5 |
| Develop and manage HR budget | 8 | 6 |
| Training and development | 7 | 10 |
| Performance appraisal | 6 | 7 |
| Employee relations | 5 | 2 |
| Develop and maintain corporate culture | 4 | 8 |
| Recruitment and section of HRs | 3 | 4 |
| External relations | 2 | 3 |
| Administrative management | 1 | 1 |

Source: Chien (2002: 13); Note: 1–10 scale (1 = least important, 10 = most important); * level of
importance (awareness); ** level of application (reality).

A more optimistic picture may be observed in the foreign-invested companies. The fact that 95 percent of the members of the self-established "Club of HRM Managers" (*Cau lac bo Giam doc Nhan su*)[1] are working for foreign-invested companies indicate that these firms are more aware of the role of HRM and hence have more interest in expecting HRM best practices. In the discussions with them, it emerged clearly that the HRM managers play an important role in the company organizations and are highly appreciated by the company management and employees. HRM managers in this sector are not confined only to handling salary and recruitment activities, as are their counterparts in the state-owned sector, but have more roles to play (Thuc Doan, 2002). As members of the board of directors, the HR director/manager in foreign-invested companies is also involved in the overall strategic planning.

In spite of positive developments in the last five years, the initiatives taken by local enterprises with regard to HRM have still been either piecemeal or not driven by a clear strategic vision. HRM techniques or principles such as job analysis, HRIS, quality of work life (QWL), ergonomics, dual career, outsourcing, employee retention, career development, job rotation, succession planning, developmental appraisal, or even pay for performance, should be put in full play and in good combination so as to create optimal impact on the firms' effectiveness.

Needless to say, the recognition of HRM's strategic role and its full integration into the corporate strategy in all phases will augur well for better performance of both the enterprise (micro level) and the country (macro level).

## Key challenges to HRM in Vietnam

The quest for quality improvement to support the country's continued drive for economic development and economic integration will present the as yet under-developed HRM with both opportunities and challenges in the coming years. The following are the most remarkable developments in HRM in Vietnam that will continue in the years to come:

1 *Proactive search for qualified personnel*: Under the pressure of competition, local firms, private and SOES alike, are taking more proactive moves in finding the best pool of applicants. They cooperate more closely with universities and training institutions in creating nursery grounds for the "best of breed," by granting scholarships for students with good academic performance, providing internship opportunities, participating in job fairs, organizing "open house" to market the

---

1 There were 95 members in mid-2002, representing a wide range of enterprises in all sectors, but mostly from foreign-invested companies. The members use the Internet to exchange views on critical HRM issues currently facing them and help each other to find a proper solution from their practical experience. The e-mail contact address of the Club is: nam_nguyen @cargill.com.

company, and announcing job openings widely in the media. In the late 1990s, these activities were considered peculiar only to foreign-invested companies (Nam Hoang, 2000).

The shift in both perception and practice in recruitment could be explained by the tighter labor market for skilled employees. The emphasis on the criticality of HRs for business success (Kamoche, 2001), the high labor demand initiated by the steady growth of the economy, and the availability of attractive job opportunities abroad have emerged as key drivers for this new type of competition (Chanh Khai, 2002; Ngoc Minh, 2002).

2  *More attention on employee retention*: At a conference on exchange of managerial experience among Vietnamese companies with top-quality prizes in 1999, three main concerns were most mentioned, one of which was the issue of retaining skilled and qualified employees (Huynh Kim, 1999). To underline the importance of this aspect on the company livelihood, Vietnamese managers have started to provide training and discuss career development with employees, and to build a corporate culture and teamwork in the company, next to monetary instruments.

3  *Using training and development as a means to build competitive edge*: While training was seen as one of the most indispensable activities to develop HRs in foreign-invested companies since their first day at work, local companies mostly relied on recruiting trained employees to acquire their HR stocks. Until recently, training and development was taken for granted by the business community as the responsibility of the government. The first public effort to call for companies to participate in training was made by a businessman with academic talent at the end of 1996 (Do, 1996). Local companies now consider training a necessary investment with good payback on future employee productivity. More companies are making proper reserves in their budget to send people to off-the-job short training courses, financing employee long-term studies or finding ways to outsource their in-house training needs.

4  *Building HRM professionalism*: Along with the growing awareness of the critical role of HRM, both the government and the business community, fully-fledged HRM departments have been added to company organizations with clarified functions and tasks. This gives rise to the development of a generation of trained professionals in HRM. In HCMC alone, there are no less than twenty foreign-initiated MBA programs which, together with local universities, introduce the concept of modern HRM in the teaching curriculum of business education. Today, many young graduates are seeking HRM careers in companies as their committed profession. They are, in effect, the vanguards who bring changes into the management system by means of practicing all HRM activities in a professional way.

Other factors may also be attributed to this change. It is generally perceived that there is a considerable gap between what the companies require and how the students are being trained by the system. Therefore, training provided by the companies is now seen as a necessary tool not only to fix this mismatch, but also to reward and retain people.

5  *Emphasizing the task of management development*: Local enterprises should have concrete and effective plans to prepare for management succession and a future stock

of managers in order to meet the growing need for competent and professional managers. This can be done by a combination of altering and adapting the teaching curriculum of the current MBA programs to the real needs of the market, campus recruitment of dynamic and promising graduates, training programs and job rotation for management potential, and creating a favorable environment for the mobility of seasoned managers from "good" to "bad" enterprises through headhunting services.

6 *Partly easing or fully lifting government control and intervention on the HRM activities of enterprises*: for example, the setting up the minimum and maximum wages and in the appointment of high level positions, so that firms can have a free hand to link compensation to performance and hire qualified managers from all available sources as the need arises, including foreign experts.

It is understandable that more and more enterprises in Vietnam have been focusing on capitalizing their human assets in the face of intensifying competition. In the long run, only companies which have paid proper attention to HRM, among other strategic adjustments, will reap the benefits of their efforts and survive the complex test of globalization in the years to come.

## Conclusion

This chapter provides an overview of how HRM has emerged over time as a critical issue, both in qualitative and quantitative terms, in all organizations in Vietnam. Due to long periods of external colonialization and internal conflict, the concern for proper management of the most valuable asset has been given due attention only after the country decided to jettison the system of central planning and subsidy. The old, rigid system was then replaced by a more flexible and market-oriented structure, well-known to the world as the *doi moi* policy, to jumpstart the country's bid for quick development and economic integration, which puts a premium on recognizing the right of private ownership, stimulating individual productivity, and rewarding individual contribution to the overall achievement of the organization, public and private alike.

As a matter of fact, the advent of significant foreign investment at the beginning of the 1990s has provided "good" models of well-functioning organizations under the forms of joint ventures and fully owned enterprises, and triggered the sense of urgency for the local firms to follow. To be fair, it should be mentioned that the SOEs, which form the driving force and represent the majority of the national economy, had pioneered with the "enterprise restructuring" campaign to streamline their cumbersome structure, downsize their unproductive workforce, and introduce more effective managerial methods in order to regain their position in the markets. However, since most of these SOEs (including the "equitized/privatized" enterprises) are so desperately and deeply rooted in the past heritage, they are not flexible and innovative enough to take advantage of the new momentum and to emerge as "equal" players in the increasingly competitive business environment. On a comparative basis, the newly established domestic private enterprises, despite their disadvantageous position as latecomers, have benefited the most from the "good" models of effective management thanks to their smaller size and willingness to learn.

To this effect, the analysis of the HRM development in the post-renovation period has underlined a significant difference, yet explainable, in the levels of adopting and practicing modern principles of managing human resources in the state sector (public agencies and SOEs) and the non-state sector (foreign-owned enterprises and domestic private enterprises). Several cited surveys indeed show that there is a wide gap between these enterprises in terms of HRM effectiveness, with a clear preference for the foreign-invested enterprises based on their long and well-proven practices in both home and host countries.

In the final analysis, all organizations in Vietnam, no matter in which status, position and stage of development they are, have begun to realize the important and/ or strategic role of HRM in the process of regaining, building or sustaining their competitiveness in the face of a market expanding toward more global integration. Arguably, such a condition requires a total transformation of the whole organization, industry, and nation, in which HRM is the most critical success factor of all, especially for an economy in transition like Vietnam.

# References

An, N.P (2002). "Looking beyond *Bien Che*: The considerations of young Vietnamese graduates when seeking employment in the *Doi Moi* era," *Journal of Social Issues in Southeast Asia* 17 (2): 221–248.

Chanh K. (2002) "Thi truong Lao dong: Cung khong du Cau" (The labor market: Supply does not meet demand), *Thoi bao Kinh te Sai Gon*, 27 June: 23.

Chien, N.N. (2002) "Chan dung con mo nhat" (The profile is still blurred), *Thoi bao Kinh te Sai Gon*, 27 June: 12–13.

CIEM, Central Institute for Economic Management (2003) Economic Integration, January 22; hrrp://www.ciem.org.vn/index.php?newlang-english.

Dang, Tran Bach (2002) "Cai cach Che do Tien luong: Mot Cuoc Cach mang That su" (The reform of the compensation policy: A real revolution), *Thoi bao Kinh te Sai Gon*, December 5.

Dinh, H. (1997) *Human resource management*, 3rd edition, Hanoi: Education Publishing Company.

Do, D.V. (1996) "Kinh nghiem Dao tao Nhan luc: Doanh nghiep Phai Tham gia" (Experience on human resources training: Enterprises should participate), *Thoi bao Kinh te Sai Gon*, 26 December: 41.

Doanh, L.D. and Tran, T.C. (1998) "The SOE reform policies in Vietnam and their implementation performance" in Ministry of Planning and Investment, *Study on economic development policy in the transition toward a market-oriented economy in Vietnam*, Phase 2, Hanoi: Ministry of Planning and Investment and Japan International Cooperation Agency, 4: 19–49.

Gross, A. and Lepage, S. (2002) "Vietnam human resources update," *Corporate Relocation News*, Pacific Bridge, Inc.

Hai L. (2001). "Chuyen khong Binh thuong duoi Mat mot Nha Dau tu" (An unusual thing under the eyes of an investor), *Thoi bao Kinh te Sai Gon*, 29 March: 19.

Ho, V.V. (1999). "Experience of SME development in Asian countries," working paper presented at the Workshop of SME Support Policies in Industrialization and Modernization Process, Ministry of Planning, Hanoi.

Hoang, V. (1995) "Compensation in private enterprises," working paper, Hanoi: University of Economics.

Hofstede, G. (1997) *Cultures and organizations: Software of the mind*, New York: McGraw-Hill.

Hofstede, G. (1998) "Think locally, act globally: Cultural constraints in personnel management," *Management International Review* 38: 7–26.

Hong, K. (2003a) "Lam viec Ngay le duoc Huong luong gap 3 Ngay thuong" (Working in holidays will be paid three times higher than the normal days), *VNExpress*, 6 June.

Hong, K. (2003b) "Luong tai Doanh Nghiep Nuoc Ngoai Toi thieu la 487,000 Dong" (The minimum wages at foreign companies is VND 487,000), *VNExpress*, 7 June.

Hung, L.N., Appold, S.J. and Kalleberg, A.L. (1999). "Work attitudes in Vietnam: Organizational commitment and job satisfaction in a restructuring economy," *Journal of Asian Business* 15 (3): 41–48.

Huynh, K. (1999) "Ba Chuyen Lo lon cua Doanh nghiep" (The three big concerns of enterprises), *Thoi bao Kinh te Sai Gon*, 18 November: 36.

Lai, X.T. and Nguyen, T.T.D. (2000) "Assessing international joint ventures performance in Vietnam", in Truong Quang (ed.) *Vietnam: The challenges on the path to development*, Bangkok: SAV-SOM Joint Publishing.

McDaniel, D.O, Schermerhorn Jr., J. and Cuoc, H.T. (1999) "Vietnam: the environment for management development in the twenty-first century," *Journal of Management Development* 18 (1): 79–93.

MOSTE (Ministry of Science, Technology and Environment) (2000) *Strategy for scientific and technological development to the tear 2010*, Hanoi.

Nam, H. (2000). "Chu dong Tim Nhan vien" (Active in searching for new personnel), *Thoi bao Kinh te Sai Gon*, 1 July: 30.

NCSSH (National Center for Social Sciences and Humanities) (2001) *Doi Moi and human development in Vietnam*, National Human Development Report 2001, Hanoi: The Political Publishing House.

Ngoc, M. (2002) "Xuat khau Lao dong qua Malaysia: Dang thieu Nguoi" (Labor export to Malaysia: A shortage), *Thoi bao Kinh te Sai Gon*, 21 March: 42.

Nguyen, Si Dung (2003) "Tu nhan cung la Quoc dan," (Individuals are also nationals), *Thoi bao kinh te Sai Gon*, November 13, p. 20.

Norlund, I. (1993) "The creation of a labor market in Vietnam: Legal framework and practices", in C.A. Thayer and D. Marr (eds.) *Vietnam and rule of law*, Canberra: Australian National University Press, pp. 173–189.

Pham, N.T. (2001) "Human resource management practice and SME performance," unpublished DBA research report, Southern Cross University.

Quang, T. (1997) "Sustainable economic growth and human resource development," *Transitions* XXXVIII (1&2): 256–280.

Quang, T. (1998) "A case of joint venture failure: Procter & Gamble vs. Phuong Dong in Vietnam', *Journal of Euro-Asia Management* 4 (2): 85–101.

Quang, T. (2001) "Vietnam: The quest for improving competitiveness," in T. Quang (ed.) *Vietnam: Gearing up for integration*, Bangkok: SAV/SOM Joint Publishing, pp. 3–14.

Quang, T. and Dung, H.K. (1998) "Human resources development in state-owned enterprises in Vietnam," *Research and Practice in Human Resource Management* 6 (1): 85–103.

Quang, T. and Vuong, N.T. (2002) "Management styles and organizational effectiveness in Vietnam," *Research and Practice in Human Resource Management* 10: 2.

Quelch, J.A. and Dinh-Tan, M. (1998) "Country managers in transitional economies: The case of Vietnam," *Business Horizon*, July–August: 34–40.

Ralston, D.A., Thang, N.V. and Napier, N.K. (1999) "A comparative study of the work values of north and south Vietnamese managers," *Journal of International Business Studies* 30 (4): 655–672.

*Saigon Times* (2002) "Employers prefer new graduates," 5 January.

*Saigon Times Weekly* (2002a) "Students care more about job opportunities," 24 June.

*Saigon Times Weekly* (2002b) "HCMC wants recruiters to charge employers, not applicants," 17 April.

*Saigon Times Weekly* (2002c) "Career Day," 15 June.

Schultz, C.J, Speece, M.W. *et al.* (2000) "The evolving investment climate in Vietnam and subsequent challenges to foreign investors," *Thunderbird International Business Review* 42 (6): 735–753.

Swierczek, F.W. (1994) "Culture and conflicts in joint-ventures in Asia," *International Journal of Project Management* 12 (1): 7.

Swierczek, F.W. and Lan Anh, T.T. (2000) "Management training needs: An assessment of Vietnam Saigon plastics association," in T. Quang (ed.) *Vietnam: Challenges on the path to development*, Bangkok: SAV/SOM Joint Publishing, pp. 237–260.

Tan Duc (2001) "Quan ly Nhan su o Doanh nghiep Nha nuoc" (HRM in state-owned enterprises), *Thoi bao Kinh te Sai Gon*, 18 October: 14.

Tan Duc (2002) "Qua Quan trong nen phai "om" het" (Too important to keep all for himself), *Thoi bao Kinh te Sai Gon*, 27 June: 14–15.

Tan Duc (2003) "Trach nhiem hon Nghiep vu" (The sense for responsibility is more important than the professional skills," *Thoi bao Kinh te Sai Gon*, 9 January.

Thuc, D. (2002) "Khong chi lo Tien luong hay Tuyen dung" (Not only taking care of salary and recruitment), *Thoi bao Kinh te Sai Gon*, 27 June: 16.

Thuy, L.X. and Doan, N.T.T. (2000) "Assessing international joint ventures performance in Vietnam," in T. Quang (ed.) *Vietnam: the challenges on the path to development*, Bangkok: SAV-SOM Joint Publishing.

Tran, K.H. and Le, V.S. (1999) "HRM and SME development in Vietnam," paper presented at Human Resource Management Symposium on SMEs, APEC, National Sun Yat-sen University, Taipei, Taiwan.

Tuan, V.V. and Napier, N.K. (2000) "Paradoxes in Vietnam and America: Lessons earned," *Human Resource Planning* 23 (1): 7–8; (2): 9–10; (3): 8–10.

*Vietnam 2001 Economic Report*, http://wwww.uk-vietnam.org/commerce/Economic%20Report.html; accessed on 13 January 2003.

*Vietnam Economic News* (1999) "Vietnam: Will equitisation succeed nation-wide?," Hanoi, 26 April.

*Vietnam Economic News* (1999) " Vietnam: Out of job," Hanoi, 8 June.

*Vietnam Economic Times* (2001) "VN manpower lacks global potency," 21 February.

*Vietnam Economic Times* (2002) "Revised labor law approved by the national assembly," 3 April.

*Vietnam Economic Times* (2003) http://www.vneconomy.com.vn/index.php?action=thongtin&chuyenmuc=03&id=030509143800

*Vietnam Investment Review* (2002) "Firms given a freehand to lift wage levels next year," 10–16 June.

*Vietnam News* (2002) "Labor code works for benefit of all," 7 June.

Vo, N.T. and Dinh, H. (1997) "Use of performance appraisal in private enterprises in Ho Chi Minh City," working paper, Hanoi: National Economics University.

Webster, L. and Tausig, M. (1999) *Vietnam's undersized engine: A survey of 95 larger private manufacturers*, Mekong Project Development Facility, 8, Hanoi.

World Bank, Asian Development Bank and UNDP (2000) "Vietnam 2010: Entering the 21st century," *Vietnam Development Report 2001*, 14–15 December.

World Investment Report (2001) *Promoting linkages*, New York and Geneva: UNCTAD.

Zhu, Y. (2002) "The reform and human resource management in Vietnam," *Asia Pacific Business Review* 8 (3): 115–134.

Zhu, Y. and Fahey, S. (1999). "The impact of economic reform on industrial labor relations in China and Vietnam," *Post-Communist Economies* 11 (2): 173–192.

# Useful websites

Newspapers and Journal:
Lao Dong (*The Worker Journal*):  http://www.laodong.com.vn
Nguoi Lao Dong (*The Worker*
  *Weekly*):  http://www.nld.com.vn
*Saigon Times Weekly*:  http://www.saigontimesweekly.saigonnet.vn
*Tuoi Tre* (*Youth Daily Weekly*):  http://www.tuoitre.cum.vn
*Vietnam Economic Times*:  http://www.vneconomy.com.vn
*Vietnam Investment Review*:  http://www.vir.com.vn

Home Pages
Vietnamese Human Resources
  Club:  http://www.vnhrclub.com
Vietnamese Labor Law:  http://www.hcmste.gov.vn/ldldhcm/cac-luat/luat-ld/luat-ld.htm
UNDP Vietnam:  http://www.undp.org.vn
World Bank Vietnam:  http://www.worldbank.org.vn

# 10 HRM in Malaysia

**KAMEL MELLAHI AND GEOFFREY T. WOOD**

Whilst there is little doubt that there has been a convergence of HRM practices in key areas – most notably in a general weakening of security of tenure – national particularities persist. This reflects the nested nature of social institutions. This chapter demonstrates that in Malaysia a range of authority mechanisms prevail at community, national and international level, shaping economic and social outcomes. This explains the continuance of various national forms of business practice, and, indeed, the unequal performance of different nations.

In recent years, it has become increasingly accepted that employees represent a core component of organizational capacity, and that the manner in which various human resource functions are carried out reflects wider organizational and social realities. The differing performance of firms, industries and nations in part reflects distinct approaches to handling employment relations and management, and the manner in which in-firm practices diffuse and are replicated across a specific economy to organize collaboration, and provide protection against overly-opportunistic behavior that might erode economic and social solidarity (cf. Marsden 1999).

Despite the shock of the Asian financial crisis of the late 1990s, and subsequent pressures towards deregulation along neoliberal lines – which, in theory at least, entails treating labor no more or less than any other commodity – the practice of HRM in Malaysia continues to exhibit a number of distinctive features. These include targeted affirmative action policies, paternalism (at both governmental and firm level) and active state efforts to promote the competitiveness of selected areas of industry. In this chapter we introduce the key features of Malaysia's political economy, and locate the practice of HRM therein. This is followed by an assessment of the various external pressures with which the system has had to contend, recent trends, and potential challenges facing HR and general managers within this emerging economy.

## Political context

Malaysia is a federation of thirteen states with a parliamentary system of government based on periodic multiparty elections in which the ruling National Front coalition has held power since 1957. The Malaysian government is a coalition of communally based political parties with the United Malays National Organization playing a pivotal role (Todd and Peetz, 2001: 1367).

The need to maintain a satisfactory relationship between the three main ethnic groups has dominated political, economic and social policies in Malaysia since World War II (Todd and Peetz, 2001: 1367). Malaysia is a multi-ethnic society consisting of 61.7 percent Malays, 27.2 percent Chinese, 7.7 percent Indians and 3.4 percent others (Malaysia, 1985). It has a population of just over 23 million. Malaysia gained her independence from Britain in 1957. Soon thereafter, Malaysia embarked on an ambitious industrial development program, with a strong emphasis being placed on diversification and sustainability. Whilst a market system dominated by ethnic Chinese persisted, targeted interventions in the industrial sector resulted in the increasing production of secondary and tertiary goods. On independence, Malaysia had inherited a well-developed infrastructure, an efficient administrative system, and a thriving primary export sector. However, the country remained an economically, politically and socially polarized and unbalanced multi-racial society. Race was identified according to economic activities. Crudely described, "Malays were paddy cultivators, Indians as rubber tappers, and Chinese as businessmen" (Abdullah, 1997). While the Chinese held economic power, the Malays held political power but with very little economic power. Abdullah (1997: 192) notes that

> the more salient and significant demographic feature of Malaysia – especially in the early years of independence, and which, to a relatively lesser extent persists today – was the association of ethnic identification and economic activities and geographic areas, namely rural and urban.

This led to the development of a plural society "which lives side by side, yet without mingling into one political unit" (Furnivall, 1956: 304: quoted in Abdullah, 1997: 192). Abdullah (1997: 189) notes that such "professional categorisation" drawn along ethnic lines has not only implied social compartmentalization but also economic stratification. The latter led to the development of a pluralistic society characterized by "differences, jealousies, suspicions and even animosities but in which people yet lived or had to live, in the same country" (Abdullah 1997: 196). The Malays, the majority and original people, felt that they were deprived from obtaining education, and employment in the thriving industrial and mining sectors.

The tensions between the different ethnic communities finally erupted on 13 May 1969 with the destruction of life and property. The government assumption that by increasing the overall size of the national income, most of the ethnic problems would be alleviated, proved unrealistic (see Snodgrass *et al.*, 2003). The response of the Malaysian government to the 1969 disturbances was twofold: on the one hand, an increasing authoritarianism with minimal tolerance or dissent; on the other hand, a paternalistic stance towards the bumiputras, presenting itself as "the protector" of their interests. Long-serving Prime Minister Dr Mahathir has justified the latter as follows:

In Malaysia it would have been easy to give a free hand to the very dynamic and business oriented non-indigenous Chinese Malaysian to develop and enrich the country. But then the indigenous people would remain poor and have a sense of deprivation. They would be bitter and angry and would rise against people whom they would regard as foreigners who had stolen wealth that rightly belongs to them. They would destroy the wealth which had been created and the country would fail to develop. In the end everyone would lose and the country would have to beg for foreign aid and accept the conditions imposed.

(Mahathir, 1999)

## Recasting racial segmentation and enhancing growth: key government policy interventions

The 1969 disturbances led directly to the introduction of the New Economic Policy (NEP) in 1971. The NEP was, quite simply, a twenty-year plan aimed at raising the status of poor bumiputras (ethnic Malays and other native races) to economic parity with the Chinese minority, through affirmative action targets. The NEP aimed to ensure that ethnic Malays achieved at least 30 percent representation in all occupations by 1990 (Jayasankaran, 1999: 52). In return, Chinese businesses received explicit guarantees that a market-based system would be retained (Le Roux, 2001: 216).

The NEP shifted the focus from pure economic development to economic advancement of the ethnic Malays. The NEP was based on the premise that the best way to achieve economic development without ethnic strife was through targeted affirmative action policies in the urban areas, coupled with rural development initiatives aimed at improving the material conditions of the indigenous population (see Kuruvilla and Arudsothy, 1995; Le Roux, 2001). For instance, according to the NEP, any firm which went public had to meet the NEP requirement of at least 30 percent bumiputra ownership. As a result the bumiputra-owned proportion of share capital in Malaysian limited companies rose from 4.3 percent to 20.3 percent during the 1971–1990 period (Lucas and Verry, 1996). Another objective of the NEP was to assist the creation of a Malay business class. For instance in 1970, Malay businesses accounted for 14.2 percent of business in Malaysia; by 1980 the percentage increased to 24 and reached 30.5 percent in 1985. The growth rate of Malay business is nearly double the growth of non-Malay business expansion (Noordin et al., 2002: 46). Throughout the 1970s, the economy grew at an average annual rate of 7.8 percent. Unemployment during the NEP period averaged around 6.5 percent. Within two decades, the proportion of the population living in poverty was reduced from more than half to about one tenth, with the emergence of an indigenous business class (Le Roux, 2001: 217). However, despite political intervention through the NEP's affirmative action, the identification of ethnic grouping with occupation and industry still persists (Todd and Peetz, 2001: 1367). The average household income for bumiputras remains lower than that of the Chinese and Indian communities, although the former enjoyed the fastest income growth from 1970 to 1989 (Lucas and Verry, 1996).

In 1981, Malaysian Prime Minister Dr Mahathir Mohamed proclaimed the Look East Policy doctrine. Simply put, Malaysia would look to Japan as its primary economic development model. Malaysian engineers and technicians were sent to Japan for formal training (Elger and Smith, 2001: 461). In practice, only limited knowledge transfer took place. Even in Japanese firms operating in Malaysia, there continues to be considerable divergence not only from the Japanese model, but also from the actual operations of their parent company in Japan. This underscores the continued importance of local economic, political and social conditions (ibid.: 460).

In contrast to the limited effects of Look East, official affirmative action policies continued to have a far-reaching impact. In 1990, the NEP was succeeded by the National Development Plan (NDP), this time a 10-year policy intervention. The NDP specified that a range of key posts should be filled by bumiputras. Although the NEP's 30 percent target had not yet been achieved, the NDP introduced new plans for extending affirmative action through the sale of selected state assets to bumiputras and via the allocation of government contracts (Morris et al., 2001). The NDP was supplemented by a further policy intervention, "Vision 2020," a plan to accelerate industrialization through sector restructuring, technology upgrading, human resource development and industry linkages. Long-range goals included doubling GNP every 10 years and achieving global competitiveness in high-tech industries by the year 2020.

Since the adoption of the NDP and Vision 2020, growth has been the government's primary strategic economic objective. The growth strategy in the 1990s was based on capital-intensive investment, aimed at supporting improvement of labor productivity and income growth. The privatization of public services and infrastructure continued as a means of improving efficiency and reducing the burden on the budget. Skills upgrading and technology development were needed to support the productivity-oriented strategy. In this context, HR development became a key component of the new development strategy. Other strategic objectives were poverty reduction, improvement in quality of life and sustainable development. An Industrial Master Plan (IMP), launched in late 1996, addressed issues to sustain and enhance growth in the manufacturing sector.

Confidence in the Malaysian model was severely dented by the Asian financial crisis of 1997. The Malaysian Ringgit severely depreciated, whilst growth declined from some from 8 percent in 1997 to –5 percent in 1998. Conversely, unemployment rose from 2.6 percent in 1997 to 4.9 percent in 1998 (Todd and Peetz, 2001: 1368).

In reaction, the government established the National Economic Action Council (NEAC) in January 1998 to manage the impact of the crisis. In August 1998, NEAC published the National Economic Recovery Plan (NERP) which defined a short-term crisis management strategy. Overall, NERP aims to restore economic development by stimulating domestic demand, maintaining progress in the social sectors and protecting the poor. The plan sought to promote a range of long-standing policy objectives: ameliorate the hardship from poverty; promote bumiputra equity ownership; expand employment opportunities; meet the challenge of expanding tertiary education; and address graduate unemployment. However, the plan also called for greater deregulation, above all in making state corporations more competitive, and for the influx of foreign workers to be curbed (NERP, 1998). While underlying contradictions were not necessarily solved, the Malaysian economy rapidly recovered, albeit at the cost of increased indebtedness (ibid.).

## Training, development, competitiveness and investment

Malaysian economic development is one of the few success stories, a story of export-led industrialization. Malaysia has recorded strong productivity growth since the late 1980s and 1990s, the 1997 financial crisis notwithstanding. Productivity increased by 5 percent during the 1991–1995 period. This in part may be ascribed to a strong emphasis being placed on skills development. A manpower survey conducted by the federal government in 1965 (with the assistance of the United Nations) indicated that there was a shortage of trained professionals, especially among the bumiputras (Morris et al., 2001). This led to a rapid expansion in technical training. By 1994, Malaysia had emerged seventeenth in national competitiveness according to the World Competitiveness Report, a rating buoyed up by the high priority placed on research and development (R&D) and on skills development and training initiatives. Malaysia has developed from a largely commodity producer to a predominantly industrialized country: the manufacturing sector accounted for around 35 percent of GDP. Malaysia has become an important center in the global electronic production network (SocGen, 1997, quoted in Noordin et al., 2002: 46).

Malaysia relies heavily on foreign direct investment (FDI), attracted by a stable economic and political business environment, combined with a friendly IR environment as well as taxation allowances. Few investors seem deterred by the Mahathir government's increasing authoritarianism. Within the manufacturing sector, foreign firms account for 44 percent of manufacturing value added and 76 percent of manufacturing exports in 1992 (Hill and Athukorala, 1998, cited in Todd and Peetz, 2001: 1368). Malaysia is "an important platform for low-cost mass production" complementing higher value manufacturing in mature industrial societies (Elger and Smith, 2001: 462).

Official policy holds that foreign investors will provide a valuable infusion of managerial knowledge, supplementing the promotion of heavy industries through direct government involvement. The Heavy Industries Corporation of Malaysia (HICOM), a public sector holding company, was formed in 1980 to go into partnership with foreign firms in setting up industries in what were perceived to be strategic sectors such as steel, paper, petrochemicals and automobiles. This directly contributed to a sizable budget deficit during the 1980–1986 period. The global economic slowdown during the late 1980s exposed Malaysia to vagaries of world market fluctuations and resulted in an enforced reduction in the deficit, resulting in HICOM's activities being scaled back. The volatile and uncertain global economy paved the way for a series of radical policy reforms, which placed a greater emphasis on the role of the private sector.

The Promotion of Investment Act of 1986 introduced new and more generous packages and incentives for foreign investors. This, and similar incentives, have encouraged successive waves of investment in standardized mass production. However, there is only limited scope for more complex variants of production activity, given the continued emphasis on cheap labor and managerial autocracy (Elger and Smith, 2001: 461). For example, Elger and Smith (2001: 460) found that Japanese-owned plants were characterized by routing mass assembly and machine minding by semiskilled operatives, supplemented by small groupings of maintenance workers, with little room being accorded for innovation. While sometimes present, quality circles have done little to broaden work roles or responsibility. However, in spheres of activity where competitiveness depends on cheapening labor, lower cost centers such as China are likely to prove more attractive in future (ibid.: 461). A real danger exists that, while proving increasingly uncompetitive in the sweatshop stakes, Malaysia lacks the managerial capacity and institutional precedents to move away from autocratic Fordism to more highly value added production paradigms. Based on an extensive multinational study (encompassing Malaysia) Przeworski *et al.* (2000) conclude that autocratic political institutions result in a higher wage gap; highly paid and skilled production and service sector work is more likely to be found in democracies. An autocratic political environment may make for robust growth, but is also likely to make for labor repression and a slower growth in personal incomes (ibid.). Quite simply, under autocracies, it is easier to ensure labor quiesence without having to make meaningful concessions in the form of higher wages and better working conditions that would necessitate the adoption of higher value added production paradigms.

## Setting labour policy: the Ministry of Human Resources

Since independence in 1957, the Malaysian government had a key role in the design and implementation of personnel policies and practices. One of the key reasons is that the government is the single largest employer in the country. In 1983, one out of every 14 workers in the country was employed by the public sector. By 1994, the number of employees in the public sector had reached more than 850,000 (Yong, 1996). The role of the Ministry of Human Resources during the 1970s was to develop labor administration and labor welfare policies. Since the mid-1980s the Ministry has been given additional responsibilities, including facilitating manpower planning through the monitoring and analysis of labor market information, and industrial training to supply the private sector with the right type of skilled and efficient labor to meet modern technological and industrial requirements. In 1997, the Ministry employed more than 3,500 employees. The Ministry formally seeks to

> develop a caring, yet an effective, efficient and proactive organisation contributing to Government's efforts, to generate and create a highly skilled, productive and disciplined workforce in an environment of industrial harmony towards achieving the goals of the vision 2020.

Its objectives as stated by the Ministry are:

> Contributing efficiently and effectively towards the Government's efforts in the planning and development of human resources to produce a skilled, competent, disciplined, innovative and an efficient workforce with positive values, consistent with the nation's industrial needs, technological changes and economic growth . . . create and maintain a harmonious industrial relations climate.

## Management culture and HRM in Malaysia

About 60 percent of Malaysians are Muslim. And similarly to other Muslim societies, management practices are influenced by key Islamic values and principles. However, over 30 percent of the population is Chinese or Indian, the former strongly influenced by Confucian values of collectivism (see Mansor and Ali, 1998). Mansor and Ali (1998: 507) argue that Malaysian management practices should be understood in the context of interposing Confucian, Islamic and western values.

The former colonial power, Britain, deeply influenced organizational cultures, especially in the public sector. By the 1970s, US dominance of management education led to an increasing Americanization of workplace organization. As noted earlier, Japanese success led to the adoption of the Look East policy in the 1980s, coterminous with moves towards indigenization. This interposition is, at times, contradictory. The persistence of religious and cultural difference has precluded any single cultural paradigm from gaining predominance; neither American nor Japanese managerial cultures have attained hegemony.

In Malaysia, collectivism comes to equate with traditional values and individualism with western management values. Malaysia is a collectivist society (Noordin *et al.*, 2002). Social relations, self-sacrifice and family integrity are very strong in Malaysia (ibid.). The Malay culture is essentially a cooperative society based on *kampung* (village) and *gotong royong* (mutual help) values (Taib and Ismail, 1982). Malaysian *kampungs* were self-sufficient, small and dispersed, creating a sense of community and need for collective work. Wolf and Arnold (1994) noted that "Malays were socialised to place the needs of the *kampung* above their personal needs." *Gotong royong* implies that people who offer help or service will expect the same service or help to be returned later on (Taib and Ismail, 1982: 109). The *gotong royong* is underpinned by the Islamic concept of the *Ummah* (Islamic religious community) where each Muslim is responsible to his fellow Muslims. Taib and Ismail (1982: 109) noted that "The unity of the Malay community thus rests on the *adat resam* (social customs), which include the institution of *gotong royong*, and the concept of *ummah* and *malu* (self-respect)." The Malay culture puts a strong emphasis on the importance of having and maintaining "face," an emphasis shared by many cultures in the Far East.

Islamic values and teaching put strong emphasis on obedience to leaders. Beekun and

Badawi (1999) noted that in Islam "at all times, the leader must be obeyed." They added that "Islam considers obedience to the leader so important that it views any kind of insubordination to be abhorrent unless in very specific circumstances." The authority of the leader or manager is thus accepted as right and proper and subordinates are expected to show respect and obedience to superiors. The majority of Muslim scholars advocate what it is called "dynamic followership." Beekun and Badawi (1999) noted that although "Islam emphasizes that followers should comply with the directives of their leader, it does not condone blind subservience." That is, although the typical Muslim worker does respect his leader, the onus in most cases is on the leader to convince subordinates that his orders are worth obeying rather than impose his will on others by administrative fiat. This is why, according to *Sharia*, Muslim leaders are asked to consult their subordinates before a decision is made. In addition, Islamic teachings put heavy emphasis on forgiveness, kindheartedness and compassion. Atiyah (1999) noted that Islamic values emphasize harmony, cooperation and brotherly relationships. Conflicts should be avoided or suppressed. The business leader, in turn, is expected to show responsibility for the quality of work life of employees and concern for their families and surrounding society. Wolf and Arnold (1994) reported that the *kampung* headman receive respect, obeisance, and loyalty but was expected, in turn, to display generosity and *anakhuah*, a fatherly concern for the welfare of his subjects. Taib and Ismail (1982: 113) noted that in Malaysian schools, the power distance factor is further reinforced:

> Malay children are normally taught to consider teachers as a figure of authority, and as kings of the institution, to be respected and obeyed . . . and the end-product is an obedient and law abiding citizen, but not an independently thinking one.

Wolfe and Arnold (1994) argue that, in addition to the above, power distance is a product of the *kampung* values where there was a strict code of behavior which applied to both leaders and followers. They noted that "recognising one's relative status and acting in accordance with one's station were the hallmarks of a *halus* person, the idealized member of society." Further, the Malays are socialized to be non-assertive and compliant, and humility, courtesy and tactfulness are strongly held values. The latter have a strong impact on HRM policies and practices. For instance, Wolfe and Arnold (1994) noted that Malay values make direct discipline at work unacceptable because it leads to the loss of face. Hofstede (1991) noted that high power distance in Malaysia was reflected in the unwillingness to make any decision without reference to the most senior executive and the high ratio of supervisory to non-supervisory personnel, and strong uncertainty avoidance as well as low individualism was apparent in the organization he studied.

The concepts of Islamic work ethic (IWE) and Islamic work values (IWV) have their origin in the Quran, the saying and practice of the Prophet Mohammad, who preached that hard work caused sins to be "absolved" and that "no one eats better food than that which eats out of his work" (Darwish, 2000). Alhabshi and Ghazali (1994) listed the following as core Islamic values: every act should be accompanied by intention (*niyat*); conscientiousness and knowledgeableness in all endeavors (*itqan*); proficiency and efficiency (*ihsan*); sincerity (*ikhlas*); passion for excellence (*al falah*); continuous self-examination; forever mindfulness of the almighty; piety (*taqwa*); justice (*'adil*); truthfulness (*amanah*); patience (*sabar*); and moderation, promise-keeping, accountability, dedication, gratefulness, cleanliness, consistency, discipline and cooperation.

Darwish (2000) notes that the IWE advocates "that life without work has no meaning, and engagement in economic activities is an obligation." The IWE views dedication to work as a virtue and puts emphasis on cooperation at work, consultation as a way of overcoming obstacles and the minimizing of risk of mistakes (ibid.). Social relations at work are encouraged in order to achieve a balance between individual and social life. In addition, work is considered to be a source of independence and a means of fostering personal growth, self-respect, satisfaction and self-fulfillment. Besides constant hard work to meet one's responsibilities, competition is encouraged in order to improve quality (Ali, 1988). Ahmad (1976, quoted in Darwish, 2000) asserted that the IWE stands not for life denial but for life fulfillment and holds business motives in the highest regard.

Values are dynamic and change over time. There has been a widespread diffusion of new management practices in Malaysia. These have taken the form of changes to the business culture, and HRM policies and practices. They have invariably been accompanied by western practices and sometimes by Japanese practices, including QCs, TQM and teamworking. The new business environment has slightly shifted management culture from collectivist behavior towards individualist practices. This has led to the erosion of some of the old HRM practices and to attempts, especially by TNCs, to westernize HRM practices through the use of western universalist best practices. Some observers have viewed this as a "western shift" towards individualism and a fracturing of previously prevailing collectivistic forms of HRM practice. In this context, there has been increasing interest in the effect of these economic and social changes on HRM practices. There has been some speculation that HRM practices in Malaysia may be becoming more individualistic in their management practices. From this perspective, the new western management practices may be seen as a direct threat to indigenous Malaysian practices. For instance Lim (1998, 2001a, 2001b, 2002) found that, while power distance in Malaysia is still high and masculinity still moderate, there is evidence to suggest that the levels of uncertainty avoidance and individualism in Malaysia have increased over the past decades. Others have argued that new forms of participation have done little to erode a tradition of autocracy and deeply entrenched managerial prerogatives (Elger and Smith 2001: 460).

Indeed, it has been suggested that the alleged drift to individualism does not necessarily lead to the eradication of traditional Malaysian practices; the impact of the individualization of Malaysian managers should not be overstated. Noordin *et al.* (2002: 46–47) note that individualism is most pronounced in the new middle class whereas the upper class pays attention to traditional collectivist values and social norms that secure and prolong its comfortable position in society.

Nonetheless, Noordin *et al.* (2002: 47) suggest that at least one facet of individualism, an emphasis on global competitiveness, has infiltrated into the collectivist values held by Malaysians. They found that harmony and social behavior as well as relationships, self-sacrifice and family integrity still appear to be important for Malaysian managers. However, while they remain inclined towards collectivism in situations involving in-groups, they appear to be individualistic in situations that involve out-groups, and the organizations they work for may fall into the latter category. They noted that Malaysian managers are basically "collectivist in relation to their in-groups, but the rapid development of the Malaysian economy has introduced another element into the Malaysian culture that is competition between members of out-groups" (p. 48). However, they argue that heightened individual competitiveness does not necessarily imply decreased collectivism (p. 49). Overall Malaysian companies pick and mix Japanese and western HRM practices to suit their needs (Mansor and Ali, 1998: 506). Table 10.1 highlights the standing Malaysia has on GLOBE's dimensions.

*Table 10.1* GLOBE social culture dimension in Malaysia (highest 7 – lowest 1)

| | |
|---|---|
| Uncertainty avoidance | 4.78 |
| Future orientation | 4.58 |
| Power distance | 5.17 |
| Institutional collectivism | 4.61 |
| Humane orientation | 4.87 |
| Performance orientation | 4.34 |
| Group and family collectivism | 5.51 |
| Gender egalitarianism | 3.51 |
| Assertiveness | 3.87 |

Source: Adopted from Gupta *et al.*, 2002. Southern Asia cluster: where the old meets the new, *Journal of World Business* 37 (16–27): 22.

The Chinese Malaysian cultural values are to a large extent similar to Malay values. The Chinese Malaysians adhere to collectivist values, respect of face, and have high power distance. Using Hofstede's four cultural factors, Lim (2002) found no significant difference between the Malays and the Chinese in work-related values. The sharp difference between the two values is in the entrepreneurial drive. While the Malays are often criticized by the Malaysian government for the lack of entrepreneurial aggressiveness, the Chinese have strong entrepreneurial traditions and a desire for financial independence.

# The industrial relations system

Malaysian industrial relations (IR) have been characterized by extensive state control, guaranteeing a high level of managerial prerogatives within the workplace, minimal overt conflict and with labor having weak bargaining power (Arudsothy and Littler, 1993; Jomo and Todd, 1994; Ariffin, 1997, quoted in Todd and Peetz, 2001: 1365). In Malaysia, approximately 13 percent of the labor force in 1980 was unionized, in many cases by unions of dubious efficacy (see Table 10.2 for details of union membership).

During the early post-independence era, IR in Malaysia reflected the British colonial legacy, with legislation providing for collective bargaining and minimum standards, while the focus of government policy was to contain conflict in the interest of economic development (Kuruvilla and Arusothy, 1995). Political strikes by unions (then registered as societies) were prohibited. At the firm level, unions' ability to strike was restricted and they had little influence on most HRM policies and practices such as promotions, lay-offs and restructuring, deemed outside the scope of unions' bargaining power. This period has been referred to as "controlled pluralism" (Kuruvilla and Arudsothy, 1995, quoted in Sarosh, 1996). Despite the fact that the government had extensive powers to control unions' activities, there was little need to invoke them.

The second phase in the development of the Malaysian IR system came in the early 1970s, 1973–1974, when Malaysia moved from its failing and expensive-to-sustain heavy industry strategy, towards an intensive export strategy based on cheap manufacturing for exports financed primarily by foreign investors. By the mid-1970s Malaysia promoted itself as a cost-effective and "IR" friendly country and enacted several IR rules and regulations to restrict union activities. New investment packages included an extension of

*Table 10.2* Number of employee trade unions and membership by gender, 1992–2000

| Year | Number of unions | Membership | | | | |
|------|------------------|------------|------|-----|--------|-----|
| | | Total | Male | (%) | Female | (%) |
| 1992 | 479 | 680,007 | 463,697 | (68.2) | 216,310 | (31.8) |
| 1993 | 496 | 693,581 | 450,828 | (65.0) | 242,753 | (35.0) |
| 1994 | 501 | 699,373 | 450,047 | (64.3) | 249,326 | (35.7) |
| 1995 | 504 | 706,253 | 450,307 | (63.8) | 255,946 | (36.2) |
| 1996 | 516 | 728,246 | 465,098 | (63.9) | 263,148 | (36.1) |
| 1997 | 526 | 734,685 | 466,549 | (63.5) | 268,136 | (36.5) |
| 1998 | 532 | 739,636 | 468,143 | (63.3) | 271,493 | (36.7) |
| 1999 | 537 | 725,322 | 461,938 | (63.7) | 263,384 | (36.4) |
| 2000 | 563 | 734,037 | | | | |

Source: Labour and Human Resource Statistics 1992–2000, Ministry of Human Resources, Department of Trade Union Affairs

tax and exemptions from several labor protection laws for foreign corporations, an alteration of the definition of wages, especially the calculation of overtime to reduce labor costs during overtime, holidays and rest days, extending working hours, and a lack of a minimum wage (and equal pay for equal work legislation) in the export-oriented sector (see Sarosh, 1996). Unions in the export-oriented sector were not allowed to affiliate themselves with other national unions or industry level union federations.

A third shift in Malaysian IR policy came in the 1980s as a result of the government "Look East." In the export-oriented sector, unions were banned, the ban only being lifted in 1988 in response to international pressures (Kuruvilla and Arudsothy, 1995). After this, only "in-house" unions were allowed at the plant rather than industry level. It was hoped that such unions would be more pliable, and "less likely to transmit wage pressures across firms and sectors" (Elger and Smith, 2001: 460). Given restrictions on collectivism, strikes are rare. For example, in 2001, only thirteen strikes involving 2,209 workers took place, according to official figures (Malaysian Ministry of Human Resources, 2002). The emergence of class-consciousness is constrained by the persistence of deep ethnic divisions (Elger and Smith, 2001: 461). However, workers have retained the right to "vote with their feet" (Wilkinson *et al.*, 2001: 692) by job-hopping, which is very common in Malaysia due to the very low unemployment rate.

## Labor market

Until the 1990s, the Malaysian manufacturing sector was predominantly labor-intensive and low skilled sector. Lucas and Verry (1996) noted that in 1980, over 70 percent of manufacturing employees had no more than lower secondary education and the figure was around 72 percent in 1987. In the early days of the NEP, 75 percent of places at Malaysian universities were reserved for bumiputras, although the quota was later lowered to 55 percent. As a result of state intervention, the proportion of bumiputra students at public universities increased from 12 percent in 1969 to around 70 percent today. The reaction of the Chinese and Indian communities has been to turn increasingly to foreign universities and to private schools and colleges (Lucas and Verry, 1996). Lucas and Verry (1996) reported that in 1988 nearly 55 percent of Chinese undergraduate students were at universities overseas.

Despite rigorous affirmative action policies, work remains both ethnically divided and gendered. The growth of export industry has led to the emergence of a Malay working class, whilst the NDP and NEP have also resulted in the creation of a bumiputra bourgeoisie. Typically, inward investors have sought to capitalize on the cheapest possible sources of labor: young Malay women from the countryside (Elger and Smith, 2001: 459) or foreigners. Table 10.3 depicts female labor force participation rates in the late 1990s. Whilst – in line with government quotas – bumiputras increasingly are found at managerial level, many firms continue to favor employing ethnic Chinese at supervisory level (Elger and Smith, 2001: 459).

*Table 10.3* Malaysia: labor force participation rates by gender,
1995–1999

| | | | Year | | |
|---|---|---|---|---|---|
| | *1995* | *1996* | *1997* | *1998* | *1999* |
| Total | 64.5 | 65.8 | 66.6 | 64.3 | 64.3 |
| Male | 83.8 | 84.8 | 85.7 | 83.4 | 83.4 |
| Female | 44.3 | 45.8 | 47.4 | 44.2 | 44.2 |

Source: Economic Report 1999/2000

## Shortage of skilled workers

The shortage of skilled workers in key areas is both qualitative and quantitative, state policies to promote HRD notwithstanding. Rapid growth, and the adoption of modern technological production processes has resulted in the need of a new breed of skilled workers who are able to absorb and adapt to new technologies and work practices. Industrialization has developed faster than the education and training system output to meet the needs of the economy. Output from industrial and vocational training institutes remains insufficient, in part due to a shortage of qualified and experienced lecturers. Employers remain reluctant to promote on-the-job training, given tight cost margins and high staff turnover. Moreover, many skilled production workers actively seek employment in neighbouring Singapore, where industrial competitiveness is less dependent on low wage rates.

## Employment of foreign workers

The 1986–1997 period of rapid economic expansion in Malaysia stimulated extensive labor flows from abroad of unprecedented proportions (Kassim, 1996, quoted in Abdul-Aziz, 2001: 89). From approximately 500,000 foreign workers in 1984, the number increased to in excess of 1.2 million by 1991 (Pillai, 1992). By the mid-1990s, foreign workers made up 15 percent of the labor force (Lin, 1996).

The Seventh Malaysia Plan gave a figure for foreigners in the labor force in Malaysia in 1995 of 650,000. Estimates have suggested that there were roughly 2 million foreign workers in the country. For instance, an estimated 60 percent of all manual workers in the construction industry were foreign nationals in 1987 (Gill, 1988) a figure which reached 80 percent in 1995 (Balaisegaram and Pillai, 1996).

In December 1991, the Ministry of HR opened up to foreigners a range of jobs in the manufacturing and construction sectors. The aim of the policy was to ensure that only appropriate foreign workers with required skills were employed and would not hinder the employment of Malaysian workers. Foreign workers could initially be employed for a period of five years. However, the private sector was asked to shift its production process from labor-intensive technology to capital-intensive technologies, in order to reduce the need for foreign workers. Automation has been at the top of the Ministry of Human Resource agenda since then: officially speaking, employers should realize the need for the "shift to automation, robotics and higher value-added technology and production process." Furthermore, firms should train existing staff and provide more competitive wages for Malaysian nationals, relocating to labor-surplus areas such as Kelantan, Terengganu and Pahang if need be. It is not certain how this policy can be squared with a continued reliance on relatively low-cost labor, and on low value-added production.

Being a signatory to the ILO Migration for Employment Convention, Malaysia is obliged to ensure employers give equal treatment and rights to foreign workers (Lee and Sivananthiran, 1996). However Abdul-Aziz (2001: 769) found that, in addition to allegations of unfair treatment, there was a wage hierarchy in the construction industry "with the Malaysian occupying the apex, followed by Indonesians, with the least favoured Bangladeshis at the bottom." Employers do not normally provide written contracts to foreign blue-collar workers, with the employment relationship being invariably *ad hoc* (Abdul-Aziz, 2001: 796).

## Human resource development strategy

It is apparent that, if Malaysia is to become a developed nation by the year 2020, a pool of educated multiskilled, disciplined and productive workforce has to be created. The demand for skilled labor has increased due to the rapid transformation of the economy during the late 1980s and 1990s. Industries are shifting to more modern technological production processes which require bold and innovative HRD strategies to meet the challenging skills requirements. The workforce has to be imbued with enhanced knowledge and modern industrial skills and be able to absorb and adapt new technologies. Todd and Peetz (2001: 1375) found a strong emphasis on training in 12 out of 16 case-studies.

Vision 2020 puts great emphasis on HRD. The National Development Policy under the Second Outline Perspective Plan for the period 1991–2000 underscored the importance of HRD to cater for the needs of an economy under transformation. *Inter alia*, the NDP seeks to promote the following: the development of an educated, flexible, innovative, numerate and multiskilled workforce to cater for rapid technological development and the shift from labor-intensive technologies to knowledge-intensive technologies; vocationalizing the education curriculum; training and developing bumiputras; motivating the private sector to invest in HRD.

To further encourage and stimulate the private sector to introduce training and development for its employees, the HRD Act 1992 requires organizations employing more than 50 employees to contribute 1 percent of their monthly payroll to a fund to promote training. In turn, the fund aims to provide financial assistance to defray part of the allowable costs in training undertaken by employers. It acts as an incentive scheme whereby grants from the fund can be provided to employers to undertake and accelerate systematic training programs to equip the workforce with high skills, knowledge and positive industrial attitudes. The fund was initially open only to the manufacturing sector but has since been expanded to the service sector.

The HR Ministry's Manpower Department and the National Vocational Training Department formulate the curriculum of training programs and supplying skilled and trained workforce to meet the needs of the economy. Their aim is to minimize skill mismatches and conduct training to supply a multiskilled, innovative and adaptive workforce, in order to facilitate the transition from labor-intensive to knowledge-intensive industries with a strong science and technology base.

## The HRM function

Yong (1996) argues that the diversity of the composition of the modern workforce in Malaysia requires more appropriate and imaginative HRM solutions than have hitherto been deployed. HRM is currently a rapidly growing field in Malaysia. Since the late 1980s, Malaysian managers have increasingly used the term HRM instead of personnel management (Todd and Peetz, 2001; Yong, 1996). In 1990, the former Ministry of Labor adopted the new term and changed its name to the Ministry of Human Resources in keeping with the international trend and "need of recognising people as a key resource for national development" (Yong, 1996). HRM departments are usually staffed by people who have general qualifications but with much working experience in the field (Todd and Peetz, 2001). Yong (1996) described a typical profile of a Malaysian HRM as "a male with social science degree plus a qualification in personnel management with five years experience and around 33 to 45 years old, able to communicate well, in Bahasa Malaysia, and English." Todd and Peetz (2001: 1373) found evidence of the increasing strategic integration of the HR function.

The Ministry of Human Resources plays a key role in shaping HRM policies and practices in Malaysia. The government is responsible for the development of labor administration policy, promotion of workers' welfare (especially bumiputras) and promoting industrial harmony. More importantly, it plays a role of coordinator with the private sector by maintaining the supply of a multiskilled, disciplined – by controlling union activities – and efficient workforce.

## HRM policies and practices

### Work organization

The organization of work in Malaysian firms is influenced by a host of factors. Todd and Peetz (2001: 1374–1375) found that work organization varied from Tayloristic with limited multiskilling style to modern flexible multiskilled style. In Japanese factories operating in Malaysia, they found an apparent influence of Japanese practices through the active use of QCs, and Just in Time (JIT) practices (see Wilkinson *et al.*, 2001 for a detailed study of work organization in Japanese firms operating in Malaysia). Wilkinson *et al.* (2001) reported that in several Japanese companies in Malaysia there is a high division of tasks. However, Elger and Smith (2001: 461) suggest that, in practice, work roles remain very tightly defined; the predominant paradigm remains low value-added production under autocratic control. This reflects the continued importance of industries centering on the assembly of mature standardized products (such as VCRs and TVs), and the production of lower value components for such products (ibid.).

### Recruitment and selection

Generally, Malaysia firms practice external recruitment (Mansor and Ali, 1998: 508). Several big companies take the initiative and recruit new graduates straight from universities. As noted earlier, managers still turn to specific ethnic groupings when seeking to fill certain jobs; even if bumiputra managers are employed, Chinese are still favoured for supervisory roles. A large proportion of production workers continue to be directly recruited from the countryside. Elger and Smith (2001: 459) argue that such segmentation "structures the social distance between management and workers and mediates the transmission of management policy."

### Rewards system

Todd and Peetz (2001: 1376) found that, although the bulk of employee's pay is based on the wage of the occupation, tenure-related increments and contractual bonus, many Malaysian companies include performance-related bonus within their pay packages. They also found that, while wages are determined via collective bargaining in unionized workplaces, management determined the wages in non-unionized firms. Wilkinson *et al.* (2001: 690–691) found in Malaysia that starting salaries for operators were around US$1,900 a year, typically around RM430 per month for an average 45-hour week, with two months' pay as an annual bonus.

# Turnover

Malaysian organizations suffer from high staff-turnover rates. In the case of blue-collar workers, this reflects a tradition of autocratic management, with little room for dissent, coupled with a high demand for labor within specific geographic areas. On the one hand, managers find such turnover helpful as it enables staffing levels to be easily adjusted to match fluctuations in demand (Elger and Smith 2001: 461). On the other hand, this limits the effectiveness of in-firm training and development initiatives. Firms are unlikely to break with autocratic Fordism if they lack the human capacity to do so, official policies notwithstanding. There is some evidence to suggest that the reluctance of a significant number of firms to devote too many resources to development, and to advance women, has resulted in intense competition for a relatively small pool of highly skilled bumiputras (Morris *et al.*, 2001; Jayansankaran, 1999). Again, this mitigates against the attainment of a predominantly high value-added production paradigm.

# Conclusion

In many respects, Malaysia represents a success story. From an economy centered on the production of primary commodities, it has developed a significant manufacturing sector. In particular, the country has assumed an important role in the global consumer electronics industry. Moreover, from a predominantly poor rural grouping, bumiputras have increasingly urbanized, and gained representation at the highest levels of industry. The Malaysian experience highlights the continued relevance of state interventions – globalization notwithstanding – and the possibilities of active industrial policy. At the same time, Malaysia's growth trajectory is fraught with contradictions. Much industrial production centers on low-value-added activity on autocratic Fordist lines, dependent on cheap labor supplies. However, Malaysia has long since lost any competitive advantage in the sweatshop stakes, with China emerging as the ultimate low-cost alternative. Whilst official HRD initiatives have had some success – above all, in enhancing productivity – chronic skills shortages persist in certain areas. Moreover, the kind of products that tend to be manufactured in Malaysia – both mature standardized products, and components thereof – do not always readily lend themselves to a more highly value-added production paradigm. Further institutional barriers to a high wage–high skill scenario include an autocratic managerial tradition, with geographic, ethnic and regional barriers being deliberately erected between managers and workforces. This is not to suggest that in certain niche areas, Malaysia may retain global competitiveness on grounds other than cost. However, the diffusion of a culture of autocracy from the political center would seem to mitigate against the emergence of a genuine culture of involvement and participation, unlocking the fullest potential of the country's human capital. In other words, HRM can only be developed if corporate and societal governance systems have the ability to support and follow through the necessary investments in physical resources and trust (cf. Marsden, 1999: 268).

# References

Abdul-Aziz, A.-R. (2001) "Foreign workers and labour segmentation in Malaysia's construction industry," *Construction Management and Economics* 19: 789–798.

Abdullah, Hj. F. (1997) "Affirmative action policy in Malaysia: To restructure society, to eradicate poverty," *Ethnic Studies Report* 15 (2): 189–221.

Abdullah, W.A.W. (1994) "Transnational corporations and human resource development: Some evidence from the Malaysian manufacturing industries," *Personnel Review* 23 (5): 50–69.

Ahmad, K. (1976) *Islam: Its meaning and message*, London: Islamic Council of Europe.

Alhabshi, S.O. and Ghazali, A.H. (1994) *Islamic values and management*, Kuala Lumpur: Institute of Islamic Understanding Malaysia (IKIM).

Ali, A. J. (1998) "A Comparative study of managerial belief about work in Arab states," *Advances in International Comparative Management* 4: 96–112.

Ariffin, R. (1997) "Changing employment structures and their effects on industrial relations in Malaysia," *Economic and Labour Relations Review* 8: 44–56.

Arudsothy, P. and Littler, C. (1993) "State regulation and union fragmentation in Malaysia," in S. Frenkel (ed.) *Organized labor in the Asia-Pacific region: A comparative study of trade unionism in nine countries*, Ithaca: ILR Press.

Attiyah, H.S. (1999) "Public organization's effectiveness and its determinants in a developing country," *Cross Cultural Management* 6 (2): 8–21.

Balaisegaram, M. and Pillai, S. (1996) "Looking beneath the surface," *Sunday Star*, Kuala Lumpur, 29 September.

Beekun, R. and Badawi, J. (1999) *Leadership: An Islamic perspective*, Beltsville: Amana Publications.

Bond, P. (2001) "The IMF and the world bank reconsidered," in J.K. Coetzee, J. Graaff, F. Hendricks and G. Wood (eds.) *Development: Theory, policy and practice*, Cape Town: Oxford University Press.

Boyer, R. and Hollingsworth, J.R. (1997) "From national embeddedness to spatial and institutional nestedness," in R. Boyer and J.R. Hollingsworth (eds.) *Contemporary capitalism: The embeddedness of institutions*, Cambridge: Cambridge University Press.

Cho, G. (1990) *The Malaysian economy*, London: Routledge.

Darwish, A.Y. (2000) "Organizational commitment as a mediator of the relationship between Islamic work ethic and attitudes toward organizational change," *Human Relations* 45 (4): 513–537.

Davi, R. (1996) *Contract labour in peninsular Malaysia*, Kuala Lumpur: Institute for Policy Research.

Economy of Malaysia (1998) "Economic report 1997–98," *The Star*, 18 October.

Elger, T. and Smith, C. (2001) "The global dissemination of production models and the recasting of work and employment relations in developing societies," in J.K. Coetzee, J. Graaff, F. Hendricks and G. Wood (eds.) *Development: Theory, policy and practice*, Cape Town: Oxford University Press.

Furnivall, J.S. (1956) *Colonial policy and practice*, New York: New York University Press.

Gill, M.S. (1988) "The features of labour utilisation and the problems of migrants and immigrant workers in the construction industry," paper presented at the Workshop on Current Issues in Labour Migration, Kuala Lumpur, 24–28 August.

Gupta, V., Surie, G., Javidian, M. and Chhokar, J. (2002) "Southern Asia cluster: Where the old meets the new," *Journal of World Business* 37: 16–27.

Hill, H. and Athukorala, P. (1998) "Foreign investment in East Asia: A survey," *Asia-Pacific Economic Literature* 12 (2): 23–50.

Hofstede, G. (1991) *Culture's consequences: Software of the mind*, London: McGraw-Hill.

Jayasankaran, S. (1999) "Easing up," *Far Eastern Economic Review* 162 (50): 52–53.

Jesudasen, J.V. (1989) *Ethnicity and the economy: The state, Chinese business and multinationals in Malaysia*, Oxford: Oxford University Press.

Jomo, K.S. and Todd, P. (1994) *Trade unions and the state in peninsular Malaysia*, Kuala Lumpur: Oxford University Press.

Kassim, A. (1996) "An overview of migrant workers in Malaysia," paper presented at the one-day workshop on foreign workers in Malaysia, organized by the Institute of Policy Research and University of Malaya, 23 October.

Kuruvilla, S and Arudsothy, P. (1995) "Economic development, national industrial relations policies, and workplace IR practices in Malaysia," in A. Verna, A.T. Kocjan and R. Lansbury (eds.) *Employment relations in the growing Asian economies*, London: Routledge.

Lee, J.-H. and Sivananithiran (1996) "Contract labour in Malaysia: Perspectives of principal employers, contractors and workers," *International Labour Review* 135 (6): 75–91.

Le Roux, P. (2001) "The IMF and the world bank reconsidered," in J.K. Coetzee, J. Graaff, F. Hendricks and G. Wood (eds.) *Development: Theory, policy and practice*, Cape Town: Oxford University Press.

Lim, L. (1998) "Cultural attributes of Malays and Malaysian Chinese: Implications for research and practice," *Malaysian Management Review* 33 (2): 81–88.

Lim, L. (2001a) "Work-related values of Malays and Chinese Malaysians," *International Journal of Cross Cultural Management* 1 (2): 209–226.

Lim, L. (2001b) "Work-related values of Malaysians and Japanese: A re-examination of Hofstede's propositions", *Journal of Transnational Management Development* 6 (3/4): 39–56.

Lim, L. (2002) "Have work-related values of Malays and Chinese Malaysians changed over the last 30 years?," paper presented at the 12th International Conference on Comparative Management, College of Management, National Sun Yat-sen University Kaohsiung, Taiwan, R.O.C, 23–25 May 2002.

Lin, L.L. (1996) "The migration transition in Malaysia," *Asia and Pacific Migration Journal* 5 (2–3): 319–337.

Lucas, E.B. and Verry, D. (1996) "Growth and income distribution in Malaysia," *International Labour Review* 135 (5): 553–575.

Lucas, E.B. and Verry, D. (1999) *Restructuring the Malaysian economy: Development and human resources*, London: Palgrave–Macmillan.

Mahathir, M. (1999) "Malaysia's experience in managing economic recovery while safeguarding the socio-economic responsibilities," paper presented by Dato Seri Dr Mahathir bin Mohamad, at the Smart Partnership Dinner, Victoria Falls, Zimbabwe, 4 October 1999 (http://www.angelfire.com/nh/saint1/mahathir7.html).

Malaysia (1985) *The industrial master plan, 1986–95*, Kuala Lumpur: National Planning Department.

Malaysian Ministry of Human Resources, *Official website*. http://www.jaring.my/ksm/key.htm#14 (downloaded 26 June 2002).

Mansor, N. and Ali, M. (1998) "An exploratory study of organizational flexibility in Malaysia: A research note," *International Journal of Human Resource Management* 9 (3): 506–515.

Marsden, D. (1999) *A theory of employment systems*, Oxford: Oxford University Press.

Milne, R.S. (1986) "Malaysia – beyond the new economic policy," *Asian Survey* 26: 1346–1382.

Morris, D., Wood, G. and Yaacob, A. (2001) "Securing diversity in human resources? Lessons from Malaysia," *Asia Pacific Business Review* 8 (1): 58–74.

National Economic Recovery Plan (1998) *NEAC, economic planning unit*, Kuala Lumpur: Prime Minister's Department.

Noordin, F., Williams, T. and Zimmer, C. (2002) "Career commitment in collectivist and individualist cultures: A comparative study," *International Journal of Human Resource Management* 13 (1): 35–54.

Peetz, D. and Todd, P. (2001) "Otherwise you're on your own: Unions and bargaining in Malaysian banking," *International Journal of Manpower* 22: 4.

Pillai, P. (1992) *People on the move: An overview of recent immigration and emigration in Malaysia*, Kuala Lumpur: Institute of Strategic and International Studies.

Przeworski, A., Alvarez, M., Chiebub, J. and Lemongi, F. (2000) *Democracy and development*, Cambridge: Cambridge University Press.

Sarosh, K. (1996) "Linkages between industrialization strategies and industrial relations/human resource policies: Singapore, Malaysia, the Philippines, and India," *Industrial and Labor Relation Review* 49 (4): 635–657.

Snodgrass, D., Yusof, Z. A. and Shari, I. (2003) *Managing economic growth amid ethnic diversity: Malaysia, 1970–1990*, Harvard Studies in International Development, Cambridge, MA: Harvard University Press.

SocGen, C. (1997) "Malaysia: Into a period of vulnerability," *Asiamoney* (London: Euromoney Publications).

Taib, A. and Ismail, M.Y. (1982) "The social structure," in E.K. Fisk and H. Osman-Rani (eds.) *The political economy of Malaysia*, Kuala Lumpur: Oxford University Press.

Todd, P. and Peetz, D. (2001) "Malaysian industrial relations at century's turn: Vision 2020 or a specter of the past?," *International Journal of Human Resource Management* 12 (8): 1365–1382.

UNCTAD, FDI/TNC database., http://www.unctad.org/en/press/pr2799t1.htm#b1 (downloaded 25 May 2002).

Willkinson, B., Gamble, J., Humphrey, J., Morris, J. and Anthony, D. (2001) "The new international division of labour in Asian electronics: Work organization and human resource in Japan and Malaysia," *Journal of Management Studies* 38 (5): 675–695.

Wolfe, D. and Arnold, B. (1994) "Human resource management in Malaysia: American and Japanese approaches," *Journal of Asian Business* 14 (4): 80–103.

Yong, A.K. (1996) "Malaysian human resource management," Eagle Trading Sdn Bhd, Malaysian Institute of Management: Kuala Lumpur.

## Useful websites

| | |
|---|---|
| Ministry of Human Resources, Malaysia: | http://mcsl.mampu.gov.my/english/fedgovt/Human_resc.htm |
| Industrial Relations Department, Malaysia: | http://61.6.32.133/jppm/ |
| Human Resources Development Council, Malaysia: | http://www.hrdnet.com.my/ |

# HRM in Singapore

NARESH KHATRI

## Introduction

Since its independence in 1965, Singapore has achieved tremendous economic advancement. From earning a GDP of S$2.15 billion in 1960 to a GDP of S$153 billion in 2001, the city-state is today a reputable financial center, a key regional trading center, the world's busiest port and a top location for investment. Singapore is one of the newly industrialized countries (NICs), which were hailed as a great economic success in the 1990s.

The total labor force in Singapore in June 2002 stood at 2,128,500.[1] It comprised 2,017,400 persons who were employed and 111,200 unemployed. Overall, 64.7 percent of the population aged 15 and above participated in the labor force. The rate of participation in the labor force has been largely unchanged from 65.3 percent in 1992. However, the stability of the overall participation rate masks some significant changes. Specifically, the labor force participation rate in the younger age group of 15 to 24 declined as more youths delayed their entry to the labor market to pursue higher education. On the other hand, there has been a rise in participation of females, particularly among those aged 45 to 59, suggesting that more females are returning to work when their children are older. Among males in the prime working age, participation has been fairly stable except for a notable increase in the older age group of 55 to 64, following the extension of retirement age. Despite the increasing trend in the participation of older persons and females in the workforce, the participation of these two groups of workers is much lower than in other countries such as Japan, South Korea, and the USA (see Table 11.1 later in the chapter).

The educational profile of the labor force continues to improve with the share of degree holders more than doubling in 2002 from 8.2 percent a decade ago. Nevertheless, it

---

1  Most of the data and discussions in this section of the chapter are derived from several publications of the Manpower Research and Statistics Division of the Ministry of Manpower, Singapore, namely, *The 2002 Singapore Yearbook of Manpower Statistics*; *Report on Labor Force in Singapore 2002*; *Labor Market, Third Quarter 2002*; *Conditions of Employment, 2002*; *Older Workers 1999*; *Women Returning to Work 1995*; and Flexible *Work Arrangements 1999*.

remains significantly below that in the USA (32 percent), UK (29 percent), South Korea (25 percent), and Japan (21 percent), but slightly ahead of Hong Kong (16 percent) and Taiwan (12 percent). A sizeable pool of 659,000 workers, forming 33 percent of employed workforce, possessed less than secondary education level. The number has come down from 702,400 or 45 percent in 1992.

The distribution of workers across industries and occupations has undergone significant shifts over the last decade in response to rapid restructuring in the economy and improvement in the educational profile of the workforce. Although manufacturing continues to play a vital role in the development of the economy, contributing between 22 and 26 percent, the sector's share of employment has fallen. In 2002, manufacturing employed 18 percent of the workforce down from 28 percent in 1992. The change reflects the shift in manufacturing away from labor-intensive to capital-intensive and the relocation of lower-end production to nearby countries. The employment share of the workforce in the services sector has increased over the decade, constituting three of every four workers in 2002, up from 65 percent in 1992. Higher skilled workers have been gaining employment share. The top three occupational groups, namely, managers, senior officials, and professionals and technicians, now constitute 12 percent, almost double the 6.6 percent in 1992.

In June 2002, the seasonally adjusted unemployment rate stood at 4.1 percent, which is substantially higher than 2.7 percent in June 2001 and 2.0 percent that was common before the onset of the Asian economic crisis. Without adjusting for seasonal influences, the unemployment rate was 5.2 percent in June 2002, up from 3.4 percent a year ago, indicating greater difficulties in the job-search efforts of this year's cohort of new tertiary graduates. Unemployment is generally higher among those less educated, as they are adversely affected by an underlying structural shift in demand in favor of those with education and skills. Nevertheless, with the spate of retrenchments affecting managers and executives in 2001 and early 2002, the degree holders have suffered the greatest increase in unemployment, underscoring the difficulties faced by displaced mid-career managers and executives in securing re-employment. For example, while the unemployment rate among degree holders was less than those with lower secondary education (6.2 percent), it has risen most sharply from 2.5 percent a year ago to 4.8 percent in June 2002. Younger persons experience higher unemployment rate. For instance, the unemployment rate in the age group 15–24 was 8.6 percent.

The Singaporean economy has made a transition from being low-end, labor-intensive to being high-tech, service-oriented, and knowledge-based. Since Singaporean educational institutions are not able to meet the demand for high-skilled workers, the government has encouraged companies to hire foreign skilled workers. Further, Singaporeans do not like to work in certain low-skilled jobs/industries, such as housemaid/construction. Companies in such industries rely on foreign workers. Thus, on the whole, foreign workers represent a significant portion of the Singaporean workforce, about 20 percent (Islam and Chowdhury, 1997). (The number of foreign workers may have grown further in the last five years.)

# Historical development and key factors influencing HRM practices in Singapore

## Singapore's economic strategy

Singapore has a unique wage system, which has evolved along with its economic strategy. In the period between 1965 and 1978, the economic strategy was to provide employment by attracting labor-intensive industries. To make Singapore more competitive than its neighbors, it put a restraint on wages. Singapore changed its economic strategy (1979–1984) from being labor-intensive manufacturing to more skill and capital-intensive manufacturing. This phase may be termed as wage correction. The government pushed for phasing out low-wage, labor-intensive industries and attracting high-wage, capital-intensive, and skill-based industries. The third phase of the economic strategy was to be more competitive in the face of increasing competition from the neighboring countries, especially Malaysia. This phase was called wage flexibility and it began in 1985. The flexible wage system has several components:

1  a basic fixed component reflecting the value of the job and to provide stability;
2  an annual wage supplement (AWS) of one month which can be adjusted under special circumstances;
3  a variable bonus based on the company's profitability and improved productivity,
4  a service increment each year for loyalty, experience, and length of service.

It is worth noting that the variable bonus in Singapore companies varies significantly. It has ranged roughly from the equivalent of one month's salary to six months' salary in recent years. Singapore has achieved one of the highest saving rates through employing a wage system in which a significant component is contributed by both employee and employer to the Central Provident Fund scheme. The Central Provident Fund contributions (both from employee and employer) have been as high as 40 percent of each monthly salary.

## Singapore's economic model

Before we can understand the role and status of HRM practices in Singapore, we need to grasp the unique Singaporean economic model and the administrative systems associated with it. Lingle (1996) characterizes the Singaporean economic model as "authoritarian capitalism." Authoritarian capitalism combines a selective degree of economic freedom and private property rights with strong-armed control over political life. It assumes that economic liberties and political liberties are not interdependent. It provides a nice contrast to its cousin, "authoritarian socialism" of Soviet Union type. While authoritarian socialism subscribes to having an economy without prices, authoritarian capitalism presides over markets without the guarantee of individual freedoms or rights. Authoritarian capitalism employs extensive interventions in the economy. Investment funds and subsidies are directed toward selective areas of economic activity. The model of authoritarian capitalism involves the politicization of commerce and the commercialization of politics. The Southeast Asian economic model has been termed as "crony capitalism" by some (Husted, 1999; Vogl, 1999). In crony capitalism, politicians, businesses, and banks develop close relationships and businesses depend heavily on their relationships with the ruling party. Economic activities involve privileged, insider access to economic data that benefit the party and also allow party functionaries to enjoy private gains. A downside of authoritarian capitalism is that it suppresses individualism and intellectual freedom, thereby impairing the formation of entrepreneurs. Crony capitalism is widely regarded as a key factor in the Asian financial crisis of 1997 (*Asiaweek*, 1999; Dale, 1999). Singapore is also called a "nanny state" in which people are supposed to do exactly as they are told. In return, the government takes care of all their basic needs.

## Singapore's administrative system

Singapore's administrative system is also unique. It may be said that Singapore has put in place one of the most elaborate management control systems. A neutral observer will find a Singaporean administrative system to resemble a military system. In fact, a number of senior officers in the military take up positions as heads of government ministries, departments, and corporations after their retirement from military. Singaporeans are proud of their disciplined, efficient, military-like administrative systems. Caning of an American citizen, Michael Fay, in Singapore in the early 1990s, brought to the fore a heated debate on Singapore's control-based management model. Although sometimes a little overexaggerated in the western media, there is some truth in Singapore's image as a controlled society. On the positive side, Singapore is one of the most disciplined societies in the world and is one of the cleanest cities in the world.

A pervasive thinking shared privately in Singapore is that Singaporeans make excellent administrators/managers and clerks, but poor leaders and entrepreneurs. This is reflected in the preponderance of scores on Myer-Briggs indicators. A large number of Singapore managers are ISTJs (Introvert–Sensation–Thinking–Judging) and ESTJs (Extrovert–Sensation–Thinking–Judging) (Ditzig and You, 1988; Tan and Tan, 1999): 31.9 and 18.8 percent respectively as compared to 13.3 and 11 percent, respectively, in the USA. Singapore's highly structured education and administrative systems have fostered a mindset of low tolerance for ambiguity. For example, the government takes pains even to the extent of specifying the weight limit of childrens primary school school bags. Still another example is where the government decided to mark the pavements with footprints from the school gates to nearby bus stops so that school children can find their way to the nearest bus stop without a problem. In a system when thought, even on such small matters, is taken away from individuals, people depend upon government instructions on most issues.

A preponderance of ISTJ and ESTJ types in Singapore results in overemphasis on formalization/bureaucracy and detailed rules and guidelines. Such a management is termed as "micromanagement." Micromanagement means managerial emphasis on routine, operational aspects of management at the expense of broader, strategic management issues (Khatri *et al.*, 2003). Even relatively minor and routine decisions are made by senior-level managers. A result is that senior managers are bogged down with routine decisions, some of which border on triviality. It is not uncommon in Singapore that an expense of a few dollars goes all the way to the top for approval. While micromanagement enhances reliability and control, it comes at a price as it chokes creativity, entrepreneurship, and initiative. Intuitive and perceptive skills, which are significantly lacking in Singapore, are important for managers to face the challenges unleashed by the forces of regionalization and globalization (Tan and Tan, 1999). Unfortunately, these skills cannot be changed or modified through weeks or even months of training. It will require a different infrastructure and years for Singapore to undo the effects of overmanagement in the past.

A *Kiasu* mentality underlies Singaporean attitudes towards education, work, and other aspects of their lives (Ho *et al.*, 1998). In education, Singaporean students are very examination-oriented and success in school is narrowly defined in terms of grades. Such an environment is not conducive for critical and creative thinking. Most Singaporeans have been brought up with many of their decisions made by government and parents on their behalf, resulting in lack of independence, initiative, and originality (Ho *et al.*, 1998). There is a general lack of idealism and enthusiasm at work.

## Multinational corporations as growth drivers

Singapore has one of the most open, trade-oriented economies. It realized the importance of the pro-business environment in 1965, which its neighbors understood much later. Its government made a deliberate choice of attracting multinationals to be an engine of economic growth. Interestingly, Asian economies are pursuing three distinct economic strategies. While Japan and Korea have a few mega companies/conglomerates that control the bulk of their economic activity, Hong Kong and Taiwan have depended on small, entrepreneurial firms for their growth and development. Singapore and Malaysia chose still another distinct path. Both have relied heavily on multinational corporations for their economic growth. For example, multinationals account for more than 70 percent of the manufacturing output in Singapore and about 95 percent of its total export.

Singapore has a good mix of multinationals from Europe, Japan, and North America. This mix of multinationals is also reflected in a mix of HRM practices in Singapore companies. Fisher and Shaw (1992) found evidence of the impact of the headquarters on HRM practices of Singaporean subsidiaries. Shaw *et al.* (1995) examined the role of Singapore government on HR practices and found that the government has taken an interventionist role not only concerning broad issues of economic policy but with respect to HRM activities as well. It has focused heavily on training and productivity improvement. The process of unquestioned selective imitation is the pervasive mindset in Singapore, encouraged by both government and professional organizations. There are some similarities between local and foreign firms in Singapore resulting from firms conforming to local government standards as well as from the mutual imitation processes operating between Singaporean and foreign firms.

Singapore's small, open economy is vulnerable to external shocks because the value of its exports is much larger than its GDP and about two-thirds of its industrial output is exported. On the positive side, the strategy of attracting multinationals has led to rapid growth in Singapore and was not possible otherwise. Multinationals bring capital, the latest technology, and excellent management practices, three most critical factors for business success. On the negative side, multinationals do not show any loyalty. If business conditions are not favorable, they move to other locations. This is what has happened in Singapore recently. Other countries in the region, such as Malaysia and Thailand, and now China,[2] have realized the importance of the pro-business environment and the role of multinationals in achieving rapid growth. The neighboring countries have greater natural resources and cheaper labor. Consequently, Singapore has been gradually losing its competitive advantage. It has been trying to create a new niche in high-tech, bio-medical sciences and high value-added services, to isolate it from the threat of competition.

Singapore has been successful in the past in transforming itself in the face of adversity. However, it is not clear at present if it will succeed in becoming an economic force in the region again. The Singaporean government and policy-makers are privately ruing not having provided an environment for local entrepreneurs. For example, in the Silicon Valley heyday, the Singaporean government and people were hoping that some of their homegrown IT enterprises and entrepreneurs would make it big on the world stage. Unfortunately, it never materialized. Part of the reason is the fact that entrepreneurs cannot surface in a highly structured Singaporean system.

## The role and status of HRM in Singapore companies

My own experiences of HRM practices in Singapore companies suggest that the HR function is in transition. Organizations have realized the importance of HRM and salary surveys show that HR executives are among the best paid in Southeast Asia. Most organizations have changed the title of the function from "Personnel" or "Administration" to "Human Resource Management." The HR department that used to be part of the finance and accounts department in most organizations in the past is being configured as a standalone function in most of them. There is an increasing trend of HR managers reporting directly to their CEOs, unlike in the past, when they used to report to the head of finance and accounts department. HR managers are also increasingly participating in strategic planning meetings and the link between strategic planning and

2  In fact, China might be affecting the foreign direct investments in the whole of Southeast Asia, including Singapore.

HR function has been strengthening. Until a few years ago, HR's role in most organizations was limited to administrative activities, such as personnel record-keeping and holiday and leave administration. However, in recent years, linkage of HR with strategic planning is growing and we see more and more organizations showing-one-way link[3] between strategic planning and HR, and some even showing a two-way link[4] (Golden and Ramanujam, 1985).

Khatri and Budhwar (2002) interviewed 35 senior managers including CEOs of nine companies in Singapore and found that two factors, HR competencies and top management enlightenment, affect the status of the HR function in an organization. HR managers felt that their competencies were important in gaining trust and strategic involvement in the organization. They also felt the need to convince the upper management that they were capable of managing the fundamental HR functions well before being invited to the strategic table. In addition, top management enlightenment (a recognition by the top management that HR function can play a critical role in formulating and implementing organizational strategies) impacts on the role and status of HR function in the organization.

## Key challenges facing HRM in Singapore

There are a number of HR challenges facing Singaporean companies. The chief among them include chronic employee turnover/job-hopping, relatively low participation rate of females and older workers in the workforce, management of Singaporeans expatriates, training and development, and overhauling management systems and HR practices that can sustain a high value-added, knowledge-based service economy.

## Turnover/job-hopping

The labor shortage has been the main feature of the Singapore economy for over two decades. A result is chronic employee turnover problem. Reports in the popular press highlighting the costs and disruptions associated with job-hopping continue unabated, and companies continue to call for help with this pressing issue. The extent of the problem may be gleaned from the fact that the issue of job-hopping was brought up in the country's parliament. In fact, there is deep concern at the national level that job-hopping is adversely affecting Singapore's competitiveness (Chang, 1996; *The Straits Times*, 1996). Foreign investors, particularly manufacturers, are concerned about the frequency of job-hopping (*Asian Finance*, 1988). According to the report of a task force on

3  In-one-way link, top management provides strategic initiatives and the HR managers design HR activities consistent with these initiatives.
4  A two-way link involves an interdependent and mutual relationship between strategic planning and the HR function.

job-hopping in Singapore, more than two-thirds of the organizations indicated that they had suffered a productivity loss of greater than 10 percent as a result of the high employee turnover (National Productivity Board, Singapore, 1988). In addition to low productivity, the survey reported a high cost of recruitment and poor quality of products and services due to high turnover. Even more important, high turnover was found to be the major source of poor morale in many organizations.

Even in the face of increasing unemployment during the Asian crisis and subsequent economic downturn in 2001–2002, resignation rates in Singapore companies have remained at alarmingly high levels. For example, overall monthly resignation rate in 2002 was 2.2 percent, which translates into a hefty 26.4 percent annual resignation rate. Annual turnover for hospitality and retail industries is as high as 55.2 and 49.2 percent, respectively (Ministry of Manpower, 2002c). HR managers and policy-makers have been hoping that the turnover problem would go away in a less tight labor market than exists at present. Unfortunately, they are puzzled by the fact that, although it has declined marginally, it remains at a high level despite unemployment climbing to 5.2 percent. Khatri *et al.* (2001), in their study of companies in three industries (retail, food and beverage, and marine and shipping), attempted to identify the root causes of turnover problem in Singapore. The authors found no evidence for the common myth in Singapore that young and educated Singaporeans have developed a job-hopping attitude because of labor shortage and that they hop from one job to the other for a few extra dollars as a result. Instead, turnover problem is caused by factors under the control of management. Especially, the authors found that companies were not doing enough to create a sense of belongingness and commitment in their employees and that their management practices were perceived as lacking in fairness and transparency.

## Participation of females in the workforce

The female participation in the Singapore labor force has risen significantly over the years. However, it is still lower than that in many developed countries. For example, only 52 percent of Singapore women aged between 40 and 49 years work compared with 71 percent in Japan, 62 percent in Korea, 79 percent in the UK, and 76 percent in the United States (see Table 11.1). Why are Singaporean women not re-entering the workforce and what can be done to encourage them to return to work? A study "Back to work – are you ready?" conducted by the National Trade Union Congress in 1995 provides the answer to this question. Reasons identified by respondents for not working include lack of a suitable job near their home, lack of part-time working arrangements, lack of required qualifications, not knowing where to look for work, problems in adjusting to working life, lack of before and after school care facilities for children above 6 years old, preference to spend more time with children, no felt need to rejoin workforce, and lack of childcare facilities for children from 2 to 6 years old. The solutions identified in the study to alleviate the problem include providing training to women to upgrade their skills, encouraging employers to provide part-time or flexible working arrangements, offering better pay and benefits, providing facilities for childcare and the aged, and changing employers' attitudes to be more receptive to career breaks. Companies in the UK and the USA provide flexible working arrangements to help female employees combine career and domestic commitments. Besides part-time working, other flexible work schedules existent there include flexitime, non-fixed starting and ending time, annualized hours, teleworking, job sharing, and a compressed work week.

The lower female participation in Singapore's workforce does not make sense, especially when one considers perennial chronic labor shortage and job-hopping problems in Singapore. HR managers in Singapore have failed to rise to the occasion and counter the problem by being proactive in their HR practices. Singapore has a large pool of highly educated female workers aged 29 to 34 who take themselves out of the workforce temporarily to raise their children. These women have to struggle to find suitable jobs when they want to return to the workforce. HR managers look at their CVs, find gaps in their employment history, and reject their applications without due consideration. Instead, they hire young, unmarried employees who keep switching jobs. HR managers need to tap the pool of highly educated, older women. Older women are much less likely to job-hop than other employees. Further, by understanding the needs of these employees and by providing them with job-sharing and flexible scheduling opportunities, it is possible to create a sense of commitment in them.

*Table 11.1* Labor force participation rate in Singapore, 2001

| Country | Females (aged 40–54) | Older persons (aged 55–64) |
| --- | --- | --- |
| Singapore | 58.5 | 45.1 |
| Taiwan | 53.8 | 41.8 |
| Hong Kong | 55.6 | 43.2 |
| South Korea | 61.8 | 59.2 |
| Japan | 70.2 | 65.8 |
| USA | 77.0 | 60.2 |

Source: *Report on labor force in Singapore*, Ministry of Manpower, 2002b.

## Participation of older workers in the workforce

In 1998, 14 percent of Singaporeans (or 451,900) were aged 55 and above. The figure is likely to reach 27 percent by the year 2020. This change will have a significant impact on the labor force. Similar to the participation of women, the participation of older workers in the labor force in Singapore is comparable to Hong Kong but lags behind developed countries like Japan, Korea, the UK, and the USA (see Table 11.1). While 80 percent of males aged 55 to 64 work in Japan and Korea, the proportion was only 65 percent in Singapore. The share of older females in the same age group at 22 percent was much lower than 50 percent in Japan and Korea and 46 percent in the USA. The older workers in Singapore are generally less educated compared with the younger cohorts because many of them have missed out on the limited opportunities available when they were young. However, future cohorts of older workers will be increasingly better educated. Although older workers have lower turnover and unemployment compared to their younger counterparts, they are more vulnerable to job loss and longer unemployment spells. This may be attributable to wrong perception among employers that they are less productive and receptive to change. Studies have shown that older workers perform better in many jobs, especially those such as retail, counseling, social services, and consultancy which involve service and human contact. Also, in jobs that require substantial training and experience such as professional and highly technical work, older workers can maintain high levels of performance well into their fifties and sixties. The growing importance of the services industry in fact augurs well for employment of older workers as the nature of work will be less dependent on physical stamina but require softer skills such as communication and service delivery.

Currently, flexible working arrangements such as flexitime, job sharing, part-time work, and teleworking are not commonly practiced in Singapore. There is considerable scope for employers to use flexible work options to allow older workers a more gradual transition from full-time work to retirement, enabling them to stay longer in the workforce. Work processes may need to be simplified to accommodate them. While various measures can contribute to the continued employment of older workers, their success hinges on employers changing their attitudes so as not to base employment decisions on age stereotypes. Employers need to be more enlightened in their attitudes toward older workers and make necessary adjustments to facilitate their continued employment.

## Management of Singaporean expatriates

An important emerging HR issue in Singapore is the effective management of its expatriates. Realizing that it has limited market and natural resources, Singapore has pursued a two-pronged economic strategy: (i) to go high-tech and (ii) to regionalize. To actualize the second prong of its strategy, Singapore is encouraging its companies to invest in regional countries. The fast-growing countries in Asia-Pacific provide ample opportunities to grow and expand. To manage overseas operations of Singaporean companies requires capable and willing Singaporeans. Currently, there are many Singaporeans working in various countries and their number is on the rise as more Singapore-based corporations set up plants and subsidiaries in other countries. Over the next few years, many of the Singapore-based companies would need about two-thirds more managers over and above the total managers involved in overseas operations at present. There are a number of major issues involved in the management of Singaporean expatriates, such as training and appropriate compensation. In fact, repatriation has been the major concern of Singaporean expatriates for two important reasons: (i) the Singaporean school system, which tends to be rigid and makes it hard for the children of expatriates to adapt after they have been away to another country, and (ii) the overseas stint of expatriates is not perceived as desirable when they return to Singapore. There are also issues of living standards and the family. Singaporean expatriates do not find living conditions to their taste when they are posted in developing countries. Moreover, their posting also poses a dilemma of what to do with the family – take them along or leave them behind. Khatri (2000a), in a study of determinants of Singaporean expatriates in China, identified several key factors contributing to their greater performance/success. While many studies of American and European expatriates have found cultural competency as more important than technical competency, this study found that technical competency plays a more important role in the success of Singaporean expatriates in China. The reason for little or no impact of cultural adaptability was that 99 percent of the Singaporean expatriates in the sample were Chinese. The second factor affecting the success of Singaporean expatriates was the nature of assignment, which includes briefing the expatriates about their overseas assignments, explaining clearly to them their role in overseas operations, and giving them greater autonomy. Another factor affecting the success of Singaporean expatriates was related to the value of assignment. Successful expatriates perceive that their overseas assignments open new career opportunities for them. They also value greatly the development of their skills during foreign assignments. The last key factor contributing to the success of the Singaporean expatriates was the expectation of immediate results from them, although the conventional wisdom in existing expatriate literature suggests that expatriate managers should not be expected to produce immediate results.

## Training and development

Singapore ranks very high in the world in its emphasis on training and development. Companies in Singapore spend about 3.5 to 4.0 percent of the payroll expenses on training and development activities. In the last decade, training consultants in Singapore have mushroomed. The emphasis on training is so much so that some companies have even created a standalone department on training along with the HRM department. One wonders though if the current training programs, with emphasis on improving operational efficiencies, are appropriate in the new economy that is increasingly knowledge-based. For example, research in the strategic HRM field suggests that different business strategies (cost reduction or quality enhancement or innovation) require different HR strategies to support them. Most of the training programs at present are designed to support the cost reduction or quality enhancement strategies. They do not support innovation strategy. As Singaporean companies attempt to move from cost-quality combination to quality-innovation combination, the nature of training programs has to change significantly.

# HRM practices in Singapore

HR managers in Singapore and many other Asian countries are facing difficult challenges. However, with challenges come opportunities. For example, MacLachlan (1996) noted that East Asia is the best place in the world to be a personnel manager because of the focus on recruiting, training, developing, and retaining staff. Unfortunately, at present there is a dearth of qualified and professional HR managers in the region. With a few exceptions, HR function is not receiving the attention from top management that it deserves. Debrah (1994) observed that the *ad hoc* nature of HRM policies and practices in companies in Singapore contributed significantly to the job-hopping phenomenon. Cunningham and Debrah (1995) reported that line managers and executives took over some of the functions of HR managers because HR managers lacked the necessary skills to manage HR function competently. Khatri (2000b) noted that companies in Singapore do a poor job, especially in recruitment and selection of employees. Companies rarely use valid recruitment and selection strategies. The most common approach to selection was unstructured interviews that have low validities. Neither is performance management a particularly well-managed function. Although there is great emphasis on training and development activities, they are not aligned with organizational strategy and culture. Consequently, it is not clear how much value training and development programs are adding to organizational performance.

The companies in Singapore may be grouped into two broad categories in their management practices: (i) multinational corporations and their Singaporean subsidiaries headed mostly by senior managers from home-country nationals and expatriates from countries such as Australia, India, New Zealand, the Philippines, and the UK, and (ii) local Singapore companies, government departments, and government corporations headed by local Singaporean managers.

# Practices in multinational corporations and their Singapore subsidiaries

As noted above, Singapore has a mix of multinationals from Europe, Japan, and the USA. The multinationals from these countries reflect a management philosophy and culture of their home countries. For example, Japanese multinationals emphasize life-long employment and use decision-making and compensation systems similar to Japanese organizations. Singaporean subsidiaries of American corporations tend to show greater goal-orientated, outcome-based management practices consistent with management practices observed in the US multinational corporations. Typically, middle and top managers of the Singaporean subsidiaries are non-Singaporeans and junior managers, and non-managers are Singaporeans, Malaysians, and other foreign workers from the region. Multinationals have enjoyed and exploited this synergy between managerial abilities from home-country nationals and disciplined and hard-working Singaporean workers to achieve a high level of performance and productivity.

# Practices in local companies, government departments, and corporations

Practices in local companies, government departments and corporations are an amalgamation of administrative systems inherited from the British and strong authority and power distance orientation of the Chinese/Asian culture. A result is a highly structured, authoritative management philosophy whose main features are discussed in the following paragraphs.

As noted earlier, one salient feature of Singaporean management style is its emphasis on micromanagement. In local companies and government departments, there is a strong tendency in managers to micromanage organizational activities. Even relatively minor routine decisions are taken to the enterprise's top for resolution.

Further, employees in Singapore have long operated in a high power distance context and have developed a mindset of unwillingness to participate in decisions. They are content with their managers making decisions and giving them instructions. Jobs are narrowly and tightly specified, giving employees little discretion. Communication takes place vertically downwards; informal and horizontal communication is quite limited. Voluntary feedback from the bottom is minimal. In a typical encounter between a superior and subordinate, the former does most of the talking and the latter merely nods his or her head in affirmation. A superior is actually expected to make decisions without consulting his or her subordinates, because subordinates may view their involvement in decisions by their superiors as a sign of incompetence or lack of authority on the part of the superior. Subordinates are unwilling to express their opinions and disagreements openly, due to fear of losing face or making someone else lose face. There exists a big chasm in communication between superiors and their subordinates because it is hard for subordinates to air their views to their senior managers. On the whole, organizational communication is quite anemic. Senior managers wield unlimited power and control over subordinates. Employees have an unquestioning, submissive attitude. Senior managers elicit respect from junior employees not because of the former's competence but because of their authority and position. However, the education level of Singaporeans has increased steadily and they are also coming into contact with the outside world. Although they are used to taking orders and instructions from above, there is a growing sentiment/resentment against the authoritative management approach in general. It is not clear how the tussle between demand for more instruction from the top by Singaporeans and their need for greater say in decision-making is going to be resolved.

## HR in the next five years in Singapore

The Ministry of Manpower, Singapore, has prepared a document, *Manpower 21*, outlining the vision and strategy of Singapore related to HR issues in the twenty-first century. The document states that the vision is for Singapore to become a talent capital, a place where the workforce makes the difference to Singapore's competitive advantage.

*Manpower 21* is a strategic blueprint to develop people and manpower as a competitive advantage, to support as well as create growth in the knowledge economy. While the new vision and strategy regarding people emphasized in *Manpower 21* are worthy goals, they clearly are a break from the past. Singapore has used a control-based management model in the past. The new vision and strategy, however, require a new management approach based on employee participation and commitment. One wonders if it would be possible to unlearn a management approach that has permeated the entire society and culture. Singaporean education and administrative systems have refined and perfected the control-based management system over the last four decades. It would be a formidable task to change the deeply entrenched values and practices of the past. The dilemma of transition from control-based approach to commitment-based approach plays in organizational settings everyday. Employee participation and empowerment schemes are implemented in a control-based context with a top-down approach with obvious disappointing results. Employee participation and empowerment initiatives end up becoming a tool of control in the hands of authoritative bosses. Companies implement performance-based compensation without clearly defining and communicating objective performance standards. Because clear and specific performance criteria that are central to the success of performance-based compensation may reduce subjectivity, they thus impair the power and control of managers inherent in their subjective discretion.

There are changes taking place in the economy in the region. The twin cities of Hong Kong and Singapore prospered using pro-business economic strategies at a time when other countries and governments in the region relied upon socialist economic philosophies. That provided them with a competitive advantage for several decades. However, other countries are following in their footsteps and opening their economies to foreign direct investment. The foreign direct investment that used to flow naturally to the two cities is not flowing at the same rate as before. Other countries are becoming more attractive because of size, natural resources as well as cheap labor. In particular, Malaysia is a major threat to Singapore and mainland China a threat to Hong Kong. Over time, Hong Kong and Singapore may or may not enjoy the advantage they have had in the past as other countries catch up with them. The Singapore government and policy makers do realize this challenge and are trying to create a niche and looking for ways how to have as big a slice as possible of the ever-bigger-growing economic pie in the Asia-Pacific.

## Websites and current references for latest information on HRM in Singapore

Three key departments/institutions involved in HRM in Singapore are: MOM (The Ministry of Manpower), SPRING (Standards, Productivity, and Innovation Board), and SHRI (the Singapore Human Resource Institute).

MOM is made up of five business groups: Manpower Planning, Manpower Development, Manpower Augmentation, Workplace Environment and Welfare, and Corporate Support.

The Manpower Planning division coordinates and spearheads national efforts to balance manpower demand with supply. Through Manpower Development, the Ministry is developing Singapore's manpower resources into one that is globally competitive and optimally employed. The Manpower Development division is responsible for developing the School of Lifelong Learning which promotes lifelong learning for employability at the national, workforce, and individual levels. As part of a national effort to enhance Singapore's competitiveness, the Manpower Augmentation group has made it a priority to attract global intellectual capital and manpower resources to fill specific gaps and roles in Singapore's economy. The Workplace Environment and Welfare group's mission is to ensure a harmonious, safe and favorable work environment for all Singaporeans and foreigners employed in Singapore. The Corporate Support group provides a variety of support services to the Ministry to help its business groups achieve their objectives. The Ministry has a website (http://www.gov.sg/mom) that provides detailed information about its activities, programs, and numerous publications.

The mission of SPRING Singapore is to raise productivity so as to enhance Singapore's competitiveness and economic growth for a better quality of life for all Singaporeans. The overall goal is to achieve an average total factor productivity (TFP) growth of 2 percent per annum for the next 10 years. To achieve the 2 percent TFP growth, SPRING focuses on three areas: productivity and innovation, standards and quality, and small and medium-sized enterprises and the domestic sector. SPRING has changed its name three times. It was first known as the National Productivity Board, which was changed to the Productivity and Standard Board. More information on SPRING can be found on its web page (http://www.spring.gov.sg).

Founded in 1965, SHRI is dedicated to raising the quality of work life in Singapore through effective HR practices that support the development of a world-class workforce. To help individuals upgrade skills and enhance knowledge, it has various certificate, diploma and degree courses in areas such as human resource management and development, people relations/skills and industrial relations. Specialized courses like the professional certificate in compensation and benefits management, certificate in applied psychology and master of applied finance are also offered to enhance the professional development of the HR people. SHRI also organizes conferences, seminars, workshops and forums to keep members abreast of current HR issues and government policies. SHRI has its own website (http://www.shri.org.sg).

In addition, Singapore has three universities, all of which offer undergraduate and graduate courses in HRM. The National University of Singapore (http://www.nus.edu.sg) is the oldest and has the most comprehensive offering of courses. The Nanyang Technological University (http://gemsweb.ntu.edu.sg/igems/public.htm) was inaugurated in 1990 and its focus is on business management, engineering, mass communication, and education courses. The Singapore Management University (http://www.smu.edu.sg) was established only a few years ago and its focus is basically on management.

# References

*Asian Finance* (1988) "Singapore: manpower shortage deters investors," 14 (9): 96–98.

*Asiaweek* (1999) "Curb the cronies," Editorial 25 (6): 14–16.

Chang, H. (1996) "In Singapore, the dreams are getting bigger," *Business Week*, 23 September.

Cunningham, J.B. and Debrah, Y.A. (1995) "Skills for managing human resources in a complex environment: The perceptions of human resource managers in Singapore," *International Journal of Human Resource Management* 6 (1): 79–101.

Dale, R. (1999) "Crisis stills apologists for corruption," *International Herald Tribune*, 21 January.

Debrah, Y.A. (1994) "Management of operative staff in a labour-scarce economy: The views of human resource managers in the hotel industry in Singapore," *Asia Pacific Journal of Human Resources* 32 (1): 41–60.

Ditzig, H. and You, P.S. (1988) "In search of the Singapore managerial style," *Singapore Management Review* 3: 35–51.

Fisher, C.D. and Shaw, J.B. (1992) "Establishment level correlates of human resource practices," *Asia Pacific Journal of Human Resource Management* 30 (4): 30–46.

Golden, K. and Ramanujam, V. (1985) "Between a dream and nightmare: On the integration of the human resource management and strategic planning process," *Human Resource Management* 24: 429–452.

Ho, J.T.S., Ang, C.E., Loh, J. and Ng, I. (1998) "A preliminary study of kiasu behavior – is it unique to Singapore?," *Journal of Managerial Psychology* 13: 359–370.

Husted, B.W. (1999) "Wealth, culture, and corruption," *Journal of International Business Studies* 30: 339–360.

Islam, I. and Chowdhury, A. (1997) *Asia-Pacific economies: A survey*, London: Routledge.

Khatri, N. (2000a) "Determinants of expatriate success in China," in C.-M. Lau, K.S. Law, D.K. Tse, and C.-S. Wong (eds.) *Asian management matters: Regional relevance and global impact*, London: Imperial College Press, pp. 319–339.

Khatri, N. (2000b) "Managing human resource for competitive advantage in Singapore: A study of companies in Singapore," *International Journal of Human Resource Management* 11 (2): 336–365.

Khatri, N. and Budhwar, P.S. (2002) "A study of strategic HR issues in an Asian context," *Personnel Review* 31 (2): 166–188.

Khatri, N., Budhwar, P.S. and Chong, T.F. (2001) "Explaining employee turnover in an Asian context," *Human Resource Management Journal* 11 (1): 54–74.

Khatri, N., Templer, K.J. and Budhwar, P. (2003) *Consequences of power distance orientation in organizations*, paper presented at the Academy of Management Conference, Seattle.

Lingle, C. (1996) *Singapore's authoritarian capitalism: Asian values, free market illusions and political dependency*, Fairfax, VA: The Locke Institute.

MacLachlan, R. (1996) "Job-hopping or industrial espionage," *Personnel Management* 2 (14): 15–16.

Ministry of Manpower, Singapore (1995) *Women returning to work*, Manpower Research and Statistics Division.

Ministry of Manpower, Singapore (1999a) *Older workers*, Manpower Research and Statistics Division, July.

Ministry of Manpower, Singapore (1999b) *Flexible work arrangements*, Manpower Research and Statistics Division.

Ministry of Manpower, Singapore (2002a) *The 2002 Singapore yearbook of manpower statistics*, Manpower Research and Statistics Division.

Ministry of Manpower, Singapore (2002b) *Report on labor force in Singapore 2002*, Manpower Research and Statistics Division.

Ministry of Manpower, Singapore (2002c) *Labor market, third quarter 2002*, Manpower Research and Statistics Division.

Ministry of Manpower, Singapore (2002d) *Conditions of employment 2002*, Manpower Research and Statistics Division.

National Productivity Board, Singapore (1988) 'Report of the task force on job-hopping'.

Shaw, J.B., Kirkbride, P.S., Fisher, C.D. and Tang, S.F.Y. (1995) "Human resource management practices in Hong Kong and Singapore: The impact of political forces and imitation processes," *Asia Pacific Journal of Human Resources* 33 (1): 22–39.

*The Straits Times* (1996) "Job-hoppers will 'drag Singapore down,'" 9 August.

Tan, V. and Tan, N.T. (1999) "Personality type and the Singapore manager: Research findings based on MBTI," *Singapore Management Review* 21 (1): 15–31.

Vogl, F. (1999) "Asian crisis stimulates establishment pressures for fundamental reforms," *Earth Times*, February: 16–28.

# 12 HRM in Australia

MARGARET PATRICKSON AND WAHYU SUTIYONO

## Introduction

Although the land size of Australia is approximately the same as that of the continental United States, its population of only 19.5 million in 2001 is less than 10 percent that of the USA. During the 1996–2001 period population growth rates have averaged 1.3 percent per annum (ABS, 2001). A little over half the population is employed (9.3 million in 2002), with a workforce participation rate of 63.6 percent and an unemployment rate of 6.3 percent (ABS, 2002a). In common with other western nations, the population is aging, with a median age of 35.4 years (ABS, 2002b).

This chapter presents an overview of Australian HRM practice in the context of the changing economic and technological parameters facing the country. Though there have been increasing inroads into the economy by MNCs, the vast majority of Australian organizations remain relatively small by global standards and consequently the take-up and penetration of emergent global HR practices remains relatively slow.

## The Australian HRM context

Australia is generally considered to be a developed country offering its inhabitants a relatively high standard of living and a relaxed lifestyle. Until 1973 Australian industry was protected against the inroads of international trade through high tariff barriers (Archbold, 2001) but by 1996 most tariffs had been reduced to less than 5 percent making the economy more vulnerable to competition from beyond its borders. Today's economic activity levels comprise a GDP of US$380 billion of which 79 percent comes from service industries (*Australia Country Profile*, 2001) with the largest service sector made up of finance, property and business services. Private consumption accounts for 60 percent of GDP. If the dotcom problems in the early 2000s are ignored, business performance in the recent past has been steady and marginally positive (Ruthven, 2002), with the country being affected only slightly by the recent economic crises in Asia. Since 2000 the national government has been pursuing a definite cooperative policy toward its neighbors in the Asia Pacific region (Commonwealth of Australia, 2002). This has coincided with an expansion of Australian business activities and an increasing involvement of multinational enterprises in the domestic economy (Walsh, 2001).

During the last two decades, manufacturing has declined both as a contributor to GDP and an employer of labor, and with this has come a change in workforce skill requirements. Jobs requiring more than a basic education and competency in modern computerized technologies continue to rise and now outnumber those needing little education (Loble, 2001). At the same time there are fewer career tracks as organizations continue to de-layer (Buchanan *et al.*, 1999).

The Australian workforce is made up of people from various cultural backgrounds (Patrickson and Hartmann, 2001). Both the population and the workforce are aging and this has led to recognition of the need to revise staff management practices to reflect this trend (Patrickson and Hartmann, 2001; DeCieri and Kramar, 2003). In common with other developed nations, workforce skill levels are high with increases recently recorded in educational attainments so that 40 percent of the population now hold a trade qualification and 12 percent hold post-graduate qualifications. Women have recorded higher levels of educational increase than men (ABS, 2000b). Yet while training and education has introduced various new skills into the labor force (De Cieri and Kramar, 2003), Australia continues to source migrants for skills which are lacking in the country and immigration policies continue to put an emphasis in obtaining skilled people (ABS, 2000a).

## Workforce characteristics

Among all wage and salary earners, 54 percent hold a post-school qualification of which 28 percent hold a higher education qualification and a further 24 percent hold a skilled or basic vocational qualification (ABS, 2000b). Women are less likely to hold a vocational qualification than men (19 percent and 29 percent respectively). This trend toward increased credentialism is nonetheless coincident with simultaneous shortages of skilled workers, especially in computing, health, teaching, tool-making, sheet metal work, hairdressing, and childcare (AGPS, 1998). Many skilled workers head overseas for higher paid jobs (Patrickson and Hartmann, 2001). The aging workforce is one of the more crucial employment issues in the new millennium as Australian baby-boomers approach their retirement age. While 2002 was the peak when they began to reach their mid fifties, in 2012 the population over 65 will grow by 4 percent and continue to do so by 2.9 percent per year until 2028. This growth rate will exceed the growth of the total population by four times (*The Australian*, 5 March 2003).

The workforce has been characterized by a series of restructuring and recurrent downsizing efforts resulting in trends toward early retirement for many (Hartmann, 1998; Patrickson, 2001) and a significant growth in the contingent workforce (Vandenheuvel and Wooden, 1999) in outsourcing (Beaumont, 2002; Benson and Littler, 2002; Charles, 2002; Cully and Phong, 2002; Gome, 2002; Howarth, 2002), and in teleworking (ABS,

2000a). Accompanying these trends have been reductions in union density in all categories (Cranston, 2000).

Diversity, in all its forms is also growing. Women now comprise 42 percent of the workforce (Vines, 2001). Yet even though their participation in the workforce has been expanding, their promotion into managerial ranks remains relatively stable and low. There are no female executives in more than half (52 percent) of the top 200 Australian companies, though women constitute a small number (8.2 percent) of board members. Just two women are CEOs (*Human Resources*, January 2003).

Ethnic diversity is also spreading with at least 25 percent of the workforce born overseas in over 160 countries (DeCieri and Olekans, 2000). Given that Australian immigration policy favors immigrants with post-school qualifications, the number of adult migrants of non-English-speaking background who have a post-school qualification is 55 percent of all workers (ABS, 2000b). Indigenous Australians, though 2 percent of the population, tend to be under-represented in the workforce.

Culturally the workforce reflects largely Anglo-Celtic values (Smith and Phillips, 2001) with English almost the exclusive language of the workplace, though there are signs this is gradually becoming more inclusive (Waterhouse and Deakin, 1995) as organizations begin to recognize and value the contribution of those from other cultures. Employee surveys tend to indicate employees seek balance in their lives (Kerslake, 2002) and view their job as a means of self-fulfilment and a place to develop and apply an expanding set of skills. Nevertheless this represents only part of the picture as other researchers (e.g. Loble, 2001) voice concern about an increasing population divide between a growing elite group of optimistic free agents with high incomes and another group less fortunate who seek their fulfillment outside the work experience.

# Recent contextual changes

## Legislative context

Patrickson and Hartmann (2001) report how in the 15 years preceding the introduction of the 1996 Workplace Relations Act, a series of continuous marginal changes had been introduced through the federal legislature in an effort to reduce the number of disputes associated with the then adversarial nature of Australian industrial relations practice. They comment that until 1983, Australia's adversarial labor system was regulated through a centralized conciliation and arbitration process, underpinned by permanent quasijudicial tribunals, employer tribunals and union representation of employees. This was gradually deregulated in the 1983–1996 period and, although the 1996 Industrial Relations Act in Australia is generally credited to have eased much of this tension, the Act was not a defining event *per se* but rather the culmination of a number of changes during the previous decade. By 1996 major stakeholders such as governments, employers and unions were ready for a more substantive change and supported the introduction of the new Act which was designed to put an end to the previous history of dispute and noncooperation.

The ambit of the 1996 Act was comprehensive and subsequent dispute activity has dwindled. The main impact of the Act has been to initiate and maintain a move toward enterprise bargaining and this has contributed to the declining power of trade unions. Despite expectations that it might lead to a worsening of circumstances for organizations and individuals, Wooden (2000) reports that, contrary to the fears of its opponents, the new industrial relations practices have not led to any reported rise in job insecurity, increased hours of work or greater income diversity. Other authors indicate the picture may be more complex in that some income recipients, especially those in very senior roles, have improved their salary relative to their subordinates. However, at the lower end, the disparity between incomes is not significant (O'Neill, 1998).

Even given the relatively strong industrial relations environment in Australia, organizations now seem to enjoy a reasonable degree of freedom to innovate in HRM practices. This is especially the case in MNCs operating in Australia (Walsh, 2001). Walsh (2001) reports that there is a higher degree of formalization in HR policies and practices in foreign-owned companies (notably British, US and Japanese) operating in Australia than their domestic counterparts. The level of investment and sophistication in HRM is demonstrated in areas such as selection, performance appraisal and grievance mechanism in British firms; innovative work practices, just-in-time approaches and joint consultation committees for Japanese firms; and in US firms in strategic approaches to HRM.

## Workplace management changes

The key changes in workplace management include declining union power, coupled with increasing formalization of HR practice. Shifts in the power balance have been accompanied by concomitant shifts in reward distribution in that, not only has the balance of power swung away from the lower ranks, but their remuneration has reduced relative to more senior levels.

## Unions

The decline of union membership and influence since the mid-1990s has meant that employers are gaining power over the conditions of employment (Patrickson and Hartman, 2001). Employees working under enterprise agreements now outnumber those working under the award system (Wooden and Hawke, 2000). Australian workplace agreements (AWAs) now cover 3,000 organizations but only a small number of employees (De Cieri and Kramar, 2003). The common law remains the major tool for regulating employment for the majority.

Gollan (2001) reported a survey of employers in non-unionized workplaces, that indicated that over 60 percent of respondents believed AWAs had enhanced management–employee relations, the introduction of change and labor productivity. His findings also demonstrated that effective consultation with employees about AWAs had created positive organizational outcomes. Though only based on small numbers of employees, the findings confirm those in the UK and North America.

Slow growth in employee numbers has tended to occur in industries with high union stronghold, while above average growth has tended to take place in those with low union membership rates (ABS, 2000a). Given that manufacturing, where the majority of unions had their base, has been in decline, this has contributed to the changing union density observed by the ABS.

## Trends toward formalization of HRM practice

McGraw (2002) reports that larger organizations tend to have more formal HR policies in place and these are likely to be aligned with corporate strategies. In recent times there have been innovations in the way in which work is organized, with a shifting emphasis toward recognizing the importance of quality in both service and product industries. Efforts at work reorganization are exemplified by the movement away from work organized around the input of individual operators toward team-based structures functioning either permanently, regularly or episodically. The incidence of work teams has significantly increased (Wang, 2001) and reflects the more sophisticated and integrated technologies that underpin modern throughput processes.

Such moves have implications for the way in which employee performance is assessed and rewarded. Contribution to team effort and the ability to work effectively with others are becoming key considerations in recruitment and promotion decisions (Glassop, 2002). Yet despite intentions to implement performance appraisal practices that are less susceptible to personal bias, reports in *Human Resources* (March 2002) indicate that only one third of 6000 organizations have employee performance management in place, of which more than half (66 percent) comprise the state and utilities sector. Over 90 percent never conduct performance management. Nevertheless, HR strategy to retain top performers suggests that about one third or 35 percent are putting in place career management strategies, leadership competencies are actively sought by 18 percent of organizations with high evidence of this from transport (50 percent) and manufacturing (36 percent) industries.

Notwithstanding this minor level of negative feedback, the majority of larger Australian organizations increasingly demonstrate the importance of human resources in strategic decision-making. *Human Resources* (March 2002) reports that among 50 top companies on the Australian Stock Exchange, those that had an HR director on the executive level recorded higher growth compared to those that did not. While this finding does not imply causality, it does indicate that larger organizations are beginning to pay greater recognition to their senior HR staff. Moreover, the value of HR function is increasing as the majority (83 percent) of organizations who were surveyed have HR directors in the executive committee (*Human Resources*, January 2003: 9).

## Changes in HRM practice

Recent trends indicate that HR practices in Australia are reflecting similar moves to practices in other global locations. New initiatives may be divided into three major trends. The first of these seeks to identify, recruit, re-train and further develop increasingly scarce individual talent, the second seeks to develop more effective team functioning and the third is focused on striving for better integration of individuals into their work environment. Programs aimed at identifying talent early, and intensive coaching of those with potential are being adopted in a number of companies. Given that salaries for top performers now significantly exceed their less successful contemporaries, such programs tend to be attractive to high achievers and aid the recruitment activities of larger companies. Awareness of the need for performance management systems has grown and led to an increase in incidence of monitoring and measurement of performance at both team and individual levels though few companies report they are happy with their current systems.

Other new programs appear aimed at developing more effective interpersonal and team activities. As in the USA, recognition of the benefits of diversity or achieving balance between life and work continue to expand and underpin many new programs aimed at promoting better interpersonal working relations between staff.

## Work/life balance and diversity management

Promotion of diversity is one of the objectives of the national government and has led to programs to raise awareness of the benefits of inclusive employment practices in the workplace. In 1998, for example, the government introduced a program that focused on diversity in language and cultural background (BRW, 2002). In a recent effort to verify take up rates, *Human Resources* (March 2002) indicates that diversity management practices are now being reflected in organizational processes, such as strategic planning (51 percent), in statements of values and mission/vision (58 percent), representation by various demographic groups (56 percent), and that such policies are supported by senior managers (69 percent). Those companies, designated as Best Practice organizations, consistently demonstrated stronger allegiance to the recognition and incorporation of diversity values. Yet except for these best practice organizations, only a small number of organizations (38 percent) indicate that the CEO regards managing diversity as contributing to the bottom line (Managing Work/Life Balance, 2002).

Other information from this study showed that organizations were paying more attention to issues of labor flexibility and achieving balance between work and family (Managing

Work/Life Balance, 2002). Yet even though the number of Australian organizations who report they are pursuing such practices continues to expand, the proportion still lags behind the global average for developed countries. Those organizations who have recognized work/ life balance as important, report they have increased the availability of flexible work options, such as part-time work, flexible starting and finishing times, study leave, paid parental maternity leave, and team work, and their employees have increasingly accessed these options. Those involved have shown a reduction of turnover by 3.7 percent, absenteeism by 3 percent and an increase of return rate from parental leave by 23 percent. However, only a few organizations (10.3 percent) have offered reduced overtime as work/life balance policy compared to a global average figure of 32 percent (*Human Resources*, February 2003). These results are confirmed through two consecutive surveys undertaken by Hay Consultants showing that organizations with a written diversity policy had increased dramatically from about 10 percent in 1998 to nearly 50 percent in 2001 (Hay, 2002).

## Remuneration levels

Chief executives' remuneration levels have slowed in 2002 compared to the two previous years, given that the technology-inspired share market boom has peaked (Johnston and Kitney, 2002). Nevertheless, the gap between blue- and white-collar remuneration is widening partly due to the weakening influence of the union movement, public scrutiny and peer pressure (Cornell, 2002).

While much of the salary explosion has been attributed to the US influence on the relationship between salary and performance, issues of governance remain a challenge. Lowe *et al.* (2002) report that within current pay practices, variable pay is regarded as receiving little emphasis in the total package. This is reflected in incentives being seen as moderate in terms of both their importance and amount. This is also the case with benefits. While there is some element of seniority in pay practices, managers are not keen to see the level increased. Rather they felt that the link between pay and performance, including group performance, should be greater than at present. There is also some evidence of a more short-term orientation in pay, though with some expectation that pay should be tied to longer-term future results. The authors suggest that for motivational purposes, Australian organizations may seek to narrow the gap between the current level and employee expectations. Holland *et al.* (2001) report that, in the Australian case, the relationship between CEO rewards and organizational performance has yet to be determined in light of the deficiencies, ambiguity and variance in remuneration disclosure.

## Training and development

International comparisons of training expenditure generally place Australia below the levels of similar countries. The 2000 ASTD report by the American Society for Training and Development placed Australia behind most European countries, though ahead of the USA and the majority of Asian countries. A more recent paper by Drost *et al.* (2002) comparing countries in terms of best practice indicates that the majority of Australian managers perceive their organizations as slow to support the softer aspects of training and development, such as team-building, understanding business practices and corporate values, and the proactive aspects of training, such as preparation for future assignment and multiskilling. Australia is similar to Canada and the USA in increasing worker productivity and in focusing training activities toward individual learning rather than team-based learning.

As issues of the aging workforce begin to bite, HR managers are facing the challenge of managing transfer of skills and knowledge to younger workers to fill the skills shortage as baby-boomers are retiring. This is happening at the same time as they face the need to provide continuing career opportunities to older workers as they phase out of the workforce (*The Australian*, 5 March 2003).

## Recruitment

In a similar comparative study on recruitment practices, Huo *et al.* (2002) report that, compared with benchmarks in the Asia-Pacific region, many Australian managers believe that a good fit between company values and ways of doing things should receive greater emphasis in their selection processes. Though other criteria, such as a person's ability to perform the technical requirements of the job, a person's potential to do a good job and a person's ability to get along well with others, are viewed as important, in practice these had not been treated as important. Australia seems to be located among countries that accord little significant relationship between hiring practices and subsequent organizational effectiveness. In common with other countries, there is a swing toward e-recruitment (Sachdev, 2000), especially in the contingent part of the labor force.

## Performance management

Practices such as benchmarking (Winkler, 1998) and the use of the balanced scorecard are becoming more prevalent in Australia. In a comparison of performance management practices, the evidence from Milliman *et al.*'s findings (2002) is that companies should put greater weight on documenting appraisal results. In common with Latin America, Australian respondents place a relatively high emphasis on the developmental aspects of performance appraisal, rather than the administrative or strategic, and still believe further improvements are needed. Practitioners report they encourage staff to participate in the process. Linkages between performance appraisal and pay are less emphasized in Australia where the major purpose is more likely to be developmental than reward linked.

# Emergent HR competencies

Ulrich's (1997) work on the efforts of the HR profession to become increasingly strategic in its operation has highlighted four main roles that practitioners undertake: administrative expert, employee champion, change agent and strategic business partner. In Australia there have been moves by practitioners away from what they regard as an entrapment in being administrative experts and employee champions towards acquiring the competence and exercising the capacity to have a greater input into business strategy. This is exemplified by the increasing qualifications held by HR practitioners and their reported switch toward a more strategic focus (Fisher *et al.*, 1999). One illustration of such increasing professionalization is the rise (6.8 percent) of the average pay of HR professionals in 2002 compared with 5.6 percent of salary increase of those of other sectors (*Human Resources*, January 2003).

The Australian Human Resources Institute (AHRI), the professional body of HRM practitioners in Australia, is presently conducting a series of focus group workshops with members, asking them to indicate which skills they themselves feel they need to further develop. Early results suggest that overwhelmingly they are reporting themselves in need of better business understanding in order that they can make recommendations to their CEOs underpinned by financial analysis, in addition to softer HR objectives. They indicate that they need to augment their professional people skills with more bottom-line arguments to demonstrate their strategic approach and how they add value.

In the public sector, increasing commercialization of public organizations and introduction of a service orientation (McGuire, 2001) have been associated with an uptake of the strategic input of HRM. This is clearly illustrated in a recent case study on the effectiveness of a corporate HR department in an Australian public sector entity (Teo, 2002) that demonstrates how the corporatization processes set the scene for the shift from an administrative personnel function to the integration of organizational strategy and HRM. Yet though this effort to take on a more strategic role resulted in a degree of ineffectiveness within the HR department, in Teo's view this was largely due to line managers not being ready to assume people management responsibilities when the HR function decentralized.

One factor driving the uptake of HRM has been the need to coordinate and manage the high incidence of downsizing and restructuring in the last few years. Despite little evidence of their involvement prior to downsizing, there is growing acknowledgment of HR practitioners as HR staff work closely with senior management in various downsizing activities, such as preparing and dealing with issues of redundancy, counseling retrenched staff and handling the restructuring processes (*Human Resources*, January 2003: 1). Participating in activities in such practices has given HR practitioners opportunities to upgrade their HR expertise and, accordingly, their profile. Despite surveys on victims indicating that the majority (81 percent) of organizations mismanaged the process of downsizing in terms of communication to employees and especially in providing clarification on various retrenchment issues (*HR Monthly*, November 2002: 7), management continues to see this as an area of HR competence. Another emergent competency involves dealing with ethical concerns but skills in this area are still embryonic as many HR managers are puzzled about the issues and actions in ethical conduct. Such doubts demonstrate an early stage of take-up in ethical matters and raise concerns about the ability of HR managers to develop programs that promote ethical issues (*HR Monthly*, November 2002: 7).

Yet, while there are many examples of increased professionalism, they are not widespread and the take-up of newly emergent HRM practices in Australian organizations is generally restricted to larger public sector organizations, MNCs and larger domestic companies, as borne out by survey results reported by Guest *et al.* (2002). According to Guest *et al.* (2002), less than 1 percent of companies (from the 784 senior managers responding to the survey) install three-quarters of 18 typical HRM practices, only 20 percent utilize more than half, and 31 percent apply less than a quarter of them. In addition, except for recruitment and selection, HR practices in general and their personnel departments are rated modestly in terms of their effectiveness. This finding is supported by a recent global survey conducted by Pricewaterhouse Coopers which states that only few organizations measure or report key people issues (*Human Resources*, February 2003: 8). In comparison to organizations globally, only about half (53 percent) Australian companies measure employee satisfaction and a quarter (26 percent) report employee cost (*Human Resources*, February 2003: 8).

## HRM in SMEs

Small and medium enterprises (SMEs) play an important role in the Australian economy (McMahon, 2001; Huang *et al.*, 2002). In conjunction with sole income earners and partnerships, they account for over 65 percent of all employment (ABS, 2002c). However, the prevalence of HRM practices in these organizations is moderate. Wiesner and MacDonald (2001) report that SMEs are modest in terms of participative HR practices, union membership, and presence of HR managers. Their recruitment practices tend to be informal. While selection activities to a greater extent are more formalized, they tend to be practiced in the medium-sized entities. Performance appraisal is not formalized and compensation practices lack a participative component. Nevertheless, these findings are dissimilar compared to SMEs that undertake organizational innovation, mainly those engaging in international operations. Case studies on innovative SMEs show the use of strategic HRM-related practices such as strategic use of rewards, career development and ongoing investment in training and development (Matthews, 2002).

# Conclusion

This review has highlighted a number of trends in HRM practice within Australia, such as the movement toward more inclusive labor management practices, adoption of behavioral codes that incorporate ethical standards, greater sophistication in the nature of the administration of recruitment, training, enterprise bargaining, remuneration and performance appraisal, efforts to benchmark practices against other countries and, underpinning all these changes, moves toward upgrading the standards of professional preparation and practice. Despite this, however, the process toward a more inclusive workplace is slow and the gains have been marginal. HR professionals seem to be on their way to the realization of being valued as business partners but they still have a long distance to travel, compared with counterparts in North America, Canada, and some parts of Asia. Isolation, coupled with the comparative smaller size of Australian organizations, means the demands on the HR professional may be less than those on their counterparts in larger economies.

Globalization has stimulated an increasing recognition that cross-cultural issues need staff management policies that reflect this growing interaction and there is some evidence of this happening. However, apart from large MNCs, such changes have generally been slow.

Despite its gains, Australian HRM remains conservative and behind the developments in other western nations. Why this is so is difficult to explain, other than in terms of its geographical isolation and a heritage of adversarial employment practices. In our opinion, benchmarking HRM globally and the increasing incidence of MNC take-over of local enterprises may hasten further progress but this prediction remains unverified at this point.

# References

*The Australian* (2003) "Exodus: Baby boomers bowing out," pp. 1–3, 5 March 2003, supplement.

Australian Bureau of Statistics (ABS) (2000a) "Work – industrial relations: Trade union members," *Australian social trends*.

Australian Bureau of Statistics (ABS) (2000b) "Education and training," *Year Book Australia, 2000.*

Australian Bureau of Statistics (ABS) (2001) *Australian demographic statistics*, Cat. No. 3101.0. December Quarter.

Australian Bureau of Statistics (ABS) (2002a) *Labour force, Australia*, Preliminary. Cat. No. 6202.0.

Australian Bureau of Statistics (ABS) (2002b) "Population – national summary tables," *Australian social trends*.

Australian Bureau of Statistics (ABS) (2002c) *Business operations and industry performance, Australia*, Report 8140.0.

*Australia Country Profile* (2001) *The economy* http://web21.epnet.com/citation.asp (viewed on 4 December 2002).

Australian Government Publishing Service (AGPS) (1998) *Skills in Australia: Trends and shortages*, Department of Employment, Education, Training and Youth Affairs, analytical series 98/5, Canberra: AGPS.

American Society for Training and Development (2000) *2000 ASTD international comparisons report*, New York: American Society for Training and Development.

Archbold, D. (2001) "Microeconomic policy and structural change in the Australian economy," *Ecodate* 15 (2): 6–9.

Beaumont, N. (2002) "Information technology outsourcing in Australia," *Resources Management Journal* 15 (3): 14–32.

Benson, J. and Littler, C. (2002) "Outsourcing and workforce reductions: An empirical study of Australian organisations," *Asia-Pacific Business Review* 8 (3): 16–30.

Brown, M. (2001) "Employee pay adjustment preferences: Recent Australian evidence," *Asia Pacific Journal of Human Resources* 39 (3):1–22.

Buchanan, J, Callus, R. and Briggs, C. (1999) "What impact has the Howard government had on wages and hours of work?," *Journal of Australian Political Economy* 43: 1–22.

*Business Review Weekly* (BRW) (2002) "Diverse challenges," 24 (29): 64–66.

Charles, E. (2002) "Leaving it to the experts," *Australian CPA* 72 (8): 44–48.

Commonwealth of Australia (2002) "Australia's overseas aid program 2002–3," statement by the Honourable Alexander Downer MP Minister for Foreign Affairs, 14 May 2002.

Cornell, A. (2002) "Up, up, and away," *Financial Review Boss* (November) 3(11): 42–46.

Cranston, M. (2000) "The terminal decline of Australian trade union membership," *IPA Review* 52 (4): 26–28.

Cully, M. and Phong, N. (2002) "Year of the flip-flop: The Australian labour market in 2001," *Australian Bulletin of Labour* 28 (1): 1–19.

De Cieri, H. and Kramar, R. (2003) *Human resource management in Australia: Strategy, people, performance*, Sydney: McGraw Hill.

De Cieri, H. and Olekans, M. (2000) "Australia," in *Managing diversity: An Asian and Pacific focus*, Brisbane: Wiley, pp. 21–36.

D'Netto, B. and Sohal, A.S. (1999) "Human resource practices and workforce diversity: An empirical assessment," *International Journal of Manpower* 20 (8): 530–548.

Drost, E.A., Frayne, C.A., Lowe, K.B. and Geringer, M. (2002) "Benchmarking training and development practices: A multi-country comparative analysis," *Asia Pacific Journal of Human Resources* 40 (1): 81–104.

Fisher, C., Dowling, P.J. and Garnham, J. (1999) "The impact of changes to the human resources function in Australia," *International Journal of Human Resource Management* 10 (3): 501–514.

Glassop L. (2002) "The organisational benefit of teams," *Human Relations* 55 (2): 225–250.

Gollan, P. (2001) "Bargain hunting," *HR Monthly*, May, 38–39.

Gollan, P. (2002) "Blue skies ahead," *HR Monthly*, May, 34–35.

Gome A. (2002) "The global squeeze," *Business Review Weekly* 24 (4): 60.

Guest, D., Michie, J., Trenberth, L., Conway, N., Brennan. L. and Sheehan. M. (2002) "Human resource management and performance in Australia," special report to AHRI as part of the United Kingdom's Economic and Social Research Council project on "Workplace reorganization, human resource management, and corporate performance.'

Hartmann, L. (1998) "The impact of trends in labour force participation on Australia," in M. Patrickson and L. Hartmann, *Managing an ageing workforce*, Sydney: Pearson.

Hay, C. (2002) "A better mix," *HR Monthly*, March: 39.

Holland, P.J., Dowling, P.J. and Innes P.A. (2001) "CEO compensation in Australia: Is there a relationship between principles, policies and practices?," *Asia Pacific Journal of Human Resources* 39 (3): 41–58.

Howarth, B. (2002) "The big handover," *Business Review Weekly* 24 (18): 54–57.

*HR Monthly* (2002) "Research bites" (November), p. 7.

Huang X., Soutar G., and Brown A. (2002) "New product development processes in small and medium sized businesses: Some Australian evidence," *Journal of Small Business Management* 40 (1): 27–43.

*Human Resources* (2002) (March) "Human resources link to bottom line."

*Human Resources* (2003) (January) "Glass ceiling holds strong in corporate Australia."

*Human Resources* (2003) (January) "Big bucks for HR professionals."

*Human Resources* (2003) (January) "Value of HR increasing in executive eyes."

*Human Resources* (2003) (February) "Proven link between effective HR and profitability."

*Human Resources* (2003) (February) "Local leaders unprepared for brave new world."

Huo, P.Y, Huang, H.J. and Napier, N.K. (2002) "Divergence or convergence: A cross-national comparison of personnel selection practices," *Asia Pacific Journal of Human Resources* 40 (1): 38–54.

Johnston, K. and D. Kitney (2002) "Executive salaries under pressure," *Financial Review*, 6 November 2002.

Kerslake, P. (2002) "The work-life balance payback," *New Zealand Management* 49 (5): 28–32.

Loble, L. (2001) "Where is the federation settlement? Work, learning and earning in the knowledge economy," *Australian Journal of Management* 26 (2): 145–154.

Lowe, K.B., Milliman, J., De Cieri, H. and Dowling, P.J. (2002) "International compensation practices: A ten-country comparative analysis," *Asia Pacific Journal of Human Resources* 40 (1): 55–80.

McGraw, P. (2002) "The HR function in local and overseas firms: Evidence from the PricewaterhouseCoopers–Cranfield HR project (1999)," *Asia Pacific Journal of Human Resources* 40 (2): 205–224.

McGuire, L. (2001) "Service charters: Global convergence or national divergence," *Public Management Review* 3 (4): 493–515.

McMahon, R. (2001) "Business growth and performance and the financial reporting practices of Australian manufacturing SMEs," *Journal of Small Business Management* 39 (2): 152–165.

Managing Work/Life Balance (2002) "Managing work/life balance survey of work/life initiatives," <http://ww3.cch.com.au:8080/dynaweb/ahrm...eneric_BookTextView/251459;pt=241172/> (viewed on 28 June 2002).

Martin, G. and Worldring, K. (2001) "Ready for the mantle? Australian human resource managers as stewards of ethics," *International Journal of Human Resource Management* 12: 243–255 (2 March 2001).

Matthews, J. (2002) "Innovation in Australian small and medium enterprises: Contributions from strategic human resource management," *Asia Pacific Journal of Human Resources* 40 (2): 193–204.

Milliman, J., Nason. S., Zhu, C. and De Cieri (2002) "An exploratory assessment of the purposes of performance appraisals in North and Central America and the Pacific Rim," *Asia Pacific Journal of Human Resources* 40 (1): 105–122.

O'Neill, G. (1998) "Issues in the design and structure of executive remuneration," in G. O'Neill and R. Kramer (eds.) *Australian human resources management*, volume 2, Melbourne: Pitman, pp. 155–170.

Patrickson, M. and Hartman, L. (2001) "Human resource management in Australia: Prospects for the twenty-first century," *International Journal of Manpower* 22 (3): 198–206.

Ruthven, P. (2002) "Profit power," *Business Review Weekly*, 24–30 October.

Sachdev, M. (2000) "E-recruitment in the new economy," *HR Monthly*, July: 34–35.

Smith, P. and Phillips, T. (2001) "Popular understandings of unAustralian: An investigation of the unnational," *Journal of Sociology* 37 (4): 323–339.

Teo, S.T.T. (2002) "Effectiveness of a corporate HR department in an Australian public sector entity during commercialization and corporatization," *International Journal of Human Resource Management* 13 (1): 89–105.

Ulrich, D. (1997) *HR champions*, Boston: Harvard Business School Press.

Vandenheuvel, A. and Wooden, M. (1999) *Casualisation and outsourcing: Trends and implications for work-related training*, Adelaide: National Centre for Vocational Educational Research.

Vines, H. (2001) "Surface tension," *HR Monthly*, February: 14–18.

Walsh, J. (2001) "Human resource management in foreign-owned workplaces: Evidence from Australia," *International Journal of Human Resource Management* 12: 425–444.

Wang, X. (2001) "Dimensions and current status of project management culture," *Project Management Journal* 32 (4): 4–18.

Waterhouse, P. and Deakin, R. (1995) "Changing approaches to workplace literacy," *Journal of Reading* 38 (6): 498–502.

Wiesner, R., and MacDonald, J. (2001) "Bleak house or bright prospect? Human resource management in Australian SMEs," *Asia Pacific Journal of Human Resource* 38 (2): 31–53.

Winkler, N. (1998) "Benchmarking the board," *HR Monthly*, April: 20.

Wooden, M. (2000) "Industrial relations reform: Do the critics have a case?," *IPA Review* 52 (3): 14–15.

Wooden, M. and Hawke, A. (2000) "Unions and employment growth: Panel data evidence," *Industrial Relations* 39 (1): 88–107.

## Useful websites

| | |
|---|---|
| Australian Human Resource Institute: | http://www.ahri.com.au |
| Australian Bureau of Statistics: | http://www.abs.gov.au |
| *Business Review Weekly*: | http://www.brw.com.au |

# 13 Transfer of HRM to MNC affiliates in Asia-Pacific

INGMAR BJÖRKMAN

## Introduction

Research on international human resource management (HRM) consists of two distinct albeit related strands, one examining differences in HRM across different countries, the other focusing on how multinational corporations (MNCs) manage their human resources worldwide.[1] While most parts of this book (chapters 2–12) consist of analyses of HRM in individual Southeast Asian and Pacific Rim countries, and one chapter (chapter 14) highlights the main challenges facing HRM in the Asia-Pacific region, the focus of this chapter is on the transfer of HRM practices to MNC affiliates in Asia-Pacific. As MNCs employ a significant part of the labor force in many countries in Asia-Pacific, the management of employees in foreign-owned firms constitutes an important part of the HRM systems found in these countries. Furthermore, MNCs may through transfer of policies and practices to their overseas units, contribute to the spread of new HRM systems in domestic firms.

The literature on HRM in MNCs is still relatively limited, albeit rapidly growing. The increase in research and writing is triggered by a growing awareness of the importance of how people are managed in foreign units for the global success of the MNC. Through their worldwide management of people, MNCs strive at achieving a number of important, yet potentially contradictory objectives: global efficiency, local responsiveness, flexibility and adaptability, and successful transfer of learning across geographically dispersed units (Schuler *et al.*, 1993; Schuler *et al.*, 2002). In this chapter, I examine the transfer of HRM policies and practices within MNCs. The following two questions are posed: (i) To what extent do MNCs tend to transfer "foreign" HRM practices to their foreign subsidiaries, and (ii) how may we explain why foreign-owned subsidiaries differ in terms of their

---

1  Some scholars (e.g. Milliman *et al.*, 1991; Schuler *et al.*, 1993; Taylor *et al.*, 1996) have termed research on HRM within MNCs "Strategic International Human Resource Management," thereby stressing the importance of linking HRM policies and practices with the strategy of the MNC.

HRM policies and practices? The focus is on HRM in the western-owned affiliates in developing countries in the Asia-Pacific.

## Conceptual issues

In the international strategy and management literature, strategy has often been conceptualized in terms of global integration (or MNC "standardization") versus local responsiveness ("local adaptation" or "localize") (e.g. Prahalad and Doz, 1987). The framework has typically been used to analyze the advantages of global integration/standardization of certain tasks versus the benefits of responding to national differences (Ghoshal, 1987). These alternatives are arguably largely incompatible, i.e. to a large extent MNCs must either standardize or localize the way in which they operate in different settings. A similar framework has been proposed for the HRM policies and practices in MNCs (e.g. Schuler *et al.*, 1993), although it has also been argued that an MNC sometimes may have an HRM strategy that blends global standardization with local responsiveness (Hannon *et al.*, 1995; Taylor *et al.*, 1996).

To transfer HRM practices that are standardized across different parts of the MNC to the focal subsidiary may entail certain advantages for the corporation as a whole. First, a consistent set of HRM practices is likely to be seen as equitable by employees in different parts of the MNC (Rosenzweig and Nohria, 1994). Second, standardized HRM practices may contribute to increased collaboration across organizational units where the employees have been selected using comparable selection criteria, have been trained in a similar way, and whose work is assessed and compensated based on similar kinds of criteria (Taylor *et al.*, 1996). Third, standardization of HRM can serve as a way for MNC headquarters to control the operations of foreign affiliates (Martinez and Jarillo, 1989). Fourth, transfer of HRM practices throughout the MNC may enable the corporation to leverage practices that already have been found to work well in other settings. It has been argued, in line with the resource-based theory of the firm (Barney, 1991), that the use of parent company HRM policies and practices may be seen as an important resource that can be used to build a global HRM system that is valuable and difficult for competitors to copy (Taylor *et al.*, 1998). Fifth, standardization of HRM across units may entail some scale and scope advantages.

However, a number of potential drawbacks to a standardized approach to HRM also exist. First, global standardization by definition precludes the possibility to be responsive to the local cultural environment. Second, the implications of institutional differences for subsidiary HRM policies and practices are downplayed or even totally neglected with this strategy. In reality, however, legal requirements may force companies to adapt locally, at least to some extent, their HRM practices. Third, labor market considerations may favor different HRM solutions in different countries. Fourth, a blind standardization of practices across MNC units may lead to a lack of fit between the characteristics of the focal subsidiary's operations and its HRM system. Hence, it may be more difficult to achieve a high degree of strategic HRM fit in the subsidiary. Fifth, there may be a backlash against "headquarters imperialism" if subsidiaries are forced to fully adopt standardized MNC practices rather than contribute to the development of the own unit's policies and practices (Martin and Beaumont, 1998). Sixth, if there are strong pressures to standardize HRM throughout the MNC, this may stifle local experimentation and development of the HRM system, thereby reducing the capacity of the MNC as a whole to develop new innovative HRM practices.

## Theoretical perspectives

Empirically, the HRM practices found in MNC subsidiaries have been analyzed in a number of recent studies to which we will return later in the chapter. A variety of theoretical perspectives have been utilized as scholars have attempted to identify determinants of the level of transfer of HRM practices within MNCs. Probably the most common has been to apply some kind of contingency-based perspective. Several scholars have argued that the international *strategy* of the MNC affects subsidiary HRM practices (either directly or through mediating variables). For instance, Schuler *et al.* (1993) and Taylor *et al.* (1996) identify two generic MNC strategies – multidomestic and global (Porter, 1986) – and propose that the choice of strategy will influence the approach taken by MNC management in the design of its HRM system. A firm follows a multidomestic strategy when overseas units are treated as independent businesses, where the operations of one unit do not significantly affect the activities of the rest of the MNC. In contrast, a global strategy entails that the firm uses the resources and competencies of one unit to create competitive advantages in other parts of the MNC. Theoretically it can be assumed that MNCs following a global strategy will be more likely to standardize HRM practices worldwide so as to facilitate inter-unit integration of operations (Taylor *et al.*, 1996).

Several studies have been designed to scrutinize how the host country *national culture*, including values, norms and beliefs, affects HRM practices. The cultural dimensions of Hofstede (1980) have been used to hypothesize how HRM practices may be expected to vary across subsidiary locations. It has been argued that MNCs need to adapt their HRM to the specific social and cultural norms of the host environment (Laurent, 1986; Schneider, 1988). Researchers have found some support for the hypothesized effect of national culture on subsidiary HRM. For instance, Schuler and Rogovsky (1998) received support for most of their propositions concerning how Hofstede's four dimensions are associated with compensation practices in MNC subsidiaries worldwide. The cultural distance between the host country and that of the MNC's home base may also influence the degree to which subsidiary HRM practices resemble those of the MNC parent as well as those of local firms. In both instances, a negative association may be expected between cultural distance (e.g. using the Kogut and Singh index 1988) and level of MNC standardization (Taylor *et al.*, 1996) and local adaptation (Schuler *et al.*, 1993), respectively.

Other scholars have examined subsidiary practices from an *institutional* (or institutionalization) perspective. Although the institutional perspective is far from homogenous (Scott, 1987), a common point of departure for most scholars is that organizations are under pressure to adapt and be consistent with their institutional environment. They are assumed to search for legitimacy and recognition, which they do by adopting structures and practices defined as, or perhaps rather taken for granted as, appropriate in their environment. DiMaggio and Powell (1983) suggest that there are three major ways in which isomorphism is produced: coercive isomorphism, where a powerful constituency (e.g. the government) imposes certain patterns on the organization; mimetic isomorphism, where organizations in situations of uncertainty adopt the pattern exhibited by organizations in their environment that are viewed as successful; and normative isomorphism, where professional organizations act as the disseminators of appropriate organizational patterns which are then adopted by organizations which are under the influence of the professional organizations. More recently, Scott (1987) has categorized isomorphic processes into those which focus on the role of external institutional agencies in the environment and those which emphasize the processes whereby those within organizations come to take certain externally validated patterns for granted and value them as ends in themselves. Thus, foreign-owned subsidiaries may be under formal or informal pressure from local institutional agencies to adopt certain HRM practices, but there may also be taken for granted practices – for example, those of the MNC parent organization – that are unconsciously introduced in the subsidiary (Westney, 1993). In other words, the subsidiary may be seen as being under institutional influence from both from the local environment and from the MNC (Westney, 1993; Rosenzweig and Nohria, 1994). IHRM researchers have mostly focused on the former source of institutionalization of HRM practices in their work.

Finally, some researchers have applied a *resource dependence* (Pfeffer and Salancik, 1978) or *bargaining power* perspective in their search for determinants of subsidiary practices. It has been argued that the greater the dependence of the subsidiary on the parent company, the more the affiliate's HRM system is influenced by headquarters (Martinez and Ricks, 1989), leading to a higher degree of MNC standardization of HRM practices. Hence, the more the subsidiary is dependent on the parent organization, for example, technological knowledge, financial resources and components for the manufacturing process, the more the affiliate's practices would be expected to resemble those of the parent organization. Studies on the effect of the equity share held by the MNC on subsidiary practices may also be categorized as being part of this theoretical perspective.

During the last decade, several efforts have been made to go beyond individual theoretical perspectives to build integrative models of (among others) the determinants of HRM in MNCs (e.g. Schuler *et al.*, 1993; Taylor *et al.*, 1996). These models have built on a variety of theoretical perspectives and models, including those discussed above. Additionally, the model proposed by Taylor *et al.* (1996), for instance, also draws on the resource-based theory of the firm (Barney, 1991). Both the Schuler *et al.* (1993) and the Taylor *et al.* (1996) models specify a number of mediating and moderating factors that may influence the HRM policies and practices in MNCs, and their work has been instrumental in furthering empirical work on international HRM.

# Review of existing research

## The characteristics of MNC HRM practices

Only a handful of studies have examined specifically the degree of MNC standardization versus local adaptation of HRM in the context of the Asia-Pacific. In these studies, subsidiary managers have been asked to estimate the extent to which the subsidiary's HRM practices resemble those of local firms and the MNC parent organization, respectively. Hannon *et al.* (1995) studied 100 subsidiaries of Japanese, US and European MNCs operating in Taiwan. In line with research on foreign-owned subsidiaries in the USA (Rosenzweig and Nohria, 1994), the researchers found that the HRM practices of MNCs in Taiwan overall were more localized than globally standardized. Other researchers have collected data on the HRM practices of both local and foreign-owned firms. This group of studies includes, among others, a study of indigenous and foreign-owned firms in Korea and Taiwan (Bae *et al.*, 1998). Pronounced differences were found between host countries and foreign firms, indicating that at least some degree of transfer of HRM practices had taken place. In sum, although MNCs tend, at least to some extent, to transfer standardized HRM practices to affiliates located in advanced western countries like the USA and newly industrialized Asian countries like Taiwan and Korea, there is some indication that the degree of localization of HRM is greater than that of MNC standardization.

However, in their study of 63 Chinese–western joint ventures situated in different parts of China, Björkman and Lu (2001) found that the HRM practices were more similar to those of the MNC parent company than to those of local manufacturing companies. The authors offer three explanations for the high degree of MNC standardization. First, the foreign executives that were interviewed expressed a strong dissatisfaction with Chinese management practices. Most respondents believed that western management principles should be implemented into their company for it to be competitive, and many looked to their own parent organizations for appropriate models of HRM to implement in China. Second, since the 1980s there had been a move away from the Marxist personnel practices that previously prevailed in Chinese state-owned companies. Currently, there appears to be no undisputed institutionalized HRM/personnel model in China (Warner, 1996). Although the affiliates were under pressure to comply with government regulations concerning issues like social security payments and formal approval of labor contracts, there was very little government influence on HRM functions like employee selection and compensation systems. As a consequence, and in combination with few codified laws, it had apparently become easier for western MNCs to introduce their own HRM systems (see also Child, 1994; Goodall and Warner, 1998). Third, the research focused on local professionals and managers, whereas many other studies on MNC subsidiaries abroad have examined the whole labor force. It is conceivable that the HRM practices for workers are, relatively speaking, more similar to those of local companies than those of the MNCs.

The results in a recent investigation of six US and six European MNCs (Braun and Warner, 2002), although not specifically focusing on MNC standardization of HRM, seem largely in line with those obtained by Björkman and Lu. The western MNCs surveyed by Braun and Warner attached high importance to HRM, and the HRM practices (in particular performance appraisal) were significantly influenced by home-country practices. Other scholars have done research on samples of both Chinese-owned and foreign-owned affiliates. In a series of studies, Goodall and Warner (e.g. 1997, 1998, 1999) analyzed HRM practices in Chinese–western joint ventures and domestic Chinese firms. Goodall and Warner (1999) established a number of differences between local and foreign-owned firms, but they also identified a number of Chinese-owned firms that recently had adopted "western" HRM practices. Overall, compared with Björkman and Lu's results (2001), Goodall and Warner (1999) seemed to find a somewhat lower degree of global standardization of HRM in the foreign firms in their sample. It is conceivable that at least some of this difference is explained by the fact that, while Björkman and Lu (2001) studied HRM for local professionals and managers, Goodall and Warner (1999) examined the whole labor force.

Research on western affiliates in other countries in the Asia-Pacific is scarce. An early study (Low 1984) compared several aspects of management practice in American affiliates and local firms in Singapore. US subsidiaries were more likely to have a formal appraisal system and focused more on formal training and development programs than did domestic Singapore firms. A study by Lawler et al. (1994) identified several differences between American, Europeans, Japanese and local Thai firms. US and European firms in their sample had the most elaborate systems for linking pay with work-related performance. In contrast, Japanese firms provided local employees with more extensive internal training. Overall, and although this set of studies has not conceptualized HRM in terms of how far the policies and practices resemble those of the MNC parent organization, they do suggest that at least some degree of transfer of HRM has taken place.

In particular, some of the quantitative studies have neglected the differences in MNC transfer that may exist between different HRM functions (such as recruitment, compensation and training and development). Whereas both Hannon et al. (1995) and Björkman and Lu (2001) created indices of standardization versus localization of the total HRM system, there is strong reason to believe that the extent to which MNCs transfer HRM practices to affiliates in the Asia-Pacific varies across HRM functions. Lu and Björkman (1997) found that western affiliates in China exhibited a higher level of MNC standardization concerning performance appraisal and criteria for promotions, while the affiliates differed more from their western parent organizations in terms of recruitment, training and financial compensation.

# Determinants of HRM policies and practices

Some of the explanatory research on HRM practices in MNC affiliates in Asia has conceptualized HRM in terms of degree of standardization (and/or localization), while other studies have applied more direct measures of the HRM practices found in MNC subsidiaries and domestically owned firms. Among those choosing the former approach, Hannon *et al.* (1995) found that the more dependent a subsidiary was on the parent organization, the more globally standardized the HRM practices were. The degree of MNC ownership moderated the relationship between the subsidiary's dependence on host institutions and HRM standardization – the higher equity percentage held by the MNC, the more the HRM practices resembled those of the foreign corporation.

In their study of the determinants of the degree of western MNC standardization of HRM practices in Chinese–western joint ventures, Björkman and Lu (2001) examined factors derived from the institutionalization perspective supplemented with a bargaining power perspective. They received strong empirical support for their theoretical framework. Among the explanatory factors consistent with institutionalization theory, acquisitions as the mode of establishment, the nationality of the foreign parent organization (US MNCs are more likely than European MNCs to standardize HRM practices), and the number of expatriates were significant determinants of HRM resemblance with practices in the corporation's home-country operations. The equity share held by the foreign parent organization and the non-capital resources provided by the MNC were also significant determinants of the HRM standardization.

Bae *et al.* (1998) studied local and foreign-owned firms operating in Korea and Taiwan. The dependent variables in their study were HR flow, work systems, reward system, employee influence and a composite measure of the HRM system as a whole. There was a strong and consistent positive effect of the extent to which management strongly valued the role of HRM and people in the organization and each of the dependent variables. A number of differences were identified between local and foreign-owned units, with significant differences also found across MNCs from the USA, Japan and Europe. Overall, US-owned firms seemed most likely to have high scores on the HRM scales, in particular in the use of performance-based reward systems.

Ngo *et al.* (1998) investigated the effects of country of origin on four dimensions of the HRM system. Included in their study were firms from the USA, Great Britain, Japan and Hong Kong operating in Hong Kong. Although the focus of this research was on the performance effects of HRM, the results indicated significant differences across the nationality of the parent company as well between indigenous and foreign-owned firms. Also the work by Lawler *et al.* (1994) in Thailand suggests the existence of MNC home country effects in affiliates of US, European and Japanese MNCs.

However, the findings in research on US and Japanese affiliates located in Malaysia, Singapore, Thailand, Indonesia and the Philippines differed to some extent from those obtained in other pieces of work. While subsidiary management's beliefs in the HRM competences of the parent organization were positively associated with the degree of similarity of HRM practices, no such relationship was observed between the method of establishment, the percentage of ownership held by the MNC, or the MNC home country and the level of standardization of HRM. Furthermore, surprisingly, the number of expatriates was negatively associated with the similarity of subsidiary and MNC parent company practices (Taylor *et al.*, 1998).

In sum, although the results of several explanatory studies conducted in different locations across the Asia-Pacific have yielded consistent findings, some exceptions to this pattern must also be noted. Hence, more research is clearly needed before any firm conclusions can be drawn concerning the determinants of HRM transfer within MNCs to their affiliates in the Asia-Pacific. Nonetheless, there is at least some indication that the following factors may increase the level of MNC transfer of standardized HRM practices to their affiliates in the region:

- the equity held by the MNC;
- non-equity resources provided by the parent organization;
- top management perception of the importance of HRM and people in the organization;
- the subsidiary has been established as a greenfield operation;
- the nationality of the MNC;
- the number of expatriates.

The studies reviewed above have enhanced our understanding of how MNCs manage people in their subsidiaries in the Asia-Pacific, and why. However, this field of study is still in its early stages of development.

## Where to go from here?

IHRM researchers probably need to pay more attention to the question of *what* they study. Much extant work on HRM practices in MNC subsidiaries abroad has used a single measure of the degree of MNC standardization and/or localization of HRM practices. However, as observed by Rosenzweig and Nohria (1994) and Lu and Björkman (1997), different HRM functions often differ in their level of MNC standardization and localization. The possibility of combining MNC and local elements (i.e. their compatibility) may also vary among different HRM functions. Therefore, there is arguably a need (also) to describe and analyze each HRM function separately rather than, as has been used in many of the international HRM research so far, using an aggregate measure of the subsidiary's HRM system.

Most research on subsidiary HRM policies and practices has centered on how much the foreign affiliate's HRM system resembles that of the home-country organization of the MNC. However, as pointed out by Taylor *et al.* (1996), the "exportation" of HRM from the parent organization to the foreign unit is not the only possible MNC–internal transfer of HRM polices and practices; MNCs may also have an "integrative" approach to IHRM by attempting to identify "the best" practices and policies within the MNC as a whole, and then transfer these to the other MNC units. In this conceptualization of IHRM, transfer of HRM policies and practices may occur between foreign affiliates as well as between headquarters and foreign subsidiaries (Taylor *et al.*, 1996).

Additionally, researchers need to be careful in terms of the level of analysis. A distinction may be made between HRM system architecture, HRM policies, and HRM practices (Becker and Gerhart, 1996; Schuler and Florkowski, 1996). Using employee compensation as an example of a specific HRM function, at the HRM architecture level of analysis the focus can be on the extent to which employee performance is valued in the firm; at the policy level, data may be collected on the extent to which incentive pay is used throughout the firm; and typical questions at the practices level of analysis could be whether 360-degree performance appraisals are used to determine bonuses, on the part of the total financial incentive achievable by an employee that is based on the performance of the team that s/he is part of (Becker and Gerhart, 1996). Research of the transfer of HRM within the MNC has predominantly been conducted at levels two and three (although with some researchers using the term "practices" also at level two). All three levels of analysis are relevant, but the results are likely to differ both in terms of the degree of HRM standardization and concerning the determinants of subsidiary HRM. To date, there is a dearth of research on the relationship between the different levels of analysis.

Few IHRM researchers seem to have deliberated on their selection of *whose* HRM practices they study and what are the implications of their choice for the generalizability of their findings. Some researchers have analyzed rank-and-file employees, a few have studied only managers and professionals, and others have surveyed HRM for all domestic subsidiary employees. To generalize across studies focusing on different groups of employees is for obvious reasons problematic. For instance, as suggested by Taylor *et al.* (1996), the perceived criticality of a certain group of employees may influence the kind of HRM practices that are used for these employees. Generally speaking, HRM for top managers and for certain categories of subsidiary professionals may be more globally standardized than for blue-collar workers. Furthermore, there may be significant differences within a subsidiary in terms of how a certain HRM policy or tool is implemented. Lindholm (2001) showed in the context of western affiliates in China that inexperienced expatriates, experienced expatriates and domestic managers differed significantly in how they implemented a standardized performance appraisal system. These results also point to the problems in using aggregate level data of HRM for MNC affiliates.

Schuler *et al.* (2002) suggest that more rigorous *research designs and operationalizations* are needed in IHRM research. In several studies HRM practices have been operationalized in a relatively simplistic manner using perceptual data (e.g. Hannon *et al.*, 1995; Björkman and Lu, 2001). Indications of actual practices in the foreign subsidiary as well as in the parent organization would give better measures of the degree of resemblance of HRM practices. Researchers choosing this approach are advised to consider carefully how to measure HRM policies and practices. If possible, researchers should try to agree on using the same questions across different studies, thereby facilitating the comparison of their findings.

Data have often been collected from only one respondent in each subsidiary data (Hannon *et al.*, 1995; Björkman and Lu, 2001). This is understandable given the challenges involved in collecting data from multiple subsidiary respondents and/or parent company representatives. Nonetheless, the systematic use of multiple respondents, e.g. one from each parent organization and one from the focal subsidiary, would significantly increase the validity of the data. At the very least, scholars should attempt to verify the data obtained through self-reported subjective questions by asking samples of headquarters and/or other subsidiary respondents to answer the same question (Roth and O'Donnell, 1996).

Longitudinal research on MNC practices has so far been virtually nonexistent. Of interest, for instance, would be to conduct *ex post* analyses of the degree of localization and global standardization over the tenure of foreign companies in a given country. Qualitative research remains an important vehicle for studying the process through which IHRM policies and practices evolve and are spread throughout the MNC (Schuler *et al.*, 2002).

There is a long-standing debate about the *impact* of multinational corporations on the host country (Moran, 1993). Most of this discussion has been on the direct economic implications of multinational firms. In spite of calls for research into the influence of the organizational patterns of multinational enterprises on host countries (Westney, 1993), there has been much less work on the impact of foreign firms' operations on non-economic aspects of the local society. We know that multinational firms tend to introduce parts of the parent company practices in their foreign subsidiaries. Although numerous studies have shown that considerable differences in HRM remain across countries due to cultural and institutional factors, also within Asia (Rowley and Benson, 2002), there are also indications of some convergence. MNCs may, through their activities in the region, significantly contribute to the diffusion of foreign HRM practices, but relatively little rigorous empirical work has been carried out so far. For instance, although several scholars (e.g. Warner 1996, 1999; Benson and Zhu, 1999) have described and analyzed some of the changes taking place in Chinese HRM (or "personnel management") during recent years, little empirical research has specifically aimed at investigating the process of diffusion of western-style HRM practices and policies among local Chinese organizations (Benson and Zhu, 1999; though see Zhu and Warner, 2000, for an analysis of the introduction and development of HRM as an academic concept in China). Björkman (2003) has developed a series of testable propositions that can be used as a foundation for future empirical research in the Chinese context, but the same set of propositions could also be tested in other parts of the region.

Although a variety of potential determinants of subsidiary HRM have been analyzed at host country, MNC, and subsidiary levels of analysis, *some potentially important determinants* seem to have failed to receive much scholarly attention. A number of scholars have noted that foreign subsidiaries play an increasingly important strategic role in MNCs (e.g. Hedlund, 1986; Bartlett and Ghoshal, 1989). Some subsidiaries play crucial roles in the MNC as a whole, both in terms of competence development and in terms of being highly integrated parts of the MNC's value chain. The development of the human resources of strategically important subsidiaries is particularly important for the MNC as a whole. Therefore, such subsidiaries may be particularly likely to have standardized HRM practices (Taylor *et al.*, 1996).

How highly regarded the subsidiary's HR department is within the firm and how deeply involved the department is in strategic planning of the unit is likely to influence the affiliate's HRM practices. The HRM practices are in turn likely to influence the capabilities of the work force of the organization in question. Unfortunately there only exists relatively limited international comparative research on the role of the HR department and its influence on HRM, and virtually no work on the role of the subsidiary HR department in MNC subsidiaries.

This book covers eleven countries and territories in Southeast Asia and the Pacific Rim. Most empirical research carried out to date on HRM in this region has focused on the operations on western corporations in the People's Republic of China. Although work also has been conducted in, at least, Taiwan, South Korea, Hong Kong, Japan, Singapore and India, the results obtained in these studies are somewhat difficult to compare due to significant differences in focus, design, and operationalizations. More *comparative work* is needed to shed light on the effects of host-country factors on MNC practices and policies.

Finally, an issue of obvious importance is the *performance effects* of how people are managed. During the last decade extensive research has been conducted on the relationship between HRM and firm performance, recently also in the context of foreign-owned units in Asia (Ngo *et al.*, 1998; Björkman and Fan, 2002). However, to date there appears to exist no research on the relationship between the levels of subsidiary HRM standardization/localization and organizational performance. An even more important and challenging task is to augment our understanding of *how* subsidiary HRM is related with organizational performance. In particular, there is a need to develop and test a more sophisticated theory of what HRM accomplishes and how. Although it has been recognized that research is needed on the intervening variables between HRM practices and firm performance, few such studies exist (Wood, 1999; Wright and Gardner, 2000; Guest, 2001; Truss, 2001). Hence, empirically tested models of the relationship between HRM, outcomes like employee commitment, employee competencies and flexibility, and firm performance should be the next step in our endeavor to better understand the strategic role that HRM may play as a determinant of subsidiary performance. Both the use of structuring modeling techniques like LISREL and longitudinal case studies are called for.

# Conclusion

How to manage local employees in overseas subsidiaries is a crucial question facing both HR and line managers. Based on a review of the existing literature, in this chapter I have discussed the transfer of "foreign" HRM practices to subsidiaries located in the Asia-Pacific. I have also reviewed research attempting to explain the extent to which MNCs introduce parent company practices in their foreign affiliates.

Unfortunately, there exists very little research-based evidence to guide MNC managers in their decisions concerning subsidiary HRM policies and practices. Nonetheless, both the conceptual HRM literature and research conducted in a domestic setting suggest that decisions concerning HRM should be made based on an analysis of, first, the ("internal") fit among HRM practices (Becker *et al.*, 1997). In other words, individual HRM policies and practices must contribute to an internally consistent and coherent HRM system. Second, the HRM system shall be constructed so as to help the subsidiary solve operational problems and implement the strategy of the focal unit as well as the corporation as a whole. Hence, the decision-makers need to analyze the *strategic* fit of the subsidiary HRM system. Third, the fit with the *cultural and institutional environment* of the subsidiary have to be considered. Although MNC subsidiaries may not necessarily need to "do as the Romans do," they should consider how MNC HRM practices fit with the local environment. The aim of this volume is to provide managers and researchers with an insightful overview of the characteristics and evolution of HRM in selected countries in Southeast Asia and the Pacific Rim, including the main factors that shape how people are managed across the region. Each of the country-specific chapters hence familiarize MNC managers with the context in which their subsidiaries will function, thereby helping decision-makers to choose appropriate HRM policies and practices in their own units.

## Acknowledgments

The author would like to thank Anna af Forselles and Randall Schuler for helpful comments on earlier drafts, and the Academy of Finland for financial support.

## References

Bae, J., Chen, S.-J. and Lawler, J. (1998) "Variations in human resource management in Asian countries: MNC home-country and host-country effects," *International Journal of Human Resource Management* 9: 653–670.

Barney, J.B. (1991) "Firm resources and sustained competitive advantage," *Journal of Management* 17: 99–120.

Bartlett, C.A. and Ghoshal, S. (1989) *Managing across borders: The transnational solution*, Boston, MA: Harvard Business School Press.

Becker, B. and Gerhart, B. (1996) "The impact of human resource management on organizational performance: Progress and prospects," *Academy of Management Journal* 39: 779–801.

Becker, B. and Huselid, M. (1998) "High performance work systems and firm performance: A synthesis of research and managerial implications," in G.R. Ferris (ed.) *Research in personnel and human resource management*, Greenwich, CT: JAI Press, pp. 53–101.

Becker, B., Huselid, M., Pickusm P.S. and Spratt, M.F. (1997) "HR as a source of shareholder value: Research and recommendations," *Human Resource Management* 36: 39–47.

Beechler, S. and Yang, J.Z. (1994) "The transfer of Japanese-style management to American subsidiaries: Contingencies, constraints, and competencies," *Journal of International Business Studies* 25: 467–92.

Benson, J. and Zhu, Y. (1999) "Markets, firms and workers in Chinese state-owned enterprises," *Human Resource Management Journal* 9 (4): 58–74.

Björkman, I. (forthcoming) "The diffusion of western-style human resource management practices among Chinese firms: The role of western multinational corporations," *Asia-Pacific Business Review.*

Björkman, I. and Fan, X (2002) "Human resource management and the performance of western firms in China," *International Journal of Human Resource Management* 13: 853–864.

Björkman, I. and Lu, Y. (2001) "Institutionalization and bargaining power explanations of human resource management practices in international joint ventures – the case of Chinese-western joint ventures," *Organization Studies* 22: 491–512.

Braun, W.H. and Warner, M. (2002) "Strategic human resource management in western multinationals in China: The differentiation of practices across different ownership forms," *Personnel Review* 31: 553–579.

Chew, I.K.H. and Teo, A.C.Y. (1991) "Human resource practices in Singapore: A survey of local firms and MNCs," *Asia Pacific Human Resource Management* 29: 30–38.

Child, J. (1994) *Management in China during the age of reform*, Cambridge: Cambridge University Press.

Child, J. and Markóczy, L. (1993) "Host-country managerial behaviour and learning in Chinese and Hungarian joint ventures," *Journal of Management Studies* 30: 611–631.

DiMaggio, P.J. and Powell, W. (1983) "The iron cage revisited: Institutional isomorphism and collective rationality in organizational fields," *American Sociological Review* 48: 147–160.

Ghoshal, S. (1987) "Global strategy: An organizing framework," *Strategic Management Journal* 8: 425–440.

Goodall, K. and Warner, M. (1998) "HRM dilemmas in China: The case of foreign-invested enterprises in Shanghai," *Asia Pacific Business Review* 4 (4): 1–21.

Goodall, K. and Warner, W. (1997) "Human resources in Sino-foreign joint ventures: Selected case studies in Shanghai compared with Beijing," *International Journal of Human Resource Management* 8: 569–594.

Goodall, K. and Warner, M. (1999) "Enterprise reform, labor–management relations, and human resource management in a multinational context," *International Studies of Management and Organisation* 29 (3): 21–36.

Martin, G. and Beaumont, B. (1998) "Diffusing 'best practice' in multinational firms: Prospects, practice and contestation," *International Journal of Human Resource Management* 9: 671–695.

Guest, D. (2001) "Human resource management: When research confronts theory," *International Journal of Human Resource Management* 12: 1092–1106.

Hannon, J.M., Huang, I.-C. and Jaw, B.-S. (1995) "International human resource strategy and its determinants: The case of subsidiaries in Taiwan," *Journal of International Business Studies* 26 (3): 531–54.

Hedlund, G. (1986) "The hypermodern MNC: A heterarchy?" *Human Resource Management* 25 (1): 9–35.

Hofstede, G. (1980) *Culture's consequences: International differences in work-related values*, Beverly Hills, CA: Sage.

Kogut, B. and Singh, H. (1988) "The effect of national culture on the choice of entry mode," *Journal of International Business Studies* 19: 17–31.

Laurent, A. (1986) "The cross-cultural puzzle of international human resource management," *Human Resource Management* 25: 91–102.

Lawler, J., Atmiyanandana, V. and Zaidi, M. (1994) "A cross-national comparison of human resource management in indigenous and multinational firms in Thailand," in D.J.B. Mitchell and

D. Lewin (eds.) *International perspectives and challenges in human resource management*, Los Angeles: UCLA.

Levitt, B. and March, J.G. (1988) "Organizational learning," *Annual Review of Sociology* 14: 319–40.

Lindholm, N. (2001) *Globally standardized performance management policies in multinational companies' subsidiaries in China*, Doctoral thesis, Helsinki: Swedish School of Economics.

Low, P. (1984) "Singapore-based subsidiaries of US multinationals and Singapore firms: A comparative management study," *Asia Pacific Journal of Management* 2 (1): 29–39.

Lu, Y. and Björkman, I. (1997) "MNC standardization versus localization: MNC practices in China-Western joint ventures," *International Journal of Human Resource Management* 8: 614–628.

Martinez, J.I. and Jarillo, J.C. (1989) "The evolution of research on coordination mechanisms in multinational corporations," *Journal of International Business Studies* 20: 489–514.

Martinez, Z.L. and Ricks, D. (1989) "Multinational parent companies' influence over human resource decisions of affiliates: U.S. firms in Mexico," *Journal of International Business Studies* 20: 489–514.

Milliman, J.M., von Glinow, M.A. and Nathan, M. (1991) "Organizational life cycles and strategic international human resource management in multinational corporations: Implications for congruence theory," *Academy of Management Review* 16: 318–339.

Moran, T.H. (1993) "Introduction: Governments and transnational corporations," in T.H. Moran (ed.) *Governments and transnational corporations*, London: Routledge.

Ngo, H.-Y., Turban, D., Lau, C.-M. and Lui, S.-Y. (1998) "Human resource practices and firm performance of multinational corporations: Influences of country origin," *International Journal of Human Resource Management* 9: 632–652.

Pfeffer, J. and Salancik, G.R. (1978) *The external control of organizations: A resource dependence perspective*, New York: Harper and Row.

Porter, M.E. (1986) "Competition in global industries: A conceptual framework," in M.E. Porter (ed.) *Competition in global industries*, Boston: Harvard Business School Press.

Prahalad, C.K. and Doz, Y. (1987) *The multinational mission: Balancing global demands and global vision*, New York: Free Press.

Rosenzweig, P.M. and Nohria, N. (1994) "Influences on human resource management practices in multinational corporations," *Journal of International Business Studies* 25: 229–251.

Roth, K. and O'Donnell, S. (1996) "Foreign subsidiary compensation strategy: An agency theory perspective," *Academy of Management Journal* 39: 678–703.

Rowley, C. and Benson, J. (2002) "Convergence and divergence in Asian human resource management," *California Management Review* 44 (2): 90–109.

Schneider, S. (1988) "National versus corporate culture: Implications for human resource management," *Human Resource Management* 27: 231–246.

Schuler, R.S. and Florkowski, G.W. (1996) "International human resources management," in B.J. Punnett and Shenkar, O. (eds.) *Handbook for international management research*, Oxford: Blackwell.

Schuler, R.S. and Rogovsky, N. (1998) "Understanding compensation practice variations across firms: The impact of national culture," *Journal of International Business Studies* 29: 159–177.

Schuler, R.S., Budhwar, P. and Florkowski, G.W. (2002) "International human resource management: Review and critique," *International Journal of Management Reviews* 4: 41–70.

Schuler, R.S., Dowling, P.J. and De Cieri, H. (1993) "An integrative framework of strategic international human resource management," *Journal of Management* 19: 419–459.

Scott, W.R. (1987) "The adolescence of institutional theory," *Administrative Science Quarterly* 32: 493–511.

Taylor, S., Beechler, S. and Napier, N. (1996) "Toward an integrative model of strategic international human resource management," *Academy of Management Review* 21: 959–985.

Taylor, S., Beechler, S., Najjar, M. and Ghosh, B.C. (1998) "A partial test of a model of strategic international human resource management," *Advances in International Comparative Management* 12: 207–236.

Truss, C. (2001) "Complexities and controversies in linking HRM with organizational outcomes," *Journal of Management Studies* 38: 1121–1149.

Warner, M. (1996) "Managing China's enterprise reforms: A new agenda for the 1990s," *Journal of General Management* 21 (3): 1–18.

Warner, M. (1999) *China's managerial revolution*, London: Frank Cass.

Westney, D.E. (1993) "Institutionalization theory and the multinational corporation," in S. Ghoshal and D.E. Westney (eds.) *Organization theory and the multinational corporation*, New York: St. Martin's Press.

Wood, S. (1999) "Human resource management and performance," *International Journal of Management Reviews* 1: 367–413.

Wright, P.M. and Gardner, T.M. (2000) "Theoretical and empirical challenges in studying the HR practice – firm performance relationship," paper presented at the EIASM workshop *Strategic Human Resource Management*, INSEAD: 30 March 2000.

# HRM challenges in the Asia-Pacific region: agenda for future research and policy

YAW A. DEBRAH AND PAWAN S. BUDHWAR

## Introduction

In a recent analysis of developments in the field of international human resource management (IHRM), Schuler *et al.* (2002) highlighted the need to examine HRM in context. In many ways, this approach was adopted to write this book. Thus, the analysis of HRM system(s) in the selected countries has been conducted in the context of sociocultural, economic, political and legal set-ups and the changing business conditions. The structuring of the chapters according to the framework introduced in chapter 1 has helped to highlight the influence of core factors on HRM policies and practices in each country, as well as the context-specific nature of HRM. For example, the economic environment significantly influences HRM in all the countries, but its impact varies from country to country. For instance, in Japan the recessionary conditions of the past decade are undermining traditional employment practices and precipitating changes in the system. India has witnessed a boom in foreign direct investment since it liberalized its economy. However, the arrival of foreign firms in the Indian labor market is forcing local firms, in pursuit of efficiency, to rationalize their HRM practices.

In the same way, the political and legal set-up of the respective countries influence HRM policies and practices in their own unique way. China allows the existence of only one national union, which functions strictly according to the wishes of the Communist Party. But, in India there are many local, regional and national unions which generally function in an adversarial way. Similarly, the country-specific chapters have revealed the unique influence of sociocultural context (for example, Islamic work principles in many Malaysian firms; Confucian principles in China and Taiwan) on HRM systems.

Thus, the chapters depict a mixture of factors including sociocultural, economic, political and legal which actively dictate the pattern of national HRM system. Each chapter also sheds light on a number of HRM challenges in the Asia-Pacific region but here we carry the discussion forward: an awareness of the HRM challenges can help practitioners to develop relevant policies and allow academics to set the agenda for future research.

# HRM challenges in the Asia-Pacific region

In spite of the fact that this book covers HRM in different countries with diverse economic and political systems, there appear to be more similarities than differences in the HRM issues discussed. Arguably, there is some degree of commonality in the impact of economic globalization and international competitiveness on HRM in the Asia-Pacific region. The evidence so far indicates that globalization and international competitiveness are driving major changes in HRM in the Asia-Pacific region. This supports Frenkel and Peetz's (1998) assertion that globalization is changing previously stable workplace systems in the region. This is evident in all the countries covered. Thus, the effects of these changes pose major challenges for HRM in the Asia-Pacific region. For instance, in China and India there is some evidence that economic liberalization arising from globalization and competitive pressures is changing the pattern of HRM, employee relations and industrial relations and labor legislation. Some of these changes are occurring both in the private and public sectors in both countries. In China, it is argued that the emergence of a market economy is undermining the "nanny employer" image of organizations, as there is a concerted effort to shift the huge welfare burden from employers to individuals. In line with this approach, then, the downsizing of organizations and changing recruitment and retention practices have resulted in insecurity for workers in China. It is expected that a similar pattern will emerge in countries like India where many of the state-owned firms have surplus labor. However, unlike China, downsizing in India will be strongly resisted both by trade unions and opposition political parties. This has been clearly evident in some of the recent cases (for details, see Budhwar, 2003). Such dynamics again highlight the context-specific nature of HRM.

Similarly, the changing business environment in Japan has put tremendous pressures on employers to change their traditional employment practices in order to survive. Accordingly, Japanese employers are restructuring their employment systems in response to low growth, globalization and international competitiveness. On these issues, Harukiyo and Hook (1998) contend that the major elements of the Japanese-style HRM – lifetime employment, seniority promotion system, enterprise unions, *keiretsu* and subcontracting relations developed essentially in response to rapid and high economic growth during the postwar industrialization boom – are being fundamentally transformed.

As Salmon's chapter on Japan indicates, this transformation is by no means smooth. In particular, Salmon asserts that, against a background of low growth, recession and rising unemployment, Japanese employers are experiencing significant HRM problems. Consequently there are calls for a critical re-evaluation of the basic framework of the established Japanese HRM model. Accordingly, in recent years some Japanese companies are cutting down the number of full-time employees and relying on temporary workers. The temporary workers are cheaper, low maintenance alternatives to lifetime employees (Graham, 1998). Similarly, older workers are being encouraged to volunteer for early retirement and new workers who possess the skills required by the companies are lured to replace them. In a break with tradition, employers hiring computer-literate staff and high-tech specialists in the use of various types of advanced technological equipment, boycott the sacrosanct hiring practices under the lifetime employment system and use temporary agencies instead. Just like their counterparts in the West, Japanese employers/companies are now outsourcing more activities and relying more on temporary employees. In this regard, Alexander (1999) notes that, for a country famous for providing lifetime employment, this is a major transformation with fundamental and long-term challenges for HRM.

The deep-seated challenges are not limited to Japan, China and India, as they are occurring through out the Asia-Pacific region. In the chapter on Korea, Rowley and Bae have identified a number of key challenges facing HR managers in that country. They discuss the historical development of HRM in Korea and the changes in traditional Korean HRM practices. They give an account of the emergence of the post-1997 "Flexibility Based Transitional" HRM. Presumably, this emerged from the ashes of the 1997 Asian crisis and is a response to the restructuring efforts, including outsourcing, downsizing, mergers and acquisitions. As elsewhere in the Asia-Pacific region, vital changes are occurring within the HR function in Korea as a result of globalization and competitive pressure.

While not every chapter can be analyzed here, the above examples provide evidence of the far-reaching implications of the globalization and international competitiveness on HRM in the Asia-Pacific region. The challenge facing HR managers who are dealing with the global forces is how they can minimize the threats posed by global competitive pressures on HRM while at the same time taking advantage of the opportunities created by globalization to restructure their HRM and employee relations practices. This would involve bold managerial proactive initiatives or responses to individual and collective employee actions in the workplace in this globalized era. These initiatives provide opportunities for researchers to examine the transformation of HRM in the region.

Globalization and international competitiveness can pose a significant threat to the productivity and morale of employees. In an attempt to explore these challenges, Rowley and Bae have proposed the use of Rousseau's (1995) three-fold typology of psychological contracts as an analytical tool. This is quite pertinent in view of the impacts of globalization and competitive pressures on HRM discussed earlier. Throughout the Asia-Pacific region, the changes in traditional employment practices have crucial consequences for HRM. These include increased stress, declining job security – as a result of downsizing and rising unemployment – as companies adopt labor flexibility strategies to reduce labor costs (Wiseman, 1998). With a high degree of uncertainty in the workplace, it becomes imperative for employers to address employees' psychological contract needs. In a competitive environment as it pertains in the Asia-Pacific, the beliefs held by an individual and his/her employer about what they expect of one another are changing. In such a changing environment, employees still expect to be treated fairly, rewarded equitably, provided with growth opportunities, to know what is expected of them and be given fair and constructive feedback on their performance (Armstrong, 2001). This is particularly the case in Japan, China, India and Vietnam. In the last three countries there are internal changes pertaining to privatization of state-owned enterprises

(SOEs), which have resulted in insecurity for workers. In the case of Japan the insecurity arises from changes in the external economic environment.

For many employees in Japan, China, India and Vietnam, the move away from traditional employment practices constitutes a violation of the psychological contract. Thus, the challenge for HR managers is how to be able to deal with the outcome of employees' responses to the perceived violations of the psychological contract – such as reduced effort on the job or output and reduced contributions in the form of loyalty and commitment (De Nisi and Griffin, 2001).

Perhaps this is going to become a much bigger challenge in information technology enabled service (ITeS) providers such as call centers and business process outsourcing (BPO) firms where problems relating to psychological contract and job stress become prominent after a while. For example, in the case of India, the majority of call-center employees are full of enthusiasm when they start their first job. However, after a while the dark side of the "rosy" picture starts to emerge and the level of staff morale declines considerably. This often results in high attrition – at times as high as 22 percent (see *The Economic Times*, 2003). To a great extent, the lack of talent development initiatives is held responsible for this (Chowdhry, 2003) as the lack of career structure provides a good opportunity for competitors to poach talented people (Prabhakar, 2003). Such emerging trends pose challenges to HR managers regarding both their recruitment and retention policies and practices. It also provides a good case for researchers to examine the topics of psychological contract, job stress and attrition. Also, it is predicted that both China and the Philippines are expected to become the next hubs of BPO (*The Times of India*, 2003). Possibly, decision-makers in such countries can learn from the experiences of the Indian ITeS sector.

Another key challenge in HRM in the Asia-pacific region is the effects of the transition from collectivism to individualism in HRM practices in countries such as Japan, India, China and Vietnam. Here, along with the managerial responses to employees' perceived violation of the psychological contract is the need for managers to develop a new culture where promotion, pay and other organizational benefits will be based on individual contributions rather than group characteristics. In this regard, it appears that globalization and competitive pressures are pushing organizations in East Asia to move towards the Australian system of determination of employee benefits. How to achieve an effective and successful change to individual-based HRM practices within the broad East Asian culture of groupism is a critical challenge for all managers in East Asia.

The emergence of the knowledge-based economy/knowledge-driven global economy is also creating a significant challenge for managers is the Asia-Pacific region regarding how to manage employees involved in it. The importance of human knowledge in economic growth is now widely acknowledged and is considered as the basic form of capital; the accumulation of knowledge, it is argued, drives economic growth (Romer, 1986; DTI, 1998). A knowledge-driven economy is one in which the generation and exploitation of knowledge play the predominant part in the creation of wealth (DTI, 1998). The two key drivers of the knowledge economy are globalization and communication technology (Houghton and Sheehan, 2000), both of which are prevalent in the Asia-Pacific region.

Singapore was one of the first countries to move towards a knowledge-driven economy (Ofori 2002, 2003) and has instituted plans/programs to develop a world-class workforce. Singapore considers its current economy to be progressing from capital intensive to knowledge-based. To a great extent, Hong Kong is also following the same model. To achieve this objective, Singapore has acknowledged the importance of talent and education, and life-long learning among other factors as the key determinant of a competitive economy. HRM has a major role to play in the knowledge economy, not least because of its ability to equip employees with skills, knowledge and attitudes to operate in a competitive environment. Moreover, as the knowledge-driven economy creates rapid and dramatic change, uncertainty and turbulence as well as adjustment problems for employees, HRM managers will have to develop new strategies for managing people. These issues would be of interest to managers in the Asia-Pacific region as they move towards knowledge-driven economies in their attempts to compete in the global economy.

Relating to the issue of knowledge-driven economy is knowledge management. It is now acknowledged that how well knowledge workers are managed is a major factor in determining the future success of organizations. Noriaka and Hirotaka (1995) argue that knowledge is the source of innovation in organizations. In their view, in order for an organization to survive, it must be capable of continuous innovation and as such must pay attention to knowledge (Armstrong, 2001). The capability to gather, lever and use knowledge effectively is a major source of competitive advantage for organizations (Trussler, 1998). The management of knowledge workers provides considerable challenges for HR managers in the Asia-Pacific regions.

Across the Asia-Pacific region, governments are trying to develop the biotechnology industry. Many of the ambitious projects are in India, Singapore, South Korea, Taiwan and China. Many cities in these countries already have thriving high-tech industries and want to ride the next big wave by creating life-science centers/hubs. Singapore, for instance, is pouring money into Biopolis, a science park for biomedical and other knowledge-based industries. In India, Hyderabad is witnessing a gathering of the elements needed to create a life-science hotspot to match its IT industry (Merchant, 2003). East Asian countries, particularly China, Korea and Taiwan are building biotech clusters to attract back to their native (East Asian) countries, expatriate scientists trained overseas (mainly USA).

As these biotech clusters take hold in East Asia, the need for knowledge workers will increase. The companies that are able to attract expatriate scientists must be capable of harnessing the knowledge of the scientists. In this respect, HR managers need to contribute effectively to knowledge management by exhibiting expertise in the area. In a changing psychological contract environment, HR managers need to be able to promote values and norms which emphasize the importance of sharing knowledge, commitment and trust. In relation to that, HR managers must be capable of developing compensation and career development structures that can not only motivate but also retain knowledge workers. In addition, HR managers must be able to develop performance management processes and organizational and individual learning programs for knowledge workers in organizations (Armstrong, 2001).

Yet another challenge for HRM managers is the issue of diversity management. In recent years, diversity management has been a burning issue in the management of HRs in the Asia-Pacific region. The issues relating to gender, age, ethnicity, among others, have assumed increasing importance. In the Australian chapter, Patrickson and Sutiyono have discussed the efforts of the Australian government to raise awareness of the benefits of inclusive employment practices (in terms of ethnicity) in the workplace. Indeed, as Bertone and Leahy (2002) argue, with large numbers of business and skilled migrants arriving in Australia in recent years, many of them Asian, there is the need for HR managers to develop policies to harness their skills in customization and niche marketing both at home and abroad. Here, one of the managerial challenges is the removal of barriers and the development of strategies to ensure that all employees in Australian organizations can contribute the full range of their skills and knowledge, whether formal or informal (Bertone et al., 1998). It is asserted that Australian employers need to acquire skills and expertise in: (a) making use of ethnic differences within the workforce to understand, reflect and respond to the different needs of a multicultural domestic market, (b) making use of language, knowledge and cultural skills within a workforce to develop and expand their export market; (c) breaking down ethnic barriers and prejudices within the workforce to enable more harmonious work relations, increased productivity, flexibility and innovation (Bertone and Leahy, 2002).

In Australia, as in many East Asian countries, it is contended that there are glass-ceiling problems in organizations. Patrickson and Sutiyono maintain that in spite of the growth in female labor-force participation rate in Australia, their promotion into managerial ranks remains relatively stable or low. The situation is no better in other Asia-Pacific countries. In fact there are serious gender discrimination problems in Japan. However, against a background of labor shortage problems in many East Asian countries, the governments are urging more women to enter the labor market. In view of the declining birth rate in many East Asian countries, it is anticipated that the female labor-force participation rate will continue to grow. If this trend continues as predicted, then HR managers face the challenge of developing a safe and secure working environment for women. It must be realized that, in order for organizations to be able to recruit, motivate and retain female employees, HR managers need to confront the issues relating to the discrimination of women in the labor market.

Perhaps the most daunting scenario regarding diversity management in Australia and East Asian countries is the looming demographic time-bomb. As Holland (2003) asserts, Asians are getting older. This is a slow, silent and unstoppable "revolution" which is reshaping Asian societies. It is claimed that in the mid-1950s, old people (65 years and above) were a rarity in most East Asian societies. However, with better health care, higher standards of living, better-educated people and an increase in life expectancy in recent years, there has been a considerable increase in old people. At the same time most East Asian countries are experiencing decreasing birth rates, an aging workforce and hence labor shortages. It is estimated that by 2050 nearly, a quarter of East Asia's population will be aged 65 or over (Holland, 2003).

Japan and Australia are particularly affected by the problems of an aging population. Currently, one in six Japanese is older than the mandatory retirement age of 65. But with a fertility rate of just 1.3 children per woman – way below the birth rate of 2.1 needed to maintain a stable population – and a life expectancy of more than 80 years and rising, it is estimated that, by 2050, more than 36 percent of the Japanese population will be above retirement age (Holland, 2003). Patrickson and Sutiyono have indicated that Australia is going through similar demographic transition and, by 2012, the population over 65 will grow by 4 percent and thereafter continue to grow by 2.9 percent per year until 2028. Thus, Patrickson and Sutiyono assert that the aging workforce will be one of the crucial employment issues in this century in Australia and indeed in the whole of East Asia.

While some countries such as Singapore, Japan and Australia have made efforts in the legislative arena to tackle the problem, others have paid little attention to it. However, aging populations pose serious challenges to HRM in the Asia-Pacific region (see Debrah, 2001, 2002; Snape and Redman, 2003). How each country responds to the issues relating to an aging workforce depends on the severity of the problem but it is likely that some countries would have to import labor or rely on immigration in order to sustain economic growth. For instance, it is anticipated that Japan will need 6 million immigrants in the next 25 years but immigration is bitterly opposed by those who equate it with crime (Pilling, 2003). Even if East Asian countries manage to delay or resist limited or large-scale immigration from both within and outside the region, the countries would most likely need migrant workers.

Currently there are legal migrant workers from labor-surplus countries such as Indonesia and the Philippines working in labor-receiving countries such as Hong Kong, and Singapore. There are also low-paid legal migrant workers from countries such as India and Bangladesh in Singapore and Malaysia. In many workplaces in the construction industry in Singapore, for instance, it is possible to find migrant workers from different countries working together in a team. The management of such multicultural work teams is one of the challenges facing HR managers. Going by current demographic trends, it is possible that the use of migrant workers is likely to increase in future with multiple implications for the management of HRM in the Asia-Pacific region.

Other interesting HRM challenges are emerging in the Asia-Pacific region. One such challenge is the HRM issues relating to the outsourcing of service jobs from industrialized countries to the developing world (Crabb, 2003). In the last decade, advancements in ICT and availability of high-skilled workforce in some developing countries have made it possible for then to attract white-collar jobs from developed countries. It is estimated that 3.3 million jobs in the USA and 2 million in western financial services will be lost as result. In the UK, 200,000 job losses have been predicted by 2008 (FT, 2003). Asia has been the major recipient of these jobs.

Lower cost locations such as India, the Philippines and China are now attracting outsourcing of much higher value-added services such as medical diagnostics, treasury management and software development (FT, 2003). Bibby (2003) also points to the offshore outsourcing of architectural services. For instance, a British company, Atlas Industries, has set up an office in Vietnam to work entirely for the UK market. The Vietnamese employees produce drawings and 3D computer-generated designs for buildings at a relatively low cost. The work is assigned or finished, product transferred through email or a password-protected website (Bibby, 2003).

In India, the main activities or areas covered by the call centers include customer care (such as remote maintenance, help desk and sales support), finance and administration (for example, data analysis, medical transcription, insurance claims and inventory management), HR and payment services (such as payrolls, credit-card services, cheque processing and employee leasing) and content development, i.e. digital content, R & D, LAN networks and application maintenance (for more details, see Chenggapa and Goyal, 2002). As the competition, both nationally and internationally, to acquire business contracts has increased considerably in recent years, HR managers working in the sector are facing enormous challenges in attracting and retaining the best employees.

At another level, HR managers face significant challenges in their attempts to utilize internal labor markets (ILMs) in organizations. Appropriate ILMs are known to be conducive to the development of long-term employment relationships, to bind employees to the organization and also help to reduce employee turnover (see Soeters and Schwan, 1990; Osterman, 1994). It is also known that ILMs make it possible for HRM practices to be consistent with a systematic and rationalized employment system. However, in the case of countries like India and China (and many other Asian economies), ILMs are generally based on social connections, political contacts, caste, religion and economic power. Thus, in the context of present business conditions in India and China, the efficiency of the established traditional ILMs is questionable. The challenge, however, is how HR managers can engineer such a macro-level change without alienating powerful members of their organizations.

The existing ILMs system has been linked to corruption in Asian countries. It is argued that the ILM system, where informality, social networks and power distance are essential elements tends to engender corruption in organizations (see Luo, 2002). This has serious implications for efficient HRM systems and HR practitioners need to pay due attention to it.

Yet another challenge revolves around the quality of research in the Asian context. In his analysis of the main limitations of research conducted in the region, White (2002) suggests that too much of research effort has been limited to simplistic comparisons, correlational analyses providing no insight into underlying processes, and skewed, idiosyncratic sampling. Such research, it is argued, does not contribute significantly to theory development. Accordingly, White (2002) highlights the need to increase both rigor and relevance of research efforts in the Asian context.

In response to this suggestion, Lau (2002) recommends the adoption of Asian-developed constructs to study local and global issues and calls for development and validation of new constructs so as to delve into the depth of Asian-based issues. Similar suggestions have been made by many others. For example, focusing on cultural values, Kao *et al.* (1999) stress the need to indigenize management practices in Asian organizations. Due to the strong influence of the sociocultural context, the authors question the applicability of western management and organization theories in the Asian context (also see Kanungo and Jaeger, 1990). To a great extent this is a core issue for western firms operating in the Asian context (see Kidd *et al.*, 2001) and sends a clear message to researchers in the field.

## Conclusion

The challenges facing HRM in the Asia-Pacific region are clearly complex and daunting. The majority of them have emerged due to the changes in the economic environment. In particular, globalization and international competitiveness have brought to the fore the need for organizations to adopt appropriate HRM practices in their quest for competitive advantage. In this globalized era, competitive pressures have laid bare the limitations of the traditional models of management in some Asia-Pacific countries. Clearly, there is some indication that HRM is undergoing transformation in the region but it is unclear what the outcome of this transformation would be. Early indications are that there is a move towards individual basis in employment systems. However, it is too early to see a clear model or approach emerging. Possibly, a hybrid system (based on a mixture of both traditional Asian characteristics and western rationalized systems) would emerge. However, it is important that any HRM system that emerges in the Asia-Pacific region should be context based.

## References

Alexander, G. (1999) "Japanese industry in a spin over Nissan's U-turn," *The Sunday Times, Business Section*, 24 October: 8.

Armstrong, M. (2001) *A handbook of human resource management practice*, London: Kogan Page.

Bertone, S. and Leahy, M. (2002) "Globalization and diversity management: Empirical evidence from Australia," in Y.A. Debrah and I.G. Smith (eds.) *Globalization, employment and the workplace: Diverse impacts*, London: Routledge, pp. 207–238.

Bertone, S., Esposto, A. and Turner, R. (1998) "Diversity and dollars: Productive diversity in Australian business and industry," *CEDA Information Paper* No. 58, Melbourne: CEDA.

Bibby, A. (2003) "Designs for western living from the East," *Financial Times*, 2 September 2003: 15.

Budhwar, P. (2003) "Employment relations in India," *Employee Relations* 25 (2): 132–148.

Chenggapa, R. and Goyal, M. (2002) "Housekeepers to the world," *India Today*, November: 18–48.

Chowdhry, S. (2003) "Bad employment practices cause high attrition rates," *The Economic Times*, 18 June (http://economictimes.indiatimes.com/cms.dll/xml/uncomp/articl . . .) (accessed on 18 June 2003).

Crabb, S. (2003) "Going East: India curries favour with UK industries," *People Management*, 20 February: 28–32.

Debrah, Y.A. (2002) *Migrant workers in Pacific Asia*, London: Frank Cass.

Debrah, Y.A. and Ofori, G. (2001) "Subcontracting, foreign workers and job safety in the Singapore construction industry," *Asia-Pacific Business Review* 8 (1): 145–166.

De Nisi, A.S. and Griffin, R.W. (2001) *Human resource management*, Boston: Houghton Mifflin.

Department of Trade and Industry (1998) "Our competitive future: Building the knowledge-driven economy," London: DTI (http: www.dti/gov/uk/comp/competitive/wh_es1.html).

*The Economic Times* (2003) "Indian firms see darker side of call centre boom," 15 July (http://economictimes.indiatimes.com/cms.dll/xml/uncomp/articl . . .) (accessed on 15 July 2003).

*Financial Times* (FT) (2003) "Western services jobs go east," *Financial Times*, 7 August: 10.

Frenkel, S. and Peetz, D. (1998) "Globalization and industrial relations in East Asia: A three country comparison," *Industrial Relations* 37 (3): 282–310.

Graham, F. (1998) "Traditional employment systems are fragmenting," *Financial Times Survey: Japan*, 14 July: 5.

Harukiyo, H. and Hook, G. (1998) *Japanese business management: Restructuring for low growth and globalization*, London: Routledge.

Holland, T. (2003) "Asia's huge unfunded gap," *Far Eastern Economic Review*, 23 January: 42–43.

Houghton, J. and Sheehan, P. (2000) *A primer on the knowledge economy, centre for strategic studies*, Victoria University, Melbourne.

Kanungo, R.N. and Jaeger, A.M. (1990) "Introduction: The need for indigenous management in developing countries,' in A.M. Jaeger and R.N. Kanungo (eds.) *Management in developing countries*, London: Routledge, pp. 1–19.

Kao, H.S.R., Sinha, D. and Wilper, B. (eds.) (1999) *Management and cultural values: The indigenization of organizations in Asia*, New Delhi: Sage.

Kidd, J.B., Li, X. and Richter, F.-J. (eds.) (2001) *Advances in human resource management in Asia*, Basingstoke: Palgrave.

Lau, C.-M. (2002) "Asian management research: Frontiers and challenges, *Asia Pacific Journal of Management* 19: 171–178.

Luo, Y. (2002) "Corruption and organization in Asian management systems," *Asia Pacific Journal of Management* 19: 405–422.

Merchant, K. (2003) "The birth of a biotech cluster," *Financial Times*, 14 August: 8.

Noriaka, I. and Hirotaka, T. (1995) *The knowledge-creating company*, New York: Oxford University Press.

Ofori, G. (2002) "Technical change and the aggregate production function," *Review of Economics and Statistics* 63: 495–502.

Ofori, G. (2003) "Preparing Singapore's construction industry for the knowledge-based economy: Practices, procedures and performance," *Construction Management and Economics* 21: 113–125.

Osterman, P. (1994) "Internal labour markets: Theory and change," in C. Kerr and P.D. Staudohar (eds.) *Markets and institutions*, Cambridge, MA, and London: Harvard University Press, pp. 303–339.

Pilling, D. (2003) "Western services jobs go East," *Financial Times*, 7 August: 10.

Prabhakar, B. (2003) "NASSCOM to curb poaching in call centres," *The Economic Times*, 25 June (http://economictimes.indiatimes.com/cms.dll/xml/uncomp/articl . . .) (accessed on 25 June 2003).

Romer, P.M. (1986) "Endogenous technological change," *Journal of Political Economy* 94 (5): 1002–1037.

Rousseau, D.M. (1995) *Psychological contracts in organizations: Understanding written and unwritten agreements*, London: Sage.

Schuler, R.S., Budhwar, P. and Florkowski, G.W. (2002) "International human resource management: Review and critique," *International Journal of Management Reviews* 4 (1): 41–70.

Snape, E. and Redman, T. (2003) "Too old or too young? The impact of perceived age discrimination," *Human Resource Management Journal* 13 (1): 78–89.

Soeters, J.L. and Schwan, R. (1990) "Towards an empirical assessment of internal market configurations," *International Journal of Human Resource Management* 1 (1): 272–287.

*The Times of India* (2003) "China can be BPO hub by 2007: Report," 24 August, (http://timesof india.indiatimes.com/cms.dll/xml/uncomp/articl . . .) (accessed on 24 August 2003).

Trussler, S. (1998) "The rules of the game," *Journal of Business Strategy* 19 (1): 16–19.

White, S. (2002) "Rigor and relevance in Asian management research: Where are we and where can we go?," *Asia Pacific Journal of Management* 19: 287–352.

Wiseman, J. (1998) *Global nation? Australia and the politics of globalization*, Cambridge: Cambridge University Press.

# Index